K.I.S.S.

DK

The Only Guides You'll Ever Need!

THIS SERIES IS YOUR TRUSTED GUIDE through all of life's stages and situations. Want to learn how to surf the Internet or care for your new dog? Or maybe you'd like to become a wine connoisseur or an expert gardener? The solution is simple: Just pick up a K.I.S.S. Guide and turn to the first page.

Expert authors will walk you through the subject from start to finish, using simple blocks of knowledge to build your skills one step at a time. Build upon these learning blocks and by the end of the book, you'll be an expert yourself! Or, if you are familiar with the topic but want to learn more, it's easy to dive in and pick up where you left off.

The K.I.S.S. Guides deliver what they promise: simple access to all the information you'll need on one subject. Other titles you might want to check out include: Playing Golf, the Internet, Gardening, Weight Loss, and Playing Guitar.

GUIDE TO

Astrology

JULIA AND DEREK PARKER

Foreword by Eric Francis

A Dorling Kindersley Book

LONDON, NEW YORK, MUNICH,
MELBOURNE, AND DELHI

FIRST EDITION
DK Publishing, Inc.
Editorial Director LaVonne Carlson
Series Editor Beth Adelman
Editor Nancy Burke

Dorling Kindersley Limited
Senior Editor Bridget Hopkinson
Editorial Director Valerie Buckingham
Managing Art Editor Stephen Knowlden

Created and produced for Dorling Kindersley by
THE FOUNDRY, part of The Foundry Creative Media Company Ltd,
Crabtree Hall, Crabtree Lane, Fulham, London SW6 6TY
The Foundry project team
Frances Banfield, Lucy Bradbury, Josephine Cutts, Sue Evans, Karen Fitzpatrick,
Douglas Hall, Dave Jones, Jennifer Kenna, Lee Matthews, Ian Powling, Graham Stride,
Bridget Tily, Nick Wells, and Polly Willis. Special thanks to Sasha Heseltine.

SECOND EDITION
Project Editor Caroline Hunt
Art Editors Justin Clow, Simon Murrell
Designer Martin Dieguez

Managing Editor Maxine Lewis
Managing Art Editor Heather McCarry
Category Publisher Mary Thompson

Copyright © 2000
DK Publishing, Inc.
Second edition 2001

Text copyright © 2000 Julia and Derek Parker
4 6 8 10 9 7 5 3

Published in the United States by
DK Publishing, Inc.
375 Hudson Street
New York, New York 10014

Library of Congress Cataloging-in-Publication Data

Parker, Julia.
    KISS guide to astrology / Julia and Derek Parker – 1st American ed.
        p. cm. -- (Keep it simple series)
            ISBN 0-7894-6044-0
1. Astrology. I. Parker, Derek. II. Title. III. Series.
BF1708.1 .P377 2000
133.5--dc21

                                                    00-008797
                                                        CIP

Color reproduction by David Bruce Imaging and The Foundry
Printed and bound by MOHN media and Mohndruck GmbH, Germany

See our complete product line at
www.dk.com

Contents at a Glance

PART ONE

Understanding Astrology

Sun and Moon and Planets, Oh My
Simply Astronomical
Simply Zodiacal: A Sun Sign Primer
Rise and Sign: Your Ascendant
The Family of Planets
You Simply Gotta Have Friends!
A House is Simply Not a Home

PART TWO

Simply Sun-sational

Simply Dazzling: The Fire Signs
Simply Fundamental: The Earth Signs
Simply Stirring: The Air Signs
Simply Soulful: The Water Signs

PART THREE

Keep-It-Simple Birth Charts

The Simple ABCs of Building a Birth Chart
Simple Interpretations

PART FOUR

The Planets at Work

The Sun at Work
The Moon at Work
Mercury at Work
Venus at Work
Mars at Work
Jupiter at Work
Saturn at Work
Uranus at Work
Neptune at Work
Pluto at Work

PART FIVE

Use It . . . Or Simply Lose It!

Using Astrology in Everyday Life

CONTENTS

PART ONE *Understanding Astrology*   24

CHAPTER 1 *Sun and Moon and Planets, Oh My*   26

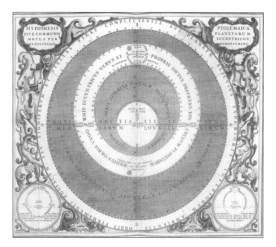

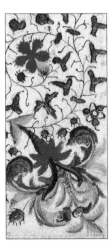

PART THREE Keep-It-Simple Birth Charts 210

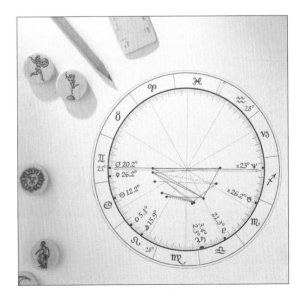

PART FIVE Use It . . . Or Simply Lose It! 388

APPENDICES 402

Foreword

EVERY NEW ASTROLOGY BOOK that is published represents a minor triumph over ignorance and narrow-mindedness. The reason for this has less to do with any particular author, and much more to do with the nature of astrology itself. Astrology causes us to open our minds and to think differently: Neither in a box, nor in a line, but rather in symbols, circles, and spirals.

Sometimes after talking to an astrology client for an hour or three or four, I remind both of us that the charts I'm working with contain about as many glyphs, in total, as the sentences you have just read. There are no small miracles, but this is a real one: Outside the box of pure logic and off the fragile strand of linear reality, there are rich rewards.

These are treasures to which Derek and Julia Parker have spent a lifetime introducing us. Julia is international patron of the Faculty of Astrological Studies, one of the longest-established teaching bodies in the world, and, with Derek, has created more than 40 books. They lack no credentials, except – some would say – for the fact that they have dared to enter the world of popular astrology. And here they do something very Promethean, which is to make the too-often-out-of-reach fire and light of astrological reason accessible to the people who will benefit from it the most, such as you and me.

Though you have picked this book up in an ordinary shop, purchased it online, or received it as a gift, for them to make this information available is more courageous than it would seem on its face. Astrology stands outside both conventional religion and conventional science, and popular astrology is the orphan child of "proper," scholarly astrology. The Parkers are among those who have not just made the world safe for the Moon, the stars, and the planets, but also those who have made the work fun, practical and most important, within reach.

This book is part of a renaissance of astrology that began in England at the turn of the 20th century. This rebirth is a natural extension of the very strong tradition of indigenous religion in the British Isles, call it what you will: Celtic shamanism, Wicca, Romany lore, or many other names. The introversion and inscrutability of the Brits could successfully hide all of this in dark days, keeping it both safe and well-preserved through the imposition of big religions and big science, even through horrendous times of diabolical persecution. In that sense, there is an unbroken chain of esoteric work, and the Parkers clearly stand in that legacy.

Each link in such golden chains is the most important; each has brought us to the present day, which is rightfully a moment of celebration for astrology. We live in an era when the ancient texts, many of them long lost in obscurity, or mistranslated, or ignored, are being brought out in affordable editions. The Internet has done something beautiful, which is to enable astrologers from around the world to band together in a community and to make vast information available anywhere there is a computer. At the same time, astronomy is looking deeper into space and picking up great subtlety, and there are astrologers assessing the personal and collective meaning of these discoveries with great care and interest. And in the contemporary revival of what you could call natural religion, astrology is being seen for what it really is: a study of the archetypes and the cycles of nature.

The Parkers are abundantly clear that astrologers need to stop looking to science for vindication. But it's also clear that such developments as chaos theory, fractals, quantum physics, and Einstein's theory of relativity, all of them purely scientific and all of them pushing reason into the purely mystical, have created mental frameworks wide enough and tolerant enough of the numinous to embrace the possibility that the planets and people share some kind of intelligent relationship. At long last, there are far stranger things than astrology – but of course, astrologers have always known that.

From these developments, we must learn to keep an open mind; for the scientist, the philosopher, and the mystic must all be accepting of the many possibilities, greeting the unknown with respect, awareness, and sensitivity. We must also subject every idea to the same basic test: Does this work? Then we can receive the rich inheritance of the cosmic order that has, by whatever grace and the dedication of Derek and Julia Parker, been passed down to us through many centuries and countless generations.

ERIC FRANCIS
Miami Beach, Florida
Planet Waves Digital Media
http://www.planetwaves.net/

Introduction

DOES ANYONE EVER READ an Introduction? Probably not. What most of us do is ignore the "instructions" and get right to work on a project – perhaps a new computer program or a do-it-yourself entertainment center. About a half hour later, in tears of frustration and anger, we throw up our hands with cries of "There must be something missing!" Only then do we turn to the book of instructions.

So of course you've already read the description of your "sign" (what we astrologers officially call your "Sun sign") in Part Two. Then perhaps you leafed through the rest of the book and came across a paragraph entitled, "Mercury's Aspects to Venus." Uh oh. And perhaps you saw the bit about Venus's conjunction to Saturn. Even worse! And then you saw all those pages of numbers, dates, and strange symbols at the end of the book. And right now you may be wondering if this book isn't just the right thickness to prop up the kitchen table's one short wobbly leg! What a pity that would be.

We've spent the best part of 30 years and over 40 books – between The Compleat Astrologer in 1971 and Parkers' Astrology Pack in 1997 – trying to convince people that real astrology, based on your time and place of birth, is much more interesting and rewarding than the "horoscopes" you read in the newspapers and magazines. But we've never been completely successful.

The problem was that learning about and understanding "real" astrology can be tough work. That is, it was tough work up until now.

What every budding astrologer needs is a hands-on, down-to-earth, let's-get-to-the-nuts-and-bolts-of-things starter kit. A starter kit that doesn't make assumptions about what you know or don't know. A starter kit that doesn't throw too much at you, too fast; or too little, too late. A starter kit that leads you by the hand through the simple A-to-Z steps of getting the job done – the job, in this case, probably being (and these are the only two assumptions we make in the whole book!) learning about real astrology and learning enough about real astrology to draw up your own birth chart.

So what you have here, with the K.I.S.S. Guide to Astrology, is the best astrological starter's kit ever devised. Hands-down! First of all, we've taken a simple "soup-to-nuts" approach to teaching you the fundamentals of astrology. We start with a basic history lesson, and we end with how to interpret your birth chart.

Along the way, we've done our utmost to keep everything simple, straightforward, and to the point. To that end we've used a system of icons (little symbols) in the text and boxes in the margins that alert you when especially important or interesting information is being passed along. So be on the lookout for these icons shown overleaf.

CAPRICORN

Finally, look for the informational "boxes" giving definitions, internet sites, and trivia in the margins of the text.

We hope this KISS Guide to Astrology entertains and inspires you, and perhaps prods you farther along the richly rewarding road of astrology. If we have gotten you even halfway through the journey, we've done our jobs . . . and we're happy.

Happy trails to you . . .

DEREK AND JULIA PARKER

What's Inside?

THE INFORMATION IN the K.I.S.S. Guide to Astrology *is arranged from the simple to the more advanced, making it most effective if you start from the beginning and slowly work your way to the more involved chapters.*

PART ONE

Here you'll find an introduction to astrology – how it got started, how it developed, and exactly what it is. We also provide the basic information and fundamental tools to allow you to begin compiling and interpreting your very own birth chart.

PART TWO

In this section we take an in-depth look at the weird and wonderful characteristics associated with each of the 12 Sun signs, with a detailed examination of how these impact on your personal relationships, family, career, and health.

PART THREE

This is where we show you the difficult bit – how to build up your birth chart step by step – and make it painless for you. In Chapter 13, you'll also find basic information that will start you off on the tricky business of interpreting your birth chart.

PART FOUR

Now you're ready to learn how to interpret that birth chart in a little more detail; in this section we run through the unique influences of each of the planets as they move through each of the zodiac signs, houses, major aspects, Ascendant, and Midheaven.

PART FIVE

In the final section of this book, we apply the use of astrology to every-day life. This is the practical section that allows you to use your birth chart as a guide to improving your career and your health as well as your relationships with friends...etc

The Extras

THROUGHOUT THE BOOK, *you will notice a number of boxes and symbols. They are there to emphasize certain points we want you to pay special attention to, because they are important to your understanding of astrology. You'll find:*

Very Important Point

This symbol points out a topic we believe deserves careful attention. You really need to know this information before continuing.

Complete No-No

This is a warning, something we want to advise you not to do or to be aware of.

Getting Technical

When the information is about to get a bit technical, we'll let you know so that you can read carefully.

Inside Scoop

These are special suggestions and pieces of information that come from our personal experience as astrologers.

You'll also find some little boxes that include information we think is important, useful, or just plain fun.

Trivia...

These are simply fun facts that will give you an extra appreciation of astrology in general.

DEFINITION

Here we'll define words and terms for you in an easy-to-understand style. You'll also find a glossary at the back of the book with the star-related lingo.

INTERNET

www.dk.com

We think that the Internet is a great resource for would-be astrologers, so we've scouted out some of the best web sites for you to check that will help with all aspects of the stars.

PART ONE

THE MILKY WAY IS OUR LOCAL GALAXY

UNDERSTANDING ASTROLOGY

IF YOU THINK YOU KNOW everything about *astrology* that you need to know . . . well, we're here to tell you that if Sun signs are the only exposure you've had to astrology, you've barely uncovered the tip of this celestial iceberg! Do you know, for instance, what planet rules your Sun sign and what that means? Do you know who were the first astrologers, and why? Do you know what a "modern" planet is? Or an aspect? Or your rising sign?

Have we got your attention? Good! Part One answers all the questions above – and more. Here you will learn about the history of astrology, get a crash course in astronomy, study the planets in-depth, learn every characteristic there is to know about a "sign," and discover why in astrology a house is never a home. Enjoy the ride!

Chapter 1

Sun and Moon and Planets, Oh My

LEARNING ABOUT ASTROLOGY is like learning a new language. You have to keep it simple and start small, with the basic building blocks of any language – everyday, commonplace words. To understand how celestial energy affects life on Earth and to learn how to separate the meaning from the mystery, metaphor from fact, it helps to know a little about the history of astrology. It's also good to start off, right from the top, with a discussion about what astrology can and cannot do. So let's first begin with a simple look at astrology's roots, then go on to tackle the facts and fictions around astrology's effectiveness.

In this chapter...

✓ Twixt the Earth and the sky
✓ From observation to science
✓ Does astrology work?
✓ What astrology can do

THE EARTH AS SEEN FROM SPACE

Twixt the Earth and the sky

ON A FOGGY PREHISTORIC RIVER BANK, *in a dank and smoky cave, the Neanderthal Ug, club in hand, made mincemeat of Sunday dinner because his wife's fillet of mastodon was overdone again. Then he stormed out into the mist to try to bag a pterodactyl for next day's supper. But he didn't go hunting when it was pitch dark. Oh no. Ug went hunting when his old friend the Sun was up – because then he could see his target. And what's more, he didn't bump into the trees. Or another mastodon.*

What does this fable have to do with *astrology*?

And then there was light

DEFINITION

*Simply put, **astrology** looks at the effects of the Sun, Moon, and the planets on the Earth and all its living things.*

What Ug had discovered, along with his other Neanderthal pals, was that with the appearance of the Sun came light – daylight – and warmth. And in the warm light, things got done more easily and safely. And Ug and his pals probably also noticed that the daylight lasted longer at certain times of the year. This made planning things like hunting and gathering a lot simpler too.

When the light was around for the longest time, the days were warmer, the plants were greener, the fruit was fatter, the animals were slower – easy pickings all around! When the days grew short and the air got chilly, the green disappeared, the fruit went to seed, and the animals got friskier – time to retreat to the warmth and safety of home fires! The Sun was a mighty entity, dictating how Ug and his pals ran their lives.

But if daylight is the most basic of all astrological effects, how did mankind go from simply noticing that life was easier if you didn't try to live it in the dark, to devising an enormously complex astrological system – one which has produced whole libraries of books and theories that make Einstein's ideas about relativity seem about as difficult as the plot of a romantic novel.

Moonstruck, too!

We can only guess that the more intelligent cavemen (and more likely, the cavewomen) also noticed that that big white ball in the night sky – the Moon – had almost as great an effect on their lives as the Sun did. When the Moon was full, it not only provided enough light to move around in at night, but it affected the rivers and sea – and thus fishing and other related activities. As the Moon changed in the night sky, so too did the tides of those rivers and seas. The waters receded at intervals, and this made clam digging and seaweed gathering a snip. But at other times the waters rose and rushed forward, dousing fires and flooding caves. Time to find a new home on higher ground!

Soon enough, the women noticed that the Moon also had an effect on their cycles – and on the emotions of those around them. And of course there were always those few Neanderthals who got downright loopy when the Moon was at its roundest.

■ **Humanity** *has always been fascinated by the Moon.*

Red light, blue light

Then there were those other bright lights in the sky (we call them planets today) – fiery red Mars and cool blue, shining Venus. It can't have been long before prehistoric men and women noticed that when Mars was particularly prominent, the very air seemed stormy and there was more violence around. When Venus shone especially brightly, people were happier and there was romance in the air. So the planets that Neanderthal man and woman could observe with the naked eye also surely began to figure – if only in a rudimentary way – in prehistoric astrology.

And while we're on the subject of planets, it's important to note that the Sun and the Moon are also treated as planets in astrology, even though they are technically – and more properly – known as luminaries. We talk more about that in Chapter 2.

The Sun? The Moon? The planets? Okay. But what about the stars? you ask. What about all those popular books and newspaper columns that promise to reveal "what the stars foretell" or to illuminate "your life in the stars."

Sorry, it simply isn't in the stars

The stars – or rather, the various constellations of stars – do have something to do with astrology: with how the Sun signs first got their names and with how the Sun was tracked through those signs in its journey around the Earth (see Chapter 3). But the stars don't have as much importance in modern astrology as most people – or most newspaper and magazine editors – think they do. For 30 years we tried to persuade editors to let us write about Sun signs rather than stars, but it's been a losing battle.

■ **Ancient people** *saw the very same view of the stars that we see today.*

Remember that what we're talking about here is genuine astrology and not "your stars," or the all-purpose horoscopes you read in newspapers and magazines, or the very popular *Sun sign* books (some of which we've written ourselves) that you find in book stores. In truth, Sun sign astrology is at the "low" end of the astrology market – wonderfully entertaining, but as far from real astrology as the Charlie Brown cartoon strip is from a novel by Tolstoy.

■ **The Sun** *is central to the solar system and has a profound effect on all our lives.*

This is not to say that studying the Sun signs is nonsense, not by any means – though we've said that from time to time, just to shock people into realizing that there's more to astrology than meets the average eye. Of course the Sun signs work; indeed, we devote a big section of this book (Part 2) to them. Sun signs, in fact, are the reason why most people go into astrology to begin with. Scratch a professional astrologer, and you'll find that umpteen years ago, he or she first got interested in the field by reading a Sun sign book. Even more, read the description of your sign in Part 2, and you'll discover that out of twenty or more sign characteristics, you can recognize at least 15 that apply to you. Nevertheless, the signs are just the icing on the astrological cake: it's the rich and varied ingredients in the cake that give astrology its depth and breadth.

The simple truth is that for all the hype about the signs and the stars, it is really the Sun, the Moon, and planets that are the major players in astrology. Think of them as featured actors in a cosmic opera. Imagine them strutting about the stage of our solar system, belting out a variety of stirring themes which affect us all. The stars – or signs – make for a wonderful backdrop to this drama; an integral part of the scenery, but far less important than the main action.

In fact, only a hundred or so of the millions of "fixed stars" we can see from the Earth have been used by astrologers through the millennia. And only a few modern astrologers pay the stars any attention at all. Even ancient astrologers gave the stars a subordinate role, and made the Sun and Moon into deities.

From observation to science

THE WAY IN WHICH ancient man's simple observations of the skies gradually became scientific theory may seem mysterious, but no more mysterious than mankind's gradual understanding over thousands of years of any other chain of cause-and-effect events.

Celestial campfire tales

Perhaps Ug's great-grandchildren remembered great-grandpapa's tales about the happy and scary adventures he and great-grandmama played out under the sway of the Sun and Moon. Perhaps these great-grandchildren began looking more closely at the movements of those mighty deities of the skies and to link those movements with events on Earth. Maybe they began to notice that a child born when Mars was prominent was very different indeed from a child born when Venus was at its most brilliant. Perhaps these great-grandchildren even began to record celestial events on their primitive stone tablets – creating the first, albeit rudimentary, astrological tables.

But a genuine astrological system couldn't be defined – and refined – until the invention of writing, mathematics, and a good calendar. Then man could do more than just admire the night skies. He could actually count and map the stars and use them, mathematically and systematically, to track the movements of the Sun, Moon, and planets through the sky. Moreover, man could then relate specific celestial events to corresponding actions on Earth. Which is just what happened – in the Middle East. There – in such exotic places as Babylonia, Assyria, and Egypt – lived the greatest mathematicians-astronomers in antiquity.

■ **The Moon** *has long been regarded as playing a significant role in our lives.*

> ## Trivia...
> *In antiquity, the Moon – which was and still is associated with feminine traits, while the Sun is considered masculine – was often depicted in illustrations as the Queen of the Sky with a small crown of stars around her head. The placement of the stars was meant to show their "subservience" or secondary importance to the Moon who, together with the Sun, reigned supreme over heaven and earth. This image of the Moon as a deity crowned with stars would be echoed centuries later in Western paintings of the Madonna and other female icons.*

We know for a fact that by the seventh century b.c., the ancient Babylonians had indeed formalized a complete system of astrology, including several centuries' worth of birth charts, all of which were inscribed on a series of stone tablets (now known as the Enuma Anu Enlil) and preserved in the royal library at Nineveh. And the Babylonians admitted to gleaning much of this information from Sumerian invaders of their country, who had arrived several thousand years earlier.

INTERNET

www.astrology.net/ parker

If you're interested in a detailed history of astrology, check out our own book on the Internet. It covers this subject from prehistoric to modern times.

Trivia...

One of the earliest astrological textbooks we have is the Tetrabiblios, _also called_ Four Books on the Influence of the Stars, _written by the Greek astronomer and mathematician Claudius Ptolemy in the second century_ A.D. _And Ptolemy was only passing on information that he had gathered and synthesized from Middle Eastern astronomers, who had recorded their findings eight centuries earlier! Ptolemy's synthesis of the extensive work of the early Middle Eastern astrologers, together with his own original theories, became the basis of modern astrology._

Astrology a science?!

That noise in the distance is the sound of scientists blowing their tops. But let's look at the Oxford Dictionary's definition of science: "A branch of knowledge conducted on objective principles involving the systematized observation of and experiment with phenomena, especially concerned with the material and functions of the physical universe." What that means is that scientists study and make theories about what causes a particular effect. Then they collect as much evidence as possible to support their theories. And finally, they tell everyone their conclusions.

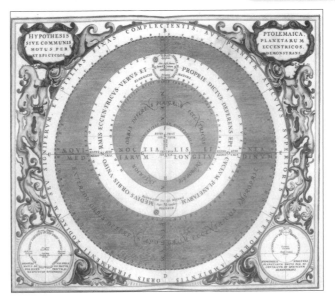

■ **Page taken from** The Celestial Atlas (1660–61), _a hand-colored engraving by Andreas Cellarius._

This is just what astrologers have been doing for thousands of years – and we do literally mean thousands of years.

Trivia...

You might think that the word "zodiac" comes from the word "zoo." In fact, it comes from the Latin word zodiacus, *derived in turn from the Greek* zodion, *and means "living creatures." The zodiac was originally thought of as a crowd of "beings" who some people have suggested were connected to the cherubim (or angels) of the Bible, that is, creatures who lived outside time.*

It was also the Babylonians who, after many centuries, produced a reliable calendar and began to devise the *zodiac* which we are familiar with today. By 235 B.C. an ancient astrologer could tell an expectant mother that, "If your child is born when Venus comes forth and Jupiter has set, his wife will be stronger than he."

While we can't go into the history of the zodiac in depth in this book, it's worth pointing out that its development was a truly international phenomenon, and the signs of the zodiac are celebrated in many cultures and languages. Gemini, for example, which was called *Mas.tab.ba.gal.gal* in ancient Babylonia, is called *Do-parkar* in Iranian, *Didemoi* in classical Greek, and *Mithuna* in Sanskrit.

Slowly, over the centuries, astrological theory became more complicated and sophisticated. It spread from Babylonia via Egypt to Greece, where the Greeks – being very good at math – contributed a great deal to its development. When astrology reached Rome, it really took off; there it was used both by ordinary people and the emperors, who consulted the zodiac for political as well as personal reasons.

DEFINITION

As the Earth turns and we look up at the sky, it seems as though the Sun is moving around it along a 360-degree path. This path is called the ecliptic, and the **zodiac** *is a belt which follows that path (stretching out on either side of it about 8 or 9 degrees). Ancient astrologers eventually divided this belt into 12 sections of 30 degrees (12 x 30° = 360° or a full circle), with a zodiac "sign" sitting in each division: Aries, Taurus, Gemini, Cancer, Leo, Virgo, Libra, Scorpio, Sagittarius, Capricorn, Aquarius, and Pisces.*

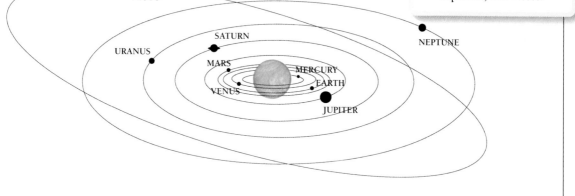

■ **In the same way** *that we have calculated the movements of the planets around the Sun, ancient astrologers marked the passage of the Sun through the zodiac belt.*

From then on, for the next eighteen hundred years, there was scarcely a country in the civilized world where astrology was not a part of life. At court, astrologers crouched behind curtains to time the first cry of a newborn prince. In Rome some of the popes used it to choose their cardinals, who in turn used it to decide when to start building their cathedrals. (A zodiac is set into the floor of the cathedral at Canterbury in England.)

In ordinary homes people used the zodiac to help them make decisions in many areas of life: who to marry; when to plant crops; where to build a new cottage; how to find a stolen cow or goat. And all this was done by interpreting one's *horoscope* or birth chart (the terms are interchangeable), which placed the planets (including the Sun and Moon) in specific signs of the zodiac – and gave special meanings to those placements. We'll teach you how to draw up your own (or a lover's or child's) birth chart in Chapter 12, but first you'll need some simple lessons in basic astronomy and astrology.

DEFINITION

*Simply put, your **horoscope** or birth chart is a diagram of the sky showing exactly where all the planets were positioned at the exact time and place you were born. While the words "horoscope" and "birth chart" are synonymous to astrologers – and, in fact, "horoscope" is the more traditional of the two terms – most nonastrologers think of horoscopes as those one-size-fits-all zodiac snapshots found in newspapers and magazines.*

■ **The Breton Calendar** *dates from 1546 and shows the passage of the Moon through the skies.*

Astronomers versus Astrologers

Once we begin talking about planets, we find ourselves smack in the middle of the old "astronomy versus astrology" conundrum. But when Ptolemy was at work, astronomers were astrologers and vice versa. It's only fairly recently – in the last couple of hundred years – that the two words were separated, and astronomers became "real scientists" who went very red in the face and began shouting whenever the word "astrology" was mentioned.

Yet for centuries it was considered extremely unwise to study the positions and movements of the planets – or the patterns and locations of the stars – without considering the effect they had on humans. In fact, it was more than unwise; it was unthinkable. So unthinkable that the two words – "astronomer" and "astrologer"– actually had the same meaning: one who studies celestial phenomena and how these phenomena affect the Earth.

Today things are very different. While every good astrologer is also an astronomer (to some extent), the opposite is far from true. Most astronomers don't hesitate to attack astrology. And those few astronomers who have a sneaking regard for astrology mostly keep their feelings to themselves. When one British astronomer dared, a few years ago, to write a book suggesting how the planets might affect the Earth, his colleagues refused to speak to him for several months!

Does astrology work?

THE THOUSAND DOLLAR QUESTION, *of course, is does astrology really work? One might ask another question in reply: Would any theory have lasted 3,000 years if it didn't work? But of course that's not a particularly good answer. People are quite capable of believing something silly for thousands of years, until they are proved wrong. Even then, some of them go on believing their silly theories. Just ask the flat-earthers even now.*

Trivia...

In fact, astrologers of the past had a motto, which they sometimes printed in the front of their textbooks: "The stars incline, they do not compel." In other words, under the influence of the planets (ancient astrologers called them stars), you may feel tired. But that planetary influence can't force you to drive your car, fall asleep at the wheel, and crash into a highway embankment.

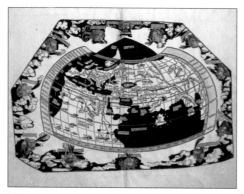

■ **A map of the world** *drawn with coordinates calculated from Claudius Ptolemy's (90–168 A.D.) Geographia.*

Yes, astrology works, but not the way most people think it does. The biggest mistake people make about astrology is believing that it can do the impossible – like foretell the future.

Shock! Horror! Astrology doesn't foretell the future? you say. But isn't that what it's for?

Yes – but not by telling you what's actually going to happen. It's not that simple. If there's a way to find out exactly what's going to happen to you at 4:30 next Wednesday afternoon, no one – including astrologers – has discovered it. Maybe foretelling the future will be possible some day. But it's not possible now. Astrology certainly can't do it. And no respectable astrologer will claim that it can.

Astrology works – within simple limits

While there may be plenty of argument about just how clearly astrology can see into the future, there's no doubt about this one simple fact: any good astrologer can see something. At the very least, an astute and practiced astrologer can tell you when you're more likely to catch a cold, when you may be exhausted and need a holiday, when you will feel particularly romantic, or when you may be careless enough to have an accident. But foretelling how sick you may get, which tropical island you may visit, when you'll meet a new lover, or what sort of accident you may have, is another matter entirely.

The sky's the limit

Having said that, we can assure you that there's practically no area in which astrology can't be helpful – starting in the cradle right through to retirement. (And we discuss this more in Chapter 24.) In fact it's fair to say that wherever human life is, so too is astrology! There really isn't any area of life to which astrology can't be usefully applied. And you'll be convinced of that as you read more of this book.

But it's important to remember that astrology has its limitations, and even those astrologers who are very good indeed at "forecasting" or "prediction" will admit this – despite the fact that there have been some spectacular examples of astrological prediction. One of the best known is the forecast made by the British astrologer Dennis Elwell of a maritime disaster he suspected would take place on March 6, 1987 – and he warned a number of shipping lines well before the date! On March 6, 1987, the British car ferry *Herald of Free Enterprise* capsized off the coast of Belgium drowning 188 people.

EARLY STARGAZER

Professor Eric Querulous,* who makes a career of attacking astrology, would say that it's an exceptional day when there isn't some shipping accident somewhere in the world. That may be true. But the "coincidence" of such a major disaster occurring exactly when Elwell said it would seems impressive to most of us. The problem for astrologers, of course – and here's where those limitations come into play – is that general predictions aren't very helpful. Unless you can say, for example, that a specific ship will sink at a particular time at a precise latitude and longitude, the forecast is generally useless: you can't expect every shipping firm to cancel all its sailings.

Eric Querulous, Professor of Closed Mind Studies at the University of Polperro, appears throughout this book from time to time. He raises the typical questions and criticisms that scientists often do about astrology and astrologers. Any resemblance between him and any living scientist is entirely intentional.

What astrology <u>can</u> do

WHAT ASTROLOGY CAN DO (*as Shakespeare's Hamlet says*) *is "hold a mirror up to nature." Astrology reveals your "real" face – and not the face you put on for the world to see. Astrology tells you the truth about yourself: your talents and your failings; your enthusiasms and your prejudices; your probable potential and your probability of success. Whether these revelations help or hinder you depends on what you do with the information. Certainly many of us hate being forced to recognize the truth about ourselves – and astrology ultimately succeeds by gently forcing us to face some basic truths – but if we can accept what's revealed to us, we almost always profit from the experience.*

Moreover, astrology never lies. And you can take that to the bank! If astrology indicates that you're pretty stingy, you'd better think long and hard about your attitude towards money – and then start thinking about your attitude towards love: because if you're stingy with your pennies, you're probably stingy with your affection.

When Professor Querulous asks what "proof" there is that astrology works, it's not very easy to produce simple statistics (though there are plenty of complicated ones). But we do like to remind him about a famous experiment set up by the British Sunday newspaper *The News of the World* in 1975. Four leading astrologers were introduced to 12 people – one for each Sun sign. The astrologers had never met these people but talked to them about their lifestyles, hobbies, careers, and families . . . anything but their birthdays! The subjects were pretty cagey, gave away as little as possible, and answered only "yes" or "no" when that was possible.

■ **The Anatomy of Woman** *from* Les Très Riches Heures du Duc de Berry *(early 15th century) shows the areas of the body reputed to be governed by each Sun sign.*

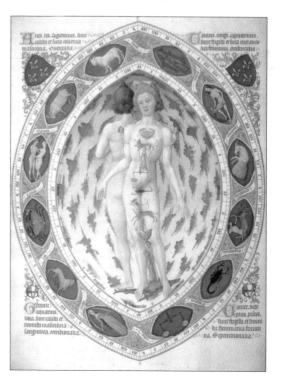

The astrologers then wrote down a Sun sign for each person interviewed. By chance alone, they might have made two or three correct assessments. But in fact, the astrologers got eight right.

At some time in the future, when Professor Querulous remembers that it's not very scientific of him to go ballistic every time someone mentions astrology, and when he decides to look seriously at the subject, it's possible that science may discover just how astrology works. For what it's worth, we believe that if it works, it must work on a scientific level, as well as, perhaps, on a psychological one.

18TH-CENTURY TELESCOPE

It really seems the height of absurdity to believe that our tightly integrated celestial family, the solar system – one Sun, one Moon, and nine planets (including Earth) which are held in perpetual attraction to one another (and have been for millennia) – don't do something significant to each other, and, in return, to us.

In the next chapter, let's put aside the astrology versus astronomy fiddle-faddle and take a look at the real cornerstone of astrology: the planets.

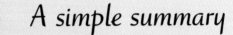

A simple summary

✓ Astrology is the study of the effects that the Sun, the Moon, and the planets have on the Earth, humans, animals, and plants.

✓ The "Sun", the "Moon," and the "planets" aren't just scientific names for celestial bodies. In astrology, these heavenly bodies are imbued with real and metaphorical energy that influences every facet of human life. Thus they are the foundation of "real" astrology.

✓ In astrology, the Sun and the Moon are also treated as planets, even though they are technically – and more properly – known as luminaries. The "stars" have little to do with real astrology, despite the fact that newspaper and magazine "astrologers" use the term in their forecasts.

✓ The history of astrology can probably be traced back to prehistoric times, when ancient man and woman first noticed that the Sun and the Moon had powerful effects on the land and sea, and thus on human life.

✔ By the seventh century B.C., the ancient Babylonians had devised a complete system of astrology, a reliable calendar, and several centuries' worth of birth charts or horoscopes. Astrology has remained popular around the world ever since then.

✔ A horoscope or birth chart is a diagram of the sky showing exactly where all the planets were positioned at the exact time and place an individual was born. The words "horoscope" and "birth chart" are synonymous to astrologers.

✔ The Sun appears to move around the Earth along a 360-degree path called the ecliptic. The zodiac is a belt which parallels that path and is wider than it. Ancient astrologers eventually divided this belt into twelve 30-degree sections with a zodiac "sign" sitting in each division: Aries, Taurus, Gemini, Cancer, Leo, Virgo, Libra, Scorpio,

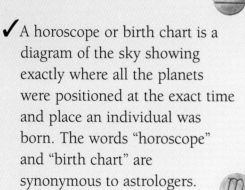

Sagittarius, Capricorn, Aquarius, and Pisces. The 12 signs are more properly known as the zodiac signs, not the Sun signs.

✔ One's Sun sign is the sign – Gemini, for example – that the Sun was in on the zodiac belt as seen from Earth at the time and place of an individual's birth. Despite its popularity, studying the Sun signs – and reading one's "horoscope" in newspapers, magazines, and books – is just a small part of the larger discipline of astrology. All the planets, in all the signs, have an effect on an individual's life.

✔ The biggest mistake people make about astrology is believing that it can do the impossible – foretell the future (though it can suggest the shape of things to come).

✔ Astrology works by showing us the "real" face behind the one we show the world. Astrology never lies. It tells us the truth about our talents, failings, romantic inclinations, enthusiasms, prejudices, and potentials for success or failure.

Orrery invented by Graham 1700
Improved by Rowley, and presented
by him to John Earl of Orrery,
after whom it was named at
the suggestion of Richard Steele.

Chapter 2

Simply Astronomical

OUR PLACE IN THE SOLAR SYSTEM may be about as important as an insect's place in the middle of the Sahara desert unless we look at the "whole picture," at how the Sun and its family of celestial bodies, including Earth, interact with one another. The Earth's solar system is comprised of the Sun – the solar system's center – and the celestial bodies, including planets, stars, and asteroids, that surround the Sun and are held in place by their attraction to it.

In this chapter...

✓ Solar simplicity: the Sun

✓ Simple lunacy: the Moon

✓ Simply old hat

✓ Simply new wave

✓ Other bits and pieces of sky

✓ It's simply not there!

18TH-CENTURY ORRERY USED FOR TRACKING STARS IN THE SKY

Solar simplicity: the Sun

THE SUN – A STAR? People tend to raise their eyebrows a
little when we say that, just as astronomers have a laugh when
they hear astrologers describe the Sun as a planet. But in fact, as
the popular **astronomer** Patrick Moore is fond of saying, the Sun
is "a perfectly ordinary star."

SUN

As we were saying in Chapter 1, the "stars" don't have a lot
to do with astrology as far as ordinary, everyday astrologers
operate. The Sun is the only star we have to think about –
but what a huge, important star it is!

> **DEFINITION**
>
> **Astronomers** *study the
> physical properties, chemical
> makeup, and movements of
> the planets, stars, and
> celestial bodies outside the
> Earth's atmosphere.*

*The Sun sits, blazing away, 93 million miles
from the Earth. And just as well that it does,
because without its 6,000 degrees centigrade of
heat, life on Earth would be impossible. From our point of view it's huge:
865,000 miles across and more than a million times bigger than Earth. In
fact, it's so large that 109 Earths could be placed inside it.*

It's not the Sun's size which makes it important in astrology, but the fact that it figures
prominently when astrologers discuss someone's personality. In fact, since the invention
of Sun sign astrology in the 1920s, nonastrologers have often thought of the Sun as the
be-all and end-all of the subject. It isn't, as we'll be pointing out later.

*But for now, suffice it to say
that the Sun is concerned
most strongly with self-
expression and creativity
and is closely associated
with the sign of Leo.
(We discuss in more detail
the astrological influences of
each planet in Chapter 5.)*

■ **Powerful modern telescopes** *have
increased our understanding of the stars.*

Simple lunacy: the Moon

MOON

CIRCLING THE SUN *are the "real" planets, and around some of the planets circle their own (sometimes very large) satellites or moons, including, of course, the most important one, our own Moon. In astrology, the Moon, like the Sun, is an honorary planet (more properly known as a "luminary"), and most astrologers would agree that it's the second most important planet that we use. Although it is tiny compared to Earth – in fact, it would take 81 Moons to equal the Earth's size – because the Moon is so close, so dazzling, and so beautiful, it has always had a very strong influence on humankind. Like the Sun, the Moon was worshiped as a god in most ancient civilizations.*

In terms of the solar system, the Moon is very close indeed to the Earth: at its closest, within 221,000 miles; at its farthest, only 252,700 miles away. The Moon circles the Earth once every 28 days or so, while the Earth and Moon together circle the Sun.

Simply old hat

THE WORD "PLANET" *means "wandering star," and for thousands of years before it was possible to look at Mercury, Venus, Mars, Jupiter, and Saturn through telescopes, ancient astronomers realized that these five planets were closer to the Earth than the stars. What they couldn't understand was how the planets, the Sun, and the Moon were "held together," because they believed the Earth was the center of the universe.*

When Galileo put forward the theory, in 1610, that the Earth, Moon, and planets revolved around the Sun, he was threatened by the Roman church, and accused of witchcraft. Now we know better and the five planets known to him and the ancients have been joined by three others, making up the solar system as we know it. Let's look at the five oldest planets first, the ones known to the ancient astronomers/astrologers.

THE RENAISSANCE ASTRONOMER GALILEO

Mercury

Mercury is the nearest planet to the Sun, and is known in astronomy (and astrology) as an *inferior* planet. Mercury is the smallest of the known planets (you could just about drop it into the Atlantic Ocean), and is only 3,000 miles in diameter. After the Moon, Mercury is the swiftest of the planets, traveling around the Sun – along an elliptical (oval-shaped) path – in about 88 days.

MERCURY

DEFINITION

Planets are called **inferior** when their orbits lie between the Earth and the Sun. Mercury and Venus are inferior planets.

Mercury can be as close to the Sun as 29 million miles, and as far away as 43 million miles. From Earth, however, Mercury always appears quite close to the Sun, and in fact, it is never more than 27 degrees away from it. At its farthest from the Earth, Mercury is 136 million miles away.

Venus

A beacon of clear, brilliant light – brighter than anything else in the night sky except the Moon – Venus has always fascinated humankind. Named for the Roman goddess of love, Venus, like the Sun and the Moon, was worshiped as a god throughout the ancient world under her many other names: Aphrodite, Ishtar, Astarte. The second of the "inferior" planets (Mercury is the other), Venus's orbit also lies between the Earth and the Sun. From the Earth, therefore, Venus always appears close to the Sun and is, in fact, never more than 48 degrees away. Unlike Mercury, which isn't visible to the naked eye, Venus can often be seen in the night sky.

VENUS

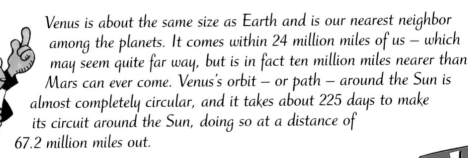

Venus is about the same size as Earth and is our nearest neighbor among the planets. It comes within 24 million miles of us – which may seem quite far way, but is in fact ten million miles nearer than Mars can ever come. Venus's orbit – or path – around the Sun is almost completely circular, and it takes about 225 days to make its circuit around the Sun, doing so at a distance of 67.2 million miles out.

In astrology, Venus is concerned with human love (emotional rather than physical), money, and possessions. It is strongly connected to the signs Taurus and Libra.

DEFINITION

In astronomy and astrology, those planets on the far side of the Earth – and thus further from the Sun than Earth – are known as the **superior** *planets. While the Earth is outside the orbits of the inferior planets, it is found inside the orbits of the superior planets. Mars, Jupiter, Saturn, Uranus, Neptune, and Pluto are all superior planets.*

Mars

Although Venus shines more brightly, Mars has a fierce red glow which makes it perhaps the most striking looking of the planets. Its angry red face is no doubt the reason why the ancients named it after Ares, the god of war. It is the first planet on the far side of the Earth, and the first of the **superior** planets.

MARS

Mars is much smaller than Earth, and at its closest comes within 35 million miles of us. It circles the Sun along a very wobbly and erratic path and takes about 687 days to makes its solar circuit. It can be as close to the Sun as 129 million miles, and as far away as 142 million miles.

In astrology Mars represents our physical life, our vital energies, and our sexual drive. It is associated with the sign Aries, and until the 1930s was also linked to Scorpio.

Jupiter

By far the largest of the planets, Jupiter is 89,000 miles in diameter, and yet it is delicate and mysterious in appearance, looking like a precious stone with warmly colored striations. Jupiter has no less than 15 moons, some of which, including the well-known Ganymede and Europa, can be seen through an average-sized telescope.

JUPITER

Jupiter is so big that you could fit all the other planets inside it. Because of its immense size, Jupiter shines more brightly than any other planet in the sky except Venus and the Moon. And this despite the fact that Jupiter is never less than 370 million miles from Earth. It is a good deal farther away from the Sun – 484 million miles away, to be exact – and it takes almost 12 years to make its solar orbit.

In astrology, Jupiter influences knowledge, wisdom, philosophy, and religion. It is strongly associated with the sign Sagittarius, and in ancient times was also associated with Pisces.

Saturn

Another of the planetary giants (second in size to Jupiter), Saturn is named after a Roman agricultural god. It is not one of the most brilliant lights in the night sky, but this mellow yellow planet is famous for its extraordinarily detailed rings (perhaps numbering in the thousands). Saturn's three main rings, made of whirling ice and rock, have been the most studied, starting as far back as 1655. Saturn also has 12 moons, the most famous (and largest) of which is Titan.

SATURN

Saturn measures almost 75,000 miles in diameter and is never less than 740 million miles from Earth. Another of the slow-moving planets, Saturn takes almost 30 years to orbit the Sun – at a distance of 888 million miles.

Simply new wave

PROFESSOR QUERULOUS *and his associates like to snigger about the fact that by 1930 astrologers were faced with the existence of no less than three new planets – Uranus, Neptune, and Pluto, commonly called the "modern" planets. How were astrologers going to reframe their "science" in light of these new planets, which had obviously been around since the dawn of civilization? Surely, Querulous and his cronies twittered, this meant that astrology had to be nonsense! Well, no, it doesn't. In fact, such an assumption would be akin to saying that the discovery of the circulatory system made all the work of medicine up until then null and void. The simple truth is, new discoveries enlarge knowledge, they don't diminish it.*

In fact, when the astrological influences of the modern planets are added to ancient birth charts, they explain some of the gaps left in those charts by astrologers who weren't aware of their influence. They also explain why some classic astrologers felt forced to assign influences to the "ancient" planets that we now know are the effects of Uranus, Neptune, and Pluto.

INTERNET

www.egroups.com/
group/all_ancient

The American astrologer Robert Hand has done wonderful work discovering ancient astrological techniques and reconciling them with modern astrology. His work is featured at the egroups web site.

In ancient astrology, Saturn marked the outer limits of the known universe, and it has, since then, been traditionally associated with "limitations" of all kinds, including inhibition and intolerance. It is strongly linked with the sign Capricorn and, until the discovery of Uranus, it was also linked to Aquarius

Uranus

Uranus is four times the size of Earth and has a system of rings similar to those of Saturn. The planet was accidentally discovered by the English astronomer William Herschel in 1781. (The glyph that represents the planet is a round ball with an "H" on top, commemorating Herschel's achievement.)

URANUS

SIR WILLIAM HERSCHEL (1738–1822)

Uranus is 29,300 miles wide and 1,600 million miles away from Earth. It is one of the three slowest-moving planets in the solar system — Neptune and Pluto are the two others — and its orbit around the Sun takes 84 years, at a distance from the Sun of almost 1,800 million miles.

In astrology, Uranus is the planet of change, panic, upheaval, and perversion. It is strongly associated with the sign Aquarius.

Neptune

Neptune was discovered in 1846, less than 100 years after Uranus, because the latter planet's rather distinctive and changeable orbit suggested that it was being influenced by another celestial body close by. That body turned out to be Neptune, the second slowest-moving planet in the solar system.

NEPTUNE

Even farther away than Uranus, Neptune is almost 2,800 million miles from the Sun and takes 165 years to make its solar orbit. Somewhat larger than Uranus, Neptune measures 31,200 miles at its diameter. One of its two moons, Triton (which takes six days to orbit Neptune), is among the largest moons in our solar system.

In astrology, Neptune is the planet of confusion and even deception, but it also encourages idealism, imagination, and creativity. It is strongly associated with the sign Pisces.

Pluto

After the discovery of Uranus, modern astronomers thought they knew all about the solar system. But no, then Neptune turned up. Now, finally, the family of planets was complete. No again. At the turn of the twentieth century, the great American astronomer Percival Lowell (brother of American poet Amy Lowell) hypothesized the existence of yet another planet (which would become Pluto) simply on the basis of mathematical calculations. In 1930, another American astronomer, Clyde Tombaugh, visually identified Pluto, the furthest planet from Earth.

PLUTO

Pluto is approximately 2,700 miles wide around its equator, making it one of the smallest of the known planets (close in size to Mercury). It is over 3,600 million miles from the Sun and takes over 250 years to make its solar orbit.

The newest planet: Chiron

For astrologers, the most important recent discovery in the solar system is that of Chiron, a small planet that was first spotted in 1977 between Saturn and Uranus, though its orbit also takes it between Jupiter and Saturn.

CHIRON

Within four years, a number of astrologers had rushed into print with all sorts of books – most of them written from personal research – about Chiron's influences in the birth chart or horoscope. These astrologers have sometimes linked Chiron to the myths connected with the Greek centaur after whom it is named. The centaur was a mythical creature who was human from the waist up, horse from the waist down. Certain astrologers thus endowed Chiron with influences that encouraged rough animal instincts combined with humane sophistication and refinement. The new planet has also been associated with astrology and forecasting arts, ecology, and healing. We believe the jury is still out on Chiron's place in astrology, but suggest that everyone keep an open mind about this latest celestial discovery.

Others bits and pieces of sky

AS FAR AS ASTROLOGICAL INFLUENCES GO, *the planets are by far the most important celestial bodies studied by astrologers. But some of the minor celestial bodies – specifically, the asteroids and comets – are also given importance in astrology (though we don't cover them in this book). Nevertheless, here's a brief look at these fascinating phenomena.*

The asteroids

Between Mars and Jupiter there's a great desert of space – a gap of three million miles, in fact – and within that gap are a number of small celestial bodies which are used by astrologers in their birth chart interpretations.

Astronomers first thought that there had to be a planet somewhere in that vast space – even a tiny one. On January 1, 1801, an Italian astronomer thought he'd found one – Ceres. But Ceres isn't really big enough to be a full-blown planet; it's only 429 miles in diameter and travels around the Sun once every 5 years or so. In fact, you might call Ceres a "planette." In quick succession, three more planettes were discovered – Pallas, Juno, and Vesta – and their discovery was soon followed by a fourth, Astrëa, in 1848. Since then, over 40,000 planettes have been identified, and they were finally renamed *asteroids*. Vesta is the brightest of these asteroids or minor planets. It is 244 miles in diameter and circles the Sun in approximately four years.

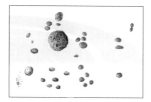

■ **The asteroids** *occupy the millions of miles between Mars and Jupiter.*

Many astrologers – in fact, most astrologers – simply ignore the asteroids. Some other astrologers, however, have worked out specific influences for these asteroids and even devised planetary tables of their movements and what they believe to be influences exerted by them. This is a highly specialized field that you're not likely to need in your study of astrology, but just for the record, here's a list of the top 12 asteroids.

THE ASTEROIDS

ASTEROID NAME	DISCOVERED	DIAMETER (MILES)	ORBITAL "YEAR"
Ceres	1801	429	4.60
Pallas	1802	281	4.61
Juno	1804	150	4.36
Vesta	1807	244	3.63
Astrëa	1845	112	4.14
Hebe	1847	106	3.78
Iris	1847	94	3.68
Flora	1847	77	3.27
Metis	1848	133	3.69
Hygiea	1849	222	5.60
Parthenope	1850	75	3.84
Victoria	1850	94	3.56

The comets

In ancient times especially – but also right up until modern times – *comets* were believed to foretell disasters of one sort or another. And indeed, their appearance in the sky often coincided with spectacular terrestrial events.

Very few astrologers use comets in birth-chart astrology – the astrology which tells us about ourselves, our personalities, and our behavior. If a comet has any effect at all, it must certainly be a symbolic one. However spectacular they may appear, comets are simply too small (often only a mile or two in diameter) to have any real astrological influence

DEFINITION

*A **comet** is a celestial body that circles the Sun along a highly eccentric and unpredictable path. A comet often appears elongated – with a "fuzzy" head surrounding a brighter, round nucleus, and a long tail (composed of ice and gases) that points away from the Sun and brightens considerably at various stages of the comet's orbit.*

Trivia...

Some comets are regular visitors to the Earth. Haley's Comet was first recorded in ancient times and has swept past the Earth many times since: its last visit was in 1986. Haley's is the only bright comet which returns to us fairly frequently. Other notable comets, such as Donati's, return only once in several centuries.

It's simply not there!

ONE OF THE MOST QUESTIONABLE *inventions of certain astrologers have been the so-called "hypothetical" planets – in other words, planets which simply aren't there! And your opinion of these "invisible planets" will depend on your opinion of mediums and the psychic world in general, because it was so-called "psychic astrologers" who invented hypothetical planets, including Admetos, Cupido, Polyhymnia, and Kronos. Madame Blavatsky, the famous theosophist, claimed to have discovered six hypothetical planets, which she called "ethereal planets," and some psychic astrologers claim that there are over a thousand hypothetical planets. They have worked out planetary tables for them and published books on these supposed planets' influences.*

■ **Helena Petrovna Blavatsky** (1831–91) *was a Russian mystic and writer.*

We admit that while it must be great fun to invent a planet, make up its astrological personality, and publish books explaining how it influences mankind, our own view is that the idea, once there, has stuck erroneously.

A simple summary

✔ Astronomy is the study of the planets, stars, and other celestial bodies outside the Earth's atmosphere.

✔ The "stars" are not the focus of astrology. The only star used in astrology is the Sun. In astrology, the Sun is treated as an honorary planet. So is the Moon. Both, however, are technically known as "luminaries."

✔ The relationships formed among the various celestial bodies of the Earth's solar system are the foundation upon which real astrology is built.

✔ The Earth's solar system includes the Sun, the Moon, Mercury, Venus, Mars, Jupiter, Saturn, Uranus, Neptune, and Pluto.

✔ Mercury, Venus, Mars, Jupiter, and Saturn are called the traditional planets. Together with the Sun and the Moon, they comprise the seven known planets used by ancient astrologers.

✔ Uranus, Neptune, and Pluto are called the modern planets. They were discovered during the last five centuries.

✔ Chiron is the newest planet, discovered by astronomers in 1977. Some modern astrologers have assigned Chiron astrological influences, but the great majority of astrologers do not include Chiron in their interpretations of planetary influences.

✔ The solar system also includes asteroids and comets. Many astrologers study the influences of the asteroids, but it is a specialized field and their effects are not included in this book. Comets, such as Haley's, appear periodically in the sky, but they are so tiny that most astrologers believe they do not have any significant effects on birth charts.

✔ A small group of "psychic" astrologers has invented a hypothetical group of invisible planets. These do not figure at all in traditional astrology.

Chapter 3

Simply Zodiacal: A Sun Sign Primer

I N ANCIENT TIMES there weren't always 12 zodiac signs. Often there were more, sometimes there were less. But for the past few centuries in the West, astrology has used the 12 familiar zodiac signs through which all the planets parade. Here, we look at how the zodiac signs were "discovered," the major personal characteristics associated with each sign, and the mythological origins of the signs.

In this chapter...

✓ Simple beginnings

✓ Aries   ✓ Taurus

✓ Gemini   ✓ Cancer

✓ Leo   ✓ Virgo

✓ Libra   ✓ Scorpio

✓ Sagittarius ✓ Capricorn

✓ Aquarius   ✓ Pisces

17TH-CENTURY MAP OF THE SKY IN THE SOUTHERN HEMISPHERE BY ANDREAS CELLARIUS

Simple beginnings

A VERY, VERY LONG TIME AGO, the star constellations that lie behind the 30-degree segments of the zodiac were given the names they now have because the star patterns were thought to resemble those figures. The zodiac signs, in turn, took on the names of the constellations in which they were placed. Through the centuries, however, and because of irregularity in the Earth's revolution on its axis as it revolves around the Sun, the sky that the ancients observed has "shifted." In fact, the fixed stars (constellations) that the zodiac signs are named after have moved slowly backward in the sky (a process called the "precession of the equinoxes"). The stars have moved so much, in fact, that the zodiac signs are no longer in their original constellations.

Astronomers like to use this fact to point out that astrology is ultimately nonsense. What they don't understand is the difference between a "sign" and a "constellation." A sign merely describes a specific 30-degree slice of the zodiac; the constellation is simply the pattern of stars which was originally used to name the sign. It makes no difference to astrologers how far the stars have moved over the last few thousand years. The fundamental astrological integrity of the signs remains intact. Still, there is often a fascinating relationship between the characteristics of a zodiac sign and the symbolic history attached to the constellation for which it was named.

Here we give you a brief taste of the major qualities associated with each zodiac sign (see Part 2 for detailed descriptions of the signs), together with its mythological history.

The 12 signs of the zodiac

ARIES

TAURUS

GEMINI

CANCER

LEO

VIRGO

LIBRA

SCORPIO

SAGITTARIUS

CAPRICORN

AQUARIUS

PISCES

Aries: the Ram

MARCH 21 – APRIL 20

KEYWORDS: Assertive; urgent; energetic; forthright; selfish; enthusiastic

The person:

Ariens are famed for their fiery, positive, outgoing natures. Considered among the most enthusiastic of the zodiac children, they have high energy levels and often fast-paced lifestyles. Ariens are straightforward in outlook, highly competitive, and enjoy taking risks. Their fiery determination to accomplish things sometimes encourages hot-headedness and rudeness. Like the light-footed ram who represents their sign and who is able to climb the most jagged of mountain sides with grace and agility, Ariens do all things in their own way, with energetic determination and regardless of obstacles.

■ **Arien scenes** *from* The Bedford Hours (*c. 1423*).

The myth:

Aries is represented by the golden Ram, an astrological animal symbol that first appeared in the zodiac charts of the ancient Egyptians. Later, in ancient Greek mythology, the golden ram surfaced again, as the illicit offspring of the sea god Poseidon (who had changed himself into a ram) and the beautiful mortal Theophane (who Poseidon had changed into a ewe). Nephele, the queen of Boetia, found the golden, half-god ram wandering around, and asked her children, Phrixus and Helle, to take him away to Colchis and sacrifice him to Ares, the god of war. They did this, and then removed the ram's golden fleece, which was hung in the temple of Ares, guarded by a dragon, until it was claimed many years later by Jason and his famous Argonauts. Zeus, in commemoration of the ram's sacrifice, made him part of the six-starred constellation Aries.

Taurus: the Bull

APRIL 21 – MAY 21

KEYWORDS: Patient; possessive; reliable; self-indulgent; persistent; warm

The person:

Taureans are famed for their romanticism, reliability, and charm, and they are often reputed to be the most beautiful people among all the zodiac children. Warm, affectionate, and sincere, they inspire confidence and loyalty in those around them. Taureans have a great need for financial and personal security. They love luxury, comfort, and beautiful things – tendencies that can encourage an obsessive possessiveness on their part. Like the Bull who symbolizes their sign, Taureans are slow to anger, but when aroused, they can be fearsome.

■ **Taurean scenes from** The Bedford Hours (*c. 1423*).

The myth:

The myth of the Bull – an extraordinary creature famed for his contradictory characteristics of fearsome strength, passionate sexuality, and graceful gentility – appears in both ancient Babylonian and Roman myths. But the Greek myth of the Bull is most famous. Zeus, the king of the Greeks' gods and goddesses, fell in love with Europa, the famously beautiful daughter of the king of Phoenicia. To get Europe's attention, Zeus turned himself into the handsomest of bulls and set about grazing in her father's herd. When Europa saw this magnificent animal, she was immediately seduced by his charm and majesty and climbed upon his back. Zeus immediately flew them away across the sea to Crete, where he changed back into his godlike form and mated with Europa, who eventually bore him three children. Grateful for the bull's help in this affair, Zeus immortalized him in the night skies as the 14-starred constellation Taurus.

Gemini: the Twins

MAY 22 – JUNE 21

KEYWORDS: Communicative; versatile; restless; witty; intellectual; sharp

The person:

Geminians are lively, restless, quick-witted, fast-thinking, mercurial creatures who rarely stay in one place – physically or philosophically – for long. They are marvelous communicators and easily sway people to their own ideas and opinions. Geminians detest boredom – indeed, they run from it – and often prefer spreading their considerable emotional and intellectual energies among a variety of tasks (and people!). This ability to do several things at once is typical of the Geminian's dual nature, aptly represented by the Twins. Poorly channeled, however, the Geminian's inability to settle down with one thing or one person can lead to the appearance of shallowness and a tendency to gloss over the important details of life.

■ **Geminian scenes from** The Bedford Hours (c. 1423).

The myth:

The Geminian Twins' origins can be traced as far back as the days of Babylonian astrology, when they were known as the Great Twins and named for the two bright and large stars in the seven-star constellation Gemini. The Twins' ancient Greek origins have been immortalized in stories and poems. As the myth goes, Zeus, the king of the gods, disguised himself as a swan and seduced the mortal Leda. From their union, Leda produced two eggs. One egg produced a god and goddess, Pollux and Helen; the other a mortal brother and sister, Castor and Clytemnestra. Castor and Pollux became inseparable friends who grew up together, were famed athletes, and later fought together. When Castor was killed in battle, Pollux was inconsolable. Zeus, moved by this brotherly love, made Castor an immortal, and placed the brothers side by side in Gemini, so they could be together for eternity.

Cancer: the Crab

JUNE 22 – JULY 22

KEYWORDS: Sensitive; emotional; protective; moody;
imaginative; loving

■ **Cancerian scenes from** The
Bedford Hours (c. 1423).

The person:

Sensitive (but often crabby), imaginatively creative
and artistically gifted (but often obsessed with the
minutiae of home and the past), Cancerians are among
the most challenging of the zodiac children to get to
know. Like the crab that symbolizes their sign, they
often present a hard, crusty, even impenetrable exterior
to the world, and can appear withdrawn, cool, and
reserved. Beneath the shell, however, lies an emotional
and sensitive soul with great reserves of compassion and
intuition. Like the crab, Cancerians are also tenacious
and protective of their home turf and make for fiercely
protective and loyal parents and friends.

The myth:

Hercules, immortalized in mythological sagas as the
greatest hero of ancient Greek civilization, also figures
prominently in the mythical origins of three zodiac
signs: Cancer, Leo, and Sagittarius. As the Cancerian
story goes, King Eurystheus of Greece assigned Hercules
12 dangerous tasks in atonement for killing his own
wife and children. The first task was to slay and skin the
much feared lion of Nemea (*see Leo*). Hercules's second
task was to kill the Hydra, a grotesque monster with the
body of a dog, nine serpent-entwined heads, and breath
so foul that it poisoned anyone who got close enough
for a whiff. Hercules had trouble slaying the Hydra
(every time he cut off a head, two more grew back in its
place!). The goddess Hera sent a giant crab to attack
him while he was fighting the Hydra. Hercules crushed
the crab underfoot and went on to dispatch the Hydra.
Grateful for the crab's help, Hera placed it within the
six-starred constellation of Cancer.

Leo: the Lion

JULY 23 – AUGUST 23

KEYWORDS: Generous; expansive; loving; bossy; creative; impressive

■ **Leonine scenes from** The Bedford Hours (c. 1423).

The person:

As majestic and impressive as the Lion that represents their sign, Leos are the natural leaders of the zodiac. Radiantly enthusiastic, magnanimous with their charm and gifts, and fiercely proud and confident, Leos love and live life to the fullest and expect, indeed need, to be at the helm at home, work, and play. Wonderfully affectionate, dramatic, and creative – there are many Leos among the actors of the world – Leos hate small-mindedness and nit-picking. But they themselves are occasionally stubborn, autocratic, and dogmatic.

The myth:

The Greek hero Hercules figures prominently in the Greek myth about Leo the Lion. As this story goes, King Eurystheus of Greece assigned Hercules 12 dangerous tasks (the famous Herculean Labors) in atonement for killing his wife and children. The first task was to slay and skin the much-feared lion of Nemea. This was no ordinary lion, of course, for he was born of Echidna the snake-woman and Typhon, the grotesquely monstrous Titan who was forever fighting the gods and goddesses. Their son, the Nemean lion, was nearly immortal. When Hercules was unsuccessful in shooting the lion with a bow and arrow, he resorted to a sword and finally to a club, but the lion simply yawned at Hercules's efforts. Hercules then decided to choke the lion to death – and finally succeeded. He removed the lion's head and skin with the beast's own claws, and wore them as armor and helmet during the period of the rest of his mammoth tasks. Zeus subsequently immortalized the Nemean lion in the 14-starred constellation Leo.

Virgo: the Virgin

AUGUST 24 – SEPTEMBER 22

KEYWORDS: Analytical; critical; modest; meticulous; intelligent; fussy

■ **Virgoan scenes from** The Bedford Hours (c. 1423).

The person:

Virgoans are modest, self-effacing, hardworking, and practical on the surface, but are often earthy, warm, and loving beneath that surface, as befits their zodiac symbol, the Virgin, a composite figure of ancient goddesses of the earth and the harvest. Quick thinking and analytical, Virgoans have so much excess mental energy that they often are subject to stress and tension. Their penchants for perfection and hard work also incline them toward being overcritical at times. The planet Mercury (the planet of communication) rules Gemini and Virgo. Virgoans are excellent and persuasive communicators who use their keen intellects to win arguments and win over people.

The myth:

Predecessors of Virgo the Virgin, one of the few zodiac signs represented by a human rather than by an animal, have appeared in several ancient cultures. In Babylonia, she was Nidaba or Shala, the goddess of the grain, depicted with a whip that trailed out over the tail of Leo in the constellation. In an ancient Egyptian zodiac, Virgo was shown holding the tail of Leo. In Greek mythology, Virgo is believed to be one of two figures. The first, Erigone, was the mortal daughter of Icarius, King of Attica, the discoverer of wine, who was murdered by drunken shepherds. Erigone so lamented the death of her father that Zeus placed her within the 13-starred constellation Virgo, along with her faithful dog Maera, now referred to as the Dog-star. Other mythologists believe that the original Virgo was Astraea (which means "starry maiden"), the goddess of purity and innocence who was long associated with justice.

Libra: the Scales

SEPTEMBER 23 – OCTOBER 23

KEYWORDS: Charming; easygoing; diplomatic; sociable; gullible; resentful

The person:

Outgoing, warm-hearted, and very sociable, Librans, like the Scales that represent the sign, are frequently concerned with achieving balance, harmony, peace, and justice in the people and in the world around them. And they are well-equipped to do that with their enormous reserves of charm, cleverness, frankness, persuasion, and easy communication. They tend at times to be too facile and laid-back and have earned an undeserved reputation for laziness. In fact, they can be hard workers and are often leaders in their fields. They are especially good at any "peacekeeping" types of jobs, because they have the remarkable gift of easily seeing (and reconciling) both sides of an issue.

■ **Libran scenes from** The Bedford Hours *(c. 1423).*

The myth:

Libra, the sign of the scales, of balance, and of justice, is not associated with any mythological figure; in fact, it is the only zodiac sign not represented by an animal or human figure. Instead, Libra is associated with a philosophical idea – the weighing of the soul on judgment day – whose origins are traced back to ancient Egypt and the *Book of the Dead*. In that book, the merit of a man's soul is measured by weighing his heart (on one side of a scale) against a feather representing truth (on the other side of the scale). The four-starred constellation named Libra lies closest to Scorpio and is overlapped by the constellation Virgo.

Scorpio: the Scorpion

OCTOBER 24 – NOVEMBER 22

KEYWORDS: Passionate; intense; intuitive; magnetic; jealous; compulsive

The person:

Mysterious Scorpios are deep-thinking, private, intense, very sexual, and always a step removed from the world. Because of their intensity and an obsessive need for privacy, there is often an aura of "danger" around Scorpios – a trait they share, of course, with the deadly Scorpion that symbolizes their sign. But this is only one facet of the rather complex Scorpio personality. They can be driven workers and achievers with the ability to overcome enormously challenging obstacles. They also value their intimate relationships and their friendships quite highly and work hard to encourage the best in those they love.

■ **Scorpian scenes from** The Bedford Hours (c. 1423).

The myth:

The great Greek giant Orion – who has a constellation of his own – was a legendary hunter and the handsomest man on Earth (in mythological times), much pursued by the Greek goddesses. Eos, the dawn-goddess, was especially enamored of Orion and in the heat of one of their meetings, he boasted to her that he was so magnificent a hunter that he could wipe out all the wild herds on Earth. This so infuriated the god Apollo (who was in charge of guarding the herds) that he sent a giant scorpion to sting Orion to death. Apollo's sister, Artemis the Huntress, who fancied Orion herself, tried to intervene by shooting the scorpion with one of her famous arrows. Unfortunately, she missed and shot Orion instead. As a memorial to the handsome giant, Artemis placed Orion in one constellation and gave the scorpion (in hot pursuit) his own seven-starred constellation, very near the constellation of Libra.

Sagittarius: the Archer

NOVEMBER 23 – DECEMBER 21

KEYWORDS: Philosophical; optimistic; intellectual;
explorative; tactless

The person:

Sagittarians love challenges of all kinds – physical or mental – and throw themselves into intellectual or physical pursuits with boundless and infectious reserves of energy. Sagittarians' interests in both purely intellectual pursuits and highly physical adventure underscore their versatile natures and are clearly related to the dual nature of the Archer who symbolizes the sign and who represents the centaur Chiron – a half-man, half-horse god who was was famed for wisdom and bravery. Sagittarians are often unabashedly optimistic extroverts who draw the admiration and affection of all those they encounter.

■ **Sagittarian scenes from** The Bedford Hours (c. 1423).

The myth:

Sagittarius the Archer is no ordinary bow-man, but is in fact one of the legendary centaurs of Greek mythology – those fabulous creatures who were half-man and half-horse. One such centaur, Chiron, a son of the god Saturn, was much admired for his kindness and great knowledge (qualities for which the lecherous and pugnacious centaurs were never famous). Chiron became a beloved teacher to some of mythology's greatest figures, including Hercules, Achilles, and Jason the Argonaut. Accidentally injured by one of Hercules's poisonous arrows, Chiron suffered all the agonies of a painful death, but, being a god, could not die. And so he gave away his immortality to the long-suffering Prometheus (who had been damned to eternal torture by Zeus), took Prometheus's place, and finally found peace in death. So that all would remember Chiron's great sacrifice, Zeus immortalized him in the ten-starred constellation Sagittarius, with the same arrow that had poisoned him.

Capricorn: the Goat

DECEMBER 22 – JANUARY 20

KEYWORDS: Prudent; calculating; practical; ambitious; disciplined

■ **Capricornian scenes from**
The Bedford Hours (c. 1423).

The person:

The Goat that symbolizes Capricorn was traditionally depicted as half-goat, half-fish. This complex dual nature is echoed in the Capricornian personality, one of the most complex characters in all the zodiac. Capricornians have two distinct natures. One side of the sign is ambitious, hard-working, and enterprising. This Capricornian is highly motivated, loves life, and is able to set high but achievable goals. The other side of the Capricornian, however, is lost in a world of real or imagined obstacles to success; further, this Capricornian often cannot find the motivation to take action. Even successful Capricornians have a tendency to whine and complain about imagined or undeserved burdens. These darker tendencies are not eased by Capricornians' introverted natures and love of solitude.

The myth:

Capricorn, often symbolized as half-man, half-goat, was known in ancient astrological works as the Goat-Fish. In Babylonia he was known as Ea, the god of knowledge, and was depicted as a man walking in a fish-shaped coat, fish head, and tail. He lived in an ocean in the Mesopotamian valley, from which he would rise up to share with man the gifts of his knowledge. In ancient Greece, Capricorn was the nature-god Pan. During one of the wars between the gods and the Titans, Typhon – the fiercest of the Titans – drove the gods into Egypt. The only way for the gods to escape Typhon's wrath was to change their shapes. Pan turned his upper body into a goat and his lower body into a fish, then jumped into the Nile River and swam away. Zeus was so impressed with the form that Pan invented that he immortalized it forever in the eight-starred constellation Capricorn.

Aquarius: the Water Bearer

JANUARY 21 – FEBRUARY 18

KEYWORDS: Independent; humane; original; honest;
inventive; distant

■ **Aquarian scenes from** The
Bedford Hours *(c. 1423)*.

The person:

Often considered the most enigmatic of the zodiac
children, Aquarians are fiercely individualistic and
independent intellectuals who rarely form permanent
relationships with anyone. Nevertheless, they are also
noted for being friendly, kind, helpful, and caring; and
they are possessed of deep humanitarian instincts. Still,
they always remain quintessentially private people.
Aquarians are gifted with inventiveness, originality, and
creativity, and they are equally comfortable working in
such disparate worlds as social work and science.

The myth:

The origins of Aquarius the Water Bearer can be traced
to several ancient civilizations. In Babylonia, Aquarius
began as a god of knowledge who was depicted with
water flowing from his hands. In Egypt he was Hap, the
god of the Nile River, who was often pictured carrying
Earth's life-sustaining waters in two large vases. In
ancient Greek mythology, Ganymede was a prince of
Troy and the most beautiful of all human men. So
beautiful was he, that Zeus, the king of the gods himself,
fell hopelessly in love with Ganymede and became
determined that no other being, god or human, would
ever have this mortal. Transforming himself into an
eagle, Zeus carried the beautiful boy away to the skies,
where he made him the immortal cup-bearer in the
12-starred constellation Aquarius. From there,
Ganymede poured wine for the gods and caused rain
to fall on the Earth.

Pisces: the Fish

FEBRUARY 19 – MARCH 20

KEYWORDS: Sensitive; imaginative; vague; kind;
intuitive; easily led

■ **Piscean scenes from** The
Bedford Hours (*c. 1423*).

The person:

Sensitive, sensual, emotional, and richly imaginative and creative, Pisceans are the other-worldly dreamers and poets of the zodiac. Deeply affected by the dual nature of their sign – symbolized by the two fishes swimming in opposite directions – Pisceans are often torn between wanting to do something real and valuable in the world (they are often drawn to humanitarian causes and artistic careers) or retreating from the world altogether to the safer harbors of their private worlds of imagination and dreams. This is an enormous pull for Pisceans, and because of its power, they are often prone to extreme nervous tension and even escapism (sometimes into alcohol and drugs). A lack of self-confidence is almost always at the root of a Piscean's inability to get on with the real world, but when this weakness can be overcome, they are found among the finest humanitarians and artists in the world.

The myth:

The Greek goddess of love Aphrodite and her son Eros were walking along the banks of the Euphrates River when they were confronted by an enraged and fearsome monster named Typhon. He was the youngest, largest, and ugliest of the race of Titans who were born to Uranus, the god of the skies, and Gaia, Mother Earth. The terrified goddess and her son called out to Zeus for help, the king of the gods, who turned Aphrodite and Eros into fish. They then leapt into the Euphrates and swam away to safety. In commemoration of the event, Zeus placed two fishes among the 11-starred constellation that came to be known as Pisces.

A simple summary

✔ The 12 zodiac signs were originally named in ancient times for the constellations of stars in which each sign was placed.

✔ Through the centuries, the stars have shifted backward in the sky (called the "precession of the equinoxes") so that the zodiac signs are no longer in the constellations for which they were named. This does not affect the astrological meaning and symbolism associated with the signs today.

 Ariens – represented by the golden Ram of Greek mythology – are energetic, enthusiastic, and forthright.

Taureans – represented by the mythological Bull, whose shape the god Zeus assumed to woo a mortal – are warm, reliable, and possessive.

Geminians – represented by the twin brothers Pollux and Castor, who are immortalized in the constellation of Gemini – are sharp-witted, restless, and versatile.

Cancerians – represented by the giant Crab who attacked Hercules when he was trying to slay the Hydra – are moody, protective, and loving.

Leos – represented by the fearsome Lion of Nemea, who was slayed by Hercules – are generous, expansive, and impressive.

Virgoans – represented by Astraea, the virgin goddess of purity and innocence, as well as other virginal earth and harvest goddesses – are modest, intelligent, and analytical.

Librans – represented by the ancient Egyptian scales of justice and balance – are charming, easygoing, and sociable.

Scorpios – represented by the deadly Scorpion who was sent by the god Apollo to kill the Greek giant and hunter Orion – are intense, intuitive, and magnetic.

Sagittarians – represented by the half-man, half-horse centaur called Chiron, beloved for his wisdom and bravery – are philosophical, optimistic, and explorative.

Capricornians – represented by the Babylonian Goat-Fish god Ea and the Greek god Pan – are calculating, practical, and ambitious.

Aquarians – represented by Ganymede, the eternal Water Bearer to Earth and to the gods – are independent, inventive, and original.

Pisceans – represented by the two fishes swimming in opposite directions (who were originally the god and goddess Eros and Aphrodite) – are imaginative, sensitive, and other-worldly.

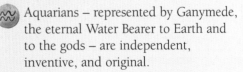

Chapter 4

Rise and Sign: Your Ascendant

JUST AS THE SUN appears to revolve around the Earth, so too does the entire zodiac. During every 24-hour period, each zodiac sign appears over the eastern horizon, mounts the sky, and then disappears below the western horizon. Because of the angle of the Earth's rotation, some signs rise more quickly than others – in the northern hemisphere, for example. In the southern latitudes, however, the signs rise more slowly. In Australia, for instance, more people are born with Scorpio rising than in England, because Scorpio takes longer to rise in the southern hemisphere. The longer a sign takes to rise, the more people who can be born during the "rising," and the more people who will have that zodiac sign as their rising sign or Ascendant (the terms are synonymous).

In this chapter...
✓ The Ascendant or rising sign

17TH-CENTURY PRINT BY ANDREAS CELLARIUS SHOWING THE POSITION OF THE ZODIAC

The Ascendant or rising sign

YOU HAVE PROBABLY READ the section on your Sun sign in Part 2. Perhaps it was even the first thing you turned to. Now it's time to look at other astrological factors which are just as important – perhaps even more important – to understanding one's personality, motivation, and behavior. And the first of those factors is your rising sign, also called your **Ascendant**. *The former term – "rising sign" – is the easiest to remember, because it's the perfect description of what the sign does.*

You probably don't even know what your rising sign is! In fact, in the past only an astrologer could determine that for you. Yet everyone knows their Sun sign (because it covers the four weeks within which you were born), together with all the major characteristics of the sign. Indeed, you can't help but know your Sun-sign characteristics almost from the time you can read: You find them on coffee mugs; inside greeting cards; printed in full color on T-shirts; and as regular entertainment staples in newspaper and magazine columns. In fact, you've probably heard about your Sun-sign qualities so often that it may be impossible not to "take on" those qualities – consciously or unconsciously.

DEFINITION

Simply stated, your rising sign – or **Ascendant** *– is the zodiac sign that was rising on the eastern horizon at the moment you were born.*

In the past, astrologers believed that the Sun sign revealed the "secret you" known only by those closest to you. In contrast, the rising sign was believed to reveal the "public you," the image you presented to the world. Today, we believe the reverse is true: your Sun sign influences your public image; the rising sign indicates the "inner you." Considered together, both signs reveal a picture of who you are, inside and out.

Aries rising

If you have Aries rising, you naturally want to beat everyone else in sight – at everything! You pour your considerable energy into anything you do, with a natural force and vigor which even you find difficult to control. This is underscored by the fact that you want to be seen as fabulously successful and as the one who calls the shots. This can lead to trouble within a family, for example, when elder children who have Aries rising assert their position and try to dominate

■ **Aries** *from the Zodiac Window, Chartres Cathedral.*

not only their brothers and sisters, but even their parents. This is mainly a problem in early childhood and most people do grow out of it in time.

You have the advantage of knowing yourself well – your virtues and your faults – and of being very adaptable. If you can properly channel your considerable energy, you can excel at using your vitality in just the right place, at just the right time, and with exactly the effect you intend.

A Sun-sign Arien's tendency to be accident-prone is translated into an oversimplification of problems with Aries rising. Similarly, while Sun-sign Ariens tend to get a good deal of minor head injuries due to careless actions, a person with Aries rising is prone to headaches or migraines caused by worry or tension.

Those with Aries rising strongly need a permanent relationship, though they are often driven to have meaningless affairs. If you engage in that kind of behavior, it's likely you suffer from guilt afterward. One part of you deeply needs to be faithful to your relationship and fair to your partners. Faithlessness is anything but fair, and you will secretly condemn yourself and be filled with self-loathing, even if you disguise those feelings successfully.

Taurus rising

Possessiveness and jealousy are the worst faults of Sun-sign Taureans. When Taurus is the rising sign, these faults are translated into a basic need to have things: to beg, buy, borrow, or even steal them, if necessary! You won't be satisfied with enormous sums of money stashed away in the bank. You need to display your wealth by driving an expensive car and by filling your (naturally luxurious) home with the most expensive furniture, pictures, and ornaments. Your home will be your castle – not only because of its beauty, but because you feel safer inside it than out in the world. You love security and routine, like most Taureans do. But the stubbornness that characterizes Taurean Sun signs is even more emphasized when Taurus rises. You are absolutely sure that you are always right. And it is difficult to persuade you otherwise, even when the evidence you are wrong is quite convincing.

■ **Taurus** *from the Zodiac Window, Chartres Cathedral.*

You have a passionate (and of course possessive) relationship with your partners, and you are very demanding. And while you need a strong element of friendship within a romantic relationship, your high emotional energy demands a thoroughly fulfilling sex life. If the latter isn't available to you inside the partnership, you may be forced to search for it outside the home.

This bears repeating: we can't emphasize enough how strongly you need sexual satisfaction, and how badly you suffer — physically and emotionally — if you don't get it. Your partner must be made aware of this. And being your partner is demanding enough. To be truly happy, the individual with Taurus rising needs a partner who not only is sexually magnanimous, but who also is a friend and confidant, lover and mistress. Only when all those ducks are in a row will a Taurus-rising partnership flourish

Healthwise, while Sun-sign Taureans sometimes have trouble with their throats, those with Taurus rising seem to have similar problems with the thyroid gland. If you suddenly start putting on weight for no reason, a visit to your physician may be in order.

Gemini rising

While Sun-sign Geminians may have a dozen ideas an hour and try to follow through on all of them, those with Gemini rising manage to keep their feet much more firmly on the ground. Any idea which occurs to you will be carefully examined from all angles and tested thoroughly before being put into practice. You also turn a searching light on your own mind, self-assessing your every emotion, attitude, response, and action.

This rigorous self-examination can be quite problematic. In trying to follow every thread of thought or emotional response that engages you, you often get so bogged down in self-analyzing that you either become thoroughly lost in your own intellectual labyrinth, or you become completely unable to take any action. You need some vigorous physical outlet to burn off this excess mental energy.

People with Gemini rising are good partners, especially with those people who are somewhat underambitious or self-doubting. You have a fine gift for encouraging friends and lovers to pursue bigger and better goals and achievements. You do this with infectious enthusiasm, and take great pleasure in any positive results. Your own enthusiastic versatility is catching, and your partners may find themselves branching out far more energetically than they might have without your encouragement.

On the other hand, you can't abide jealousy or possessiveness in a relationship, even though you're sometimes the very cause of it. It's not that you're prone to having numerous affairs; it's just that you're naturally interested in other people – and your partners may mistake your friendships for something more. Sun-sign Geminians like using their hands and are dexterous. Those with Gemini rising, however, are prone to arthritis, and any chronic pain and/or stiffness in the fingers or joints should be assessed by a doctor. You may also be prone to asthma, possibly precipitated by nervous tension.

■ **Gemini** *from the Zodiac Window, Chartres Cathedral.*

Cancer rising

The pleasure that a Sun-sign Cancerian takes in the home is emphasized when Cancer rises. In fact, this inclination may be so strong that you concentrate solely on your home life and your family – and neglect or reject the outside world altogether.

Luckily, your love for and connection to home and family is protective rather than possessive – and this is in marked contrast to some "pure" Cancerians. You don't nag your partner to work closer to home, nor do you suffocate your children with emotion and try to keep them at home for as long as possible. On the other hand, when your children do leave home, you may worry excessively about them – though without being clinging or overprotective. (This is true, by the way, for males and females.)

A person with Cancer rising who doesn't have a family must find some release for these nurturing and caretaking impulses. Charitable work is often a good outlet, but the obvious choice is a career or volunteer work in one of the caregiving professions. On the subject of work, take heed: when Cancer rises you may work almost too hard to further the ambitions of your partner; on the flip side of this tendency, Cancer rising may alternately encourage a certain emotional coolness (and seeming disinterest) in even the closest relationship. A partner should not hesitate to point this out if it becomes a problem.

With Cancer rising, you are very vulnerable to other influences shown in the birth chart – especially those of any planet in the first house, particularly if it forms a conjunction with the Ascendant. This can be a real problematic aspect, so be on the alert for it.

Leo rising

With Leo rising you probably have superb organizational skills – and you know it. This can lead to your being especially self-assured, to the point of pomposity. You frequently believe that you know best, and you make that clear to everyone. Humility is a difficult lesson to learn, but a lesson you may have to tackle nevertheless if you want to get on in the world (and with other lesser mortals!).

You badly need success and will sacrifice far too much to gain it – including some of your own talents. Remember that you need to exercise your creative gifts as well. Too much time and energy spent on achieving prosperity will be wasted time if your inner life isn't as rich as your checking account.

■ **Leo** *from the Zodiac Window, Chartres Cathedral.*

You have great inner strength and supreme confidence. Both qualities make it safe for you to engage in some healthy self-criticism from time to time, which you should do to help maintain a balance between your drive for success and your need for creative exploration. Your confidence also helps you survive even the most scathing criticism from others, something else you should heed, especially during those times when you tend to be pompous and autocratic. A trusted partner may be your best foil.

As far as partnership goes, you really need someone who has a strong and independent mind, and who won't simply roll over for you and give in to your every wish. For your part, you take great Leonine pride in a partner's achievements and are an enthusiastic cheerleader.

Given your driven need to succeed and the conflicts this may cause at home between you and loved ones, it should come as no surprise to you that you may have some psychological difficulties. They may signal themselves at first as vague and general aches and pain, particularly in the back or neck. People with Leo rising who find themselves chronically worrying (or being criticized) about balancing career, home, and personal fulfillment – especially if there are persistent headaches or back pain – should get a physical and psychological check-up.

Virgo rising ♍

The main problem for people with Virgo rising is often a crippling lack of self-confidence. You have a tendency to inwardly question and criticize every move you make, every thought you have. The end result is that you often have to work overtime to convince yourself that you have any virtues at all, or anything to contribute to the world. This is a far greater problem for rising-sign Virgoans than it is for most Sun-sign Virgoans. At best, this constant carping at yourself may cause chronic anxiety and stress; at worst, it can lead to actual physical illness.

If your parents were very critical of you as a child, this problem may be intensified. When you are interpreting your birth chart, look for other planetary influences that may strengthen your self-confidence and encourage you to praise yourself.

In your personal relationships, you may well find it easier than Sun-sign Virgoans to be warm and outgoing. You are tender and loving, with a wonderfully gentle and warm quality.

One last thing to watch out for: You tend to give in way too easily to others and to retreat from arguments and conflicts. But there's help at hand. When Virgo rises, Gemini – which is the other sign ruled by Mercury – is often found at the top of the chart (the Midheaven). This placement of quick-witted and communicative Gemini will help you to knit together opposing viewpoints (rather than retreat from them) and see yourself as a whole personality with real potential. The Mercury influence will encourage you to be outgoing, to communicate your ideas, and to think of yourself as a worthwhile asset to society.

■ **Virgo** *from the Zodiac Window, Chartres Cathedral.*

Libra rising

The simple and sad truth here is that the effects of Libra rising are not very strong at all in a birth chart. Libra is not an assertive sign at the best of times. When it rises, the positive effects it does have are greatly inhibited and often overshadowed by stronger influences elsewhere in the chart. Moreover, these negative, inhibiting qualities affect every characteristic associated with the sign.

Take, for example, your innate need for someone to lean on, for a partner who can be used as an emotional crutch. This tendency is so strong with Libra rising that you rush into a relationship with absolutely no thought at all. Too often, the partners you choose are terribly wrong for you.

The situation is not helped by the fact that those with Libra rising are more sexually active than many Sun-sign Librans; this also can attract unsuitable partners. Finally, you can be so in love with the idea of love that, again, you rush prematurely into a relationship. So be warned: Take your time before making an emotional commitment.

■ **Libra** *from the Zodiac Window, Chartres Cathedral.*

Oddly, perhaps, you can be rather self-satisfied and either fail to recognize your faults or simply ignore them. Because you're so charming, you often get away with this – but never for long. A lovingly critical partner or friend may help dissuade you from this tendency – if you really listen to them!

Quite a few people with Libra rising will have Neptune close to the Ascendant in their birth chart and even in the first house. In either placement, Neptune can further encourage you to take the line of least resistance – so be careful. On the other hand, Neptune will also strengthen your more tender, compassionate impulses. This is a wonderfully gentling influence, if you turn those feelings into positive, constructive action; not so wonderful, however, if you use the same feelings to escape reality.

And while we're on the subject of escapism: If Neptune is in Libra in the 12th house in your birth chart, beware – you may seek escape through drug use. It will better for you to channel your more "slippery" emotions through some creative art form.

Scorpio rising

When Scorpio rises, all the strongest personality traits of the sign will be seen – and make themselves felt. While you have the keenest sense of purpose, you also question your own motives incessantly (and secretively). You dislike anybody knowing too much about you. You do, however, turn self-knowledge into very positive action. When faced with a challenge, you know yourself so well that you can quickly accentuate your strengths and curb your weaknesses to fit any situation.

Beware of knowing yourself too well, however, and don't go overboard by taking an inventory of your faults and failings. People with Scorpio rising may all too easily slip into self-loathing rather than healthy self-awareness.

Your famous love of privacy will extend to your personal relationships. Tender and true, you won't display your more vulnerable traits to anyone outside your home. You can, however, be possessive and jealous, and your addiction to secrecy makes it difficult for you to discuss any problems with your partner. Unresolved difficulties may manifest themselves physically: as anxiety, at best; impotency, at worst.

When Scorpio is rising and Leo is on the Midheaven, the drive and emotional resources of Scorpio are enriched by Leo's organizational powers and capacity for leadership. This is fine – provided you don't translate these qualities into a real need for power and a tendency to dominate. Positively used, these energies can be your most valuable asset; used negatively, they make for an autocratic and even power-mad individual.

■ **Scorpio** *from the Zodiac Window, Chartres Cathedral.*

Sagittarius rising

Sun-sign Sagittarians need challenge; when Sagittarius is rising, the need for challenge is even greater. You can easily rise to the top of any profession, and you use your gifts to the maximum. Positive and optimistic, you're naturally self-confident, but never complacent. You easily recognize (and work on) your shortcomings; in fact, you're eager to know yourself as thoroughly as possible. You trust your instincts and don't hesitate to act on them at any time.

Your level-headedness endows you with considerable character, and your harmonious outlook on life is often in stark contrast to the attitudes of some Sun-sign Sagittarians. This all sounds ideal. But those with Sagittarius rising can trip themselves up by the very self-awareness they so prize. You may falsely conclude sometimes that you know yourself so thoroughly that you're ready to tackle anything.

You need friendship as well as physical satisfaction from your partner. Indeed, you thrive on intellectual challenge and intellectual freedom, and you love to argue about the bigger issues. Life itself must always be challenging for you: you need to be intellectually and physically engaged at all times. When life slows down for you or simply gets too quiet, traveling to new and exhilarating environments is a happy remedy to your restlessness.

■ **Sagittarius** *from the Zodiac Window, Chartres Cathedral.*

Capricorn rising

People with Capricorn rising often present the curious anomaly of being overconfident in some ways and underconfident in others; or being positive on one day and negative on another day. For example, a successful businessman with Capricorn rising will deal thoroughly and decisively with a problem involving millions of dollars, but the next moment agonize about the message to write on his wife's birthday card.

This "hot-and-cold" problem can extend into various aspects of your life. You may be extremely competent at work, for instance, but doubt whether you can maintain a satisfactory personal relationship. The root of this problem lies in your not being able to look at yourself objectively, and your tendency to underestimate your capabilities and achievements.

No end of compliments, reassurances, promotions, or salary increases can offer you reassurance. You must regularly remind yourself that you're immensely capable and no doubt highly successful.

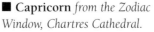

■ **Capricorn** *from the Zodiac Window, Chartres Cathedral.*

With Capricorn rising, you are more warm and caring in personal relationships than are Sun-sign Capricorns. You express your emotions more freely, and your attitude to your partner is more tender and loving. You also find it easier to regard your family simply as family, rather than as possessions and symbols of your place in society.

Healthwise, you may have digestive problems and even stomach ulcers. Tension can be a problem, too, and a carefully considered routine of exercise, relaxation, and simple pleasures is the best remedy. You're somewhat pessimistic and may be prone to depression. Physical exercise is a good corrective.

Aquarius rising

If you have Aquarius rising, you are even more private than a typical Sun-sign Aquarian. Lovers and friends may feel like they never get really close to you, and that's especially problematic for lovers. You must learn the difference between healthy independence and unhealthy isolation.

Your best Aquarian qualities – kindness, tenderness, love – shine when you work to help others, and you can be among the finest of humanitarians. Oddly enough, however, you don't accept offers of love, tenderness, and kindness well. Instead, you may push away friends and lovers. You must work hard to dismantle this emotional barrier. Easier said than done, of course, because you find making changes enormously difficult. On the worst end of the spectrum, you can be downright pig-headed, even vain, about the cold and independent stance that you sometimes are inclined to take.

In a close personal relationship, all these tendencies are very near the surface and can be potential life-wreckers. Look for countering influences in your birth chart that will encourage you to be more receptive to love and affection. Or find a partner who's perfectly happy being solely on the receiving end of your attentions!

■ **Aquarius** *from the Zodiac Window, Chartres Cathedral.*

You can be generous to a fault, but again, you need to take the lead when it comes to giving. Your inability to accept another's outpouring of generosity is very difficult to live with for any partner. And if you can't "give way" from time to time, you'll find yourself beached on some very sharp rocks.

Healthwise, watch out for one of two possible developments: either a hypochondriac tendency to worry about your health excessively and unnecessarily; or a total disdain for doctors and medical care, even when you are in fact seriously ill. You may be devoted to alternative medicine and unconventional health cures even when conventional treatments are the best option. The circulatory system is ruled by Aquarius, and vigorous, regular exercise is extremely important for you.

Pisces rising

Remember our little ditty from the first chapter? "The other day upon the stair, I met a man who wasn't there . . . " Well, he probably had Pisces rising!

People with Pisces rising are so good at taking on the color of their surroundings that they practically disappear. At worst, other people will tend to forget you exist; at best, they'll simply ignore you. That would be a pity, because you're extremely helpful, know how to get things done without a fuss, and can be the backbone of many a committee or organization. You must work on building up your self-confidence and recognizing your value in society.

You are not a natural leader, so your instincts about taking a back seat in certain situations are right on the mark. You do far better working quietly away in the background, and if anybody offers you a position of leadership, think long and hard about whether you really want to accept the responsibility.

■ **Pisces** *from the Zodiac Window, Chartres Cathedral.*

Actors often admit to enjoying the profession because when they're onstage they can hide their true selves behind their characters. A person with Pisces rising shares a similar viewpoint. Indeed, you often seem to play a part with such conviction that you begin to forget who you really are!

Those around you, too, may never get to see the genuine you. There is no real harm in this type of role playing, as long as it doesn't lead to self-deception. But do remember to take your mask off once in a while, at least in private, and give yourself the chance to discover who you are at heart, and what you really want from life.

A friendly warning: with Pisces rising, you may tend to be very critical of your lovers, even to the point of destroying what could be a perfectly good and happy liaison.

A simple summary

✓ The rising sign, also called the Ascendant, is the zodiac sign that was rising on the eastern horizon when you were born.

✓ Your Sun sign influences your public image; your rising sign indicates the "inner you." Together, the two signs reveal a complete picture of who you are.

♈ People with Aries rising are assertive, energetic, and selfish.

♉ People with Taurus rising are patient, possessive, and self-indulgent.

♊ People with Gemini rising are communicative, versatile, and restless.

♋ People with Cancer rising are emotional, protective, and loving.

♌ People with Leo rising are generous, bossy, and creative.

♍ People with Virgo rising are analytical, modest, and fussy.

♎ People with Libra rising are charming, easygoing, and gullible.

♏ People with Scorpio rising are passionate, intense, and jealous.

♐ People with Sagittarius rising are philosophical, optimistic, and intellectual.

♑ People with Capricorn rising are prudent, disciplined, and calculating.

♒ People with Aquarius rising are independent, humane, and distant.

♓ People with Pisces rising are sensitive, imaginative, and vague.

Chapter 5

The Family of Planets

GETTING TO KNOW THE PLANETS and how they work is as important as getting to know the zodiac signs and the rising signs. We've said it before, but it bears repeating; astrology is the study of the influence of the planets on the Earth and all Earth's creatures (including you!). Astrology is not simply the study of Sun signs. When you focus only on your Sun sign, you're like the diner who passes on the meat and potatoes so he or she can fill up on dessert. Deliciously fun, once or twice, but not a diet you can live on for long. When you construct your birth chart, you will discover that there were lots of planets in other parts of the sky; in other words, you don't just have the Sun in one particular sign, you also have all the planets in several of the signs.

In this chapter...

✓ Astrology's family of planets

DECORATIVE WHEEL SHOWING ELEMENTS AND ZODIAC SIGNS

Astrology's family of planets

AS WE LEARNED IN CHAPTER 2, the family of seven planets which the ancients knew – the Sun and the Moon (always considered "planets" in astrology), and Mercury, Venus, Mars, Jupiter, and Saturn – were joined over the last four centuries by the "modern" planets – Uranus, Neptune, and Pluto. Astrologers study the influences of all ten planets in a birth chart; both their singular influences and, even more importantly, the influences they exert in combination with one another and within the zodiac signs.

If your Sun sign is Virgo, you probably also know that Mercury is Virgo's ruling planet. And you no doubt recognize that many of the Virgoan qualities you embrace are the effects of Mercury.

But Mercury also rules Gemini, and its effects there are quite different than those in Virgo. Indeed, the two signs are different in character, though they share certain skills.

In both cases, the planet has not changed an iota, any more than the constellations of Virgo and Gemini have. Astrologers liken these changeable effects of the planets in the signs to the way sunlight changes the colors in a stained-glass window as it filters through. Similarly, the influences of the planets are "colored" by the sign they occupy . . . and vice versa. Besides having "rulership" responsibilities which directly affect the qualities of the zodiac signs in a birth chart, the planets may also be *personalized* in a chart, which is a phenomenon that gives them

■ **The Moon** *is always a "personal" planet in astrological terms.*

DEFINITION

*In addition to ruling a specific Sun sign, every planet also has a particular sign in which it works especially well and its influences are somewhat more pronounced than with other planets. In such a sign, the planet is said to be in **exalt**. The Sun, for example, rules Leo and is exalted in Aries. (See the chart of Planet Relationships on p. 86.)*

■ **A computer-enhanced image** *of the Earth, the Sun, and Moon.*

especially important meaning to an individual; and their influences can also be magnified (known as in *exalt*) or diminished (known as in *fall*), depending on the zodiac sign in which they are placed in a chart.

DEFINITION

*Besides ruling a specific Sun sign, every planet has a sign in which it may work less well than expected and its influences may be less pronounced. In such a sign, the planet is said to be in **fall**. Mercury rules Gemini and Virgo and is in fall in Pisces. (See the chart of Planet Relationships on p. 86.)*

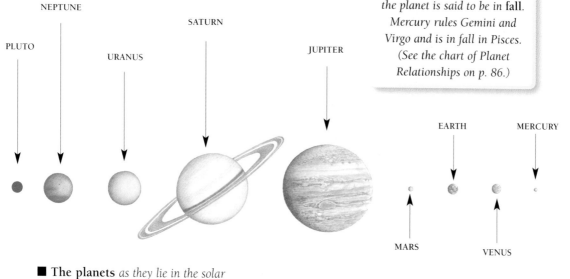

NEPTUNE

SATURN

PLUTO

URANUS

JUPITER

EARTH

MERCURY

MARS

VENUS

■ **The planets** *as they lie in the solar system, with Mercury closest to the Sun.*

THE RULING PLANETS

Each planet "rules" a particular sign – Mercury and Venus rule two each, and before the three "modern" planets were discovered, Mars ruled Scorpio as well as Aries, Jupiter ruled Pisces as well as Sagittarius, and Saturn ruled Aquarius as well as Capricorn. The planets' influences are particularly strong in the signs they rule, so it's a good idea to learn the ruling planet list below:

ZODIAC SIGN	RULING PLANET	ZODIAC SIGN	RULING PLANET	ZODIAC SIGN	RULING PLANET
ARIES	Mars	LEO	Sun	SAGITTARIUS	Jupiter
TAURUS	Venus	VIRGO	Mercury	CAPRICORN	Saturn
GEMINI	Mercury	LIBRA	Venus	AQUARIUS	Uranus
CANCER	Moon	SCORPIO	Pluto	PISCES	Neptune

THE PLANETS AND THEIR GLYPHS

- SUN
- MOON
- MERCURY
- VENUS
- MARS
- JUPITER
- SATURN
- URANUS
- NEPTUNE
- PLUTO

PLANET RELATIONSHIPS MADE SIMPLE

PLANET	SUN SIGN	SIGN OF EXALTATION	SIGN OF FALL
SUN	Leo	Aries	Libra
MOON	Cancer	Taurus	Scorpio
MERCURY	Gemini and Virgo	Virgo	Pisces
VENUS	Taurus and Libra	Pisces	Virgo
MARS	Aries	Capricorn	Cancer
JUPITER	Sagittarius	Cancer	Capricorn
SATURN	Capricorn	Libra	Aries
URANUS	Aquarius	Scorpio	Taurus
NEPTUNE	Pisces	Leo	Aquarius
PLUTO	Scorpio	Virgo	Pisces

Herewith, a brief look at the mythological origins and astrological significance of the ten planets that span the zodiac. The Sun and Moon are included in the list of planets.

The Sun

KEYWORDS: self-expression, vitality

The Sun represents our vitality and self-expression. Its importance is underlined by its commanding physical presence in our lives throughout history. Almost every civilization since the world began has worshiped a sun god. In Western mythology, the most famous sun god is Apollo – the son of Jupiter – who is represented as a handsome nude athlete, pure, innocent, and strong.

Believed to be governed by the archangel Michael, the Sun rules Leo, is exalted in Aries, and is in fall in Libra. It is associated with the metal gold and rules the heart. A well-placed Sun encourages generosity of heart, creativity, joy, affection, healthy self-esteem, and magnanimity. Badly placed, however, the Sun may encourage self-admiration, selfishness, pomposity, conceit, and ostentation. Those with a strongly placed Sun are generous and often found in positions of influence and power.

■ **Apollo** *is perhaps the most famous mythological sun god.*

■ **The Sun** *is regarded as a planet for astrological purposes.*

The Moon

KEYWORDS: instinct, intuition, emotion, vacillation, responsiveness

Known as the great mother-goddess throughout all ancient civilizations, the Moon is considered "female" and appears in classical myths under the guise of various goddesses – Ceres, Hecate, and Selene – who could be both kind and cruel.

The Moon rules Cancer, is exalted in Taurus, and is in fall in Scorpio. It is associated with the metal silver, and rules the breasts, digestive system, and the lymph glands. Powerfully linked to the subconscious, the Moon encourages natural, instinctive behavior, strongly affects the emotions, and is associated with imagination and sensitivity. When the Moon is strong in a birth chart, the individual is likely to be rather inward-looking, sensitive, impressionable, and vacillating.

The Moon can make us patient and sympathetic, but also unreliable. Although some individuals with a strong Moon seek out prominent positions in public life, most other individuals with a strong Moon are likely to be private people who love the seclusion and security of their homes.

Mercury

KEYWORDS: intellect, communication

In Greek myth, Mercury was the messenger of the gods and the god of travelers. He was a splendid athlete and is usually depicted in ancient statues wearing only the winged sandals, which gave him his speed, and the magic helmet, which protected him as the bearer of important news.

Mercury rules Gemini and Virgo, is exalted in Virgo, and is in fall in Pisces. It is associated with the metals mercury and nickel, and rules the hands, arms, lungs, and nervous system. Mercury influences the intellect, communication, emotional and physical energy, and versatility.

When Mercury is strongly placed in a birth chart, it encourages quick and agile thinking, good communication skills, perceptiveness, imagination, and analytical ability. Badly placed, Mercury may also incline an individual towards overcriticism, argumentativeness, sarcasm, and deceit. "Mercurial" people are not necessarily great thinkers; rather, they are able to respond quickly and cleverly to situations or stimuli. They are mentally agile and facile, love to engage in verbal exchanges, and are easily bored by those slower than themselves.

Venus

KEYWORDS: love, harmony, consensus

Venus, the Roman goddess of love (synonymous with Aphrodite, the Greek goddess of love), ruled not only sexual love, but love of family and spouse. In the grounds of the goddess's temples throughout the ancient world, there were always hidden nooks and corners where her worshippers could make love.

Venus rules Taurus and Libra, is exalted in Pisces, and is in fall in Libra. It is associated with the metal copper, and governs the body as a whole – but especially the lower back and the thyroid gland. Venus underscores the "feminine" aspects of the personality, and the spiritual and sensual sides of love (rather than the sexual side).

Strongly placed in the birth chart, Venus encourages gentleness, friendship, tact, diplomacy, and romance. Badly placed, Venus inhibits communication and encourages laziness. The planet also affects our attitudes toward work, ideas, and abstract concepts. Individuals with a well-placed Venus are invariably good-looking, creative, and popular with the opposite sex.

Trivia...

The glyph that symbolizes Venus is the internationally recognized symbol for the word "female."

Mars

KEYWORDS: physical energy, initiative

Mars, the ferocious Roman god of War (named after Ares, his Greek equivalent), was fortunate in battle, but unfortunate in love. Although originally a Roman god of farming, Mars is always depicted in full battle dress, even when he is engaged in one of his many flirtations.

The planet Mars rules Aries, is exalted in Capricorn, and is in fall in Cancer. It is associated with the metal iron, and governs the head. A strongly placed Mars encourages hard work, optimism, dynamic energy, courage, assertiveness, and enthusiasm.

The planet also has a strong connection to physical sexuality, the sexual glands and organs, and acts of aggression. Strongly or weakly placed, Mars also encourages a quick temper, anger, and rudeness. Mars is primarily concerned with physical energy and how that energy is channeled – in work and in play.

Trivia...

The glyph that symbolizes Mars is the internationally recognized symbol for the word "male."

Jupiter

KEYWORD: expansion

Jupiter was the powerful ruler of all the Roman gods and goddesses (his Greek equivalent is Zeus), as well as the special protector of the ancient city of Rome. There at his temple, Roman soldiers came for Jupiter's blessings before they went off to battle. Jupiter could also be a cruel and punishing god, and he is often depicted as angrily hurling thunderbolts from the sky.

In antiquity, Jupiter ruled both Sagittarius and Pisces. In modern astrology the planet rules Sagittarius, is exalted in Cancer, and is in fall in Capricorn. It is associated with the metal tin, and governs the hips, thighs, and liver. Strongly placed, Jupiter encourages a positive, expansive outlook, optimism, loyalty, high-mindedness, justice, generosity, and fidelity.

The planet is powerfully concerned with learning, philosophy, languages, morality, and problem solving. Badly placed, Jupiter encourages self-indulgence, a lack of inner and outer discipline, a weak moral character, and foolhardiness. Traditionally known as the planet of expansion, Jupiter is associated with physical size (too much "physical size"), and, arcanely, with baldness and hirsuteness!

Saturn

KEYWORDS: stability, restriction, limitation, control

In classical mythology Saturn, a Roman agricultural god, was the father of Jupiter, the king of the gods. Saturn is famously associated with the ancient Roman festival of Saturnalia, held in his honor in mid-December and later adopted by the Christian church and renamed Christmas.

In ancient times, Saturn ruled both Aquarius and Capricorn. In contemporary astrology, Saturn rules Capricorn, is exalted in Libra, and is in fall in Aries. It is associated with the metal lead, and governs all the bones in the body, but especially the knee bones. Saturn is traditionally associated with limitations and boundaries and thus is often thought of as having generally inhibiting influences.

Strongly placed, however, it encourages high practicality, dependability, pragmatism, and honesty. Saturn is also keenly associated with perseverance and tenacity. Badly placed, Saturn's inhibiting effects have full sway and tend to dampen or obstruct positive feelings and actions.

Uranus

KEYWORDS: change, disruption, shock

Uranus is the first of the "modern" planets, discovered in 1781 by the British astronomer William Herschel, who called it "George's Star." (George III was the King of England at the time). For many years astronomers had referred to an unknown, hypothetical planet which they called "Ouranos," and eventually Herschel's "new" planet came to be known as Uranus. Astrologers were quick to associate the planet with its mythological namesake, Uranus, the ancient god of the skies, who mated with Mother Earth to create the first living beings and who later fathered Aphrodite, the Greek goddess of love. In a bloody coup, Uranus was dethroned (and castrated) by Saturn.

Uranus rules Aquarius, is exalted in Scorpio, and is in fall in Taurus. It is associated with the metal aluminum, and governs the shins, ankles, and circulatory system. Above all, Uranus is the planet of change — both personal change and societal change. Strongly placed, the planet encourages heightened (and often eccentric) levels of originality, versatility, and independence.

Uranus is traditionally associated with revolution, upheaval, and lawlessness. Badly placed, Uranus encourages eccentricity, rebellion, crime, violence, perversity, and sexual deviation. The planet also has a celebrated association with space exploration and science fiction.

Neptune

KEYWORDS: cloudiness, unreality

Neptune, another of the "modern" planets, was discovered in 1846. After some consideration, astrologers decided that its influences were somewhat "watery" and gave it rulership over the highly emotional Pisces. In mythology, Neptune was the Roman god of the oceans, lakes, and rivers (his Greek equivalent was Poseidon), who later took the form of a horse so he could romance Ceres (Demeter in Greek mythology), the Roman goddess of agriculture, who was herself a horse at the time.

Neptune rules Pisces, is exalted in Leo, and is in fall in Aquarius. It is associated with the metals platinum and tin, and governs the feet. Strongly placed, it encourages pure idealism, great imagination, and keen sensitivity. Fittingly, it is traditionally associated with artists, writers, poetry, and dancing.

Pluto

KEYWORDS: elimination, eruptive change

The newest of the "modern" planets, Pluto was discovered in 1930, and it was not – as some people may have you believe – named after Mickey Mouse's dog! In fact, Pluto was an ancient agricultural god who had the additional (dark) task of ruling the mythological Underworld (the land of death), where all departed souls eventually traveled along the murky Styx River. Pluto also had the power of invisibility.

Pluto rules Scorpio, is exalted in Virgo, and is in fall in Pisces. It is associated with the metals steel and iron, and governs the genitals. Strongly placed, it encourages individuals to confront and overcome obstacles – whether psychological, physical, or societal.

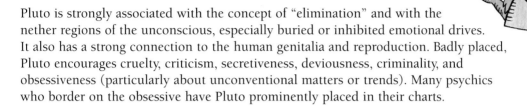

Pluto is strongly associated with the concept of "elimination" and with the nether regions of the unconscious, especially buried or inhibited emotional drives. It also has a strong connection to the human genitalia and reproduction. Badly placed, Pluto encourages cruelty, criticism, secretiveness, deviousness, criminality, and obsessiveness (particularly about unconventional matters or trends). Many psychics who border on the obsessive have Pluto prominently placed in their charts.

A simple summary

✔ Knowing about the planets is as important as knowing about your zodiac sign and your rising sign.

✔ For your birth chart, or horoscope, you have both the Sun and nine planets in various zodiac signs.

✔ The Sun, Moon, Mercury, Venus, Mars, Jupiter, and Saturn were the seven traditional planets known to all ancient astrologers; the three "modern" planets comprise Uranus, Neptune, and Pluto, which joined the family during the last four centuries.

✔ Each planet rules a specific zodiac sign. Each planet may also be "personalized" in a birth chart, or in "exalt", or in "fall" (see definitions), depending on which sign the planet is "in."

The Sun rules Leo and is associated with joyfulness, generosity, self-expression, and vitality.

The Moon rules Cancer and is associated with emotions, instincts, intuition, and responsiveness.

Mercury rules Gemini and Virgo and is associated with communication, intellect, reason, and versatility.

Venus rules Taurus and Libra and is associated with beauty, gentility, harmony, and love.

Mars rules Aries and is associated with aggression, decisiveness, initiative, and physical energy.

Jupiter rules Sagittarius and is associated with expansiveness, extravagance, justice, and optimism.

Saturn rules Capricorn and is associated with caution, control, stability, and tenacity.

Uranus rules Aquarius and is associated with change, eccentricity, independence, and originality.

Neptune rules Pisces and is associated with idealism, imagination, sensitivity, and carelessness.

Pluto rules Scorpio and is associated with elimination, eruptive change, secretiveness, and sexuality.

Chapter 6

You Simply Gotta Have Friends!

BESIDES THE CHARACTERISTICS exhibited by each sign and planet, the signs and planets have other characteristics which give another layer of meaning to the birth chart. The signs receive these qualities from four traditional groupings. The influence of the planets is further affected by the distances (degrees) that separate them in a birth chart, allowing them to form aspects. The effects of the planets, signs, and aspects occur within the boundaries of four major angles of the birth chart, which also exert influences. Here we look first at the sign groupings, the planetary aspects, and then the four main angles of the birth chart.

In this chapter...
- ✓ Getting to know groupings
- ✓ Planetary aspects...really!
- ✓ The aspect patterns
- ✓ Simply no aspects at all!
- ✓ Other riders in the sky – the heavenly angles

LATE 18TH-CENTURY SEXTANT USED FOR MEASURING ANGLES BETWEEN STARS

Getting to know groupings

OVER THE YEARS, *the 12 zodiac signs have traditionally fallen into four groupings or relationships within which they share certain basic characteristics that complement or contrast with the characteristics of other signs in their group. The four groupings are gender (or duality), element (or triplicity), quality (or quadruplicity), and polarity.*

The genders

The first grouping of signs is by gender. Traditionally, the zodiac signs were said to be either masculine/positive or feminine/negative, and astrologers still respect this tradition.

The masculine/positive signs are Aries, Gemini, Leo, Libra, Sagittarius, and Aquarius. The feminine/negative signs are Taurus, Cancer, Virgo, Scorpio, Capricorn, and Pisces. Here, the word "gender" does not refer to the male or female sex (a woman may have a masculine/positive sign; a man a feminine/negative side), but rather to the archetypal attributes associated with the masculine and the feminine in everyone. The masculine zodiac signs tend to be more extroverted, sociable, and outwardly driven; the feminine signs more introverted, less sociable, and inwardly focused.

The elements or triplicities

The second grouping of signs is by the four essential elements of life: fire, earth, air, and water. Three signs are assigned to each element: Aries, Leo, and Sagittarius are the fire signs; Taurus, Virgo, and Capricorn are the earth signs; Gemini, Libra, and Aquarius are the air signs; and Cancer, Scorpio, and Pisces are the water signs. The fire signs represent enthusiasm, the earth signs practicality, the air signs intellectualism, and the water signs emotionality. The elements are also called the triplicities.

Trivia...

The notion of astrological gender or duality is an ancient one, and in Western tradition is traced back to about 500 B.C. and the Greek mathematician Pythagoras. In fact, the theory is probably far more ancient than that. Symbolically, astrological gender/duality is very similar to the 4,000-year-old Chinese concept of yin and yang, the primal elements of the universe: yin symbolizes the feminine, dark, closed, wet, and cold; yang the masculine, light, open, dry, and hot.

FIRE   EARTH

AIR

WATER

Though we violently oppose the common belief that certain Sun signs simply cannot have a good relationship with certain other Sun signs, people who share the same element – for example, two fire-sign people – do tend to get on especially well.

The qualities or quadruplicities

The third grouping of signs is by three types of energy called the qualities – cardinal, fixed, or mutable. Four signs are assigned to each quality: the cardinal signs are Aries, Cancer, Libra, and Capricorn; the fixed signs are Taurus, Leo, Scorpio, and Aquarius; the mutable signs are Gemini, Virgo, Sagittarius, and Pisces. The cardinal signs tend to be spontaneous and sociable; the fixed signs determined and somewhat rigid; and the mutable signs versatile and flexible. These qualities are also called the quadruplicities.

The polarities

The fourth grouping of signs is by polarity. Each zodiac sign is paired with its distinct polar or opposite sign (found directly across from it in the zodiac circle). The polar pairings are: Aries/Libra, Taurus/Scorpio, Gemini/Sagittarius, Cancer/Capricorn, Leo/Aquarius, and Virgo/Pisces.

Though "opposite" across the zodiac, the polar signs are by no means psychologically opposite; indeed, there's usually a special link between them, especially in the area of business partnerships or other types of work relationships. When someone with one sign forms a working relationship with someone whose Sun sign is their polar opposite, the two people generally find that they understand each other's attitudes and motives quite well, even if they don't agree on absolutely everything.

On a personal note, one of the authors of this book has Gemini for a Sun sign, while the other author has Sagittarius, Gemini's polar sign, as a rising sign; so far, they have been happily married for almost 45 years.

INTERNET

www.efn.org/~patricia

This light-hearted web site offers some delightful tips for people in a relationship – or thinking of starting one – about how to compare birth charts for compatibility.

Planetary aspects . . . really!

BY NOW, YOU PROBABLY won't have much difficulty seeing some of the major components and patterns in a birth chart. In fact, it's relatively easy to spot in which zodiac signs and houses the planets are located; or in which houses the zodiac signs are placed.

The relationships or *aspects* between the planets themselves (measured in degrees) are slightly more difficult to spot, but have considerable impact in a birth chart. With some practice you will easily be able to see whether one planet is in aspect to another. There are nine aspects that planets may form, categorized by type (positive or negative) and strength (powerful, strong, moderate, or weak). Here's a brief look at all nine aspects – how they are made and their general influences.

DEFINITION

*When two planets in a birth chart have a specific number of degrees between them – measured around the circumference of the birth-chart circle – one planet is said to be in **aspect** to the other (see chart below). Total circumference of the circle is of course, 360 degrees. One degree equals 1/360th of the circle.*

POSITIVE AND NEGATIVE ASPECTS

ASPECT	GLYPH	TYPE	DEGREES APART	ORB
Conjunction	☌	Positive or Negative	0°	8°, up to10° with ☉ and ☽
Trine	△	Positive	120°	8°
Sextile	✶	Positive	60°	6°
Opposition	☍	Negative	180°	8°, up to10° with ☉, ☽, or ruling planet
Square	☐	Negative	90°	8°
Semi-square	∠	Negative	45°	2°
Quincunx	⚻	Negative	150°	2°, up to 3° with ☉, ☽, and personal planet
Sesquare	⊡	Weak – Negative	135°	2°
Semi-sextile	⊻	Weak – Negative	30°	2°

DEFINITION

*For two or more planets to be in aspect, they must be a certain number of **degrees apart** (see chart). For example, a sextile is made when two or more planets are 60 degrees apart. However, exact distances don't often occur. Astrologers have therefore devised an allowance of degrees for each aspect, within which the aspect can still be made. For the sextile, the allowance is 6 degrees – in either direction. That is, two planets can form a sextile if they are between 54 degrees and 66 degrees apart. This degree allowance is called an **orb**.*

The aspects

CONJUNCTION The simplest aspect of all is the conjunction. This occurs when two or more planets occupy the same – or almost the same – degree in the chart. For example, if both the Sun and the Moon are on the same degree of a sign – say 6 degrees of Aries – they are said to be conjunct. The conjunction, which may be positive or negative, is the most powerful of all aspects and greatly intensifies the influences of whichever planets are involved.

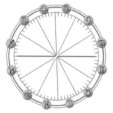

Planets aren't often exactly the number of degrees apart needed to make an aspect. Two planets don't have to be on the same degree to be conjunct. But they must be no more than 8 degrees apart. When this happens, this degree allowance is called an orb.

OPPOSITION The second easiest of the aspects to see occurs when two planets are 180 degrees apart and are said to be in opposition. This is a powerful negative aspect that often signals disruption and conflict, but it also encourages strength of character and the willingness to fight for change.

TRINE One of the more powerful positive aspects, a trine occurs when two or more planets in a chart are 120 degrees apart. The trine encourages balance and harmony, and generally helps make life easier.

SEXTILE Another of the powerful positive aspects, a sextile occurs when two or more planets are 60 degrees apart. The sextile is similar to the trine in its beneficial influence; it encourages a stress-free approach to life and open expression of the positive qualities of the planets aspected.

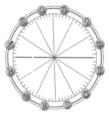

SQUARE One of the more powerful of the negative aspects, a square occurs when two or more planets are 90 degrees apart. It may indicate significant obstacles and challenges in a person's life, but can also encourage fortitude and persistence.

SEMI-SQUARE A less powerful negative aspect (than the opposition or square), the semi-square occurs when two or more planets are 45 degrees apart. It indicates stress and tension within the birth chart.

QUINCUNX Another less negative aspect, the quincunx occurs when two or more planets are 150 degrees apart. Similar to the semi-square, the quincunx weakly underscores stress and tension, and also encourages unpredictability.

SESQUARE A weak negative aspect, similar in effects to the semi-square, the sesquare occurs when two or more planets are 135 degrees apart and is usually associated with negativity and tension.

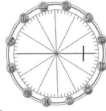

SEMI-SEXTILE A mildly positive aspect, the semi-sextile occurs when two or more planets are 30 degrees apart. It is also associated with tension and negativity, but to a lesser degree than the sesquare.

The fact that some aspects are called "negative" and others "positive" doesn't mean that they always have negative or positive effects. For example, the opposition and square – both powerfully negative aspects – generally don't work in your favor, but under some circumstances can have quite positive effects, challenging you to face difficult situations head-on and thus encouraging personal growth and strength of character.

The aspect patterns

SOMETIMES WHEN YOU LOOK at a birth chart, you will see that the planets in aspect with each other are not only separated by a specific number of degrees, but actually seem to form patterns within the birth chart. These are called aspect patterns, and they can have a powerful influence – negative or positive – on an individual. You will see from our illustrations that sometimes three and even four planets are involved in the aspect patterns. In some special cases, however, more than four planets are involved. When this happens, the effects of the pattern are greatly strengthened. The major aspect patterns described here are the tee-square, the grand trine, the grand cross, the pointer, and the stellium.

The tee-square

TEE-SQUARE

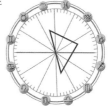

When two planets are in opposition, and a third planet makes square aspects to both of them, the pattern they make is called a tee-square. The effect of a tee-square varies according to the nature of the planets involved. It can certainly add drive, vigor and determination, but often holds the individual back, preventing a positive flow of potential.

The grand trine

DOUBLE TEE-SQUARE

A group of three trine aspects might seem on the face of it an excellent thing to have in a chart, but as is so often true, an "easy" grouping of planets can work against you. This pattern encourages charm, but sometimes also weakness of character, and may indicate a tendency to be too nonchalant and laid-back, and a belief that you can get away with anything (which you often can!). With this pattern, look for some "grittier" indications elsewhere in the birth chart – ones which will encourage character and strength.

The grand cross

DOUBLE GRAND TRINE

Here, four planets are spaced roughly 90 degrees apart: they make two opposition aspects which form a cross in the birth chart; simultaneously, each of t he four planets makes a square aspect to the others. This is a fairly rare occurrence, and it is sometimes said to have the effect of making or breaking an individual. On the one hand, it can encourage you to be extremely brave, energetic, powerful, and successful. Other individuals, however, cannot cope with the energetic strength of this pattern and simply give way under its influence.

GRAND CROSS

Because of its uniqueness, the grand cross is ascribed three different qualities (the same energy qualities that the signs are assigned); cardinal, fixed, and mutable. These qualities are critical in determining how the grand cross will affect an individual.

CARDINAL A cardinal grand cross is inhibiting. You may want to release an abundant reserve of energy, but will be unable to do so.
Self-confidence must be nurtured here.

FIXED A fixed grand cross makes for extreme stubbornness. It is often the case that you were put down once too often as a child by parents or teachers. Your initiative and confidence have been severely undermined, and again, self-confidence, together with self-motivation, must be built up.

MUTABLE A mutable grand cross can bring confusion. You may yearn for an uncomplicated and fulfilling life, but somehow never realize your aims; curiously, acting as if you have a strong sense of duty is often an excuse for inaction and a mask for total lack of confidence. There is great potential here, but an overall sense of inadequacy must be conquered.

Recognizing the influences of the grand cross is halfway to overcoming them. Indeed, those who are determined and resourceful enough to use the energy of the grand cross to rise above their circumstances are often extraordinary individuals indeed.

The pointer

This is a stressful configuration: A planet in an opposition is contacted by quincunx aspects from two others, forming an arrow-head shape. It is also possible for these two planets to form semi-sextiles to the base planet.

This configuration might symbolically be said to "show the way," indicating the direction the subject should take by centering on the affairs of the house in which the point of the pattern falls. Do not rely completely on this theory, but remember that the pointer planet always marks a very stressful area of the subject's chart, and the more negative side of all aspects' influences will be present in the personality.

The stellium

When a group of three or more planets appear in one sign or house, they form a stellium – rather like a traffic jam in the chart. In general, the characteristics of the sign where the stellium occurs will be emphasized, and the area represented by the house concerned will be under much stress. The Sun sign is usually involved, because it is the Sun, Mercury, and Venus which are most often in the same sign. In that case, you not only have the characteristics of the sign in your personality, but you think and love in the manner of the sign. Should the Moon be in the same sign as well, you also react to situations in the manner suggested by the sign.

The influence of the stellium is so strong that it can throw the personality out of kilter. Both the positive and negative qualities of the sign in question are very strong and overly emphasized. With the appearance of the stellium, look carefully at the positions and influences of other planets and signs in the chart for stabilizing and countering effects.

INTERNET

www.astroadvice.com

If you want to find out more details about aspects, this web site provides excellent, comprehensive information.

Simply no aspects at all!

SOMETIMES – *not very often – when you look at a planet's position in a birth chart, you see that it makes no aspects at all with any other planet or angle. We call such a planet "unaspected," and you might reasonably assume that left alone like that, its influences would be relatively benign and the planet itself not important. You'd be wrong.*

An unaspected planet is very important indeed. In fact, you will experience the effects of that planet particularly strongly. Its influences will feel markedly different and take on a rather eccentric and erratic force that won't be easy to deal with. In general, and unsurprisingly, unaspected planets encourage emotional stress and psychological difficulties.

Other riders in the sky – the heavenly angles

IMAGINE THE ROUND FACE *of a clock marked with only four points: the first at the 9 o'clock position, due west; the second at the 12 o'clock position, due north; the third at the 3 o'clock position, due east; and the fourth at the 6 o'clock position, due south.*

Now put on your astrological glasses and look at the clock again. In traditional astrology, the 9 o'clock point is called "sunrise," and it is the home of the Ascendant degree; the 12 o'clock point is called "noon," and it is the home of the Midheaven degree; the 3 o'clock point is called "sunset," and it is the home of the Descendant degree; the 6 o'clock point is called "midnight," and it is the home of the Imum Coeli.

These angles or degrees – especially the Ascendant and Midheaven – exert their own unique influences in a birth chart and form aspects with various planets.

The Ascendant

The Ascendant is located at the far left-hand side of the birth chart – at the "9 o'clock" position on our imaginary clock, or the "sunrise" position on the astrological clock. The Ascendant is one of the first lines drawn on a birth chart and marks the beginning of the zodiac segment that contains your rising sign. Fittingly, the Ascendant reveals your inner self, the "you" known only by those closest to you, if even then. Symbolically, the Ascendant also stands for the foundation of your very personality and is the strongest indicator of how you adapt to your environment. Any planets near or planetary aspects with the Ascendant should receive careful consideration. (In the birth chart, the term "Ascendant" is often shortened to "Asc.")

The Midheaven

The Midheaven or Medium Coeli – which means the "middle point of the heavens" – called MC for short, is located at the top of the birth chart – at the "12 o'clock" position on our imaginary clock, or the "noon" position on the astrological clock. The Midheaven indicates those personal qualities and areas of life with which we most keenly identify.

The Descendant

The Descendant is located directly opposite the Ascendant at the far right-hand side of the birth chart – at the "3 o'clock" position on our imaginary clock, or the "sunset" position on the astrological clock. It is always on the cusp of the seventh house of partnerships and is thus strongly connected to that house's concerns about personal and professional relationships.

PTOLEMAIC SYSTEM FROM THE
CELESTIAL ATLAS

The Imum Coeli

The Imum Coeli – which means the "lowest part of the heavens" – called IC for short, is located directly opposite the Midheaven point, at the bottom of the birth chart – at the "6 o'clock" position on our imaginary clock, or the "midnight" position on the astrological clock. It symbolizes our roots and ancestral background and is strongly related to the fourth house of home, family, mother, and land.

Now that we've met all the major players in astrology – the zodiac signs, the rising signs, the planets, the sign groupings, the planetary aspects, and heavenly angles – it's time to take a stroll through the houses they live in.

A simple summary

✓ Besides their general characteristics and influences, the signs and planets have additional unique qualities which may give them special meaning in a birth chart.

✓ The signs receive these additional qualities from four traditional groupings in which they are variously placed.

✓ The first grouping of signs is by gender (masculine/positive or feminine/negative).

✓ The second grouping is by element (fire, earth, air, or water), also called triplicity.

✓ The third grouping is by quality (cardinal, fixed, or mutable), also called quadruplicity.

✓ The fourth grouping is by polarity (or opposites), in which each sign is paired with its polar opposite directly across the zodiac.

✓ The planets' influences are further enhanced or inhibited by the number of degrees that separate them in a birth chart and allow them to form specific aspects. The nine planetary aspects are the conjunction, opposition, trine, sextile, square, semi-square, quincunx, sesquare, and semi-sextile. Aspects may be positive or negative in effect; powerful, strong, moderate, or weak in influence.

✓ Planetary aspects often form patterns within the signs that also exert strong effects in the birth chart. The most important planetary patterns are the tee-square, the grand trine, the grand cross, and the stellium. Planetary patterns may be positive or negative in effect and are almost always powerful in influence.

✓ Four major angles or degrees in the birth chart – located in the south ("noon" position), west ("sunset" position), north ("midnight" position), and east ("sunrise" position) of the birth-chart circle – represent key aspects of an individual's personality. The four angles or degrees are the Ascendant (east), the Midheaven (south), the Descendant (west), and the Imum Coeli (north).

Chapter 7

A House is Simply Not a Home

WE'VE ALREADY POINTED OUT that the planets not only govern specific Sun signs – that is, one of the 12 segments of the zodiac circle named after the constellations – but are also associated with the 12 houses of the zodiac. When you draw up your birth chart in Chapter 12, you'll be numbering these houses from one through 12 (counterclockwise), starting with the first 30-degree segment just below the Ascendant line (or "nine o'clock" line). And probably one of the first things you'll notice is that the signs and the houses don't coincide. That's because the first house always begins below the Ascendant line or degree. But the zodiac signs fall in different houses, depending on what and where your rising sign (also called your Ascendant) is. And your rising sign is always placed in the first house. (More about that in Chapter 12.)

In this chapter...

✓ Dividing the houses

Dividing the houses

THERE ARE VARIOUS FORMS of "house division." In this book we use the Equal House system, which is the oldest system – and seems to us to be the simplest as well. One of the most popular house systems, the Placidus system, has certain anomalies; for instance, in very northern latitudes it's impossible to calculate a rising degree.

The houses represent 12 specific areas of human life; they therefore add another important layer of meaning to the birth chart. For instance, the fifth house represents creativity and pleasure. If you were born with the Sun in Virgo but also have Mercury in Libra in the fifth house, we'd expect you to have a love of beauty (the influence of Libra), and to be good with your hands (the influence of the Sun in Virgo), but also to have considerable creative ability (the influence of the fifth house itself).

Houses made simple

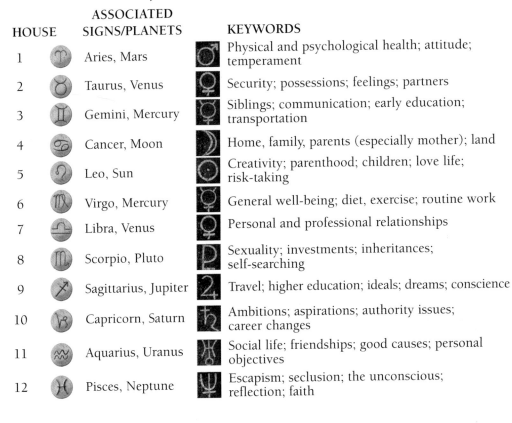

HOUSE		ASSOCIATED SIGNS/PLANETS		KEYWORDS
1	♈	Aries, Mars	♂	Physical and psychological health; attitude; temperament
2	♉	Taurus, Venus	♀	Security; possessions; feelings; partners
3	♊	Gemini, Mercury	☿	Siblings; communication; early education; transportation
4	♋	Cancer, Moon	☽	Home, family, parents (especially mother); land
5	♌	Leo, Sun	☉	Creativity; parenthood; children; love life; risk-taking
6	♍	Virgo, Mercury	☿	General well-being; diet, exercise; routine work
7	♎	Libra, Venus	♀	Personal and professional relationships
8	♏	Scorpio, Pluto	♇	Sexuality; investments; inheritances; self-searching
9	♐	Sagittarius, Jupiter	♃	Travel; higher education; ideals; dreams; conscience
10	♑	Capricorn, Saturn	♄	Ambitions; aspirations; authority issues; career changes
11	♒	Aquarius, Uranus	♅	Social life; friendships; good causes; personal objectives
12	♓	Pisces, Neptune	♆	Escapism; seclusion; the unconscious; reflection; faith

The first house

ARIES AND MARS

This is the most important house of the horoscope. Because it contains your rising sign, this house expresses your personality, your temperament, and general attitude toward life, as well as your physical health, overall well-being, and physical characteristics. If there is also a planet in this house, especially if it is within $8°$ to $10°$ of the Ascendant, it will have a particularly strong influence on your personality, appearance, and behavior, as well as on the effects of the rising sign itself.

The second house

TAURUS AND VENUS

The second house reveals your attitudes about possessions, security, and partners (but not love affairs; they're covered in the fifth house). Here we discover how important security is to you, how possessive you are, and whether you view people (as well as objects) as possessions. Here there is also a powerful association between emotional security and financial security. Money and love are clearly linked in a number of astrological indications (see Chapter 17, "Venus at Work," for example); this house is just one of those indications. In particular, planetary and sign influences in this house will indicate whether there is a balance in your life between emotional security and financial security, or whether you sacrifice one in favor of the other.

The third house

GEMINI AND MERCURY

The third house is concerned with all your nearest relatives (except your parents): brothers and sisters, grandparents, uncles, aunts, and cousins. Any problems or issues with these close relations will be indicated in the third house. This house also shows how children will respond to school life and can provide important clues for parents about early education. The house is additionally concerned with communication (the influences of both Gemini and Mercury), and with transportation and environment. If, for example, you are planning to move, the third house will offer advice about what type of environment would be best for you – town or country; noise or solitude.

The fourth house

CANCER AND THE MOON

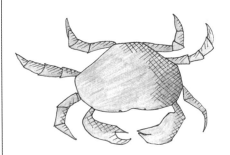

The fourth house is associated with your home and family, and with your parents (who are also featured in the tenth house, which is the house of authority). The fourth house clearly reveals how you react to your parents and whether the child-and-parent relationship is a success or a failure. In accurately interpreting any family dynamic, however, it's important to have the birth charts of all members, particularly if there are problems that need resolution. Nevertheless, this house hints most strongly at your real feelings about your parents. This is also the house of home and property, and your home life may be highlighted here. If this house is very strongly emphasized in your birth chart, you may have an obsession with the past.

The fifth house

LEO AND THE SUN

This is the house of creativity. And creativity isn't only related to the arts: you may be especially creative in the kitchen, or in the garage, or in the board room. Creativity is often stimulated by one's parents, and this house is concerned with a parent's feelings about their relationship with a child (in contrast to the fourth house's emphasis on a child's feelings about a parent). The fifth house also has a strong association with pleasure, particularly with regard to your attitudes about love affairs, the act of love, and having children – that is, with all the ways you translate emotional and spiritual love into physical form.

The sixth house

VIRGO AND MERCURY

The sixth house, like the first, is related to health. But while the first house is concerned with physical health, the sixth house is strongly associated with hygiene and diet, and the bowels – all may or may not be linked to physical well-being. This house also indicates how you handle everyday work and routine, whether in business or in raising a family. It indicates how disciplined you are when faced with daily routine, and whether you are a slave to routine or a victim of disorganization. Traditionally, the sixth house also revealed your attitudes towards servants – no longer (if ever) a politically correct concept. The house does, however, indicate how we treat those who help us run our lives more smoothly: carpenters, plumbers, electricians, contractors.

The seventh house

LIBRA AND VENUS

This house primarily highlights your attitudes and feelings about emotional relationships or partnerships. In particular, the seventh house reveals your deep-rooted needs in the area of love, what kind of partner you look for, and how easy or difficult it is for you to maintain harmony and fairness in a partnership. It also indicates how self-contained and independent you are within an emotional relationship. The seventh house should always be interpreted together with the fifth house (the house of creativity and love affairs), which indicates your attitudes toward the act of love and having children. Personal rapport and understanding are primary concerns of this house and will also influence how you deal with other types of partnerships – friendships and work relationships, for example.

The eighth house
SCORPIO AND PLUTO

The eighth house is sometimes referred to as the House of Death. But in this case, "death" is symbolic of change, new beginnings, rebirth, and/or coming to terms with deep-rooted problems. There is also a strong association with endowments, inheritances, and big lottery wins! Consult the eighth house whenever you are thinking of investing or buying insurance. Crime, research, and investigation are also highlighted here. This is traditionally the house of the primal "life force," and as such it is inevitably linked with sex. Sexually, the emphasis is on an individual's deepest, most fundamental (and sometimes most difficult to accept) sexual urges, rather than the simple lovemaking.

The ninth house
SAGITTARIUS AND JUPITER

Here we find clues to your philosophical outlook on life, and your attitudes toward religion, spiritual matters, and ongoing education. Long-distance travel is also emphasized here, and the ninth house is a great source of advice if you're thinking about taking a year off to explore the world – whether it's the world of your mind or a trip around the globe. This house is traditionally consulted when someone is planning to live or study abroad, work in the travel or export industry, or pursue a career in teaching, especially at the university level. Literature, law, publishing, language skills, and dreams and inspiration are other primary concerns of the ninth house.

The tenth house
CAPRICORN AND SATURN

Here we find the house of hopes, progress, and responsibility. The tenth will reveal how well you are getting on in the world – not just financially, but in terms of fulfilling your deepest aspirations. Here you will discover how well you deal with responsibility and authority, and what you really think about family, traditional values, and social status. If a personal planet appears in this house, you probably have a strong need to be emotionally involved in a career. Fittingly, the tenth house often indicates if you will make a major career change or experience a substantial increase in either social status or work responsibilities.

The eleventh house

AQUARIUS AND URANUS

The eleventh house reveals how you relate to other people socially, and is much concerned with friendship and society. This house strongly emphasizes how you "engage" with the world – that is, your attitudes about issues like ecology, political and social oppression, and intolerance. For example, look to this house for clues about how likely you are to give time and energy to working for charitable or humanitarian causes. The eleventh additionally reveals whether your charitable impulses are genuine or merely pursued in the interests of self-aggrandizement. Here you will also learn how well you work with others, particularly in large groups or on committees, and whether you have an affinity for public office.

The twelfth house

PISCES AND NEPTUNE

This is the house of escapism, seclusion, and isolation. Traditionally, it is linked to hospitals, prisons, and mental institutions – all places where we can experience deep loneliness and isolation. The twelfth house is also the house of mystery, of the unconscious mind, and of the root causes of psychological problems. Here you will find startling clues about the fundamental nature of deep psychological difficulties (while the eighth house shows you how to deal with those difficulties). Look at the segment of the zodiac containing your rising sign. If there is a planet placed there – especially if it is very close to the Ascendant line – this is a clear indication that a "buried" problem must be excavated. Review that planet's influences for clues about how to go about doing that. The notion of sacrifice is very strongly present in the twelfth house, but it is the kind of sacrifice that leads to a strengthening of character and the resolution of long-standing problems.

A simple summary

✓ The planets not only govern specific zodiac signs, each planet is also strongly associated with one of the 12 houses of the zodiac.

✓ Each zodiac house represents a particular area of human life. The houses provide another personalizing influence on the planets, one which often has strong psychological effects.

✓ There are various forms of "house division," some more complex than others. In this book we use the Equal House system, which is the oldest and the simplest.

NEPTUNE

MERCURY

The first house governs psychological motivation and well-being and is the house of Aries and Mars.

The second house governs possessions and emotions and is the house of Taurus and Venus.

The third house governs brothers, sisters, early education, the environment, and transport, and is the house of Gemini and Mercury.

The fourth house governs home, domestic life, and parents (especially the mother), and is the house of Cancer and the Moon.

The fifth house governs creativity, pleasure, love affairs, risk taking, children, and the father, and is the house of Leo and the Sun.

The sixth house governs health, diet, exercise, hobbies, and routine work, and is the house of Virgo and Mercury.

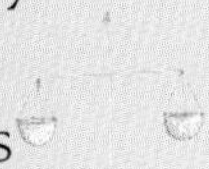

The seventh house governs partners and relationships and is the house of Libra and Venus.

The eighth house governs sex, investments, and heritage, and is the house of Scorpio and Pluto.

SATURN

PLUTO

The ninth house governs ideals, higher education, challenge, long-distance travel, and dreams, and is the house of Sagittarius and Jupiter.

The tenth house governs ambitions and aspirations, and is the house of Capricorn and Saturn.

The eleventh house governs friends, social life, social conscience, and objectives, and is the house of Aquarius and Uranus.

The twelfth house governs faith, escapism, seclusion, and institutions, and is the house of Pisces and Neptune.

PART TWO

MEDIEVAL DEPICTION OF THE SUN GOD

SIMPLY SUN-SATIONAL

So . . . HERE'S everybody's favorite part of astrology – the Sun signs – in all their blazing and confounding glory. And here we've taken a bit of a departure from the typical way the Sun signs are presented – we've divided up the 12 Sun signs by their *element* (fire, earth, air, and water), with three signs to a group. (Traditionally, signs sharing the same element have a strong association.)

Within each sign you'll find all its time-honored astrological associations and in-depth discussions about the effects of the sign in major aspects of your life. We guarantee you'll learn something you never knew before about your Sun sign, and that you'll have great fun in the process.

Chapter 8

Simply Dazzling: The Fire Signs

ARIES, LEO, AND SAGITTARIUS – respectively ruled by assertive and dynamic Mars, the regal and ego-centered Sun, and grand and extravagant Jupiter – are the most energetic and enthusiastic of the zodiac signs. Simply – and deservedly – known as the "fire signs," Aries, Leo, and Sagittarius make for people with a powerful, natural magnetism and an almost insatiable zest for life. They thrive on work, action, innovation, and challenge, and they are often found among the great leaders, explorers, athletes, and artists of the world. At their best they benevolently and selflessly draw others in to share the gifts of their intoxicating light; at their worst they can be self-absorbed, ruthless, and disinterested.

In this chapter...
✔ Aries personality
✔ Leo personality
✔ Sagittarius personality

ARIES, LEO, AND SAGITTARIUS ARE FIRE SIGNS

Aries personality

THE ARIEN DETERMINATION TO WIN, *to come first in any contest, will affect many areas of your life. This can, of course, be a wonderful characteristic, whether it encourages you to become a leader in your profession or an excellent athlete.*

But your fierce determination also brings with it the responsibility not to allow the desire to win to become so strong that you tread over other people in order to do so.

Remember that Ariens tend to think first of themselves and their place in the world, which brings with it the tendency to turn selfishness into a "career." And that won't endear you to friends, family, or colleagues. With Arien determination also comes the risk of being stubborn – something else to watch out for. You like to be busy and probably work well in the sort of noisy, dynamic environment which others find distracting. Your energy level is high, and if you're not to become quickly restless and dissatisfied, you'll have to find ways of expressing this energy positively. Some Ariens do this through sports, others through sex, and others through jobs that involve a great deal of bustling about.

If all this suggests that you're a serious and single-minded career man or woman with no time for friendship or pleasure, you're mistaken. In fact, you have a splendid sense of humor, often satirical and absurd, and you'll usually be the center of laughter and fun.

♈ ARIES
(MARCH 21 – APRIL 20)

KEYWORDS Assertive, forthright, selfish, urgent
RULING PLANET Mars
POSITIVE
DUALITY OR GENDER Masculine
TRIPLICITY OR ELEMENT Fire
QUADRUPLICITY OR QUALITY Cardinal
BODY AREA Head
COUNTRIES Denmark, England, France, Germany, Japan, Poland, Syria

CITIES Birmingham (England), Brunswick, Capua, Florence, Krakow, Leicester, Marseille, Naples, Utrecht, Verona
STONE Diamond
COLOR Red
TREES Holly, fir; thorn-bearing trees or bushes
FLOWERS AND HERBS Arnica, bayberry, broom, bryony, furze, honeysuckle, hops, geranium, juniper, leeks, milk thistle, mustard, nettle, onions, peppermint, rhubarb, tobacco, witch hazel
FOODS Beer; leeks, onions, tomatoes; most strong-tasting foods

Love and sex life

One of the generalizations about Ariens, which is often true, is the assertion that they tend to fall in love at first sight – and, indeed, fall in lust. Ariens do need an active and fulfilling sex life and are quite likely to pounce quickly on anyone they fancy. This can lead to disaster in more than one way.

The need for sex is often so strong that simple courtship is ignored. Ariens forget that many people prefer a little gentle wooing and a comfortable bed to a quickie in the back of the car. The guy who satisfies himself, then turns over and goes to sleep without thinking of his partner, may well be an Arien. It's also true that some Ariens tend, too quickly, to turn an initial spark into a commitment, which can burn out all too soon.

Rushing into what seems to be a permanent relationship can be a great mistake. Having said that, a really sound and lasting Arien commitment to a lover – who's equally enthusiastic, lively, and ready to experiment – can be pretty good!

Your partner may – almost certainly will – have to put up with a degree of selfishness. But this isn't too difficult for you to correct as long as your partner tactfully points it out. And such selfishness won't be worrying enough to outweigh the sheer fun that is likely to be part of the relationship, because your capacity for enjoyment is second to none.

Family

■ **Mars is** *Aries's ruling planet.*

Sorry if this is getting boring, but selfishness is again likely to be the most important factor for you to control. You may tend to put your hobbies or enthusiasms first and your family second, and if they don't realize that this is just you being Arien, it may lead to regular spats. For example, Ariens tend to be enthusiastic do-it-yourselfers, with a definite love for knocking things down and building other things up. The chaos this can cause may occur too often for comfort where the rest of the family is concerned. Having an interest in which your partner and children can share is one solution. Restlessness can be a difficulty, too. When you suspect you're in a rut, you may feel the need to get out of it – fast. And this can mean sudden – and unsettling – changes for the family, especially for your partner.

The important thing to remember as far as your partner is concerned is that he or she is your partner, and you should share things.

You also need to remember that there's a certain amount of aggression in every Arien, and if this quality is present elsewhere in your birth chart, it will likely show itself in all arenas: at home or at work, while you're driving, or playing sports. Look for other influences in your chart to off-set this.

A short fuse often comes along with aggression, so it's important to watch your temper.

Finally, money may tend to burn a hole in your pocket. It's a good idea to make sure you regularly set aside a reasonable amount of cash for groceries, gasoline, and the usual bills. It's also a good idea for Ariens to have at least one savings plan, or your money may vanish without your even knowing where it's gone.

Career

Imagine a job with a nice, comfortable, rather stuffy office and a regular routine. Not what you fancy? That's understandable, because all Ariens feel the same way. You need to work in an open environment with a lively atmosphere. And you need to do work – physical or mental – that calls on and uses all your enthusiasm and energy.

You particularly need a job where you're able to climb your way to the top – whatever that means for your particular line of work. Being a managing director or foreman are typical Arien goals. In fact, your ambition may make you rather ruthless. Try to control this. Though you cope well with tension, there's no point in encouraging it by upsetting people.

Ariens definitely don't find it easy to settle into work which needs a high degree of patience. So what sort of job works best for you – and you for it? Engineering and any kind of metal work will often intrigue Ariens. They also make first-rate car mechanics, fire fighters, and railway workers.

Those Ariens who are attracted to the arts usually enjoy craft work. Other artistic endeavors will show typical Arien traits: Painters will work broadly and boldly, rather than in watercolor or miniatures, while musicians will prefer the trombone or trumpet rather than the violin or harpsichord.

■ **Leeks and onions**
are foods associated with the Arien Sun sign.

Surprisingly, perhaps, Ariens seem to make excellent psychiatrists, psychologists, dentists, and hairdressers!

Health, diet, and exercise

The key to Arien good health is to make sure all your energy is positively used. If you can balance your physical life properly, you should have very few health problems – other than the occasional headache (though some fortunate Ariens simply don't know what a headache is!). If you are plagued by headaches, it will be worth your while to have a check up; a minor kidney disorder may be the cause. It's a rare Arien who hasn't fallen on his or her head at one time or another. In fact, you seem almost to enjoy bumping your head and cutting or bruising yourself – sometimes simply because you are too hasty and slightly careless.

So watch it, for example, when you're working in the kitchen with sharp knives and boiling water. And if you're into sports, be prepared for the occasional missing tooth, muscle sprain, or even a broken bone.

Apart from the bruises and sprains you bring upon yourself, you do tend to be accident-prone. Mars, which rules Aries, can make things worse. You probably find it difficult to slow down in any activity you do, so be sure to take appropriate precautions; always use pot holders, safety helmets, and eye shields where appropriate. You probably enjoy spicy foods – be careful; they can overheat your blood – and you need plenty of protein. Your taste will be for savory rather than sweet foods, and instead of sweets you may enjoy dried fruits.

■ **Sheep are** *the animals traditionally associated with Aries.*

Sports will be important to you – ideally, competitive sports, which allow you to go out and win. You'll enjoy boxing, wrestling, and the martial arts, but also aerobics and working on machines that build strength and muscle power.

Child and parent

As an Arien you may occasionally put your own activities first and spend less time with your children than you should or could. In fact, you may need to work out a specific schedule that allows you to have regular leisure time with the kids. If you don't, the children – and you – will suffer.

There are cases of Ariens so caught up in their own hobbies and pleasures that their children end up just watching television or playing video and computer games. This is a pity, since the one thing you certainly don't lack when you're with your children is enthusiasm. And that enthusiasm is contagious.

But do remember that patience isn't your thing. Impatience and shortness of temper can be a problem, especially when the children are young.

Fortunately, any storms are over quickly – but try not to blow them away! You'll probably enjoy getting involved in PTA work. As a high achiever yourself, you'll want to see your children do well at school. Arien children will be noisy, sometimes selfish, always active, and full of energy. As you already know, Ariens can be accident-prone, so be prepared with a first-aid kit and a cuddle when your children fall down, bruise themselves, knock their heads . . . Oh yes, they'll certainly knock their heads!

Arien kids are easily bored when they aren't interested in something, and teachers will find it difficult to engage their attention during lessons in which Ariens have little interest. Watch out for this tendency in your Arien children and remind them that learning the basics at school is essential to success – which you covet later on in life.

Leisure and retirement

Your leisure time may be spent extending your work hours. For example, if you're a car mechanic, you may well spend your weekends working in the garage and your evenings working with oily bits of car on the kitchen table! Sports may take up quite a lot of your leisure time as well. As we've already suggested, working out in a gym or participating in team sports will help you get rid of any surplus energy or latent aggression!

If you get bored with working out or feel you've just had enough of it, you might think about getting a dog. Long country walks, or even city strolls, will be enjoyable.

You'll probably never lose your interest in do-it-yourself jobs, and home brewing may appeal to you. If you have some savings you can spare, you might like to play the stock exchange. Insurance, mining, or steel will probably be good investments for you. As far as more thoughtful relaxation is concerned, you may enjoy debating and arguing (sometimes rather too spiritedly!). You'll be good at committee work, too, provided you keep your cool. And you find astronomy fascinating. And if you become interested in astrology, you'll have to learn about astronomy anyway!

■ **The honeysuckle** *is an Arien plant.*

Leo personality

Every Sun-sign Leo needs a kingdom over which to reign, and in one way or another you'll find it, whether it's a giant conglomerate or a small workshop. And you'll take enormous pride in whatever you do there. Your outlook on life is generally very positive and happy, and any depression about setbacks won't last long. You live every minute to the fullest and won't waste time in useless recriminations or regrets.

The major Leo fault is believing that "you know best." Well, of course you do. But it isn't always a good idea to insist on it. And you do tend to feel that you should be in charge not only of your own life but of everybody else's.

You're a splendid organizer, and you not only want, but positively need, to be at the center of things. You're very good at energizing others, and when you manage to be tactful, they'll be glad to follow your lead. But you can be dogmatic and bossy – especially with people who are negative and overcritical. This can naturally lead to trouble with those silly enough to disagree with you.

In general, your enthusiasm is your best and most useful asset. Don't curb it, even under criticism, but do remember that overenthusiasm can be one of your problems as well!

Indeed, you have a tendency to be showy in all sorts of ways, and you should watch this: Leos are inclined to go well over the top where "gold and glitter" are concerned. Watch out for a tendency to overdress or to dress inappropriately. Otherwise, especially later in life, some Leos may appear to be . . . well, not so much hamburger dressed as filet mignon, but perhaps king dressed as prince!

LEO
(JULY 23 – AUGUST 23)

KEYWORDS Creative, impressive, powerful, dictatorial
RULING PLANET Sun
POSITIVE
DUALITY OR GENDER Masculine
TRIPLICITY OR ELEMENT Fire
QUADRUPLICITY OR QUALITY Fixed
BODY AREAS Heart, spine, back

COUNTRIES Czechoslovakia, Italy, Lebanon, Romania, Sicily, Southern Iraq, South of France
CITIES Bath, Bombay, Bristol, Chicago, Damascus, Los Angeles, Madrid, Philadelphia, Portsmouth, Prague, Rome, Syracuse
STONE Ruby
COLOR The color of the Sun, from dawn to dusk
TREES Bay, citrus, olive, palm, walnut
FLOWERS AND HERBS Almond, celandine, helianthus, juniper, laurel, marigold, mistletoe, passion flower, peppermint, pimpernel, rosemary, rue, saffron, sunflower
FOODS Meat; vegetables with a high iron content

Love and sex life

When Leos fall in love, they really fall. And if that love is reciprocated, life will be idyllic. But of course sometimes it isn't, and the Leo heart is often bruised and sometimes broken – and it takes Leos longer to heal than some other Sun signs. You need to be a little careful not to overwhelm your partners with love. "But you can't have too much of that," you think. Well, that's true. But less positive and less assertive people than you may feel that they're struggling to stay afloat in a welter of emotion.

Just as you'll spend more than you can afford on your loved one, you'll also tend to go over the top emotionally. This needs a little watching, especially in the early days of a relationship. You don't want to scare him or her off!

■ **The Sun is** *Leo's ruling planet.*

You're naturally very faithful, but you do ask a lot of your partners – emotionally and sexually. You may feel shortchanged if your desires aren't met, and the atmosphere can turn a little sour. You may make the mistake of expecting too much. You certainly need a responsive partner who can match your enthusiasm in every area of a partnership – companionship, friendship, and sex.

But it's important to remember in love that you are a couple – not just one person (you!) with another loosely attached appendage (him or her!). Sharing is what a relationship's all about. It's definitely not about your deciding – for the both of you – what to do and how to feel!

Family

You need to be aware that you tend to take the lead in any relationship – whether with your partner or your children – and that tendency can go too far. If your partner really finds it difficult to make decisions, then it's fine for you to take the initiative. But if he or she is normally assertive, they won't like always having to go along with what you suggest.

Indeed, you can damage family relationships by being too overbearing, dogmatic, and stubborn.

Having said all that, life with a Leo partner and parent is never dull, and no one's going to be bored. However little money is available, you'll make the most of it: A cup of coffee at the kitchen table will turn into just as elaborate and celebratory an occasion as brunch at the Plaza!

You'll also encourage your partner and children to make the most of their lives in every possible way, and their success will be as exciting for you as for them. In fact, you so like to be able to admire your family's achievements that you may get more than a little short-tempered if they aren't as eager as you to push forward and rack up achievement after achievement.

In light of that tendency, it may surprise your family to discover that you yourself are so easily hurt. Indeed, if you're let down by a family member, your whole world can seem to fall apart. Try not to hero-worship your partner or children; then if you are let down, the blow won't be so hurtful that it can't be repaired.

Career

Above everything else, you're a showman – or, of course, a showwoman – and this characteristic will emerge in whatever career you enjoy (and "enjoy" is the operative word here!). However dull your job is, you'll be able to find an opportunity, somewhere, to show off your talents, flair, and enthusiasm. You're ambitious, and you want to get to the top. Moreover, you'll do it positively and not engage in intrigue or stepping on other people's toes. You're a hard worker, and that, together with your natural enthusiasm and emotional involvement with your work, should ensure success.

When you do end up in charge of other people, you'll expect them to follow your own high work standards, and you may become rather impatient when they fail to measure up. You'll have to learn to be tolerant of these lesser human beings!

It's a mistake, of course, to believe that people with certain Sun signs can't succeed in certain jobs – while other Sun signs excel in specific careers. Nevertheless, Leos do tend to thrive in jobs that require creativity and a certain amount of extroverted charm. Many Leos work in the theater (as actors, directors, and designers), while others work in the world of fashion. Flamboyant Leo chefs camp it up in fine restaurants or on lively TV shows, while serious-minded Leos can be found in the higher echelons of the armed services. Leos also make effective and dramatic preachers.

Health, diet, and exercise

Leos usually have a pretty robust constitution, but you tend not only to hate cold weather but to suffer slightly from poor circulation. You usually walk tall (the Leo sense of pride), and that's very good for you. But your spine can give you a certain amount of trouble. You may suffer from back pain, for example, if you have to spend many hours at a desk, and yoga or simple stretching routines are excellent remedies.

■ **Marigolds and celandines** *are Leo's flowers.*

The heart is ruled by Leo, and you should exercise regularly to keep it in good condition. This also helps the circulation. Most Leos love dancing, and a good dance class is an excellent form of exercise for you – partly because it's a form of creative exercise, unlike jogging or stepping on and off a platform.

You'll also enjoy team sports, provided you manage to get yourself elected captain. When you are, watch out that you don't overdo things. You'll naturally want to show everyone that you can do everything better than they can. That can lead to pains and strains.

Once you have found a form of exercise that you enjoy, you'll probably stick to it well into your 90s. You'll get to know your body really well and learn to channel your energy better and pace yourself. Try to avoid showing off at the gym (and anywhere else for that matter). Such behavior won't win you any popularity contests – and you may end up with injuries.

■ **Lions are** *symbolically associated with Leo.*

Child and parent

Leo is traditionally the sign of fatherhood, and your children will have a wonderfully enthusiastic parent who always keeps them busy, encourages them to make the most of their talents – and expects too much of them! In some ways, this Leo tendency is quite a good thing, provided you don't get too disappointed when your children can't meet your very high expectations for them. This is most likely to happen when you "use" your children to achieve a goal you yourself have failed to conquer. Always a mistake.

One good thing about Leos is that they usually remember very keenly what it was like to be a child, and this should enable you to make allowances for your children. Always remember that they may not be nearly as self-confident or ambitious as you are.

You'll spend readily on your children's education and on after-school activities, such as sports, theaters, museums, and travel. You'll want to see your children make the most of their formative years, learn as much as they can, and enjoy life as fully as possible.

If you have a Leo child, remember always to praise him or her as enthusiastically as possible whenever anything is achieved – and to criticize very tactfully. Leo children bruise easily!

Above all else, make sure that their self-confidence is firmly established from an early age. This will enable them to bear those unpleasant moments when, inevitably, they discover that they can't possibly achieve every high ambition they set for themselves.

Leisure and retirement

Leos, it's sometimes said, don't have hobbies – they just have careers. And that's more or less true. In fact, it's difficult to suggest particular activities which will interest you in your spare time or when you retire. (Not that Leos ever really retire; they just use the newly available time to set up another career or two!).

The problem, if you want to call it a "problem," is that you tend to regard pursuing a hobby as just as important as earning a living – and you will want to be equally successful at it.

For example, if you study archaeology or embroidery in your spare time, you'll search out the very best teacher, attend the most important digs, buy the most expensive silks. And you'll strive to achieve the most complete and dazzling techniques – whether restoring the most delicate and damaged ancient Greek vase or stitching the most beautiful bishop's miter ever embroidered!

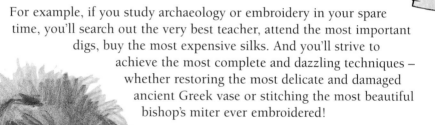

On the whole, when it comes to leisure and retirement, the keyword to bear in mind is "creative." You should be an asset on any organizing committee and will more than likely end up as chairperson. You'll also enjoy activities where you can make a positive contribution and be easily recognized by as many people as possible. An amateur dramatic or operatic society is one obvious possibility. But equally rewarding would be the study of astrology – which could obviously begin with this book and possibly end with your getting a diploma at one of the recognized schools listed in the Resources section of this book!

■ **In mythology, the Nemean lion** *was awarded his place among the stars by Zeus.*

Sagittarius personality

IT'S NOT FOR NOTHING that one of the keywords for Sagittarius is "free." And this penchant for freedom can lead to difficulty as well as delight. You tend to be so intent on leading life your way that your unconventional behavior may from time to time embarrass even yourself!

You'll also be more than a little careless – driving, for instance, with a sort of casual enthusiasm which won't make passengers particularly comfortable. Indeed, you'll tend to enjoy risk taking, almost for its own sake, and since you also enjoy sports, you should be prepared for bruises and sprains.

But you're not a raving extrovert. You also have a philosophical bent. Intellectual pursuits will probably be quite as important to you as the physical life – though you'll approach intellectual endeavors in a physical way whenever this is possible. The Eastern martial arts – with their blend of philosophy and action, and their cool, unemotional use of physical energy – may well appeal to you. The challenge of competition will also be inviting.

You are enormously versatile, to the point that you really should try to control the impulse to be good at everything. Otherwise, life may be full of half-achieved objectives.

Since it's also important to you that you complete everything you set out to do, you may have to learn how to take on less than you feel able to cope with. Your enthusiasm is indeed a great asset, but your blind optimism is not. Neither is your characteristic restlessness or your belief that the grass is always greener on the other side of the fence. It ain't necessarily so.

SAGITTARIUS
(NOVEMBER 23 – DECEMBER 21)

KEYWORDS Casual, free, philosophical, searching
RULING PLANET Jupiter
POSITIVE
DUALITY OR GENDER Masculine
TRIPLICITY OR ELEMENT Fire
QUADRUPLICITY OR QUALITY Mutable
BODY AREAS Hips, liver, thighs
COUNTRIES Saudi Arabia, Australia, Hungary, Spain, Yugoslavia

CITIES Avignon, Bradford, Budapest, Cologne, Naples, Nottingham, Sheffield, Stuttgart, Toledo (in Spain and in the United States), Toronto
STONE Topaz
COLOR Dark blue, royal purple
TREES Ash, chestnut, birch, lime, mulberry, oak
FLOWERS AND HERBS Balm, bilberry, borage, cinnamon, dandelion, dock, mosses, mullberry, pinks, sage, thistles
FOODS Asparagus, celery, leeks, onions, tomatoes

Love and sex life

A lot of energy is needed to keep up with a Sagittarian lover: you're passionate, versatile, and experimental. All this makes for a lot of fun, but it's not for someone who likes a placid, steady, slightly dull life.

You're highly susceptible to the "call" of love and sex when you're young, and you will find it very easy to be knocked sideways by a beautiful girl or handsome boy. You won't be slow in coming on to them, either. In fact, you'll express your love with an exuberant sexiness that should knock them sideways, too. When you're a little older, you'll recognize the quieter pleasures of conversation and companionship, and you'll find it easy to express your love satisfactorily within a permanent relationship.

However, your partner may sometimes feel that you don't take the relationship very seriously. Indeed, your need to express your versatility may lead you "astray" from time to time.

But the fact that you're occasionally rather casual about your love doesn't mean that you can't love steadily and long. Your partner simply needs to learn that this is just a part of your characteristic freewheeling nature.

■ **Jupiter is** *Sagittarius's ruling planet.*

In fact, your partnership, while not necessarily "open," must be a little elastic. Any hint of claustrophobia will be killing to a Sagittarian – as will any suspicion of jealousy (even with some cause!) You just don't understand jealousy at all, and a jealous partner will infuriate and anger you. Remember that your partner may not have the same approach to love and sex as you do. So watch it!

Family

Almost the worst thing for any Sagittarian is to get the idea that they're trapped within a tight family circle: "Don't fence me in" is the Sagittarian anthem. You simply can't cope with what feels like claustrophobic boundaries, and your partner must recognize this fact in order for the relationship to succeed.

Boredom is another problem for the Sagittarian. A routine life – getting up at 6:30, catching the 7:43 to the office, breaking for lunch at 1:00 – is as fatal to your Sagittarian heart as is staying at home and doing dreary housework day after day.

A Sagittarian's family life can't be dull or routine, either, and you'll do your level best to make sure that it's not. As long as you can energize your family and persuade them to join in your activities with almost as much enthusiasm as you do, all will be well. Otherwise, something, or someone, will explode! Shared activities are, in fact, very important to you. The Sagittarian family that plays together will have a good chance of staying together, and you'll all enjoy challenging each other on equal terms.

This is particularly important for you and your partner. You must feel that he or she is more or less your intellectual equal. If you feel inferior – perhaps because of a partner's expertise in an area where you don't excel – you'll find it very difficult to cope. Indeed, your response will be to redouble your efforts to catch up and level the field. A wise partner will recognize this trait of yours and encourage you.

Remember, mutual challenge within a partnership can be marvelously productive.

Career

Sagittarians are very keen on being able to see the road ahead and anticipate any difficulties which may lie along the way. You won't be happy with a predictable routine or a claustrophobic office. You also need to be able to do things your own way.

In other words, you need freedom of expression on the job. And you also need challenge. If you do find yourself in a rather dull job, set yourself unthinkably high goals and fight your way toward them. Even if you don't achieve them, the fight itself will do you good!

Any job which involves travel should suit you. You'll be able to get out and about and avoid dull hours at a desk. You may have a natural flair for languages, and you're also good at planning – whether for yourself or other people. You're good with general details, too, but a grasp of fine detail may sometimes elude you – or you may get a little careless .

Many astrologers suggest that Sagittarians are the natural athletes of the zodiac, and it's true that your determination can fuel success in that area. You're good at selling, as well, and work as a salesperson – especially if it involves travel – may be enjoyable and successful. The challenge of competition will be good for you.

Health, diet, and exercise

Exercise is probably more important for a Sagittarian than for any other sign. If you don't get it, your whole system tends to get heavy and dull – and depression may build up.

The thing to do is find an exercise routine that really appeals to you, so that you'll be happy to devote time and energy to it. Ideally, join a really good gym, where it'll be impossible to get bored. You can swop from one class to another, one exercise machine to another. Change your workout regimen from season to season – Nautilus machines in the fall to free weights in the spring. And switch sports with the weather – basketball to tennis to swimming.

The hips and thighs are the key Sagittarian body areas, and the connection with weight gain will be obvious to women readers, if not to men! An exercise routine, again, is the answer, coupled with a sensible diet. Sad, because you certainly enjoy your food – and drink. The latter indulgence can be especially unhealthy, when taken to excess, because a key Sagittarian body organ is the liver. If a strict diet does become necessary, think of it as a challenge. You love a challenge and are good at facing one head on.

■ **Mythological** *Sagittarius is half-horse, half-man.*

You have a tendency to be accident-prone, and this can be a problem if you go at your exercises too violently. Older Sagittarians should pace themselves well if they don't want problems with torn muscles and sprained backs as a result of their exercise routines!

It's also a good idea for you to try to include energy-building, high protein foods in your diet. But keep an eye on your sweet tooth! Sure, sugar builds energy – but it also builds fat! Junk food is particularly bad for you, but citrus fruits, especially grapefruit, are wonderfully good! And take plenty of supplemental vitamin C.

Child and parent

Sagittarians make marvelous parents. Your natural enthusiasm and zest for life really appeal to children. Additionally, you find bringing up children a fascinating business, and you're happy to give time and attention to it.

However, Sagittarian parents do have one small problem with child rearing, and it's probably most acute for Sagittarian mothers. You do great when your baby is tiny. But when he or she becomes a toddler, you may be driven to distraction by their endless prattle, especially when you're imprisoned with them for 24 hours a day.

Remember, you aren't the most patient of people. Add to that the fact that a child of three or four simply can't offer you the kind of mental stimulus you need, and you have a recipe for disaster. So you must find a good baby-sitter – or enlist your partner – to take the child off your hands for at least an hour or two a day. This will give you back your sense of freedom and encourage you to keep your mind busy and active.

Beware, also, of asking too much from your growing child. And watch out for a tendency to get bored and annoyed if your child doesn't seem to grasp every opportunity offered. Children do, occasionally, just like to waste time!

If you have a Sagittarian child, remember that he or she must be taught the difference between splendid natural enthusiasm and just plain overexcitement. Inevitably there will be some tears before bedtime when young Sagittarius has simply been overactive. But don't despair. Once you discover your Sagittarian's natural interests, you'll have no difficulty encouraging them. Indeed, you may have to restrain them from time to time when outside interests interfere with school work. And it won't be easy!

■ **Deer** *are closely associated with Sagittarius.*

■ **Bilberries are** *representative of Sagittarius.*

Leisure and retirement

Challenge will be as important in hobbies and leisure activities as it is in work, so try to achieve a balance between the separate demands of work and spare time. If your work mainly involves intellectual efforts, your hobbies should include physical activity – and vice versa.

You have a naturally adventurous spirit, and hobbies such as rock climbing and paragliding should appeal to you. Travel may be attractive, too. And if you can't travel, reading travel books will fascinate you. You're often described as the hunter of the zodiac, and this can apply to any type of "hunting," whether for antiques or for rare collectibles.

You may well go on educating yourself into extreme old age. Adult education classes of all kinds appeal to you, and you'll work at them consistently and enthusiastically.

■ **The oak is** *associated with Sagittarius.*

But remember, like Gemini (your polar opposite across the zodiac), you can be a little superficial about your approach to learning. You may end up knowing a little about a large number of things, rather than being a really thorough student in one area. Nothing wrong with that, if it satisfies you. But it's not the kind of attitude that makes passing examinations easy. So if you're after some additional degrees or qualifications, you may have to teach yourself to concentrate!

■ **Sagittarius is** *the polar opposite of Gemini in the zodiac.*

A simple summary

✓ Aries, Leo, and Sagittarius are known collectively as the fire signs. People influenced by these signs are active and dynamic. They thrive on work, action, innovation, and challenge, and they often excel at anything they do.

✓ Ariens are determined to win, sometimes at all costs. They are full of energy and creativity, and need careers and activities that enable them to use up all that drive. Watch out for a tendency toward selfishness.

✓ Leos are positive and happy, and waste no time on regrets. They are great organizers and faithful partners. The pitfall here is that they tend to take the lead in everything – romance, career, parenting, and relationships.

✓ Sagittarians are carefree, versatile, and passionate. They like activities that combine the active and the philosophical. But they do have a fear of getting trapped – into a routine, a relationship, or responsibilities.

Chapter 9

Simply Fundamental: The Earth Signs

TAURUS, VIRGO, AND CAPRICORN – respectively ruled by sensitive and sensual Venus, stimulating and communicative Mercury, and practical and cautious Saturn – are the most down-to-earth and least complex members of the zodiac family, appropriately known simply as the earth signs. They are the world's planners, organizers, and keepers-of-the-hearth. They thrive on hard work and are renowned for their dedication, determination, practicality, and reliability. The earth signs are the indefatigable front-line workers of the world, the people that other Sun signs depend on in every-day life to get the job done and keep the home (or office) fires burning.

In this chapter...
✓ Taurus personality
✓ Virgo personality
✓ Capricorn personality

TAURUS, VIRGO, AND CAPRICORN ARE EARTH SIGNS

Taurus personality

THE WORST TAUREAN FAULT is possessiveness. *What you have, you hold, and sometimes a great deal too tightly. A lover, for instance, can end up feeling like just another one of your possessions – something you tend to have a lot of! It may be that one of the basic reasons for this is that you need security.*

Surrounding yourself with possessions gives you the feeling that you're safe. The same is true of any money you make. You need the security it gives, and so you tend to hold on to it. This can make you seem almost entirely materialistic, which isn't of course the whole truth. What you are, in fact, is a very stable and "safe" sort of person. You run your daily life like a well-oiled machine, and you're extremely reliable – and dependable – when dealing with other people.

You take no short cuts, nor should you. Taking risks when investing, for example, isn't for you. Indeed, you're not a risk taker in general. In fact, you're so steady that sometimes you seem too safe to be true, even to the extent that you become rather set in your ways. But you also have enormous patience – and enormous charm. You may sometimes seem a little slow – in conversation, for instance – but if people listen to what you say, they almost always find it interesting.

Your mind works carefully, deliberately, methodically, and your greatest potential probably lies in the steady construction of a career and the shaping of a life just as you want each to be.

TAURUS
(APRIL 21 – MAY 21)

KEYWORDS Possessive, permanent
RULING PLANET Venus
NEGATIVE
DUALITY OR GENDER Feminine
TRIPLICITY OR ELEMENT Earth
QUADRUPLICITY OR QUALITY Fixed
BODY AREAS Neck and throat; thyroid gland
COUNTRIES Capri, Cyprus, Egypt, Greek Islands, Iran, Ireland, Switzerland

CITIES Bologna, Dublin, Eastbourne, Hastings, Leipzig, Lucerne, Mantua, Palermo, St. Louis
STONES Emerald
COLORS Pale blue, green, pink
TREES Almond, apple, ash, cyprus, fig, pear, vine
FLOWERS AND HERBS Alder, artichoke, beans, brambles, cloves, columbine, daisy, elder, foxglove, marshmallow, mint, poppy, primula, rose, sorrel, violet
FOOD Cereals, particularly wheat; apples, berries, grapes, pears; spices

Love and sex life

Taurean charm and good looks give you an excellent start when it comes to personal relationships.

Indeed, Taureans have the reputation of being the best looking of the 12 signs. When someone spots you across a crowded room, for instance, they will quickly find an excuse to get a little closer. And if they attract you, in turn, they will seem to be on to a good thing.

You are the classic romantic about whom everyone dreams. You enjoy – and are happy to share – good food, good wine, and all the other comforts, even luxuries, of life. And courtship is one area in which you're happy to spend, spend, spend.

When things get more intimate . . . well, there will be no disappointments there either. Taurean lovers have a splendid attitude toward lovemaking and aim to give as much pleasure as they get. So you will impress your partner as being caring, considerate, and cherishing.

■ **Venus is** *Taurus's ruling planet.*

But once a relationship has been established, things may tend to go downhill. It's not that you will be any the less attentive or less happy to make a comfortable, even luxurious home for you and your partner. The Taurean qualities of good loving and good living are almost always a given.

But Taurean possessiveness will almost certainly rear its head as well. And no amount of good sex, good food, and good living will compensate your lover for the feeling that he or she is always being watched or treated as a possession.

Jealousy may become a problem, too; not necessarily sexual jealousy, but your feeling that your lover isn't completely yours. Watch it! Once your lover begins to feel hemmed in, claustrophobic, or "kept," trouble will almost certainly follow.

Family

Everything we've said about your love life also applies to your family life. When you are settled into a family situation, you'll feel emotionally stable. What's more, you'll believe that all will be well. And indeed it may be – provided you allow your partner and your children the freedom they need to live their own lives. For example, they may have

interests which are not yours. Don't ignore this fact. Try to show at least some curiosity in what your family enjoys doing, and join in if you can.

Above all, don't allow your preoccupation with making money turn into working so many hours that you have no time for the family.

Remember, too, that while you may tend to be somewhat traditional when it comes to family and life in general, your partner and children may not. In fact, they may not always like to play it safe and behave as everyone else does! Be prepared for this and don't overreact.

It's especially important that you never assume your partner is going to be as conventional as you. You may have a husband who would be quite happy to look after the children while you earn the money. Or you may have a wife who much prefers having a career to having children. Remember that just because you probably want children – and will be very good at looking after them – doesn't necessarily mean that your partner also wants a family. Be sure to work all this out before you make a serious commitment.

Whether you're male or female, you'll want to establish a home that is as comfortable as it is secure. And visitors to a half-Taurean household may always be sure of good food, good drink, and a comfortable armchair!

Career

Taureans are ambitious for success, partly because success usually means a secure, steady, and hopefully substantial income – all of which makes you feel safe. You'll probably be happiest working for a large firm or corporation in a traditional area of big business: Banking or international pharmaceuticals, perhaps. A job with regular hours, a predictable routine, and no surprises . . . that's for you.

■ **Poppies and foxgloves** *are associated with Taurus.*

But if you can find a relatively risk-free way of raising money to invest in a business – the financial details of which you will carefully work out to the last penny – you will be very good at running your own show.

If you do start up your own business, think about a partnership – preferably with someone who's not as traditional and unadventurous as you! (No, we didn't say dull.). It's important for Taureans not to let excellent business opportunities slip through their fingers simply because an element of risk may be involved. While you do find it difficult to take risks, you must learn to steel yourself for inevitable changes, keep an open mind, and be flexible.

As for the traditional Taurean occupations, you always seem to do well in any business involving luxury or beauty products. You make excellent beauticians, for example, and working behind the counter in a large store is by no means unappealing. Traditionally (don't you just love that word?), Taureans have worked well in town and country planning. Architecture, accounting, farming, and agriculture in general are also appealing to Taureans. This is also one of the most musical of signs, and many successful professional musicians have their Sun in Taurus.

Health, diet, and exercise

■ **The bull is** *symbolic of Taurus.*

Taurus, as we've pointed out, is alleged to be the sign of the most beautiful people, so you have the responsibility of keeping those good looks and that splendid figure which slay the rest of us. But this also is one of the signs that seems to encourage overeating. You probably love food – rich, sweet food, such as chocolate – and of course this can lead to weight problems.

If you do allow yourself to binge from time to time, a good exercise program is a must, as is a reasonable diet to which you can stick between those occasional five-course dinners.

Excess weight may also be a problem if, like many Taureans, you have both a slow metabolism and a disinclination to exercise. Think fruits and veggies! In the long run, sweet fruit is better than sugar; fiber better than cake.

You probably move well, and a regular dance class may appeal to you. At the gym, exercise machines won't bore you as much as they do some folk; the very regularity of that kind of workout will suit you. And a good massage after exercise really will do you good, as will a relaxing sauna.

The Taurean body area covers the neck and throat. As you know perfectly well, a cold will signal itself by a really sore throat. Remember that the Taurean gland is the thyroid. If you suddenly begin to put on weight and find it impossible to lose, it'll be well worth checking that your thyroid is working efficiently.

Child and parent

As we've already said, you are likely to want, and to love looking after, children. You'll work very hard to provide them with the security you yourself enjoy – sometimes forgetting that they may not be nearly as keen on stability as you are.

Remember, too, that while you are disciplined and may want to instill a sense of discipline in your children, they may need more freedom than you find it easy to allow them. When you do have to

discipline your kids, be careful to explain the reason behind your rebuke and try not to overdo any punishment you hand out.

Your enjoyment of luxury, food, and drink will extend to your wanting your children to enjoy these things, too. You may shower them with more presents, clothes, and outings than are really good for them. On the plus side, your own cautious attitude towards money will probably lead you to encourage them to save up for any "extras" they want.

From infancy on, Taurean children will be patient, good-natured, and pretty content. They'll bolt all the food you put before them and ask for more. And it will be all too easy for you to bribe them with sweets or candy. Resist the temptation – or at least don't succumb too often.

You'll find your Taurean children well-organized and methodical – even somewhat slow in their approach to life. Don't try to rush them, especially where school is concerned. Allow them to develop at their own pace.

But do watch out for laziness! Remember that a Taurean child will be naturally skilled at using his or her charm to get out of doing something they don't want to do. Learn to resist!

Leisure and retirement

As a patient Taurean you'll cope well with hobbies and leisure activities that would bore the pants off most other Sun signs. You'll be perfectly happy putting together an intricate model schooner with spider's thread rigging, or embroidering a huge piece of petit point with 14 stitches to the inch!

Interestingly, although you may be big and stocky enough to appear downright clumsy, you're nevertheless attracted to – and successful at – small, delicate tasks. And if you're musical (and show us a Taurean who isn't), you'll love being a member of a choir or operatic society.

Taureans also enjoy working with their hands and often make good sculptors or potters. They make excellent gardeners, too, with a special love for flowers. You'll especially enjoy making your own wine or brewing your own beer (and, of course, drinking it), and your appreciation of fine food will make you an excellent cook, and in particular good with rich sauces and desserts. Where sports are concerned, when you're young you'll enjoy competitive team games. Later in life, golfing or bowling may have a strong appeal.

■ **Artichokes and grapes**
are associated with Taurus.

147

Virgo personality

VIRGOANS HAVE THE REPUTATION of being modest, prudish, shy, introverted, and fussy. If there aren't strong influences in other areas of the birth chart to counteract these tendencies, you may find it difficult to be outgoing and assured. And sadly, your many positive characteristics may never get a chance to show themselves. With any luck, however, this won't be the case.

Instead, the best characteristics of a Virgo Sun sign – practicality, careful attention to detail, and sharp intelligence – will help you overcome your less positive tendencies. They'll be particularly helpful in allowing you to put aside an overcautious attitude to life – which can prevent you from being successful, as can a lack of self-confidence.

And there are many opportunities for personal and professional success available to the intelligent, analytical Virgoan. For instance, you excel in argument and debate, marshaling facts and presenting them in such a logical and clear way that you usually win over most opponents.

But you must always take care not to argue so forcefully and critically that you alienate people before they've taken in what you have to say. Remember, too, that both your analytical talent and your tendency towards perfectionism may sometimes be interpreted as coldness or harshness.

♍ VIRGO
(AUGUST 24 – SEPTEMBER 22)

KEYWORDS Analytical, critical, fastidious, modest
RULING PLANET Mercury
NEGATIVE
DUALITY OR GENDER Feminine
TRIPLICITY OR ELEMENT Earth
QUADRUPLICITY OR QUALITY Mutable
BODY AREAS Nervous system, stomach, intestines

COUNTRIES Brazil, Crete, Greece, Iraq, Mesopotamia, Turkey, Virgin Islands, Yugoslavia
CITIES Athens, Boston, Corinth, Heidelberg, Jerusalem, Lyons, Paris, Reading; spas and health resorts
STONE Sardonyx
COLOR Brown, dark gray, navy blue
TREES All nut-bearing trees
FLOWERS AND HERBS Those ruled by Gemini, particularly bright blue and yellow flowers
FOODS Those ruled by Gemini; vegetables grown under the ground, especially carrots and potatoes

You're famous for not being afraid of hard work, as well as for working selflessly. Indeed, many Virgoans spend their lives working for others – which can sometimes have its downside. In certain ways, Virgo can become a caricature of the old-fashioned "little woman" whose whole life is devoted to the home and to worrying about and making life easier for his or her partner. Think twice before you go down that road. It can be stifling and unproductive, whether you're male or female.

Love and sex life

Your key problem in love and sex may well be that you can't imagine anybody ever falling for you. After all, your "inner critic" often tells you that you aren't handsome/pretty/intelligent/interesting enough to attract anyone. Well, the proper retort to that is a resounding "of course you are!"

You really must get over that Virgoan trait of paralyzing self-criticism. Modesty is a very attractive quality – but only up to a point!

While we're on the subject of modesty, it is true that some Virgoans suffer from puritanical inhibitions where sex is concerned. You may well need a partner who is prepared to be tactful and patient, and who will help you relax into the physical pleasures of love.

■ **Mercury is** *Virgo's ruling planet.*

Once committed to a relationship, you are a very faithful lover, though again, you must learn to relax and not spend all your time worrying about whether the bedroom is clean enough or the wine is good enough!

The greatest danger for a Virgoan in love is your unhealthy tendency to criticize your lover – too frequently and too harshly – albeit often unintentionally. For instance, you can blow those irritating little habits of your partner's quite out of proportion.

If you find yourself continually exasperated with your lover, try to work out just why you're feeling that way. It may have more to do with your own attitudes and weaknesses than with your lover's supposed faults.

Remember, there is more to life than trying to teach your partner to put the vacuum cleaner back in its place. You're far too interesting a person to waste your energy on silly and destructive complaints.

Family

You'll be prepared to work day and night for your family and to make a home which measures up to your own ambitious ideals. Most Virgoan women with their own careers don't have a problem balancing their lives and making time for partner, children, and home life. But some Virgoans decide that home is more important than career. If you're one of those people, be absolutely sure that you want to deprive yourself of outside interests, just to ensure that the house is spotless and the children perfectly turned out!

OAK LEAVES

One excellent attribute of Virgo is that you won't ever find it difficult to express yourself. When problems arise in the home you quickly analyze the situation, present it logically to the family, then offer a ready solution. There definitely won't be any moody silences in your house!

But again, you must watch out for your Virgoan tendency to criticize and fuss about anything and everything. This can really irritate your partner and children.

BEECH LEAVES

Remind yourself that non-Virgoans don't necessarily share your own feeling that "life is real and life is earnest." In fact, sometimes it's good – for you and your family – just to hang out and casually relax with no agenda whatsoever.

Having a hobby can help, especially one that calls on the explorative and stimulating sides of your natures. And even though you may believe that your spare time should be spent constructively and logically, other Virgoans learn to enjoy the simple pleasures of listening to music or reading a light romance.

■ **Small bright flowers,** *such as buttercups and crocuses, are associated with Virgo.*

Career

You'll want a career which offers you a certain amount of security, but you'll almost inevitably worry about holding on to your job. If you choose work which really taxes your mind, you'll have less time and energy to think negatively about the future.

One obvious career choice for a Virgoan is that of secretary or administrative assistant. Attention to detail comes naturally to you, and working in a one-on-one relationship is often easier for you than working with a group of colleagues. For one thing, the people in such a group may have a hard time measuring up to your high standards, and you will find the temptation to criticize them irresistible. Traveling that road can only lead to trouble.

However, don't feel that you have to get stuck in some kind of subservient role. There are careers in which you can rise almost effortlessly to the top simply by using your natural Virgoan qualities of intelligence, diligence, practicality, and reliability. Virgoans make first-rate teachers, for example, but again, you must watch that tendency to be overcritical, especially when working with children. Investigative journalism and market research are often satisfying career choices, too, as are politics and labor relations.

Virgoans are also usually interested in food, health (alternative medicine in particular), and hygiene – other rich fields for you to explore. And you may well have a feeling for nature and the outdoors, so work in agriculture, landscaping, or horticulture may suit you.

Incidentally, if you find yourself unemployed, don't just sit around worrying about it. Organize your day so that your time is filled with reading the newspapers, writing cover letters, and sending out resumés. Take action, and turn finding a job into a positive goal. Inaction will only feed your natural apprehension about job insecurity.

Health, diet, and exercise

You have naturally high levels of physical and nervous energy which must be channeled properly. The problem is, if you don't have enough to think about, or you don't have enough to do (when work isn't preoccupying you), physical and emotional stagnation can set in and will almost inevitably lead to health troubles.

Your nervous system and stomach are ruled by Virgo, which means that when anything goes wrong with your life, the first sign will be an upset stomach and a tendency to become tense and fidgety. Then the headaches come along, then the worry about the headaches, then a stomachache because of the worry – a vicious circle which is very difficult to break.

Your nervous and physical energy must be positively managed: the first by a satisfying intellectual life; the second by proper attention to diet and exercise.

For instance, you need a lot of roughage. That stagnation we talked about earlier can also extend to your intestinal tract, and you'll find whole foods attractive and satisfying for keeping everything moving. You may even choose to be a vegetarian. And you need plenty of exercise. Rather than going to an indoor gym, you may prefer walking, jogging, or cycling.

Young Virgoans will probably enjoy team sports and fast-moving games, such as squash, tennis, and badminton. If you have a light build you might enjoy gymnastics. More artistic Virgoans find ballet classes more rewarding than aerobics. Later in life, golf may appeal to you. And gardening also can provide excellent exercise. Whatever you choose, work out a regular regimen and stick to it. But remember, you will need some variation in your exercise routine to prevent boredom.

Child and parent

As parents, Virgoans are eager to fill their children's lives with activity, fervently believing that their kids must want to be as busy as they themselves like to be. This isn't always true. Remember that children always need some free playtime every day.

■ **Virgoan foodstuffs**
include carrots, potatoes, and rutabaga.

You must also be careful not to let your critical tendencies run away with you. It's not necessary to critique your child's drawing as though it were a second-rate Rembrandt. Criticism can destroy a child's will to succeed, unless it's carefully and tactfully applied. Your child may need positive, warm encouragement much more than detailed analysis.

Most Virgoans have an element of the teacher about them – which is splendid. You'll make sure your children always have something to do, they'll be less inclined to lounge around in front of the television. Unlike non-Virgoan children, the Virgo child will hate having nothing to do. In fact, long holidays and summer breaks can be real trials, unless parents are very good at organizing spare-time activities that can keep young Virgoans busy. They're very versatile children and can, in time, take to almost any area of interest.

Incidentally, it's a mistake to think that Virgoan children (unlike many other Sun-sign children) aren't perfectly capable of paying attention to two or three hobbies at the same time. In fact, they're famous for successfully juggling several tasks simultaneously.

A Virgoan child will tend to be neat, clean, and attentive. His or her notebooks will be well organized, without blots or smudges, and the handwriting will be clear and legible. At school he or she will seem to be on the side of authority, and it may be necessary to nurture individuality if there aren't to be accusations from other children of being teacher's pet.

Leisure and retirement

Virgoans are often far more involved with their pet hobbies than with other people. In addition, Virgoans also need a wide variety of hobbies and leisure-time interests, and these should be a good mix of both the physically challenging and the intellectually stimulating.

■ **All domestic pets,** *including cats, are under the rule of Virgo.*

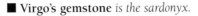

■ **Virgo's gemstone** *is the sardonyx.*

Don't forget that you need at least one hobby to which you can turn when you feel tension building up because of excessive worry. This hobby needs to keep you physically active, but it must also be relaxing. An obvious choice is gardening, and since many Virgoans love the outdoors and are attracted to growing things, you may find this the best of all possible hobbies.

If you don't have a garden – or space for a garden – you can always work with potted plants. We can't guarantee success: Some of you have decidedly green thumbs, and plants perk up and start smiling the moment you come into the room; others of you seem to be the kiss of death for anything that grows. You'll find out, soon enough, into which category you fall! And so will your plants.

■ **Herbs associated** *with Virgo include lavender and aniseed.*

You'll probably be very good at any hobby that involves your hands – sewing, quilting, embroidering, crocheting, knitting. You may also be attracted to pottery making, wood carving, and modeling in clay.

But remember that you have a tendency to cut corners and rush to finish things too fast – which will leave you less than happy with your final product. And you are your harshest critic!

You'll also enjoy reading, and you may want to consider bookbinding as another hobby with which to fill happy hours of retirement.

■ **The symbol of Virgo** *is a young maiden.*

Capricorn personality

CAPRICORNS ARE OFTEN CHARACTERIZED as austere, unbending, ambitious, and self-confident – with very little time for the simple pleasures of life. Well, that characterization is probably overdoing things just a little! But you may certainly be more attentive to your duties and more single-minded than the average person is inclined to be. Because of (or despite) these qualities, when it comes to your approach to life, you'll probably fall into one of two typical Capricorn styles.

Either you'll be single-mindedly ambitious about succeeding at anything – and well on your way to success; or you'll be equally ambitious for success – but never quite seem to make it, very possibly because of a lack of self-confidence.

Capricorns who fall into the latter camp tend to blame everyone and everything – except themselves – for their failures: "I didn't have the right education; I haven't had the same opportunities; I've been worn down by other responsibilities." More confident Capricorns, however, will be self-educated, will make their own opportunities, and will find ways of delegating responsibilities so they can pursue their own interests.

Remember that self-confidence must be nurtured. Remind yourself that you're reliable and you're disciplined, and you can be a success in any career which needs those qualities. And what career doesn't? In fact, you need to be successful. And the more successful you are, the more confident you'll become.

♑ CAPRICORN
(DECEMBER 22 – JANUARY 20)

KEYWORDS Ambitious, calculating, prudent, querulous
RULING PLANET Saturn
NEGATIVE
DUALITY OR GENDER Feminine
TRIPLICITY OR ELEMENT Earth
QUADRUPLICITY OR QUALITY Cardinal
BODY AREAS Bones, knees, skin, teeth

COUNTRIES Albania, Bulgaria, India, Lithuania, Macedonia, Mexico, Orkney, Shetland, Thrace
CITIES Brussels, Delhi, Ghent, Mecklenburg, Mexico City, Oxford, Port Said; administrative centers of all capitals
STONES Amethyst, turquoise
COLORS Black, dark brown, dark green, gray
TREES Aspen, elm, pine, poplar, willow, yew
FLOWERS AND HERBS Amaranthus, belladonna, comfrey, hemlock, henbane, medlar, onion, pansy, quince, rye, wolfsbane
FOODS Malt, meat, starchy foods

Unfortunately, however successful you are, you may be a grumbler, and this can really bore other people! You aren't averse to a little social climbing either, which can also alienate friends and work colleagues (and isn't always as helpful as you may think).

On the plus side – and contrary to popular opinion – you do have a sense of humor! Use it, in your own offbeat and unusual way. It can do a lot to win people over. And remember, just because you like to conform to society's given standards, doesn't mean you have to be a slave to conformity!

Love and sex life

"When I fall in love, it will be forever," as the old song goes, and it may well be Capricorn's motto when it comes to love. But you won't go overboard romantically without careful consideration. You examine your emotions at length, as they develop. And you'll be quite sure of your ground. You'll also have made sure (as far as you can) how your potential lover feels about you, because you hate the thought of rejection. In fact, you'd rather make no move at all than put yourself in a vulnerable position.

Your lover will realize pretty soon that you're also careful with your money. While you'll want to impress your lover, you also won't want to throw money away (as you'd put it) on overexpensive meals or presents. Your lover needs to recognize that coolness is natural to you. But once the relationship is established – and you relax – there'll be no shortage of fun.

■ **Saturn** *is the ruling planet of Capricorn.*

Don't forget, there's a strong connection between Capricorn the goat and Pan, the goat-footed god. And Pan never shied away from an opportunity for fun and games. Ideally, neither should you!

All will be well in love, if you can convince yourself that romance has just as important a place in your relationship as do more down-to-earth considerations. (The prenuptial agreement must have been a Capricornian idea!). Remember, too, that you may need to express your emotions more openly than seems natural for you – especially in bed. Above all, try not to regard emotion as something you dole out only in regular, small portions, like a financial allowance. Learning to "let yourself go" – on all fronts – is perhaps the best goal you can set yourself where a lover is concerned. You won't find it easy, but who said life was easy?

Family

The main danger to family life that a Capricorn must look out for is your tendency to be too intent on earning enough money to make your family secure.

Ironically enough, too much work means that you have too little time to enjoy the family pleasures that you've worked so hard to achieve and maintain!

Of course you take your family ties very seriously indeed, and you're a formidably stable partner. But that doesn't justify throwing so much time and energy into the demands of a career that there's too little time left over to enjoy your partner and your children. And though it's wonderful to be able to shower presents on your family – and you'll certainly be inclined to do that – gifts (no matter how lavish) are no substitute for physical affection, especially where your children are concerned!

And while we're on the subject of affection, your difficulty in showing your feelings can hinder your relationship with your children, just as it may with your partner. Remember that, from time to time, those you love need to be told you love them. And if your partner suggests that you spend more time at home – getting to know your children and having some fun with them – you'd be advised to take their advice.

And speaking of partners, watch out for the strong Capricorn tendency to marry a spouse who is a father or mother figure. There's nothing basically wrong with that; many people successfully and happily marry spouses who mirror the better qualities of a parent.

■ **Goats and pigs** *are associated with Capricorn.*

But Capricornians also have a tendency to seek out a relationship for reasons other than romance. The man who marries the boss's daughter, for instance, may well have more than a touch of Capricorn about him.

Such relationships may sometimes work out on a personal level – but the chances of success are slim. And if forging such a cynical partnership appeals to you in the name of furthering your career, consider whether making two people miserable isn't too high a price to pay for a place on the board of directors!

Career

One tends to think of the typical Capricorn and the typical business person as a natural fit, and this is often the truth. You cope well with routine, and your need for security may well lead you into big business or politics. You also manage well in rather lonely positions of power, and so you'll make a very good chairman or managing director. (There's also no shortage of Capricornian principals and deans!). Property management, real estate, dentistry, and osteopathy are all suitable careers, too.

You also work well under spartan, difficult conditions, and many self-made successes who started in basement offices are also Capricorns.

You have a very powerful, even overwhelming, ambition to succeed, and though you're unlikely to take risks without carefully calculating the odds, you'll be more than willing to take on the responsibility of running your own business. Going it alone will suit your temperament very well, and "self-made man/woman" is a synonym for "Capricornian."

When your self-owned business grows to the stage of expansion, think long and hard before you take on a partner. Going into a partnership will be a dangerous step for you. Remember your strong tendency to be self-absorbed, unbending, and single-minded. These qualities may serve you well when dealing with subordinates, but they can become problematic when dealing with an equal partner.

Certainly you're capable of working with others. But you do far better working solo – or as the leader of a team – than you do working with someone who has an equal share in the business. When and if you do go into a business partnership, remember that you will need to build the same kind of good rapport with your partner as you have built with your spouse or lover.

Health, diet, and exercise

The only major problem you need to watch out for – as you grow older – is a stiffening of the joints. The knees and shins are the key Capricornian body areas. As a child you'll simply collect plenty of bruises, cuts, and knee injuries. But as you grow older, you could find yourself less mobile. If you have to spend many hours sitting behind a desk, exercise becomes especially important to keep your joints and tendons strong.

WILLOW

In fact, "keep moving" is the best motto for a Capricornian where exercise is concerned. You'll enjoy jogging more than exercising in a gym. And the fact that running is inexpensive will appeal to you! You also enjoy distance walking and even taking part in a marathon or two.

Capricornians often make excellent athletes, and mountain and rock climbing are special favorites of this Sun sign – as is golf, which also can have its social advantages! Whatever you choose, remember to keep exercising regularly and keep moving as long as you possibly can; that way you'll remain mobile well into old age. Traditionally, teeth and bones are also related to Capricorn, so regular dental visits are advisable. The skin is also associated with this sign, and extra care should be taken to protect it. Always use a good sunscreen when you're outside, and get in the practice of using a moisturizer regularly (both men and women!). This is especially important because you don't mind – and may even enjoy – being out in extremely cold weather, and this will play havoc with your skin.

In fact, you may even like your home to be cool, or what others would call cold! But the cold really isn't good for you. It can bring on all kinds of rheumatic joint pain, to which Capricornians are especially sensitive.

Indeed, common sense suggests that it's best for you to live in a warm climate – even an artificial one, if necessary. If you want to remain flexible, you really must keep yourself comfortably warm.

Child and parent

We hate to repeat ourselves, but this warning bears repeating: Capricornian parents can be so driven about succeeding in their careers and making money that they leave themselves little time to enjoy the company of their children. That tendency, along with the Capricornian traits of sometimes being stingy with your feelings and heavy-handed with discipline, can spell disaster for the health of the parent-child relationship. At its worst, it can create an unbridgeable generation gap that you will come to regret very deeply later on in life.

It's important to remind yourself that your children need regular and open displays of your love, affection, and appreciation. It's not enough that you want your children to succeed – and will do anything to help them toward that goal. That's a given fact where Capricornian parents are concerned. You also have to cultivate the ability to enjoy the simple, and even aimless, pleasures of parenting. Always remember to set aside regular time with your children for unstructured play and communication.

Above all, remember to rein in your tendency to be an overly strict and rigid disciplinarian. Of course you have high moral standards – and want your children to develop similar values – but temper your approach to discipline with flexibility, open

CAPRICORN

communication, and your famous offbeat sense of humor, especially during your children's teenage years.

For their part, Capricornian children aren't likely to give you much trouble. They are among the most loyal and conventional of the Sun-sign children, and they tend to approach life with a remarkable degree of patience, prudence, and self-discipline.

Indeed, your greatest parenting challenge may well be trying to encourage your Capricornian child to develop a sense of fun and a real enjoyment of life for life's sake — while at the same time surrounding them with the security and structure they desperately crave. They also may well be short on self-confidence, and you'll need to constantly find ways to bolster their egos and self-esteem. More importantly, gently teach them how to express their feelings more openly than their Capricorn natures incline them to.

Capricorn children will be eager to make good progress at school, but they will do so slowly. Don't expect spectacular academic feats from them, but do encourage them to enjoy the learning process and any small achievements they make along the way.

Leisure and retirement

"You mean you have time for leisure!?" a Capricornian may well ask. Indeed, many Capricornians scorn the notions of leisure and retirement. You often are so involved with your work and with your life objectives that recreational interests are unimportant.

If you do have outside interests, they may well be allied to work: Taking up golf, for instance, because it puts you in touch with valuable clients — or even with the boss! You also may enjoy a good party, concert, or afternoon at the races, but only if they provide you with something to talk about the next day with your senior colleagues; or better yet, if someone important notices your attendance at such an event and gives you a nod of recognition.

Where they do exist, your leisure interests may well be connected to the Earth and natural materials. You'll probably enjoy gardening, pottery, or wood carving; studying geology and geography may also interest you. The sign of Capricorn is also strongly associated with music. Your favorite reading will probably involve the classics, or long family sagas. But, as the shortness of this paragraph indicates, it's really difficult to think of you as having much time for any of these pursuits!

A simple summary

✔ Taurus, Virgo, and Capricorn are known collectively as the earth signs. People influenced by these signs are ambitious, dedicated, determined, practical, modest, and conventional. They are the "do-ers" of the zodiac, and are often the most dedicated to work and family.

✔ Taureans are warm-hearted, charming, and determined. They enjoy both personal and financial success, and love luxury and comfort. But they must watch for a tendency toward possessiveness and overindulgence.

✔ Virgoans are practical, modest, intelligent, and analytical, and they are among the great communicators of the zodiac. Often content to remain "behind the scenes," Virgoans are natural teachers, scientists, and healers. On the downside, they must watch out for a sometimes paralyzing tendency to self-denigrate and an equally strong urge to criticize others.

✔ Capricorns are reserved, disciplined, cautious, and practical, and they are the most devoted of lovers and spouses. Many Capricorns are found among the great, self-made successes of the world because they are so single-minded. Some short-change their families in favor of work.

Chapter 10

Simply Stirring: The Air Signs

GEMINI, LIBRA, AND AQUARIUS – respectively ruled by intellectual and versatile Mercury, personable and romantic Venus, and original and innovative Uranus – are the most energetic and quixotic of the zodiac's children, quite simply and aptly known as the "air" signs. Collectively renowned for their ebullient energy, quicksilver minds, and aggressive sociability, Gemini, Libra, and Aquarius are the world's quintessential communicators, intellectuals, adventurers, lovers, and rebels.

In this chapter...

✓ Gemini personality

✓ Libra personality

✓ Aquarius personality

Gemini personality

ALL GEMINIANS DISPLAY *a certain degree of duality. They can (and should, and do) read more than one book at a time, do the crossword while watching TV, listen to music while driving. All this is good for you and can be a distinct advantage. You will often make a success of two careers simultaneously, or at least have more than one job during a lifetime. And you may frequently change jobs or responsibilities within a career.*

A major reason for this concentration on variety is your low boredom threshold. You hate boredom and will do almost anything to escape it. The disadvantages of your dual nature are fairly obvious – a tendency to be superficial and an inability to stick to one task or one person – and we talk about all that in more detail below.

You will enjoy a very lively lifestyle, but you'll be inclined to live on your nerves alone, which can lead to a certain amount of tension and strain. As long as you realize that this can happen, you'll be able to counter it, perhaps by using relaxation techniques. Your mind is kinetic, keen, positive, and logical, and you must find ways to use it constructively.

If you don't find a positive outlet for all that nervous mental energy, it can turn nasty and lead to deceit and even fraud.

You have a decidedly skeptical nature and will accept nothing at face value. You want to examine every statement made to you, look into every mystery, take no-one's word about anything – unless and until you have learned to trust them implicitly (and perhaps not even then).

GEMINI
(MAY 22 – JUNE 21)

KEYWORDS Adaptable, communicative, restless, versatile
RULING PLANET Mercury
POSITIVE
DUALITY OR GENDER Masculine
QUADRUPLICITY OR QUALITY Mutable
TRIPLICITY OR ELEMENT Air
BODY AREAS Arms, nerves, shoulders

COUNTRIES Armenia, Belgium, Lower Egypt, Sardinia, United States, Wales
CITIES Bruges, Cardiff, Cordoba, London, Melbourne, Metz, New York, Nuremberg, Plymouth, San Francisco, Versailles
STONE Agate
COLOR All bright colors, but especially yellow
TREES All nut-bearing trees
FLOWERS AND HERBS Aniseed, azalea, balm, bittersweet, bryony, caraway, elfwort, fern, haresfoot, lavender, lily-of-the-valley, maidenhair, myrtle
FOODS Most nuts, especially hazel and walnut; most vegetables (except cabbage)

Love and sex life

Once you set your eyes on someone you fancy, you'll not find it difficult to make contact. In fact, the object of your affection will find themselves deluged with phone calls, letters, e-mails, and faxes. Ease of communication isn't a problem for you!

However, your lover – whether in the first stages of a romance or in a permanent relationship – will have your duality to deal with, and it won't necessarily be easy.

You may nod approvingly in the direction of faithfulness, but with the Geminian's hatred of boredom, the idea of complete fidelity for a lifetime is basically alien. It is only fair that you try to make your prospective partner understand this.

■ **Mercury** *is also Gemini's ruling planet.*

At the least you should be able to talk about the situation. Intellectual rapport is as important as sexual rapport in a Geminian partnership: You must have something to talk about . . . afterward.

Putting aside your tendency to wander, your partner will never complain that you don't communicate your love in every way. Indeed, you'll continually inquire about your partner's well-being and tell him or her that you love them. And you'll do this even though you sometimes find it difficult to express your love profoundly, viewing such a declaration as slightly embarrassing.

Sexually, Geminians are versatile and excitable – sometimes rather too excitable. You may need to learn the art of leisurely love-making. Geminians are also curious where sexuality is concerned. And though no astrological signature has been found to indicate homosexuality, even on the basis of a full birth chart, it can probably be said that a Geminian is more likely than most to take the view that you should try anything once.

Family

As the paragraph on love suggests, your partner must realize that any unfaithfulness on your part, whether physical or psychological, is less a criticism of them and more a reflection of your low threshold for boredom.

If your lover is really hurt about your unfaithfulness, watch out for the tendency to say something like this: "Well, of course you're marvelous, and of course I love you! But would you really want to live only on filet mignon and nothing else?" This argument isn't as persuasive as you may think. You must remember that you can hurt others badly by entering into a one-sided commitment.

It goes almost without saying that living with you will never be dull. Life will be a series of emotional and physical extremes on all levels, with intense ups and downs. If your family accepts these highs and lows as part and parcel of living with a Gemini, they will find life with you exciting and full of surprises. But when differences do occur, your partner – and children – will find it difficult to confront or have a good fight with you. You can't cope with fighting, preferring instead to engage in debate. And because you're uncommonly quick-witted, you have a good chance of winning all points. Keep in mind that this tactic may simply leave your loved ones more irritated with you than ever. Remember, too, that you can be very stubborn, which also isn't much help.

■ **All nut-bearing trees** *have associations with the Sun sign of Gemini.*

Friendship and comradery within the family are as necessary to you as is sexual attraction between you and your partner. You also value shared common interests among family members. Above all, you can't tolerate jealousy at any price, whether it's jealousy of another man or woman, or of a hobby to which you're passionately addicted.

Career

A safe job with a predictable daily routine and no chance whatsoever of any difference between one day and the next is the typical Geminian's idea of hell! If you find yourself in such a job, get out of it as quickly as possible.

In fact, we can't emphasize this warning enough: Any job that involves a regular routine, regular hours, and the same tasks day in and day out, is NOT for any self-respecting Geminian. Moreover, such a job can only lead to trouble!

On the other hand, any job involving communication will suit you – whether it means dashing about from one sales call or media assignment to another, or merely planning itineraries for others. Work as a travel guide or in the travel industry is an obvious possibility, as is work in telecommunications, the Internet, or journalism. Many Geminians find a niche in radio or television, and they also make excellent advertising executives and copywriters. In fact, most work involving day-to-day contact with the public appeals to Geminians, including working in a book shop, at a newsstand, or behind a sales counter.

With your keen communication skills, teaching is also a good choice for you. And your need to alleviate any possible boredom makes you a lively and stimulating presence in the classroom. But you work best in higher education, since you have little patience with very young children. Geminians also have a high degree of manual dexterity, and many first-rate surgeons have their Sun in Gemini. Your good communication skills also help make you excellent doctors and psychologists.

Health, diet, and exercise

You're usually a pretty wiry and healthy type. Major difficulties often only arise when you don't properly channel all that nervous energy of yours – another reason why a dull, repetitive job isn't for you.

You must find outlets for that high metabolism of yours, otherwise you run the risk of burning out and becoming sluggish and dull, dozy and depressed.

Vigorous daily exercise is often the best antidote, and you'll probably enjoy running, cycling, squash, and tennis. Remember, though, to set aside some time for simple relaxation, too. You definitely won't enjoy repetitive exercise routines. Spending hour after hour on Nautilus machines or in aerobics classes will bore the pants off you. If you can find a large gym that offers a variety of exercise options – preferably one with squash courts, a pool, and an indoor running track, you'll be fine. Otherwise devise your own exercise regimen. Whatever you choose to do, cultivate the discipline to work your body on a daily basis – even though this won't be easy for you!

The key Geminian body areas are the shoulders, arms, and hands – all of which can be vulnerable to accidents. Take care of your hands in particular, wearing safety gloves when appropriate and protecting them in cold weather. Gemini rules the lungs, too, and you may experience problems with bronchitis. Geminians should regard smoking as akin to jumping out of a plane without a parachute. And if either of your parents suffered from a lung ailment, get your doctor to check out your chest regularly.

Child and parent

■ **Butterflies are** *symbolic of Gemini.*

As a Geminian parent you'll have no difficulty with the generation gap. Indeed, you'll be childlike yourself with your kids, as fascinated as they with the new and adventurous, and as ready as they to change your opinion and mood to fit the moment. And while it's difficult to overstimulate a child, you – among all the Sun signs – are more than likely to do that.

Remember that other Sun signs, and especially your non-Geminian children, simply aren't endowed with your speed-of-light ability to embrace new situations and challenges. Remind yourself to allow slower minds to work at their own pace. They'll very likely work more thoroughly than your own!

If you're a Geminian mother you'll suffer more than other Sun signs about being house-bound when your child is very young. Try really hard to find someone to look after him or her so that you can escape and find more mental stimulation than your six-month-old provides! A Geminian child can be a real trial to parents with more sedate

Sun-sign characteristics. It will be difficult to keep up with their energetic minds and bodies, and it will be a continual challenge (and a real education for you) to find new and different games, activities, and social outings that genuinely engage their interest.

Amidst all this bustle, watch out for superficiality in Geminian children and discourage this tendency should it arise: In the long run, it can hurt your child's social and academic development.

Remember that young Geminians are very good indeed at giving the impression that they know everything about anything, when in fact what they often do is dress up a superficial knowledge of things in the most showy Geminian fashion.

A final note of caution: Geminians are wonderfully friendly and outgoing, and endowed with an abundance of curiosity about the world. More than most Sun-sign children, your Geminian child need to be warned about the dangers of being too friendly with strangers. A sad cautionary note, but a true one.

Leisure and retirement

"Retirement? And what might that be?" you may well ask. Geminians never retire. You may be forced, at an advanced age, to stop working at the job to which you've devoted your first 50 years. But you will simply turn your mind to new areas. And because you always carefully plan how to spend your free time, you may view retirement as a matter for rejoicing. Now you can give more time to that favorite hobby of yours, which may well be more fascinating than work.

You should make sure that your spare-time activities are as different as possible from your daily work. This is the best way for you to keep the dreaded dragon boredom in his lair!

■ **Budgerigars** *are associated with Gemini.*

Any club or committee which involves chatting and argument is a good choice for you. A debating society or a political club will exercise your mind as well as keep your tongue well-oiled (which really isn't a problem for you, most of the time!). You may well love learning new languages and taking classes. Geminians often have an interest in fashion, too, and you may enjoy designing and making your own clothes. Driving can be a hobby as well as a necessity, and improving driving skills by taking advanced courses or going full throttle on a police driving course can be enormously rewarding.

A final note of warning for the retired Gemini: Perseverance is as important with your hobbies as with everything else. If you don't persevere with them, your house – and your life – will be littered with half-finished projects.

Libra personality

ESTABLISHING GOOD AND SOLID *personal relationships is very important to you. Indeed, many Librans just don't seem to function properly unless they are relating harmoniously to another person. You probably feel a very strong urge to share your life with someone (more about that later), but this need is strongly related to your hatred of loneliness. This doesn't mean that you can't be content in your own company, but on the whole you are a rather gregarious person who craves companionship. Luckily, building up a good circle of friends won't be difficult for you, since you're generally helpful, kind, and tactful, and always ready with a helping hand.*

On the other hand, you do tend to impose harsh conditions on your friendships, and you need to watch out for this tendency. You expect people to acknowledge how valuable your friendship is, to be grateful that you are their friend, and to show appreciation for every little thing you do for them. In fact, you crave this kind of appreciation, and if you don't get it you can easily turn resentful: "See what I've done for him! And not so much as a word of thanks!"

Perhaps the main disadvantage of a strong Libran personality is indecision: You really are a champion fence-sitter! You tend to treat all problems by assuming that if you just wait around long enough, they'll go away. Not always true, of course, and you must watch out for this character trait. Not only does it absolutely infuriate everyone around you, but it can actually hold you back in all areas of life.

LIBRA
(SEPTEMBER 23 – OCTOBER 23)

KEYWORDS Balanced, resentful, sympathetic
RULING PLANET Venus
POSITIVE
DUALITY OR GENDER Masculine
TRIPLICITY OR ELEMENT Air
QUADRUPLICITY OR QUALITY Cardinal
BODY AREAS Kidneys
COUNTRIES Austria, Myanmar, China, Indo-China, Japan, some South-Pacific Islands, Tibet, Upper Egypt

CITIES Antwerp, Copenhagen, Frankfurt, Freiburg, Leeds, Lisbon, Nottingham, Vienna
STONE Sapphire
COLOR Pale blue, green, pink
TREES All vines, ash, cypress
FLOWERS AND HERBS Those associated with Taurus, excluding red and pink flowers
FOODS Those associated with Taurus, particularly fruit and milk, but excluding alcohol, starches, and sugar

Love and sex life

If there's one thing you really enjoy, it's being in love – you fall easily, and you fall often. This, of course, can lead to trouble. It's all too easy for you to decide that "he/she is the one," long before there's any real indication that this is true.

One reason for this Libran tendency is that you take people at face value. If someone flirts with you, for example, you find it difficult to tell the difference between simple flirtation and a genuine declaration of true love. Taking that path may lead to disaster!

Similarly, when you're in love, keep at least one corner of your mind cool and clear. While it's delightful to plan the most charming of wedding ceremonies, you must also give some thought to what comes afterward!

■ **Venus is** *Libra's ruling planet.*

You're a true romantic, and it's always a joy to be wooed by you. You shower your loved one with presents, set up the most romantic dates, and spend considerably more than you can afford on someone you love. And you need that love to be reciprocated, not only romantically but sexually. You're very happy to please your partner, but you do need to hear his or her cry of delight or sigh of contentment. Even more, you tend to treat any suggestion that lovemaking be postponed for an evening as a personal criticism. And while you love a well-balanced relationship, you occasionally come down too heavily on your side of the scales!

Family

Once you make a commitment, and it seems to be working out, you are very happy indeed. But you must remember that your partner may not have the capacity – every moment of the day – to demonstrate how pleased they are to be with you and how grateful they are for everything you do for them. Even when your partner is fully appreciative, you still need reassurance. Indeed, many Librans have a tendency to provoke silly quarrels just for the sake of making up. This may be fun – once or twice. But your partner won't stand for it time after time. Try to recognize this tendency and keep it under control.

We can't stress enough the fact that you can endanger a relationship by continually insisting that your partner show how much he or she loves you.

Of course, some partners will find it relatively easy to satisfy your need for reassurance, but many others may not. If you have chosen someone a little more reserved than you, for goodness sakes, make allowances.

Once settled into a relationship, you'll be eager to make your home as comfortable and beautiful as possible, whether you live in a castle or a tiny stable. And if you do live in the latter, it will be the most comfortable and well-appointed stable in the "kingdom." You can adapt to living almost anywhere, provided you're with the right person and surrounded by pleasant neighbors.

Career

You'll have gathered by now that the thing you dislike more than anything else is being alone. A job as a lighthouse keeper would certainly not be for you! For the same reason you don't take easily to positions of power, which are often rather lonely and isolated. You do have a distinct feeling for glamour, and working in the fashion industry, hairdressing, or cosmetics often appeals to you. So too does work in the glamorous professions of film, television, or theater – with the caveat that of course these professions often turn out to be extremely unglamorous once you're on the inside!

■ **Cypress trees** *are closely associated with the Libran Sun sign.*

You may be most successful running a small business of your own, but if possible, find a partner with a keener eye for practicalities than you have. You'll shine when dealing with customers, because you're so good at making others feel comfortable and at ease.

Librans also make good teachers. You're most effective, however, in one-on-one situations or with a small class; you simply don't cope well with too many students at once. You can also make excellent agents and arbitrators, and the diplomatic service is a natural home for a Libran. Interestingly, many Librans reach the top ranks of the armed services. Some astrologers find this difficult to explain, but the association is probably related to your connection with fiery Aries – which is your opposite, or polar, sign across the zodiac.

Health, diet, and exercise

Librans need balance in everything, and diet and exercise are no exceptions. You have abundant energy, but you should aim to use that energy steadily and evenly; then you can do an enormous amount of work without exhausting yourself.

One reason for regular exercise is that you may put on weight too easily. And though your ruling planet, Venus, has endowed you with more than a modicum of beauty, extra fat can ruin those good looks. For the same reason, try to keep that Libran sweet tooth under control, as well as your love of good food and good wine! Discipline is not a pleasant word to Librans, but balance should, however, come naturally. So take everything in due proportion.

Libra rules the kidneys, and if you feel off-color on a chronic basis – and are having headaches, in particular – a visit to your doctor is a good idea. Your ruling planet, Venus, governs the parathyroid gland, which balances body fluids. If there is an imbalance in those fluids, or problems with elimination, your health can suffer. If you begin to feel heavy and slow, it will be well worth your while to get a thorough checkup.

You probably have a slow metabolism. Engaging in exercise that stimulates your metabolism is a good idea, but, unfortunately, you may well have a strong natural dislike of all exercise. Nevertheless, find some form of working out that you enjoy doing – and stick with it. One solution is to put up with the physical regimen at a good gym or sports club, if only to savor the relaxing and/or social activities that are also available; a massage, a facial, or just chatting in the bar over a fresh orange juice!

Child and parent

■ **Mint** is *a Libran herb.*

Your children may find you very easygoing indeed. And while this may be true, it isn't because you don't care about your kids or you're overindulgent. Instead, when you appear to be easygoing, you're just having your usual difficulty making up your mind. So when your child asks for something, you may revert to your typical state of having two (or more) opinions about whether they should have it. Worse, you happily take your time making a decision. This tendency can be maddening to those around you.

For example, by the time you write that note giving permission for a school visit to France, your child's class may have already spent a week in Paris and come back home again!

Too much laid-back procrastination can make for missed opportunities, so keep a keen eye on this Libran tendency.

On the other hand, you may also give in too easily to children just for the sake of that peace and quiet you love so dearly; you simply hate upsets of any kind. (And try not to wriggle out of making decisions by referring your children's requests to your spouse!)

Having said all that, you are keen to teach your children the virtues of kindness and consideration, and you happily spend a good deal on their clothes and any after-school activities.

It goes without saying that Libran children should be encouraged from a very early age to be decisive. When they ask you, "What do you think, Mommy?", give them the facts and insist that they make up their own minds. They have a lot of charm, and they are eager to please – but they may also be too laid-back for their own good and perhaps positively lazy. Encourage them to get really involved in school and social activities – especially after-school activities – or they can all too easily become couch potatoes.

Leisure and retirement

Leisure is important to Librans; in fact, they can almost make a career out of it. So you will look forward to retirement and spend a lot of time working slowly and steadily toward a particular goal. If you have an ear for music, you'll find it delightful to learn a musical instrument. And since you love entertaining your friends, gourmet cooking may be a skill you enjoy acquiring. On the other hand, many outwardly charming Librans may need some kind of vigorous physical activity as an outlet for their inner aggression. That's right, we said aggression!

It's a surprising fact – but a true one: Librans tend to have a very deep-rooted and natural aggressive tendency that's at odds with their otherwise charming, sociable, and laid-back natures. It's a good idea, therefore, to use leisure-time activities to externalize this aggression, so that it isn't expressed in road rage, physical or verbal altercations, or any other self-destructive habits.

Both men and women will enjoy judo. Libran women especially enjoy – and are good at – learning self-defense techniques. Libran men often become extremely adept at karate. Aggression can also be channeled positively in fast-moving games, such as soccer, tennis, and squash.

Librans usually have a strong creative streak, and this may well be expressed in photography – an activity that often strongly appeals to Librans. They enjoy not only taking photographs (glamorous portraits, beautiful landscapes), but also doing their own developing and printing. Librans make good dressmakers and fashion designers, too, and they seem to have a natural instinct for making clothes that soon become the very latest fashion trends.

■ **All forms of lizards**
are closely associated with Libra.

Aquarius personality

THINK AQUARIUS AND YOU THINK GLAMOUR – *cool, distant glamour – and the kind of person who makes heads turn when he or she enters the room. The problem is that while you do have that special aura, people – including your closest friends – also may find you rather remote and unapproachable. The simple truth is that it's sometimes almost impossible to get to know you intimately.*

It's not that you aren't friendly. On the contrary, you're the kind of person to whom people can turn in any emergency, because you're always ready with sympathy, advice, and practical assistance. Typically, however, this approachability isn't the result of any great emotional empathy on your part, but because you tend to assess situations calmly and logically and thus know just the right thing to do at just the right time.

Aside from offering cool and logical advice when asked, you guard your privacy with your life. You develop exactly the lifestyle you want and allow nobody to disrupt it. You may even avoid emotional commitments because you can't bear the thought of all the disruption such a relationship will cause in the measured routine of your days.

Despite your cool and distant demeanor, you're positive and optimistic in your approach to life – and you may well be the kind of person who's ahead of his or her time. On the other hand, you may also have an equally strong tendency to establish fixed beliefs early in life and never veer from them, giving people the impression that you're old-fashioned

♒ AQUARIUS
(JANUARY 21 – FEBRUARY 18)

KEYWORDS Distant, eccentric, humane, independent
RULING PLANET Uranus
POSITIVE
DUALITY OR GENDER Masculine
TRIPLICITY OR ELEMENT Air
QUADRUPLICITY OR QUALITY Fixed
BODY AREAS Circulation, shins, ankles
COUNTRIES Ethiopia, Iran, Israel, Poland, Russia, Sweden

CITIES Bremen, Hamburg, Moscow, Salzburg, St. Petersburg
STONES Amethyst, aquamarine
COLORS Electric blue
TREES Fruit trees
FLOWERS AND HERBS Those associated with Taurus and Capricorn, especially elder, goldenrod orchids, and sorrel
FOODS Those associated with Taurus, especially those which preserve well, such as apples and citrus fruits, dried fruits, frozen foods

and fuddy-duddy. So do keep up with current opinion and changing trends. No forward-looking Aquarian wants to really fall behind the times!

Love and sex life

Like a magnet, you both attract and repel at the same time. Few people can resist the captivating force of your Aquarian personality, but once captivated and ready for a closer look, many people will find themselves out in the cold! In fact, you often seem ready to flash a big "Trespassers Will be Prosecuted" sign at anyone who tries to get closer to you than you allow – which may not be very close at all. Illogically, while warning them off, you may secretly want them to come on, yet not be sure how to invite them in!

You have a hard time letting your true emotions rise to the surface, so beware of sending mixed signals: You may lose out on finding the love of your life!

■ **Uranus is** *Aquarius's ruling planet.*

Indeed, when you do fall for someone, you fall very heavily. And once you have made up your mind to welcome someone into your life, the pair of you should have an exciting and fulfilling relationship. Your choice of partner, incidentally, may surprise others. You seem drawn to lovers who are somewhat out of the ordinary or very different from you – someone of another ethnic group, for instance.

When it comes to love, you must try to show your emotions more openly than you normally do – or feel you can. Like the other air signs, Aquarians tend to throttle back on emotions. This makes it difficult to throw yourself into a physical relationship with the enjoyment and enthusiasm your lover needs.

■ **All citrus fruits** *are connected with Aquarius.*

Family

Once you have committed yourself to a partnership and to a family, be prepared for some big changes!

You're simply going to have to give a little – maybe even a lot – when it comes to family. Since the days when you were a toddler and cautiously guarded your toys from the children next door, you have carefully cultivated regular habits and patterns that make your daily life invulnerable to outside interference. Well, a commitment to partner and family is an invitation to interference.

You'll not only have to change your lifestyle to accommodate your new situation, but you'll have to accept that change is necessary to the success of your family life. Certainly your partner needs to recognize the fact that you'll always need a certain amount of privacy, but be sure to discuss that before you commit yourself to a long-term relationship.

If you revert back to your tendency to be self-protective, particularly shielding important areas of your life from your partner, there'll be trouble on the home front. This tendency often stems from your instinctive aversion to letting people get too close to you. But closeness, after all, is the whole point of a relationship, if you want that relationship to succeed. You must communicate freely and openly with your partner every day. Yes, this is difficult for you, but work at it: The reward is a happy family atmosphere.

You're always ready to encourage a partner in anything they want to achieve, and your kindness and consideration are second to none. Sometimes you also have a tendency to be rather unpredictable, and that can be exciting and interesting. On the other hand, you have an equal tendency to be stubborn and inflexible, and this can cause occasional problems within a relationship.

STARFRUIT

Career

Your splendid humanitarian instincts and sympathetic understanding of others' problems will be wasted if you don't work directly with people every day. You may become a first-rate social worker, for instance, using your sympathy and natural concern for others to make their lives easier and more bearable. You need to be able to work independently, however, and in your own distinctive way. Indeed, you become downright irritable if you have to put up with a crowded office and its continual chatter and disturbances. And you definitely won't welcome too much interference or advice – however kindly meant. This doesn't mean that you can't work well with others. In fact the opposite is true: You make a splendid team player, provided you're allowed a certain amount of freedom.

You are another of the Sun signs who only work well when you're really involved in what you're doing. If you find a job dull, you simply switch to automatic pilot and often don't accomplish anything. Work that is challenging and engaging is therefore especially important for you to pursue.

Many Aquarians have a natural aptitude for science, and those who work in scientific research and development can really make their mark through inventiveness and originality. Communications technology also attracts many Aquarians, as does work in the airlines industry. Your keen humanitarian instincts may well draw you to international, philanthropic organizations, such as the United Nations and Doctors Without Borders.

All in all, you have a natural originality and inventiveness, and the word "brilliant" is often applied to you – albeit with the word "eccentric" following quickly on its heels!

■ **All birds of prey,** *including the falcon, are associated with Aquarius.*

Health, diet, and exercise

Aquarius and its ruling planet, Uranus, are strongly associated with the circulatory system. Take good care of yours, or you may experience a variety of related problems: Varicose veins and hardening of the arteries, to mention just two. Your polar (or opposite) zodiac sign also has a certain effect on your health (as does everyone's polar sign), and in your case, your opposite sign has particular significance.

Leo is your polar opposite, and Leo rules the heart. The relationship between a healthy heart and a good circulatory system is almost too obvious to need mentioning. Since your sign is characterized by this double emphasis on the heart, you would do well to adopt heart-healthy practices early in life: Low-fat foods, regular exercise, and no smoking are your best preventive allies.

And always wrap up well in cold weather, which isn't good for you – no matter how much you may like it. (Leo also rules the back, so take extra precautions to avoid lower back strains and pains.)

To keep your circulatory system moving freely, it's important that you keep moving too. (You're also prone to arthritis and rheumatism, by the way.) Aerobics and dance classes will suit you, but watch out for those Aquarian ankles, which can be damaged easily. You also enjoy swimming, and in fact are drawn to most sports, especially when you're young, that favor individual performance over team playing.

■ **Leo** *is the polar opposite to Aquarius in the zodiac.*

Aquarians are almost always drawn to holistic medicine and alternative health regimens, particularly in the area of natural alternatives to conventional drugs. Though you have a deep respect for traditional science, you may have an equally deep mistrust for prescription medications, and you may well have used natural remedies, including herbs, for years. As for food, a light diet is best for you (though you tend to like rich dishes). You won't find it easy to regulate your diet, but do it. And when you manage to shake off surplus pounds, resist celebrating with a giant binge!

Child and parent

Independent-minded yourself, you encourage your children to think for themselves; you definitely won't be the kind of parent who insists that the children think just like you. Indeed, a child who is a mirror-image of you would strike you as very dull. You allow your children perfect freedom of expression and sometimes perhaps almost too much physical freedom.

On the other hand, many Aquarians make the mistake of too readily assuming that their children are just like them. In fact, your child may be far more conventional by nature than you. Don't be depressed or distressed if your children like to follow orders, easily fall into line, or want to be like the kids next door. However unlike you this conventional tendency of theirs may be, respect it.

■ **Sea birds** *are also associated with Aquarius.*

Fortunately, respecting others' viewpoints often comes easily to you. And you are eager to be fair to your child and always ready to listen to his or her point of view. Another great Aquarian plus is your total honesty: You won't dismiss any child's curiosity or questions with silly remarks. When a question is asked, an answer will be given, and that's valuable for you and your child's relationship. Equally valuable is a regular show of real affection, which you may find much more difficult to do. Work hard at overcoming your natural mistrust of showing emotions.

The Aquarian child will always be "different" in some way, and should be allowed to develop his or her originality. An Aquarian child should do well at school as long as the regimen isn't repressive or the pupils stifled by silly rules for which there are no good reasons. You should guard against unpredictability and stubbornness.

Leisure and retirement

Aquarians need and insist on variety. If you don't get it at work, you'll certainly seek it out in your spare time. You probably enjoy entertaining others, and with your innate dramatic flair and glamour you'll be an asset to any amateur dramatic or operatic society. You enjoy big occasions, so celebrity concerts, first nights, and other celebratory occasions will attract you. And your good nature and desire to help others can be well expressed by working on charity committees. You are especially drawn to ecology campaigns and the green movement in general.

You take great pleasure in giving hospitality to others, and with the help of Leo, your polar sign, you provide some lavish dinners and nights out. As a cook, you enjoy experimenting far more than slavishly following printed recipes, and though the results may often best be described as . . . well . . . unusual, they'll certainly be enjoyable.

All these pastimes can be extended into retirement, and there's no reason why they can't be carried on for as long as you wish. Your instinct to stay active and not get tied down to routine is not only natural but very good for you.

Do remember, however, to keep some time free. Not only do you need to unwind regularly, but you also love to do things on the spur of the moment. So always leave some "just-in-case" space in your busy schedules.

A simple summary

✓ Gemini, Libra, and Aquarius are known collectively as the air signs. People influenced by these signs are energetic, intellectual, eccentric, freedom-loving, aggressively social, and great communicators. They love knowledge and intellectual pursuits and are powerfully adept at translating ideas and theories into words and actions.

✓ Geminis are witty, lively, nervous, intellectual, and inquisitive. They excel in any area that requires good communication skills and personal charm, including the media, sales, and advertising. Watch out for their tendency to be fickle, especially in love, and to settle for superficial knowledge.

✓ Librans are diplomatic, romantic, easygoing, and sociable. They hate the idea of being alone and have a marvelous facility for harmoniously bringing people together. They must keep a check on their tendencies to be gullible, indecisive, and too laid-back.

✓ Aquarians are inventive, independent, friendly, and humanitarian. While they're always willing to offer a helping hand, at heart they enjoy solitude – sometimes too much. They often choose a career – scientific research, for example – where they can work independently and draw on their keen inventive skills. The drawback here is that solitude and independent thinking can easily turn into seclusion and intractability.

Chapter 11

Simply Soulful: The Water Signs

Cancer, Scorpio, and Pisces — respectively ruled by the compassionate and emotional Moon, mysterious and eruptive Pluto, and sensitive and idealistic Neptune — are the most emotional and sensitive of the zodiac's children, simply and wonderfully known as the "water" signs. Collectively famed for their deep compassion, love, sensuality, intuition, and imagination, Cancer, Scorpio, and Pisces are the world's quintessential mates, mothers, lovers, artists, researchers, and dreamers.

In this chapter...
✓ Cancer personality
✓ Scorpio personality
✓ Pisces personality

Cancer personality

MANY PEOPLE FIND that the Cancerian personality is particularly difficult to define. When we first meet you, you often seem rather aggressive and unsympathetic. And it's very easy to put you on the defensive with a casual and harmless remark which seems to rub you the wrong way. When that happens a barrier immediately comes down which forces us to back off.

Of course, as most people soon discover, that Cancerian barrier isn't as strong as it seems. If we persevere, it crumbles easily, revealing a receptive and sensitive person who is enormously aware of others' problems and very ready to offer sympathy and positive help.

You definitely have a reputation for being moody. One moment you're chatty and cheerful; the next moment you're silent and scowling. Or you initially offer us a friendly welcome when we come to visit; then you act like you wish we had thought twice about coming over! These Cancerian storms are quickly past, however, and whatever it was that was upsetting you (which often has nothing to do with us!) is soon forgotten, and you're in the kitchen, cooking us a delicious omelet or fixing our favorite drink

Your extraordinary imagination is often at the root of your moodiness and defensiveness. The Cancerian imagination is generously vivid and colorful – and it can be one of your greatest assets when used positively. Used negatively, however, it can turn sour and encourage you to worry – often irrationally – about anyone and anything. And that tendency can be an enormous liability.

♋ CANCER
(JUNE 22 – JULY 22)

KEYWORDS Melancholy, protective, sensitive
RULING PLANET Moon
NEGATIVE
DUALITY OR GENDER Feminine
TRIPLICITY OR ELEMENT Water
QUADRUPLICITY OR QUALITY Cardinal
BODY AREAS Alimentary canal, breasts, chest
COUNTRIES Algeria, Holland, New Zealand, North Africa, Paraguay, Scotland, West Africa

CITIES Algiers, Amsterdam, Berne, Cadiz, Genoa, Istanbul, Magdeburg, Manchester, Milan, New York, Stockholm, Tunis, Venice, York
STONE Pearl
COLORS Pale blue, silver, smoky gray
TREES All trees, especially those richest in sap
FLOWERS AND HERBS Acanthus, convolvulus, geranium, honeysuckle, lilies, saxifrage, waterlilies, white poppy, white rose
FOODS Fruits and vegetables with a high water content, such as cabbage, cucumber, lettuce, melon, mushroom, pumpkin, turnip

It's very important, then, to channel your imaginative energy in a positive fashion, and this is often best done by marrying it to your creativity – which can be marvelously inventive and original.

Love and sex life

A satisfactory love life will transform a Cancerian's world completely: Your powerful emotions will be strongly focused on your partner, sometimes to the extent of your caring too much and becoming overprotective. You are a true romantic, and your courtship will be full of beautifully expressed sentiments and wonderfully inventive moments.

Your emotions can run away with you, however, and when a partner, for one reason or another, doesn't respond to you with equal feeling, difficulties can arise – and there may be some highly dramatic scenes!

■ **Maple trees** *are associated with the Cancerian Sun sign.*

Difficulties also may occur when your delight in caring for your lover creates a claustrophobic atmosphere.

Although any Sun sign can have a wonderful relationship with any other sign, but one can imagine that an independent Aquarian or Sagittarian might have a tough time with an overcaring Cancerian. In fact, this tendency of yours to smother another with an excess of emotion and concern extends to any partner of yours, whatever his or her Sun sign. You must remember to give your lover some physical and emotional freedom.

Sexually, Cancerians have a wonderfully warm sensuality, and you are as intent on pleasing your partner as on being pleased yourself. But! If your partner doesn't react appreciatively to your lovemaking, or is insensitive to your efforts, you may counter with a sharp remark which will thoroughly puncture the pleasure.

■ **The Moon** *is Cancer's ruling planet.*

Indeed, any low-level tension in your life may explode in the bedroom, since you simply can't leave your overactive imagination and tendency to worry at the bedroom door!

Don't be surprised, then, if you provoke an equally sharp reply from your partner. And with the atmosphere now thoroughly ruined, you may as well turn on the light and settle down with a good book.

Watch out also for your tendency to cling to the romantic past and your subsequent reluctance to move a relationship forward. Try not to be too sentimental, and remember that, like everything else in life, a relationship needs to develop and change.

Family

Family is enormously important to a typical Cancerian. In fact, even the most ambitious Cancerian businesswoman can be seduced away from a career and then find herself becoming what she never thought she could be: A housewife or mother – pure and simple. That kind of purity and simplicity can pall after a while, however, and you must find ways to keep your mind sharp and inventive.

Think twice before deciding to devote yourself entirely to home and family. You may need outside stimuli more than you realize.

Remember, however, that you will always need to feel at home in any environment, whether in a job or a situation with a partner or lover, to which you commit yourself. If you feel that your lifestyle, in or out of the home, is threatened in any way, your typical Cancerian insecurities and moodiness will rise to the surface.

Putting all those caveats aside, Cancerians do love settling into a relationship, and both men and women make wonderfully caring partners. You enjoy expressing love through marriage, and you work very hard to make the relationship work, especially if you hit a rocky patch. Any problems there are may arise if your partner wants to make a change such as moving house. You are set in your ways and reluctant to move on.

■ **Waterlilies and convolvulus** *are Cancerian flowers.*

191

This can present special difficulties when children grow up and move out. You may find yourself clinging to a large house which you no longer really need, just because you can't bear the thought of moving.

You tend to cling to other possessions as well; the Cancerian attic, basement, or garage is a museum of useless objects – every one of which will be linked in your mind to an important event in your life. The all-time hoarder of the zodiac, you just can't bear to get rid of anything.

Career

You enjoy variety and change, and yet you need a degree of continuity in your daily work. The Cancerian personality is so strongly associated with the idea of nurture that the caring professions are an obvious first choice; nursing, of course, obstetrics, or working with children.

Cancerians also have the reputation of making the best cooks; so a career as chef or caterer – or at a simpler level, a cook in a school or business organization – should suit you well.

Incidentally, Cancerians are not especially known for evenness of temper – a trait they seem to share with many chefs! Marrying your instinct for caring with the usual Cancerian love of the sea suggests work afloat, maybe as a steward, a purser, or a tour director on a luxurious cruise ship. This latter provides a certain amount of excitement – even a sense of danger – and both will suit your personality.

■ **Crabs and shellfish** *are both associated with Cancer.*

Cancerians are often fascinated with the past, and the antique trade might interest you. Indeed, running a stall in an antique market would make a first-class part-time occupation. Working to repair or preserve antiques may also interest you, as might general museum work. You're very shrewd and have a good business sense, so running your own business – of any kind – shouldn't be difficult (or unprofitable). Giving business advice to others can be equally satisfactory as a career. Just remember that for Cancerians, fulfillment is more important than making money!

Health, diet, and exercise

You're pretty tough, and worry is the only thing that can upset your system – if you let it! Cancerians are more prone to worry than people of any other Sun sign. In fact, even before you realize you're worried about something, stomach upsets and general moodiness will announce the fact.

You must get a handle on your tendency to worry unnecessarily. At its best, worry can cause itching or other skin problems, and while these minor ailments may be psychosomatic in origin, they can be problematic none the less. At its worst, worry can cause ulcers and play havoc with your immune system and stress levels.

So try to watch it. No doubt you've heard – once too often – a friend or lover say, "For goodness sakes, pull yourself together and stop worrying!" This advice, as you know too well, simply doesn't work. But realizing how prone you are to worry – often irrationally so – is the beginning of learning how to solve the problem. Listening to your intuition, which is usually very sound, will also help.

There is absolutely no connection between the Sun-sign Cancer and the disease of that name. You are no more prone to cancer than anyone else. Nevertheless, it's better to be safe than sorry. The Cancerian body area is the chest, and the sign also rules the breasts. It's especially important, therefore, that Cancerian women check their breasts regularly. The Moon, Cancer's ruling planet, is associated with the alimentary system: The esophagus, stomach, gall bladder, bile ducts, pancreas, and intestines.

■ **Milk and turnips** *are Cancerian foodstuffs.*

It's worth keeping an extra keen eye on all these areas. And see your doctor immediately if you suspect any problems.

Your natural tenacity and toughness should carry you through to old age, despite any tensions, strains, or illnesses, and those Cancerians who have to struggle with serious illnesses do so with a courage and determination which often sees them through.

Child and parent

Most Cancerians seriously want to start a family, and you may persuade your partner to do this sooner than he or she intended. You are an excellent parent, and the only real problem to watch out for (as in your intimate relationships) is your tendency to be overprotective and to stifle your children by being too emotional.

In fact, your emotions may make it difficult for you to be logical and rational when it comes to dealing with your children and their problems. You hate it when they have to start kindergarten. You hate it more when they decide to leave home.

Try to train yourself to anticipate these moments, and keep a lid on excessive worrying and emoting. Otherwise you may provoke difficulties and differences. Worse, an unbridgeable gap may develop between you and your children – which for a Cancer is especially tragic.

Your good points as a parent are so strong that it is well worth the effort to let your children develop in their own way. You will inevitably give them a good start on life with your solid love and nurturing. And your extraordinary imaginative skills – which make you a marvelous storyteller and inventive playmate – will act to stimulate their minds and encourage their developing interests.

A Cancerian child of either sex will "mother" its brothers and sisters. It's touching to see a six-year-old boy assume responsibility for his eight-year-old sister. Watch out for your young Cancerian daughter, however, and make sure she doesn't become too maternal too early. Encourage her courageousness by offering her the opportunity for adventure away from the doll's house. Of course, the same is also true where boys are concerned. Children of both sexes enjoy keeping an animal as a pet. This gives them a sense of responsibility and a practical expression for their domestic instincts, which will emerge early.

■ **The pearl is** *the gem associated with Cancer.*

Leisure and retirement

You shouldn't have any difficulty developing ideas for leisure activities. Above all, don't limit yourself and do be adventurous: the world's your oyster!

The maple, rich in sap, comes under Cancer.

As we've already pointed out, Cancerians are the champion hoarders of the zodiac, and one obvious hobby you are likely to embrace is being a collector of some kind. You'll not only find this compulsively interesting and time consuming, but your collection – of stamps, coins, dolls, or antique kitchen tools, to name just a few examples – may turn out to be extremely profitable.

Indeed, if you start your collection when you're still working, by the time you retire you may be able to sell it at a huge profit – and start a brand new, and more lucrative, collection! You'll find you not only enjoy searching for and acquiring objects, but researching their history and becoming an expert in the area – whatever it is.

Cancerian women are often superb craft workers and especially good at sewing. Men, too, may enjoy petit point or embroidery. These kinds of activities often appeal to the side of Cancerians that enjoys peaceful, quiet periods. So fishing, too, is very attractive to members of this water sign. And though a Cancerian might find working in the kitchen of a restaurant a little too noisy and provocative, working in your own kitchen is an entirely different matter. A course in Cordon Bleu cooking could be the start of a hobby which will please your friends as much as it will delight you.

Cancer, *with images of her elements, foods, fruit, and flowers in her garb.*

Scorpio personality

OH YES – SEX! Well, of course. It's probably the sign's strong association with the sexual organs, which it rules, that has encouraged people to think that Scorpio is the sexiest sign of the zodiac. And in fact, nobody will argue that Scorpios aren't interested in sex. But please, don't go mad trying to fulfill your Scorpio reputation. People sometimes assume Scorpios are almost wholly sexually driven, an assumption that has endowed this sign with rather dark and sinister aspects only. This is a mistake.

In fact, what you have in abundance is a deep reserve of emotional, mental, and physical energy, which needs to be channeled in various ways if you're to feel happy and fulfilled. And, of course, there are other ways of doing this than in bed!

For example, you're the archetypal career person, determined and positive, entirely involved in your work (whatever that work may be). Work can be a wonderful outlet for excessive mental and physical energy. Even the old-fashioned housewife devoted to home and children can be the most satisfied of Scorpios, provided her mental and physical energy is thoroughly engaged. But when a Scorpio hasn't found positive ways to express his or her energies, then things may go terribly wrong. The dark side of the sign – resentfulness, jealousy, suspicion, a deep and brooding dissatisfaction with life in general – emerges, and in spades. The rather sinister reputation of Scorpio might be justified under the weight of those dark qualities, but they are by no means inevitably ingrained or wholly negative.

SCORPIO
(OCTOBER 24 – NOVEMBER 22)

KEYWORDS Intense, jealous, passionate
RULING PLANET Pluto
NEGATIVE
DUALITY OR GENDER Feminine
TRIPLICITY OR ELEMENT Water
QUADRUPLICITY OR QUALITY Fixed
BODY AREAS Sexual organs
COUNTRIES Bavaria, Korea, Morocco, Norway, Syria, South Africa, Uruguay

CITIES Baltimore, Cincinnati, Dover, Fez, Halifax, Hull, Liverpool, Milwaukee, Newcastle-upon-Tyne, New Orleans, St. John's (Newfoundland), Stockport, Valencia, Washington, D.C.
STONE Opal
COLORS Maroon, dark red
TREES All bushy trees, blackthorn
FLOWERS AND HERBS Those associated with Aries, particularly dark red flowers, figwort, peppermint, wild thistle
FOODS Those associated with Aries, especially tomatoes, onions, and spices such as cayenne, paprika, and chili

Yes, jealousy can be a major problem for you – not only within a relationship, but at work. Jealousy on the job may work to your advantage, encouraging you to work harder and beat the person you envy. On the other hand, jealousy may also make you bitter and frustrated.

Resentfulness and dissatisfaction may be welcome red flags, alerting you to the fact that you need to open up and discuss your problems with a loved one, thus strengthening communications and the relationship.

Love and sex life

Jealousy, which we've already mentioned, is the singular difficulty for a Scorpio in love. Putting that caveat aside, of all the Sun signs you're the most able to express your deepest and most passionate feelings, both physically and emotionally, and through words, gifts, and special occasions. Indeed, being wooed by a Scorpio is an experience and a half. In any relationship with you, there will be moments of enormous happiness. But the relationship will inevitably be stormy, too, in one way or another.

You are at your stormiest when your partner doesn't respond to the relationship as enthusiastically as you do.

In fact, the relationship won't last long if your partner isn't prepared to throw him- or herself into it wholeheartedly. When this kind of blip occurs, your famous jealousy will more than likely make an appearance.

■ **Pluto is** *the ruling planet of Scorpio.*

This is not to say you don't need a sexually compatible partner, perhaps more than most other people do. But you (and your partner) also need other interests outside the bedroom – both shared interests and ones pursued independently of each other. And don't make the mistake of thinking that jealousy is always sexual! If your partner needs outside interests which you can't share, there may be trouble again.

We can't urge you enough to be conscious of the dangers of jealousy. Learn to trust. A partner who has to work with someone else, or admires someone else, isn't necessarily shutting you out. Nor do they believe that the other person is better at their job than you, or worse, better in bed than you. Indeed, that notion is ridiculous – isn't it?

Family

Again, we must repeat ourselves: No matter how enthusiastically you go into a permanent relationship, no matter how determined you are to succeed, and no matter how certain you are of your partner's love – all of which will give your relationship a good start – jealousy, that unlovable and wasteful emotion, will sometimes rear its ugly head. Trust will fight it, and trust is what you must establish, early and firmly.

You need interests outside the home. Your energy is so abundant that it's difficult to expend it all in a tightly-knit family situation. If you can manage it, try to find an interest which you can share with your partner. If this isn't possible, and your partner quite innocently finds an outside interest of his or her own, it'll be all too easy for jealousy or paranoia to arise. Instead, even if your partner's interest doesn't appeal to you, try to act interested. You have a strong, natural capacity for encouraging others to go forward and succeed, and here's an opportunity to do just that.

■ **All bushy trees** *are associated with Scorpio.*

Career

The key to fulfilling work for you is to feel thoroughly involved in whatever you choose to do. You hate having to traipse off to the office every morning on the same train, sit at the same desk, and do precisely the same dull job – day in and day out. That kind of routine will bore and frustrate you in no time.

You need to be able to express your imagination, even in careers such as banking or insurance. And big business can indeed fascinate you! In fact, you have a marvelous business sense, and you can thoroughly relish building a career and making money.

Even if you are forced into a career which doesn't strongly appeal to you, you'll enjoy making it work for you, applying your imaginative skills and mental energy, and building a reputation for efficiency.

A career in the army and navy (despite their devotion to routine) may also satisfy you. And your imagination can be put to excellent use in police work; you love digging for details and would make an excellent detective. Indeed, you could make an excellent criminal – there is also that tendency in Scorpio – though too much success in that arena might mean you'd end up in circumstances of claustrophobic boredom (i.e., jail). Traditionally, the mining industry, engineering, and the wine trade are all associated with Scorpio. Other Scorpios may go on to become brilliant surgeons and psychiatrists.

Health, diet, and exercise

The Scorpio association with the genitals means that men, in particular, should regularly and carefully check their testicles. The gonads are the Scorpio glands, also connected with the reproductive system; any problems in this area should be checked out medically.

We've already mentioned your high levels of physical and emotional energy, and it goes without saying that exercise is more than good for you – mentally and physically. But don't go overboard! Always match your physical regimen to your age and capabilities.

Young Scorpios enjoy intense team sports, boxing, and the martial arts – all of which provide a safe outlet for those aggressive and violent tendencies that sometimes lie just beneath the surface of a Scorpio personality. Unfortunately, these same forms of exercise tend to do a little damage to the body in the form of minor bumps, bruises, and torn muscles, so take some care.

Water sports also provide an excellent outlet for Scorpios, who enjoy both high diving and scuba diving. And finally, you may find that you are very good at billiards, in which keenness of the eye and manual dexterity are joined.

When Scorpios fall ill, it's often because of some kind of blockage – physical or psychological. On the physical end, don't fall into the trap of being overconcerned about constipation. It's scarcely ever serious, but if it does become chronic, consult a doctor. If your work involves long periods of sitting at a desk, you also may have trouble with hemorrhoids; take any such symptoms seriously. Similarly, standing for long periods of time may cause varicose veins, which also should be treated medically.

Child and parent

You'll be keen to make your children as enthusiastic and hardworking as yourself, and to ensure that they are always occupied, whether in school or out.

Well, that's fine – for some children, mostly Scorpio children. But be careful with your non-Scorpio children. They may find it difficult to satisfy your demands, and this can lead to explosions of dissatisfaction and anger which will make them feel insecure – and will hurt your relationship with them.

Be careful about discipline, too. Some children can take – and indeed need – a high degree of discipline, but it can be counterproductive with other children.

As for affection, you'll love your children, but you may love them too intensely. You must learn to be a little light-hearted at times and simply just have fun. You have a wonderful imagination – use it!

Scorpio children will be highly active and energetic, and will need to be kept busy. Sports and exercise will probably play a major role in their lives – and should! Sometimes, however, a Scorpio child will fall into what seems like an uncharacteristically introspective mood. Don't worry about these "down" times, but do try to get to the bottom of the problem. It may reflect some difficulty at school or in coming to terms with their developing minds and bodies. At other times, Scorpio children may feel that their energy isn't being as positively used as they instinctively wish, and they may need advice and guidance about how to channel their abundant energy more appropriately.

■ **Onions** *are among Scorpio's foodstuffs.*

Leisure and retirement

A Scorpio's energy and vivid imagination can be applied, of course, to any sport or pastime. The key here is to choose leisure -time activities in which you are almost compulsively interested and through which you can channel your abundant physical and mental energy.

Exercise is absolutely essential, and sports will probably take up quite a lot of your time when you are young. Intellectual energy can be turned to any number of subjects, provided they demand real attention and study, and use your prodigious sleuthlike talents.

As a water sign, Scorpios love fishing, sailing – all water sports, in fact. But motorcycle racing and car racing also attract you, even if you stay in the stands. It's probably fair to add flirtation to the list of leisure-time activities as well. However happily partnered you are, there's always time for a harmless flirtation – and for giving your partner (for once!) the opportunity to be mildly jealous! In retirement you also might turn your keen business sense to good use by helping to run a charity organization. There are always plenty of helpers around to serve on such committees, but few have the organizational ability and enthusiasm that a Scorpio does.

■ **Scorpions are** *the symbols of this star sign.*

Pisces personality

KIND, CHARITABLE, CREATIVE, CLEVER, and self-sacrificing, you easily set aside your career or ambitions for the sake of raising your children. Hooray for Pisces! Well . . . yes. But on the flip side of all these admirable qualities is the fact that you sometimes have to be prodded to face reality, if only for your own good, and you often need help organizing yourself and getting your life on track. You do tend to live in a dream world of your own making, and you're definitely not the person to whom others turn for fixing a leaky faucet or even changing a light bulb.

It's also true that although you may be extremely talented, that talent often isn't expressed. You find it difficult to believe in yourself, and you're too often swayed by emotion. Like the other water signs, Cancer and Scorpio, your imagination easily runs wild, causing you too often to worry about nothing and sapping your energy to boot.

Pisceans are at their best when expressing their considerable creative potential, though it may take a stronger personality – a partner, perhaps – to show you the best way of expressing your talents. Traditionally, Pisceans are known as the poets of the zodiac – "poets" in the broadest sense of the word: those who use their creative gifts in any and every area of life. But again, you do need direction if you are to fully realize your potential.

The symbol of your sign is two fishes connected by a cord but swimming in opposite directions! The symbolism of the zodiac signs often tells the truth, and in a Piscean's case, it is precisely on the money!

 PISCES
(FEBRUARY 19 – MARCH 20)

KEYWORDS Ambiguous, deceitful, impressionable
RULING PLANET Neptune
NEGATIVE
DUALITY OR GENDER Feminine
TRIPLICITY OR ELEMENT Water
QUADRUPLICITY OR QUALITY Mutable
BODY AREAS Feet
COUNTRIES Portugal, Sahara, Scandinavia, small Mediterranean islands

CITIES Alexandria, Santiago de Compostela, Seville
STONE Moonstone
COLOR Soft sea-green
TREES Those common to the seaside; ash, birch, chestnut, mulberry, Norfolk pine, oak, willow
FLOWERS AND HERBS Dandelions, lichens, lime-flowers, mosses, pinks, waterlilies; also herbs associated with Cancer and Sagittarius, including sage, saxifrage
FOODS Those associated with Cancer, including cucumbers, melons

For instance, you may well work out the best way to go in life – the way that will fully utilize your unique gifts – but then set off determinedly, inexplicably, (and perversely) in the opposite direction. And that's a big no-no when it comes to your personal happiness – and the happiness of those around you. Our advice, dear Piscean, is to pull yourself together, recognize your own worth, face things as they really are, and learn to cope. If you don't embrace your positive qualities (and they are well within your reach), you may end up taking the easy way out of life. In Piscean terms, that translates, at best, to taking the line of least resistance in the face of life's challenges; or at worst, to opting for complete inaction when problems arise. You'll deceive yourself (and worse, deceive others) into believing that your passive approach to difficult situations is the easiest way out. In fact, taking that path only makes matters worse.

Love and sex life

Your lover will be the happy recipient of a generous display of emotion. You're a sensual and caring partner, eager to give pleasure as well as receive it. Indeed, you can positively overwhelm a lover with affection. Keep a keen eye on the latter tendency.

Your emotions can run so high and so close to the surface that a less than enthusiastic response from your partner – or a trivial remark or gesture – may well precipitate some truly terrible bedroom scenes.

■ **Neptune is** *the ruling planet of Pisces.*

And while we're in the bedroom, it's important to note that your physical passion tends to be focused on the romantic rather than on the sexual. In fact, your interest in sex has its limits, and while there will be great sensual highs at the beginning of a relationship, after the first ecstasies have passed, you may find you want to settle down to a fairly calm sexual life. That suits you eminently, and it does have its charming and sentimental side, but it may not be all that exciting for your partner. Make sure that your romantic approach to sex doesn't disappoint or alienate a partner who is more enthusiastic in bed than you.

On the other hand, being a great romantic – and you are among the greatest – has distinct advantages. You thoughtfully and imaginatively woo a prospective partner, and with any luck, your gentle romanticism will continue after you've made a permanent commitment. Nevertheless, keep the following caveat in mind:

When you fall in love, you immediately put on your favorite pair of rose-colored glasses. Unfortunately, they can often provide a less than clear view of your lover. Consequently, you may all too easily fall for – and be let down by – unscrupulous people. Or you may find it difficult to recognize your partner's faults – and everyone has some faults!

Family

Just as romance is the name of the game when you're wooing, so it remains in the foreground when you've made a commitment to partner and family. You go to great lengths to make the partnership work and to nurture it for the rest of your life. Because you believe this kind of lifelong romantic nurturing is very important, you'll worry excessively if your partner doesn't share the same view – and in confronting him or her you may well cause some unpleasant scenes.

Conversely, your innate ability to intuit people's needs and desires can be very keen, and you should give it full reign. It's an invaluable asset to any family dynamic, making it fairly easy for you to deduce what your partner and children really want, need, and mean when they reach out to you. At the

PISCEAN SYMBOL

same time, do try to keep a lid on your equally innate tendency to paralyzing indecision and excessive worry. A wise partner will encourage you to stand on your own two feet when a decision needs to be made, whether it's financial, social, or domestic. And you must learn both to welcome and to follow through on that encouragement. The consequences of not doing so can be disastrous.

Remember, when things go wrong, your immediate reaction is to be evasive and vague, to sit on the proverbial fence in a thick cloud of doubt, worrying yourself immobile about what action to take.

Again, a partner can lead you toward making your own decision. If you have no partner, making a decision and taking action is up to you. Beware of sitting on the fence too long and believing that the difficult situation will go away. It usually doesn't. If you're dealing with a situation that could damage your relationship, try to avoid – by any means possible – the Piscean tendency to lie as an easy way out! Lying may work in the short term, but will make problems far worse down the road. Instead, work very hard at keeping life uncomplicated, straightforward, and honest. Such an approach is not a basic instinct of yours, but it's one well worth cultivating.

Career

Pisceans are at their best working in the background – offstage, rather than center stage – in a variety of work arenas. But ironically, there are also quite a few first-rate Piscean actors, comedians, and impersonators. As is so often the case with Sun signs who are cautious about revealing their abundant, hidden, emotional reserves, putting on a mask allows Pisceans to hide their own personalities while exploring the emotional facets of other, and perhaps more extroverted, individuals (albeit make-believe ones!).

Because instinctively caring about others is one of Pisces' strongest suits, you are a natural for the caring professions and make excellent nurses, counselors, and pastoral assistants.

There is a traditional link between Pisces and the early Christian church, which was symbolized by the fish and emphasized service to others. Many Pisceans have a keen appreciation of beauty and aesthetics and are found in the fashion and cosmetic trades. In any work, a flexible routine suits you best, together with a variety of tasks within the job itself. You may believe that job security is all important, but beware of an occupation which makes you feel claustrophobic. Remember that you often need direction – which you take quite well – when you're first starting out on a new job or task, and you will blossom under the tutelage of a good mentor or manager. In fact, if you're an especially attentive student, you may move on to positions of authority yourself, shining as a foreman, department head, or managing director.

FISH: SYMBOLS OF CHRISTIANITY

Remember to keep in mind that the Piscean sign is characterized by duality (as are Gemini and Capricorn). Many Pisceans easily manage two jobs at the same time. Whatever you choose to do, you definitely need an occupation that provides plenty of variety and diversity. You're amazingly versatile, and provided you channel this versatility positively, it can be a great bonus in any profession.

Finally, make sure that you set aside time and space to develop the creative potential with which you've been richly gifted. Given your innate tendency to indecisiveness and inaction, your creative talents could easily lie dormant and unfulfilled throughout your life.

Health, diet, and exercise

You're likely to have a fairly sensitive system, easily affected by outside influences. Your ruling planet, Neptune, is related to the general nervous system, and in particular to the thalamus, which transmits stimuli to and from the sensory organs. Thus you react really strongly to external circumstances and conditions. Indeed, someone may only have to remark that you look a bit peaky for you to feel the need to see a doctor. Even simple criticism can make you feel awful, develop a headache, or suffer a stomachache.

The Piscean body area is the feet, and most Pisceans suffer occasionally from blisters, malformed toes, bunions, and other foot ailments. You tend to like comfortable shoes and to wear sandals – even in cold weather. And you'll have nothing to do with uncomfortable fashions such as ultra-high heels and pointy-toed boots. And rightly so!

When it comes to your general physical health, we can't emphasize strongly enough how badly Pisceans often react to prescription drugs. Monitor your reactions to antibiotics in particular, and even to such common drugs as aspirin.

It's worth noting that many Pisceans dislike drugs so much that they refuse to take them, but this can be dangerous. When there's real illness present, work with your doctor to explore all the treatment options open to you. Be careful about what you put into your system when you are stressed – and you will be tempted to do that, given your sensitivity to outside influences and your propensity for worrying. Self-medicating stress and worry about legal drugs doesn't solve the cause of those conditions and leads to health damage and substance abuse. This sign has an association with addiction. Pisceans should avoid smoking and excessive drinking.

Child and parent

■ **The willow** *is a Piscean tree.*

You'll be tremendously eager for your children to succeed, and you'll do everything you can to encourage them. Your good intentions, however, may be colored by a hidden motive: Wanting them to excel in an area where you were less than successful. Nothing is more sad and self-defeating than the misdirected actions of an amateur dancer forcing her daughter to be a professional ballerina, or a failed medical student encouraging his son to be a surgeon. Try not to succumb to this Piscean tendency. Instead, channel all that love and encouragement in the direction that your child really wants to go.

Remember that your tendency never to make up your mind about anything can drive your children to distraction, while your lack of firmness may easily be translated into lack of backbone . . . or morals. Children need a role model, and if you can't be one for them, another far less admirable person may take your place. And this would be a pity.

Your Piscean child wants to please you, and this may lead him or her to agree too easily with everything you say, rather than develop an individual and independent personality. Feeling forced to agree may also encourage your child to lie in order not to upset you. If you're a Piscean yourself, you may have a sneaking kind of sympathy for this behavior and be tempted to let it go. But it's not a good path for your child to travel, so correct him or her firmly but kindly. Their motives are right, even if their means aren't.

You have a keen appreciation of beauty – in nature and in art – and you should do all you can to communicate this sensibility to your Piscean children. When your young Piscean displays a creative streak, encourage it whatever it is; it's vital for Pisceans to express, not suppress, their creative potential.

Be mindful, too, that these children may appear slightly slow at school. Piscean children sometimes find it difficult to concentrate on real life and prefer to live in their own inventive fantasy worlds. Convince them to keep at least one foot firmly in the real world. The real world, after all, is where they have to live, love, and work.

Leisure and retirement

Retirement and leisure time offer Pisceans the opportunity to explore all the creative potential and artistic interests that they've been unable to exercise at work.

Watch out, however, for your tendency never to start a creative project because you believe you simply don't have the time for it: in "Piscean speak," this often means that you don't think you're talented enough.

Make the time, and the talent will follow. Having a creative, artistic hobby or activity to which you're devoted will open up your life to an astonishing degree.

It may be particularly good for you to get involved in a dance or movement class. Yoga will be especially rewarding, as will any discipline that helps you develop your inner strength and center your personality. Craft work is usually an excellent way of using any spare time, since you have a strong artistic bent which must be satisfied in one way or another. Pisceans are usually great readers, too, and as the poets of the zodiac there's no reason you can't write some verse as well as read it.

Finally, involvement in charity or justice work will be deeply satisfying to you. Indeed, saving the planet will seem like a matter of course to you, and you'll be eager to help. Working behind the scenes of such movements is probably a better bet for you than going before the public; your tendency to get carried away emotionally may make it difficult for you to be persuasive.

A simple summary

✔ Cancer, Scorpio, and Pisces are known collectively as the water signs. People influenced by these signs are compassionate, loving, sensual, and imaginative. They are found among the world's great mates, parents, lovers, artists, researchers, and dreamers.

✔ Cancerians are loving, nurturing, imaginative, and protective. They are natural-born parents and carers who have a deep love for the past and for tradition. They thrive on the home front, but also in business, teaching, and the caring professions. They can, however, be overprotective, moody, and clinging.

✔ Scorpios are intuitive, incisive, powerful, passionate, and magnetic. They are the famed lovers of the zodiac, with a deep and often mysterious sensuality, but they often make a successful career in the "straight" world of big business. A Scorpio's singularly worst trait is jealousy – in the bedroom, in the living room, in the board room, in the gym – and it can be the downfall of an otherwise wonderful life.

✔ Pisceans are sensitive, artistic, otherworldly, and sympathetic. They are the poets of the zodiac and often apply their considerable creative talents to a variety of situations and careers. Like Cancerians, Pisceans are natural nurturers who often make their mark in medicine, psychiatric counseling, and pastoral work. They are also frequently found among the great actors of the world. The darker side of this dualistic sign is a tendency toward escapism, evasiveness, oversensitivity, and deceitfulness.

PART THREE

KEEP-IT-SIMPLE BIRTH CHARTS

O N OUR HONOR – this part of the book will not be as painful as you think. (Well, you may rip out a few strands of hair when it comes to placing the Moon in your birth chart, but then, so do we!)

Yes, drawing up your *birth chart* (or a spouse's or friend's chart) is the most challenging task you will face in this book. It's also the most absorbing and mentally stimulating, and, we believe, ultimately the most fun. All you need is a birth date, a birth time, and a birth place.

 No mean feat, indeed! But we walk you through the process, simple step by simple step, giving lots of examples and loads of short-cuts and easy advice. And the tables in the back of the book – which will help you construct your birth chart – are the simplest ones we could devise. Again, we promise: By the end of this section, you will joyfully spread your celestial wings and feel genuinely confident about casting a birth chart for anyone.

SHARP
Scientific calculator EL-553
MEMORY SAFE GUARD / AUTO POWER OFF
CNST
S.CALC
STAT
2ndF
CNST
DRG
FSE
OFF
ON/C
hyp
sin
cos
tan
CE
EXP
D°M'S
%
DATA
RM
M+
CD
RND
QUOT/REM

Chapter 12

The Simple ABCs of Building a Birth Chart

YOU WILL LEARN HERE how to cast your horoscope. We will walk you through this step by step – and most of it will be painless – promise!

In this chapter...

✔ What is a horoscope?

✔ John Doe's birth chart

✔ Drawing your birth chart

✔ Placing the zodiac signs

✔ Finding and placing your Midheaven

✔ Finding and placing your Sun

✔ Finding and placing your Moon

✔ Finding and placing the other planets

✔ Putting in the extras

What is a horoscope?

OF COURSE, *there are software programs and web sites that can cast your* horoscope *if you plug in the right information (and sometimes pay a small fee). These options to hand-casting a birth chart are tempting and fun but they lack the human touch – intuition, empathy, and plain old life experience. Plus, many people still don't have access to a computer.*

Finally, there's nothing like drawing up your own chart to help you learn the fundamentals of astrology and chart interpretation. With each birth chart you draw and interpret, the deeper your knowledge grows. That's why experienced astrologers still draw up charts by hand.

> **DEFINITION**
>
> A **horoscope** *is a map of the sky that shows the precise locations of the Sun, the Moon, the planets, and the zodiac signs at the time and the place you were born.*

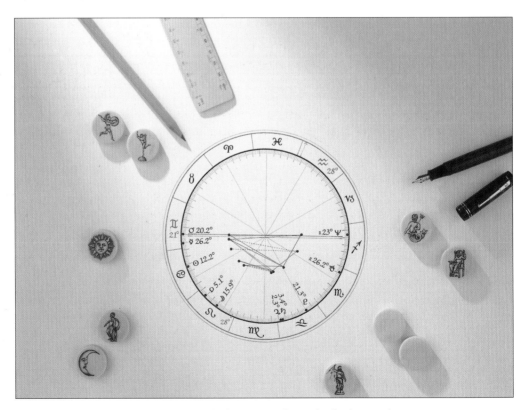

■ **Creating your own birth chart** *is the best way to learn the fundamentals.*

To help you learn the basics of drawing a birth chart – and insure that your first chart will be as accurate as possible – we feature prominently in this chapter a completed birth chart we've drawn ourselves, for one John Doe. Think of John's chart as a teaching aid. If you find yourself stuck trying to get through your own birth chart, or you're simply having problems reading those dreaded tables in the back, you'll find mirrored examples in John's chart of all the steps you're going through (and all the proper answers, too).

But first: a little fable to get you in the "birth charting" mood . . .

Imagine (if you can) that your mother gave birth to you in an open field at night, and that she was sitting (more or less) precisely in the center of the horizon line. Imagine also that at the moment of your birth, when she heard your first cry, your mother looked straight up into the sky. Imagine that she saw all the planets and signs, represented by their symbolic *glyphs*, in the same positions that they appear in the six 30-degree segments of the zodiac found in the top half of your birth chart. Below her (where she could not see), beneath the horizon line, were the other six 30-degree segments of the zodiac, in the bottom half of your birth chart.

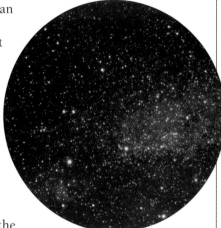

IMAGINE THE NIGHT SKY
DIVIDED INTO 12 SEGMENTS

To the east, and to your mother's left, was the Ascendant – the point of the zodiac that was rising over the horizon as you were born. To the west, and to your mother's right, was the Descendant – the point of the zodiac that was dipping below the horizon as you were born. Right above your mother, at the top of the chart, was the Midheaven (traditionally called the Medium Coeli, or "middle point of the sky"). And directly below your mother, at a point on the other side of the zodiac world, in fact, was the Imum Coeli (the "lowest point of the sky").

When you draw your birth chart, you join together the two pieces of night sky – the seen and the unseen, above and below the horizon – that were whirling about your mother's universe as she gave birth to you. You will see what she never could: absolutely everything that was happening everywhere in the zodiac when you took your first earthly cry. Awesome? Absolutely! So fasten your seat belt . . .

> **DEFINITION**
>
> *Just to remind you, the symbols used by astrologers to represent the various planets, zodiac signs, and aspects are called* **glyphs**. *For example, ☉ is the glyph for the Sun, ♉ is the glyph for Taurus, and ☌ is the glyph for the conjunction aspect of planets.*

John Doe's birth chart

LET'S BEGIN OUR FIRST LESSON in drawing a horoscope by taking a walk around John Doe's birth chart, just to get the lay of the land. Later, when you begin to construct your own birth chart, piece by piece, you will use parts of John's chart as examples to help you along the way.

Around the outside of John Doe's birth chart is a circle divided into 12 segments and in each of them is one of the glyphs representing the 12 signs. Notice that they go counterclockwise, rather than clockwise, around the circle, and that they don't coincide with the numbered 12 wedges inside the circle. These are the houses of the birth chart.

Just as each of the sections of the outside circle represent the 12 signs, which are connected with our personality, so the inside segments represent the various areas of our lives. These are counted counterclockwise from just below the horizon, with the first segment below the horizon being known as the first house.

The inside of the zodiac circle is marked out in 10-degree segments, 30 degrees to each house, while the planets' positions are marked by dots on the inner circle, with the glyph for each planet attached to the dot.

Because of the layout of the chart, every planet lies inside one of the outer segments of the chart (representing the circle of the signs), and also inside one of the inner segments (each representing a house). When you interpret the chart of a person, look first at where each planet is located, starting with the Sun.

In John Doe's chart, for instance, the Sun is in the sign of Scorpio and in the eleventh house. So when you begin to interpret this chart, look first at the characteristics that the Sun will give John when it's in Scorpio. Then determine how those Sun-in-Scorpio characteristics will specifically play out in the eleventh house.

Follow this same procedure for every planet's position in a sign and/or house.

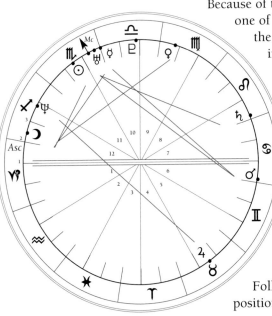

JOHN DOE'S BIRTH CHART

Apart from the signs and houses, you also have to consider the aspects each planet makes to all the others. (We cover the aspects in detail in Chapter 6 and review them again later on in this chapter).

Those are the basics of John's birth chart. Let's move on to yours.

Drawing your birth chart

Redraw, trace, or photocopy the blank chart shown here.

Numbering the houses

Number the houses, counterclockwise, 1 through 12, starting with the first 30-degree segment under the double horizon line.

Your rising sign

Turn to the tables on p. 414 to begin finding your rising sign (or Ascendant).

INTERNET

www.astro.com

Click on "atlas" to find the same information as any good atlas does, only much faster and more easily.

You will need an atlas for this step. If you have access to the Internet, you can also use the web site featured to the left. There are also atlases on CD-ROM.

First, in your atlas, find the latitude (the north-south line) for the city or town of your birth. If your city or town isn't displayed, choose the latitude of the nearest major city. Now turn to the tables on p. 414 and find the line of latitude closest to your birth latitude.

Second, under the date column, find your date of birth; under the time column, find your time of birth. (If you don't know your time of birth, use noon of the day you were born.)

■ **Draw a line**
between your date of birth and the time of your birth.

Third, take a pencil and ruler, and draw a line between the two points. Note where your penciled line crosses the Ascendant line on the chart. Right opposite this will be the glyph of a zodiac sign; this is your rising sign. Note whether the line crosses the top, middle, or bottom third of the section.

If you were born in spring, summer, or fall, remember to take Daylight Savings Time into consideration! Your local library will have records of this. Or you can get help at the web site featured on the previous page.

Fourth, on the birth chart, at the lefthand side of the horizon (horizontal) line is a segment marked "12," which is subdivided into three sections – "1", "2," and "3." If, when you found your rising sign in the tables, the line you drew crossed the top third of the table section, write the glyph of your rising sign in the section marked "1" on the birth chart; if the line you drew crossed the middle third of the table section, write your rising sign in the section numbered "2" on the birth chart; if the line you drew crossed the bottom third of the table section, write in your rising sign in the section numbered "3" on the birth chart. You have now correctly placed your rising (or Ascendant) sign. For further clarity, mark this segment "ASC," which is shorthand for "Ascendant."

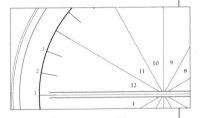

■ **Divide segment 12**
into three equal sections.

Note well: This is the basic procedure you will follow to find and write in the positions of all the planets on your birth chart.

Example

Let's look again at John Doe's birth chart. John was born in New York, at a latitude of 40°-43' N. In the tables, the nearest latitude is the one for Salt Lake City, at 40°-45' N. John was born on November 6, and his birth time was 11:19 a.m. When we draw a line between these two points, the line crosses the Ascendant line in the top third of the section for Capricorn, so you would write in the glyph for Capricorn in the segment of the birth chart marked "1."

CAPRICORN IS JOHN DOE'S RISING SIGN

Placing the zodiac signs

FIRST, LOOK AT YOUR BIRTH CHART. In the segment marked "12," you wrote in the glyph of your rising sign in section "1", "2," or "3." Put a dot on the inner circle on the birth chart where your rising sign is, and then draw a line from it to the outer circle.

Example

In John Doe's chart his rising sign is Capricorn, and it is rising in the top third of the segment in the section marked "1."

Starting with the rising sign line which you just drew, you are going to divide the outer circle (or ring) into 12 equal segments.

Beginning at the rising sign line, and going counterclockwise, count off three divisions on the outer circle and draw a line from the outer to inner circle (that is, within the outer ring). Count off three more divisions and draw another line. Continue going counterclockwise and drawing in a line at every third division, until you have 12 equal segments in the outer ring. Your birth chart should now look like the one on the right.

The first of the 12 segments in the outer ring is marked with the glyph of your rising sign. Place each of the remaining zodiac signs (which are represented by their respective glyphs) in the segments 2 through to 12 (again, going counterclockwise), in their traditional order, but starting after the rising sign.

■ **Mark off the** 12 *segments of the birth chart counterclockwise.*

219

Look at the chart for the zodiac signs and their glyphs on the facing page; the planets are listed in their traditional order.

Now, if your rising sign is Cancer, for example, Cancer is placed in the first segment of the outer ring. In the traditional order of planets, Leo follows Cancer, therefore Leo is placed in the second segment of the ring. Traditionally, Virgo follows Leo, and so Virgo is placed in the third segment of the outer ring. Continue placing the signs in this manner. After you enter Pisces (the last of the 12 zodiac signs), begin the procession again with Aries (traditionally, the first of the signs), then Taurus, and so forth, until all 12 segments are filled in.

Example

In John Doe's birth chart, Capricorn is the rising sign and is placed in the first segment. Then Aquarius is placed in the second segment, Pisces in the third segment, and so forth.

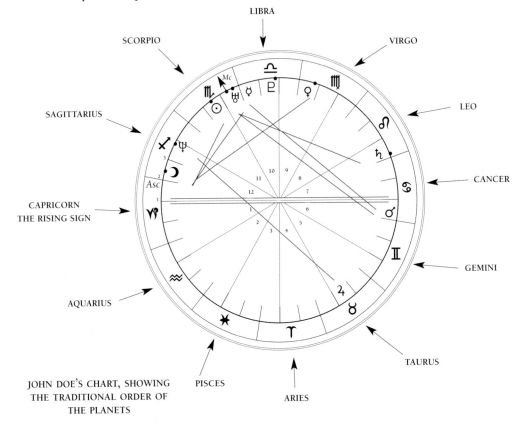

JOHN DOE'S CHART, SHOWING
THE TRADITIONAL ORDER OF
THE PLANETS

ZODIAC SIGNS AND PLANETS

As another reminder, here are the glyphs for the zodiac signs and the planets:

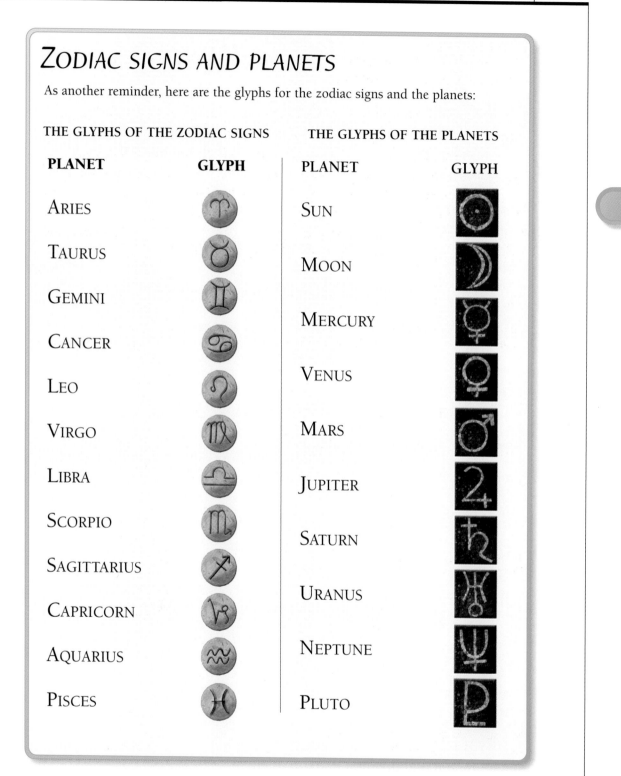

THE GLYPHS OF THE ZODIAC SIGNS		THE GLYPHS OF THE PLANETS	
PLANET	**GLYPH**	**PLANET**	**GLYPH**
ARIES		SUN	
TAURUS		MOON	
GEMINI		MERCURY	
CANCER		VENUS	
LEO		MARS	
VIRGO		JUPITER	
LIBRA		SATURN	
SCORPIO		URANUS	
SAGITTARIUS		NEPTUNE	
CAPRICORN		PLUTO	
AQUARIUS			
PISCES			

Finding and placing your Midheaven

TURN TO THE TABLES on pp. 416–417 to find your Midheaven. You will need an atlas or access to the web site www.astro.com.atlas.

You find your Midheaven in exactly the same way you found your rising sign, but this time you use the longitude (the east-west line) of your place of birth or of the nearest major city. Turn to the tables and find the line of longitude closest to your birth longitude.

DATE	MIDHEAVEN	TIME OF DAY	
DEC 30 10	♑	♋ 12 1	KANSAS (VIRGINIA) 94° 38'W
JAN 20 30 10	♒	♌ ♍ 2 3	HOUSTON (TEXAS) 95° 23'W
FEB 20 29 10	♓	♎ ♏ 4 5	
MAR 20 30 10	♈	♐ ♑ am 6 7	DALLAS (TEXAS) 96° 48'N
APR 20		♒	

■ **Draw a line** *between your date of birth and the time of your birth.*

Under the date column, find your date of birth; under the time column, find your time of birth. (If you don't know your time of birth, use noon of the day you were born.) Draw a line between your date of birth and your time of birth. You will find the zodiac glyph for your Midheaven sign at the point where your penciled line crosses the center of the Midheaven line in the tables. As with the rising sign, your penciled line will also have crossed the top, middle, or bottom third of the table section.

Look round the outside of the birth chart (in which you have now placed all the zodiac signs) and find the sign/glyph that matches your Midheaven sign. Place a dot in the appropriate top, middle, or bottom third of the sign segment, and mark the dot "MC." This is the astrological shorthand for Medium Coeli ("the middle point of the sky"), which is the traditional name for the Midheaven. To make the MC position clearer, you can mark it with an arrow from that the dot to the outside of the circle

Example

John Doe was born in New York, and its longitude is 74°-00' W. The nearest longitude line in the tables is Jersey City, at 74°-02' West. John was born on November 6 at 11:19 a.m. When a line is drawn between the date and time of John's birth, it crosses the Midheaven line in the top third of the Scorpio segment. On his birth chart, John's Midheaven is then marked in the sign of Scorpio, in the section which is marked "1."

■ **Mark the MC** *with an arrow.*

Finding and placing your Sun

YOU KNOW YOUR SUN SIGN ALREADY, RIGHT?

Or do you? If you were born on the day the Sun changed signs, you may not! Look at the tables starting on p. 402 and check this out by finding the year of your birth in the top column and the month of your birth in the lefthand column.

Read down and across to where they meet, and you will discover when the Sun moved into your Sun sign. If your birthday falls within the first 10 days of the sign, mark the position of the Sun – using its glyph – in the middle of the first third of your Sun sign. If it falls in either of the two remaining sections of the table, place the Sun in the corresponding second or third portions of your Sun sign (going counterclockwise).

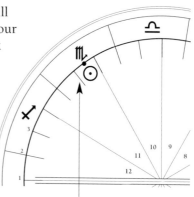

■ **Mark the Sun** *on your chart using its glyph.*

Example

In John Doe's case, his birthday is November 6, 1975. Using the Sun tables, we look at 1975 in the top of the column and at 11 in the lefthand column (November is the 11th month of the year). Reading down, we find that the Sun moved into Scorpio on October 25, so by November 6, the Sun had been in Scorpio for 13 days. This means that it falls in the second section of the sign – and that's where we've placed it on his birth chart.

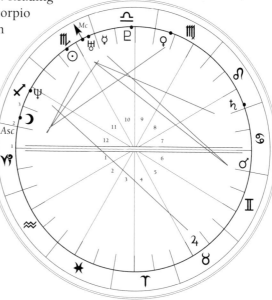

■ **Mark the place** *of your Sun sign as shown below in John Doe's chart, where the planet falls in the second section of Scorpio.*

Finding and placing your Moon

*ARE YOU FEELING STRONG? – This is going to be just a
tad difficult. Despite the title of this book, calculating the position
of the Moon may be your most challenging task. Because the Moon
moves so quickly in and out of the signs, precise calculations are
hard to come by – but very necessary. You need to know the position of the Moon
within a margin of just a few degrees, so you can calculate the important aspects
it makes to other planets in your chart.*

*We've devised a system for doing this that's easier than most, but it
takes some concentration and some practice. And there are quite a few
steps! But we promise you that after a few attempts, you'll find this
relatively easy to do. And furthermore, once you have your Moon in
place, you're more than halfway to the finish line!*

So first turn to the Moon tables on p. 413, which list the years 1920–2020. If you read
across the columns horizontally, you will see that the tables indicate the year, the
month, the day of the month, the hour of the day, the sign in which the Moon was
placed when it changed signs, and the number of hours the Moon spent in any
particular sign – the duration.

Read down the tables until you reach the year of birth you need. Because the Moon
doesn't change signs every day, you must look for the date just *before* your birth date
when it did change signs. Of course it may have changed signs on one particular day
at any time within the 24 hours – so you need to find the time also. The easiest way
of explaining this is to use our example – the birth date of John Doe. As you remember,
he was born in New York City on November 6,. 1975, at 11.19 in the morning.

So, take a very deep few breaths. Now we're going to calculate approximately where the
Moon was on John Doe's birthday.

Step 1

Look down the Moon tables and find the year 1975 in the first column.

Step 2

Next, find the month of November in the second column.

Step 3

Find Libra in the Zodiacal tables.

Step 4

Look in the Moon table for the day 6 (the day of John Doe's birth). In the "Add" column beside it is the figure 2. This means that you have to add two signs to the sign you have already found from the Yearly tables.

Step 5

Find Libra again in the Zodiacal Glyphs table and count two more signs, which will bring you to Sagittarius. This means that John's Moon is in Sagittarius, and since the figure in the "Add" column changed the next day (7th), the Moon will be in the latter half of Sagittarius.

The information is plotted and the glyph for the Moon is written near the two-thirds line of Sagittarius (counting counterclockwise) in the inner circle of the birth chart.

So where are we?

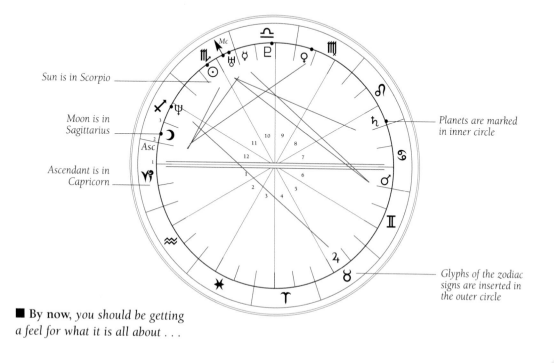

Sun is in Scorpio

Moon is in Sagittarius

Ascendant is in Capricorn

Planets are marked in inner circle

Glyphs of the zodiac signs are inserted in the outer circle

■ **By now**, *you should be getting a feel for what it is all about . . .*

Finding and placing the other planets

Mercury, Venus, Mars, and Jupiter

To find and place Mercury, Venus, Mars, and Jupiter on your chart, refer to the tables starting on p. 402, just as you did for the Sun. There is a set of tables each for these four planets. In each planet's table, find your year of birth at the top of the table and your month of birth on the lefthand side. Read down and across to where they meet, and you will see what signs the respective planets moved into on the day of your birth.

You will also see that the lines showing the changing signs are shaded from light to dark to light again. This shading indicates where in the birth chart the planet should be placed within the zodiac sign (going counterclockwise): the lightest shading indicates placement in the first third of the sign; the middle shading in the middle section of the sign; and the darkest shading in the last third of the sign. Place a dot for each of the planets – Mercury, Venus, Mars, and Jupiter – in its corresponding zodiac sign, in the appropriate section of the sign (top, middle, or bottom third). Write the glyph for the planet next to the dot.

MERCURY

John Doe was born on November 6, 1975 as Mercury moved from Libra through Scorpio to Sagittarius. Because of the limitations of these simple tables and methods we can't be sure whether Mercury was in Libra or Scorpio when John was born. Here we've put his Mercury on the line between Libra and Scorpio.

VENUS

Venus started out in Scorpio and moved into Libra on November 9. John's Venus was in the last degrees of Virgo when he was born.

MARS

Mars was in the lightest section of Cancer, and so is placed in the top third section of Cancer on the birth chart.

JUPITER

Jupiter was in Taurus for the whole of November 1975, and it is in a lightly shaded square, so is placed in the top third section of Taurus on the birth chart.

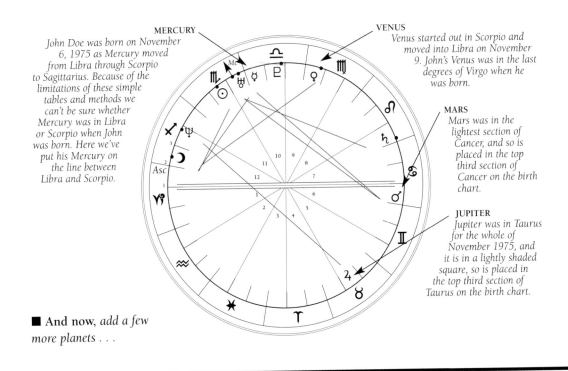

■ **And now,** add a few more planets . . .

Saturn, Uranus, Neptune, and Pluto

Saturn, Uranus, Neptune, and Pluto need far shorter tables than the other planets to reveal their positions, because they move so much more slowly. We simply give the dates on which they change signs, because the chance that one of them changes signs on the precise day you or any friend of yours was born, is pretty small.

To find and place Saturn, Uranus, Neptune, and Pluto on your birth chart, refer to the tables starting on p. 402, just as you did for Mercury, Venus, Mars, and Jupiter. There is a set of tables each for these four planets.

In each planet's table, find your year of birth at the top of the table and the nearest date before or on your birthday in the tables themselves. As before, the shading in the tables indicates where in the birth chart the planet should be placed within the zodiac sign (going counterclockwise): the lightest shading indicates placement in the first third of the sign, the middle shading in the middle section of the sign, and the darkest shading in the last third of the sign.

Place a dot for each of the planets – Saturn, Uranus, Neptune, and Pluto – in its corresponding zodiac sign, in the appropriate section of the sign (top, middle, or bottom third). Write the glyph for the planet next to the dot.

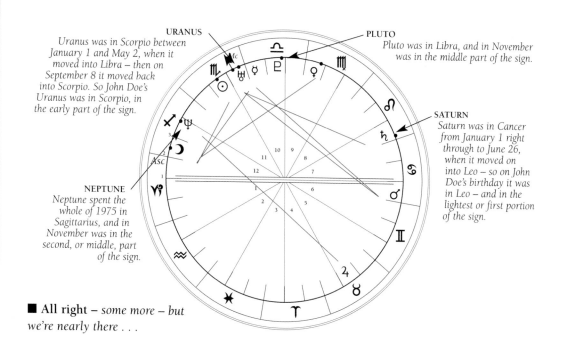

URANUS
Uranus was in Scorpio between January 1 and May 2, when it moved into Libra – then on September 8 it moved back into Scorpio. So John Doe's Uranus was in Scorpio, in the early part of the sign.

PLUTO
Pluto was in Libra, and in November was in the middle part of the sign.

SATURN
Saturn was in Cancer from January 1 right through to June 26, when it moved on into Leo – so on John Doe's birthday it was in Leo – and in the lightest or first portion of the sign.

NEPTUNE
Neptune spent the whole of 1975 in Sagittarius, and in November was in the second, or middle, part of the sign.

■ **All right** – *some more – but we're nearly there . . .*

Almost there . . .

Your birth chart circle is almost complete, with all the zodiac signs, Ascendant, Midheaven, and planets in place. Just a few more pieces of the puzzle to fit in, and then you're done. Promise!

How accurate is our shortcut method of finding the planets' positions? Well, just as a test, we got out our computer to calculate the precise positions. Here are the results for John Doe's chart:

OUR SHORTCUT POSITIONS	THE COMPUTER POSITIONS
ASC – middle of Capricorn	13° Capricorn
MC – end of first of Scorpio	8° Scorpio
Sun – second of Scorpio	13° Scorpio
Moon – Sagittarius	25° Sagittarius
Mercury – Libra or Scorpio	00° Scorpio
Venus – last of Virgo	20° Virgo
Mars – first of Cancer	2° Cancer
Jupiter – second of Taurus	16° Taurus
Saturn – first of Leo	2° Leo
Uranus – first of Scorpio	3° Scorpio
Neptune – second of Sagittarius	0° Sagittarius
Pluto – second of Libra	10° Libra

Not bad!?

Putting in the extras

IN CHAPTER 6 we discussed in detail all the traditional factors associated with the zodiac signs, as well as the key aspects which planets make to each other. Both the traditional factors and the aspects contribute additional and often powerful layers of meaning to the birth chart.

Traditional factors

Refer to Chapter 6 and to the Sun-sign listings in Part Two, to find all the traditional factors associated with the zodiac signs in your birth chart. Remember to include the following factors for each sign in which the Ascendant, Midheaven, and planets fall:

✔ the sign's duality (gender) – masculine or feminine

✔ the sign's element – earth, air, water, and fire

✔ the sign's quality – cardinal, fixed, or mutable

Write these details onto the birth chart. Note the ruling planet of the chart (also called the "ruler of the chart"); this is the planet that rules the rising sign (or Ascendant). If Cancer is your rising sign, the Moon is the ruling planet of your chart (because the Moon rules Cancer). Note the ruling planet's location, in both sign and house.

Also note any rising planets (a rising planet is one which is on or very near the Ascendant) and the polar sign, which is the one directly opposite the sign in which the Sun is placed. Also write these details on the birth chart.

Redraw, trace, or photocopy this chart to record your details.

THE FOUR ELEMENTS

PLANET		ASPECTS									
		☉	☽	☿	♀	♂	♃	♄	♅	♆	♇
SUN	☉										
MOON	☽										
MERCURY	☿										
VENUS	♀										
MARS	♂										
JUPITER	♃										
SATURN	♄										
URANUS	♅										
NEPTUNE	♆										
PLUTO	♇										
ASCENDANT	ASC										
MIDHEAVEN	MC										

Finding the aspects

Refer back to Chapter 6, which covers in great detail the main aspects between planets that we cover in this book. Those aspects include the conjunction, opposition, trine, square, and sextile.

The conjunction and the opposition are very easy to spot. A conjunction occurs when two planets occupy the same (or almost the same) degree or segment on the birth chart. An opposition occurs when two planets are exactly (or almost exactly) opposite each other across the chart.

To help you with the trine, square, and sextile – which are more difficult to spot – trace the shapes on p. 99 – exactly to the size shown – and transfer them to stiff paper or cardboard to make permanent templates.

Write the name of each aspect on your template. You'll see that they're small enough to fit within the inner circle of your birth chart. By repeatedly turning them, so that one corner points at each planet in turn, you will easily see whether the other points of the template fall on or near any other planet. If they do, you probably have an aspect.

Drawing the aspect lines

You will see that there is a little collection of lines inside every completed birth chart. These are to remind you of the aspects in the chart. Traditionally, the positive aspects (conjunctions, trines, and sextiles) are drawn in red, and the negative ones (squares and oppositions) in black. They may seem a bit tricky to draw at first, but again, practice will make them easier.

POSITIVE
SYMBOL

Look at John Doe's full birth chart opposite. To draw the aspect line showing, say, the square negative aspect between the Moon and Venus in his chart, take your pencil and make two new dots opposite the dots showing the planets' positions, but a half an inch inside the circle. Then join these with a single red line. Do the same for Mars and the MC, but this time, because the aspect is a positive trine, use a red pencil.

NEGATIVE
SYMBOL

If you have a pair of compasses, set them so that when the point is in the center of the chart, the pencil dots are a half an inch inside the outer circle. Then use them to make your pencil dots.

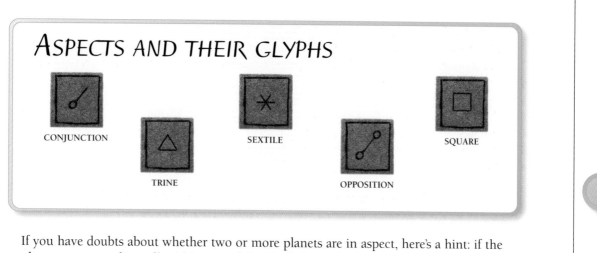

ASPECTS AND THEIR GLYPHS

CONJUNCTION

TRINE

SEXTILE

OPPOSITION

SQUARE

If you have doubts about whether two or more planets are in aspect, here's a hint: if the planets concerned are all within one of the shaded portions of the tables, they are most likely in aspect. Note any planetary aspects in the aspect table provided on the chart. Start with the Sun. On the righthand side of the diagonal line of the figure on page 229, across from the Sun, write the glyph for any aspects that the Sun makes to the other planets in the square immediately below the planets aspected.

For example, if Mars is trine to the MC, draw a little triangle in the square under Mars and across from the MC. Do this for each of the planets, as well as for the Ascendant and Midheaven.

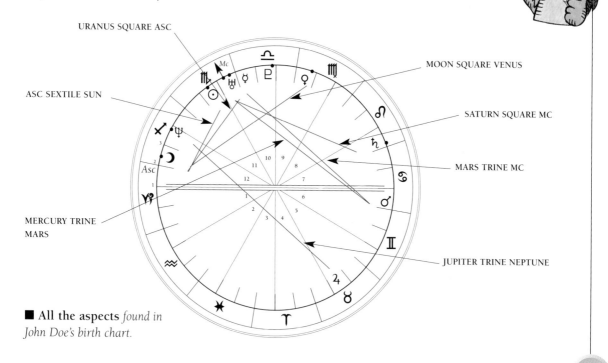

URANUS SQUARE ASC

MOON SQUARE VENUS

ASC SEXTILE SUN

SATURN SQUARE MC

MARS TRINE MC

MERCURY TRINE MARS

JUPITER TRINE NEPTUNE

■ **All the aspects** *found in John Doe's birth chart.*

Completed tables with aspects

The completed aspect tables and traditional factors for John Doe looks like this:

ASPECTS TABLE

PLANET		ASPECTS									
		☉	☽	☿	♀	♂	♃	♄	♅	♆	♇
SUN	☉										
MOON	☽				□						
MERCURY	☿					△					
VENUS	♀										
MARS	♂										
JUPITER	♃									△	
SATURN	♄										
URANUS	♅										
NEPTUNE	♆										
PLUTO	♇										
ASCENDANT	Asc	✳									
MIDHEAVEN	MC					△		□			

TRADITIONAL FACTORS

The Ascendant is in Capricorn – earth, cardinal, feminine.

The Midheaven, Sun, Mercury, Venus, and Uranus are in Scorpio – water, fixed, feminine

The Moon and Neptune are in Sagittarius – fire, mutable, masculine

Mars is in Cancer – water, cardinal, feminine

Jupiter is in Taurus – earth, fixed, feminine

Saturn is in Leo – fire, fixed, masculine

Pluto is in Libra – air, cardinal, feminine.

So in John's birth chart, there are six water planets, two earth planets, three fire planets, and one air planet. There are three cardinal signs, seven fixed signs, and two mutable signs. There are nine feminine and three masculine signs. His Ascendant is Capricorn, and the planet that rules Capricorn is Saturn, so Saturn is the ruling planet of the chart. The ruler's house is the seventh, because Saturn falls in the seventh house of John's birth chart. No planet is in conjunction with the Ascendant, so the chart has no rising planet. The polar sign is Cancer.

Write all these details and a similar summary on a separate piece of paper. Now you have a complete chart, with all the necessary details drawn or written on it. Now, all you have left to do is find out what it means! Help is on the way: Chapter 13 gives you some brief guidelines for setting about the task of interpreting a birth chart. Onward . . .

A simple summary

✓ Drawing up your own birth chart can be easy.

✓ Take it step by step. Study a pre-drawn chart before attempting your own.

✓ Web sites and computer programs can draw up birth charts, but will not be as accurate or individual in their interpretation as you will.

✓ Build up a complete picture of the skies at the time of your birth by considering each element separately.

✓ Learn to draw up your own chart and those of your friends. Find and place your ascending star. Place the Zodiac signs. Recap on the symbols (glyphs) that are used for ease on a birth chart.

✓ Find and place your Midheaven, Sun sign, and Moon. The latter is hard, so take a deep breath and work slowly through the calculations to get an accurate result.

✓ Find and place the positions of the other planets. There are two sets of charts for the planets. Place the traditional factors and aspects on the birth chart.

✓ Look at your finished chart and check it for accuracy of calculation.

✓ Then turn to the next chapter and discover what it means . . .

Chapter 13

Simple Interpretations

Y OU NOW HAVE all the information you need to start interpreting a birth chart. This is one of the most entertaining (but serious), absorbing (yet difficult) tasks you can attempt. Before you start, it's very important to remember some basic facts about interpretation. This chapter will provide you with this basic information, before you go on to the detail found in part 4.

In this chapter...

✓ *Balancing the elements*

✓ *Interpreting the key elements*

✓ *Interpreting the traditional factors*

✓ *Interpreting the planets' effects*

Balancing the elements

FIRST AND FOREMOST, try to balance all the elements in the chart. It is very easy indeed to leap out of your chair and cheer with delight at what seems the dead-on indications which leap off the page at you. But before you make any critical judgments about the subject of a birth chart, you must remember to consider all the influences of the traditional factors, sign locations, planetary positions, house influences, and planetary aspects in the chart.

Copy the details of your chart onto this empty birth chart for ease of reference.

You are going to be taking lots of notes, so get the largest sheet of paper you can find and divide it into separate sections for notes that deal with specific aspects of your subject's life: personality, love, family, work, money, health, hobbies, and so forth.

It's a good idea to use colored pencils when making notes. Use red for very strong influences, blue for moderate indications, and yellow for the more subtle suggestions.

3

2

1

IF YOU HIT A GLITCH!

Because we haven't taught you the complicated business of calculating a chart with complete accuracy there is the possibility that you will not be absolutely sure in which sign a planet should be placed. This happened, you'll remember, with Mercury in the case of John Doe's chart.

If you hit this kind of glitch, study the influences of the planet in both areas of the chart where you think it might belong. In John Doe's case, for example, you would go to Part 4 of this book, "The Planets at Work," and in Chapter 16, "Mercury at Work," read the discussions about both Mercury in Libra and Mercury in Scorpio. Armed with this information, decide which sign best fits the subject of your birth chart.

Moonshine: a caveat

Calculating the Moon's position is the most problematic area you come up against when casting your first birth charts. The Moon moves so quickly through the signs that it is simply impractical to provide a listing of the signs it passes through each year. We've given you (in Chapter 12) the simplest method of calculation we could devise, though it seems quite daunting at first glance. With practice, however, you will get good results with our calculations.

So how do you start to interpret a birth chart? Start with the simple stuff first.

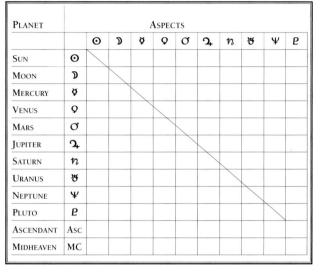

PLANET		ASPECTS									
		☉	☽	☿	♀	♂	♃	♄	♅	♆	♇
SUN	☉										
MOON	☽										
MERCURY	☿										
VENUS	♀										
MARS	♂										
JUPITER	♃										
SATURN	♄										
URANUS	♅										
NEPTUNE	♆										
PLUTO	♇										
ASCENDANT	ASC										
MIDHEAVEN	MC										

■ **As with the table** *showing John Doe's chart information on p. 232, copy the information from your birth chart onto this table for ease of reference.*

Interpreting the key elements

BEFORE YOU BEGIN interpreting the more complex influences of the planets in the signs, houses, and in aspect (in Part 4, "The Planets at Work"), first write down these key elements in a birth chart:

✔ the rising sign (or Ascendant), which is always in the first house

✔ the Sun's sign (AKA the Sun sign) and the Sun's house position

✔ the Moon's sign (the sign the Moon is in) and the Moon's house position

✔ the ruling planet's sign (the sign the ruling planet is in) and its house position

Then write down the sign and house placements of the other planets in the chart, that is, Mercury, Venus, Mars, Jupiter, Saturn, Uranus, Neptune, and Pluto. Review the characteristics of the signs and houses in question in light of the individual whose chart you are interpreting.

Interpreting the traditional factors

After you have made notes about the key elements in the chart, take a look at the traditional factors (covered in Chapter 6) associated with the signs and planets, including the following:

✓ the genders (dualities) – list which signs are masculine (positive) and which are feminine (negative); note any predominance of one gender over another.

✓ the elements – list how many planets are in fire signs (enthusiastic), earth signs (practical), air signs (intellectual), and water signs (sensitive); note any clusters or predominance of like elements.

✓ the qualities – list how many planets are in are cardinal (outgoing), fixed (inflexible), and mutable (adaptable); again, note any clusters or predominance of like qualities.

Though the effects of the traditional factors in a birth chart are not as important or as strong as those of the key elements and the planets, taken together – and especially if there is a predominance of certain factors – they can indicate subtle trends or personality characteristics that may add another layer of meaning to the chart interpretation.

Interpreting the planets' effects

PART 4, "THE PLANETS AT WORK" (which follows this chapter), *discusses in great detail the influences of each of the ten astrological planets in the signs and houses, and in aspect to other planets and elements in the chart. Think of that section as your "bible" for interpreting a birth chart. Here we briefly highlight the key characteristics, qualities, and influences you should be looking for when you study the planetary positions in a chart.*

Before you begin studying the planets' influences, however, remember to list the personal or "personalized" planets in the chart and note their locations in the signs and houses. The influences of personal planets are strengthened, and thus those planets will have special meaning in a chart.

The personal planets are the Sun; the Moon; the planet ruling the rising/Ascendant sign (also called the ruling planet or chart ruler); the planet ruling the Sun sign; and the planet ruling the sign occupied by the Moon.

Interpreting the Sun's effects

KEYWORDS: Vitality; self-expression

The Sun signs

The Sun sign (as we've said before) is not the most important factor in a birth chart. Though it certainly affects an individual's personality, those affects are always modulated by other influences in the chart. In general, the Sun sign reveals our "public self," the image we present to the world, the way we want, and even need, to be seen by others. The Sun works most strongly for an individual when it is in Leo.

The Sun through the houses

The Sun influences our vitality and self-expression, which in turn are affected by the house in which the Sun is placed. The house reveals the areas of life where we will direct most of our solar energies. The first and fifth houses are the ones from which the Sun works most powerfully.

The aspects of the Sun

The aspects made by the Sun to the other planets reveal the way in which we express the Sun's powerful influences in our lives. Aspects between the Sun and the ruling planet of the chart (which is always the planet that rules the rising sign/Ascendant) are particularly important.

Interpreting the Moon's effects

KEYWORDS: Intuition; emotion; instinct; change

The Moon through the signs

The Moon sign – the sign in which the Moon is located in a chart – usually reveals the facets of our character that we inherit from our parents. If these lunar influences are inhibiting, we must work to free ourselves from them. Generally, the Moon sign encourages us to act out its characteristics almost instinctively, and it powerfully affects our intuitive abilities. The Moon works most strongly from Cancer.

The Moon through the houses

The house position of the Moon indicates those areas of life in which we will act instinctively and intuitively, rather than (or as well as) rationally and reasonably. The fourth house is the most powerful home for the Moon.

The aspects of the Moon

The Moon's aspects affect our reactions, sharpening them (in aspects to Mars), adding caution (in aspects to Saturn) or encouraging enthusiasm (in aspects to Jupiter). The Moon personalizes any planet to which it makes an aspect, and personalized planets work very strongly for the individual concerned.

Interpreting Mercury's effects

KEYWORDS: Communication; versatility

Mercury through the signs

Mercury is the planet of the mind, and from the sign in which it is placed we can discover the way our minds work: rationally or intuitively; logically or instinctively. The Mercury sign also reveals the best ways for us to make good decisions and to communicate effectively. Mercury works most powerfully from Gemini and Virgo.

Remember that because of its "inferior" orbit (between the Earth and the Sun), Mercury can only appear in the same sign as the Sun, or in the one just before or just after it. If it appears anywhere else in your chart, you've made a mistake somewhere!

Mercury through the houses

The house in which Mercury is placed shows the area of life in which our intellectual energy will be most positively used. The planet works most strongly when it's in the third or sixth house.

The aspects of Mercury

The influences of any planet that is in negative aspect with Mercury may be a possible source of tension and stress. All of Mercury's aspects generally affect the way the mind works. It usually sharpens our wits and gives us the ability to express our ideas in a lively and dynamic way.

Interpreting Venus's effects

KEYWORDS: Harmony; love; unison

Venus through the signs

Venus, strongly associated with Taurus and Libra, deals
with love, personal relationships, and the feminine side of our natures. The planet
encourages gentleness, tact, and friendliness. Under strain, however, it can encourage
indecisiveness, carelessness, over-romanticism, and dependency.

*Like Mercury, Venus's "inferior" orbit lies between the Earth
and the Sun. Venus can only appear in the same sign as the
Sun, or in the two signs just before or just after it. If it appears
elsewhere in your chart, you've made a miscalculation!*

Venus through the houses

The house position of Venus reveals which areas of life will most engage our gentle but
persuasive powers to win over people. Venus's influence is strongest from the second
and seventh houses.

The aspects of Venus

It's always possible that Venus may work too charmingly in our lives, and its aspects
will indicate whether we are likely to ride through life on a cushion of charisma or the
strength of our character. Venusian aspects also enhance our expression of love and our
ability to handle money.

Interpreting Mars's effects

KEYWORDS: Physical energy; initiative

Mars through the signs

Mars, originally the god of war, is strongly associated with Aries. Correspondingly, the
planet influences aggressive tendencies, positivity, the masculine side of our natures,
and sexual vigor. It may also encourage us to be rude and too aggressive.

Mars through the houses

Mars will focus its formidable energies on the areas of life governed by the house in
which it is placed and encourage us to expend a great deal of aggressive personal energy
(positive or negative) on those areas.

The aspects of Mars

The positive and negative effects of Mars's energy are very different, and the aspects Mars makes to other planets will reveal how you make those energies work for you: in a positive, optimistic fashion; or with an aggressive twist that encourages stress and strain.

Interpreting Jupiter's effects

KEYWORDS: Intellectual and physical expansion

Jupiter through the signs

Jupiter is associated with a love of learning, languages, and philosophy. The planet encourage optimism, loyalty, and justice, but can also make us overly optimistic, extravagant, self-indulgent, and conceited. Jupiter works most strongly from Sagittarius.

Jupiter through the houses

Jupiter's keyword is "expansion," and this influence is strongly revealed in the house in which the planet is placed. In the second house, for instance, Jupiter encourages us to make money but also to take financial risks; in the sixth house, Jupiter often encourages us to put on weight!

The aspects of Jupiter

If Jupiter receives positive aspects, the personality can really be sharpened. Unfortunate aspects, however, can encourage discontent, dishonesty, and a tendency to overreact. Regretfully, Jupiter's negative aspects often work more fiercely than its positive ones.

Interpreting Saturn's effects

KEYWORDS: Stability; control; restriction; limitation

Saturn through the signs

Saturn represents authority. The planet is associated with limitation, and it tends to restrict actions and thought, but also strengthen perseverance and tenacity. Saturn can make us cautious and practical, but also narrow-minded, selfish, and even cruel.

Saturn through the houses

Saturn strongly encourage serious-mindedness about the areas of life ruled by the house in which it is placed. These areas often represent powerful obstacles in our life. And though we often deal successfully with them – and learn a great deal in the process – we may frequently find ourselves fighting uphill battles throughout life.

The aspects of Saturn

Saturn's aspects color a whole generation's behavior and thought; this influence is serious, even solemn. Aspects with Saturn frequently inhibit our behavior or dampen our ambitions, but they can also be stabilizing forces, encouraging us to see things in a practical (but not necessarily pessimistic) light.

Interpreting Uranus's effects

KEYWORDS: Change; consternation; disruption

Uranus through the signs

Uranus is strongly associated with sexual excess, deviation, perversion, rebellion, and nervous breakdown. None of these eventualities is inevitable, but the tendencies are there nevertheless. On a more positive note, Uranus encourages originality, versatility, and independence. Uranus appears in the same sign for over seven years, so it influences a whole generation of people.

Uranus through the houses

Delays, unexpected twists, and sudden changes can take place in any of the areas of life governed by the house in which Uranus is placed. We often have to force issues to remove obstacles, especially if personal planets are concerned. Uranus often brings tension which needs to be turned into positive action.

The aspects of Uranus

Most of the aspects of Uranus stay in force for a long time, affecting large numbers of people. However, the planet can have a personal effect as well. If Uranus's influences are enhanced or strengthened by the house and the sign in which it is placed, those influences will figure prominently in a person's character and personality.

Interpreting Neptune's effects

KEYWORDS: Unreality; cloudiness

Neptune through the signs

Neptune creeps through the same zodiac sign for 14 years before it moves on to the next sign. Neptune therefore mostly has a "generational" influence on a great number of people. Any personal influences it makes are seen most clearly in the house it occupies.

Neptune through the houses

Neptune lends uncertainty to the areas of life governed by the house it which it is placed. It encourages personal uncertainty about how to act in many situations, an inability to make firm decisions, and a tendency to take the easy way out of problems and challenges.

The aspects of Neptune

The aspects Neptune makes to the Ascendant or the Midheaven can be quite powerful in effect – though subtly felt – and should be studied carefully.

Interpreting Pluto's effects

KEYWORDS: Elimination; volatile change

Pluto through the signs

Pluto stays in the same sign for 13 to 32 years, and it therefore has a powerfully strong generational influence. Any personal influences will depend on the house it occupies and the aspects it makes.

Pluto through the houses

The areas governed by the house in which Pluto is placed won't be easy for anyone to handle. Just as we are moving forward on a personal action or ambition, we may find ourselves stopped in our tracks and marooned on rough terrain. Pluto also encourages overreaction, which exacerbates any problematic situation.

The aspects of Pluto

A correct birth time is vital when dealing with the aspects of Pluto, since the planet can only make aspects to the Ascendant or Midheaven. (Its relationships to other planets are covered by the aspects they make to it!) While Pluto's influences in aspect to either the Ascendant or Midheaven can be very powerful indeed, they are so subtle and complex that a professional reading may be necessary.

Time to move on to our final section – and some serious chart interpretation! – all the planets "at work" in all the signs, houses, and aspects.

A simple summary

✓ Expert birth chart interpretation comes with practice, but it always involves balancing all the elements and influences in a chart, rather than looking at each element and influence in isolation.

✓ Begin interpreting a birth chart by first studying the key elements in the chart. These include the rising sign (or Ascendant), the Sun sign, the Sun's house position, the Moon's sign, the Moon's house position, and the ruling planet's sign.

✓ After reviewing the key elements in the chart, write down the sign and house positions of the other planets in the chart: Mercury, Venus, Mars, Jupiter, Saturn, Uranus, Neptune, and Pluto.

✓ When you have finished studying the key elements and the planets' positions in the signs and houses, review the traditional factors which appear in the chart. This includes listing each sign's gender (masculine or feminine), element (fire, earth, air, or water), and quality (cardinal, fixed, or mutable). Note any clusters or predominance of like factors.

✓ Before you begin studying a specific planet's influences, list any "personal" planets in the chart and note their locations. The influences of personal planets are considerably strengthened. The personal planets are the Sun; the Moon; the planet ruling the rising/Ascendant sign; the planet ruling the Sun sign; and the planet ruling the sign occupied by the Moon.

✓ When you begin studying the specific effects of each planet in the chart, remember the keywords and primary characteristics associated with that planet, and then study the planet's potential effects in light of those characteristics in its respective sign and house, and in its aspects to other planets.

PART FOUR

THE NIGHT SKY REVEALS THE PLANETS

THE PLANETS AT WORK

Y OU HAVE CONSTRUCTED your first birth chart. And you have written up your preliminary notes. It's all spread out before you: the planets in the signs; the signs in the houses; the aspects between the planets; the *Ascendant* looming majestically over there to your left; the *Midheaven* staring imperiously down at you from overhead. There's Venus in Libra; the Moon and Cancer over in the fifth house; Leo's peeping over the horizon; something's conjuncting with the Ascendant. What does it all mean?!

Here we tell you what it all means. Consider Part Four your "bible" for interpreting the birth chart. Each chapter deals with one planet and its unique influences in each of the 12 zodiac signs, the 12 houses, the major aspects to the other planets, the Ascendant, and the Midheaven. If you don't feel like a pro after this, we haven't done our job properly.

Chapter 14

The Sun at Work

THE SUN, the most important "planet" in astrology, is actually the huge and magnificent star – or luminary – around which all the other planets in our solar system, including the Earth, revolve. Almost every known ancient civilization worshiped the Sun as a supreme god. And wisely so. It makes our existence possible and is the very center of our little universe. It should come as no surprise to anyone that the Sun symbolizes primal energy, vast power, supreme ego, ultimate authority, sweeping magnanimity, and, ultimately, the life force itself – including our physical lives and our more subtle inner lives.

In this chapter...
✓ *The Sun through the houses*
✓ *The aspects of the Sun*

IN MYTHOLOGY, THE SUN RULES THE HEAVENS

The Sun through the houses

BECAUSE THE SUN represents the primal life force, our vitality, self-expression, and ego, the areas of life governed by the house in which the Sun is found are critically important in a birth chart. It is there that one's most essential and uniquely individual energies are focused; it is the place that is home to the heart; and it is from there that an individual can begin to build all other aspects of life. See p. 108 for the houses.

The Sun in the first house

With the Sun in the first house, your Sun and rising signs will probably be the same, and you appear to fit your Sun sign description so closely it seems like magic. The first house is associated with Aries, and you have the typical Arien "me first" attitude. You really want to win, at anything and everything, whether the prize is first place in an egg-and-spoon race at the family picnic, or the CEO's corner office at a multimillion dollar company.

The Sun in the second house

The Sun in the second house of possessions and partners suggests someone very house-proud and pleased to show off his or her possessions. It's quite likely that you are so turned on by the idea of owning things that you think of your husband, wife, or children as personal property – rather than as people with a will of their own and a need for freedom. Beware of that tendency. You're also a pleasure seeker, and you never hold back where food, wine, clothes, and entertaining are concerned.

The Sun in the third house

You really are keen to use your mind, especially if you're still in the early stages of education – high school, for instance. If you weren't especially satisfied with your formal education, you work hard now to correct the situation and fill in any academic "black holes." You have a strong need to get through to other people. The way you do that will depend on your Sun sign.

The Sun in the fourth house

The fourth house is all about home and family, and there's a very strong emphasis on parenting. There may well be so strong an attachment to home that you'll find it difficult even to think about leaving it. With the Sun in the fourth house, it's especially important to look at your relationship with your children. Draw up their birth charts as well, and compare the father's, mother's, and children's charts for potential areas of both agreement and discord.

The Sun in the fifth house

The house of creativity and children is also the house of love affairs, and since it's specifically associated with Leo and the Sun itself, the Sun in this house can throw a really splendid influence over the whole birth chart. You shouldn't have many sexual problems, because love, affection, and sexuality will be well-balanced. This is an excellent influence, since you need a very full and fulfilling sex life, and you may take emotional risks to achieve it. Sometimes those risks will pay off; at other times they won't. This house is also often associated with physical activities, such as sports, and with creativity.

The Sun in the sixth house

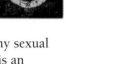

In the house of health, diet, and exercise, the influence of the Sun will affect your general well-being. There is also a distinct emphasis on duty and routine. You may have a strong sense of responsibility and favor regular routines. There may be a distinct advantage to working in the field of communication – print journalism or television news, for example.

The Sun in the seventh house

This is the house of love relationships, but also of friendships and business associations. In love, you need a lasting and emotionally secure relationship with a partner. With this combination of Sun and house you'll probably mate for life, or at least believe you're making a lifetime commitment. If a relationship – with a lover or a friend – does fall apart, you'll have more difficulties dealing with such breakdowns than you would if the Sun was in another house.

The Sun in the eighth house

This house is associated with self-searching, self-examination, and "the meaning of life." You are fascinated by your own personality and motivations – to the extent that you may spend far too much time gazing fiercely at your own navel. Remind yourself that too much introspection is counterproductive – and it's a fault shared by many people just starting out in astrology. In the end, gazing too long at your own birth chart is just another form of contemplating your bellybutton!

The Sun in the ninth house

The ninth house is very concerned with self-improvement, often through further education, sometimes through travel or what you would call "taking journeys." Such journeys may very well be journeys of the mind, and new horizons may be intellectual ones rather than – or in addition to – geographical ones. You want to satisfy your curiosity about life and the meaning of the universe as thoroughly as possible, and you continually work at your own personal system of philosophy and religion.

The Sun in the tenth house

The tenth house is associated with material progress, social status, tradition, and a sense of duty – and you're probably much concerned with all these things. You especially need to make a mark in the world, and one of the most important things in life, for you, will be to be satisfied with the sphere in which you have to work, to feel that it's worthwhile, and to be emotionally involved in the daily round. You can achieve much, and if the Sun is in a fire sign, your motivation will be so strong that you will infect those around you with your own enthusiasm.

The Sun in the eleventh house

You almost certainly are a shaker and a mover, associating with others to enjoy but also to improve the society in which you live. You may join both international aid groups and parish councils, and you're a distinct advantage in either group. You're extremely good at motivating others, provided you remember that you're a part of the group, and not necessarily its leader or even the "power behind the throne."

The Sun in the twelfth house

You need a generous amount of time to yourself, and one way or another you make sure you get it. The downside to this tendency is the possibility of your engaging in too much self-analysis and introspection. Remember that this can sap your self-confidence. You're also one of those people who works best behind the scenes. You have a great facility for downplaying your own accomplishments and achievements in order to persuade others to put their ideas and objectives into action.

The aspects of the Sun

ASTROLOGICALLY, THE EFFECT *that the planets have upon the influence of the Sun is extremely important. The planets subtly – and sometimes not so subtly – affect the way in which the Sun's influences are felt; sometimes an aspect will intensify the Sun's effects, other times it will modify them. A major aspect (such as the conjunction) in which the Sun and a planet are very close, will have a strong and significant effect on the Sun's influence on an individual's life.*

The Sun's aspects to the Moon

Conjunction

You experience the characteristics of the Sun sign intuitively and instinctively, and when responding to situations you do so in the classic behavioral patterns of your sign.

Positive aspects

A trine aspect in which the planets concerned are of the same element can make for a positive flow of natural enthusiasm (fire), practicality (earth), intelligence (air), or emotion (water). A sextile can also be helpful, emphasizing extroverted or introverted qualities, depending on whether it's in a positive (masculine) or negative (feminine) sign.

Negative aspects

Restlessness and a general feeling of discontent can be difficult to deal with, and moodiness and changeability can cause difficulties (sometimes in emotional relationships).

The Sun's aspects to Mercury

Conjunction and semi-sextile

Because Mercury is so close to the Sun (it can never be
more than 28 degrees away), only a conjunction or minor semi-sextile can be formed
between the Sun and Mercury. If Mercury is in the sign before or after the Sun sign, you
will likely exhibit the mental characteristics of that sign. If the conjunction is a very
close one – within five degrees, for example – you may have been slow to develop as a
child, and in fact may still be rather slow and plodding. On the other hand, these
aspects encourage enthusiasm, optimism, and a determination to succeed.

The Sun's aspects to Venus

Conjunction, semi-sextile, and semi-square

Because Venus is so near the Sun (they can never be
more than 48 degrees apart), the two planets can only
form a conjunction, semi-sextile, or semi-square. (In this book, with its more simple
approach to interpreting a birth chart, we do not discuss the semi-square.) If the Sun
and Venus are in the same sign, they heighten your capacity for love and affection. The
conjunction encourages warmth, affection, and a love for the luxurious pleasures of life.
The conjunction in combination with the semi-sextile (a weak but positive aspect) is
associated with an appreciation for art and music.

The Sun's aspects to Mars

Conjunction

This aspect between the Sun and Mars is associated
with powerful reserves of energy which must be
positively channeled through physical exercise, sports, or hard physical labor. The Sun
contributes vitality; Mars encourages physical energy. Emotional energies may also be
high, especially if the two planets are in a water sign (Cancer, Scorpio, or Pisces). You
have a lively sex life, are daring and brave, but must guard against selfishness,
overwork, and risky behavior.

Positive aspects

Here, again, there are tremendous reserves of physical – and often
emotional – energy, but there is far less of a tendency to work too hard
or to take risks.

Negative aspects

The tendency to overwork will be quite marked here, and the results are often tension, strain, and a very quick and dramatic temper.

The Sun's aspects to Jupiter

Conjunction

Traditionally, this was called a lucky aspect, but the word "luck" is rather out of fashion with astrologers today. We prefer to say that if you have this aspect, you are probably very fortunate in life indeed. What's more, you have an uncanny ability to find money (whatever your circumstance) whenever it's needed.

Positive aspects

Here we find influences similar to those in the conjunction, but you may be hesitant about expanding your intellectual horizons – perhaps preferring chess or crossword puzzles to more serious work.

Negative aspects

You prefer to take a very broad overview of a situation or problem, rather than grapple with the finer details that can offer direction and solutions. Your decisions, therefore, are often based on insufficient evidence and thought. You also have a strong tendency to exaggerate.

The Sun's aspects to Saturn

Conjunction

The Sun and Saturn could scarcely be more different from each other. In classical astrology, they are often considered "enemies." The Sun is all generosity, extroversion, and cheer; Saturn is all restriction, caution, and gloom. Generally, with this conjunction, the Sun's positive actions are somewhat limited by Saturn or channeled in subtle ways. For example, the more fiery influences of the Sun may be dampened by Saturn. Look for aspects from other planets which can cheer up the general picture and make Saturn more of a stabilizing – rather than an inhibiting – force.

Positive aspects

Common sense and practicality are heightened here. Natural enthusiasm may be dampened, however, and you may find yourself fearful when confronted by challenges.

Negative aspects

Here we have out-and-out combat between natural enemies, the Sun and Saturn: not a pretty sight, and frustrating to boot!

The Sun's aspects to Uranus

Conjunction

This powerful aspect can provoke rebelliousness, eccentric behavior, and unpredictability. You may have a desire for power that will drive you to extremes of behavior.

Positive aspects

You're alert and enthusiastic, but usually under rather odd circumstances that don't encourage constructive behavior!

Negative aspects

Negative aspects between the Sun and Uranus (especially the square) encourage perversity, stubbornness, and willfulness. You probably have the reputation of being difficult, especially when you're tense.

The Sun's aspects to Neptune

Conjunction

The characteristics of the Sun sign are somewhat toned down when Neptune shares it. There is added sensitivity and a tendency toward otherworldliness. Look for a shot of practicality from somewhere else in the birth chart.

Positive aspects

Here we have plenty of inspired imagination, but you also have a possible tendency to daydream and to be too laid-back.

Negative aspects

Self-deception is underscored here, as well as out-and-out lying (possibly because you see it as an easy way out of trouble). Under pressure, you'll be tempted to use addictive drugs – at best, tobacco; at worst, alcohol and illicit drugs.

The Sun's aspects to Pluto

Conjunction

A conjunction between the Sun and Pluto in your birth chart, especially if it's in Scorpio, indicates that you have a deep need to examine every corner of your personality, and to analyze the motives behind even the most ordinary, everyday actions or reactions.

Positive aspects

Here your ability for successful self-analysis is quite strong. And you make successful changes in attitudes and directions – for the betterment of your life. You may engage in self-examination and continue to grow – psychologically – throughout your life.

Negative aspects

These aspects can lead to a psychological blockage which makes it difficult for children to talk to their parents, or for a lover to "open up" to a partner.

The Sun's aspects to the Ascendant

Conjunction

If the Sun and the Ascendant (your ruling sign) are in conjunction, you must have been born within a half an hour or so of sunrise. In fact, it's quite likely that your Sun sign and Ascendant are the same. This means, for example, that you get a double whack of Gemini, or Aries, or Scorpio, etc. If the Sun is in the first house, you are a very sane person indeed, well-balanced and psychologically integrated. If the Sun is in the twelfth house, you need a degree of privacy and seclusion, and you won't be good at self-motivation. The house position in the chart is very important when you're interpreting this unique aspect.

Positive aspects

Again, look carefully at the house position, and take it into account when interpreting the effects of the positive aspects. The aspect to the Ascendant will unite and strengthen the link between the Sun and Ascendant. You will see this effect most strongly when the Sun is in the fifth house – its natural home – where positive expression and real fulfillment are indicated.

Negative aspects

An opposition from the sixth house to the Ascendant may indicate poor health and will encourage mental strain and tension. But if the Sun is positively aspected by the ruling planet, by the Moon, or by Mars, this aspect could actually invigorate you. If an opposition comes from the seventh house, your relationships may be affected.

The Sun's aspects to the Midheaven

Conjunction

Anyone with this aspect will have been born at about noon, and all the Sun's mighty energy and drive will be channeled into the achievement of ambitions – and those ambitions will be high. You are self-confident, but you may also be big-headed and pompous. Watch out for those tendencies. (Read the effects of the Sun in the tenth house.)

Positive aspects

You easily identify with the qualities of the zodiac sign located at the Midheaven (the topmost point of your chart), and you should be able to realize your ambitions without resorting to ruthlessness.

Negative aspects

While it may not be easy for you to identify with the qualities of the Midheaven sign, you fight to make them a part of your life – a struggle, by the way, that you may well win. But you need to work hard to succeed.

A simple summary

✔ The Sun is the most important planet in astrology (though technically it is a star), and it symbolizes – often to the ultimate degree – energy, power, ego, authority, magnanimity, and life itself. The Sun is also strongly associated with stamina, vitality, generosity, warmth, affection, creativity, joy, and self-esteem.

✔ Those areas of life governed by the house in which the Sun is found are critically important, because it is in those areas that an individual fully focuses his or her most essential and individualistic energies.

✔ In aspect to one another, the planets can have a subtle but potent effect on the Sun's influence. Some aspects greatly heighten the Sun's effects while others modify them. A major aspect, such as the conjunction, that is very close to the Sun, will have an especially strong and significant impact on the Sun's effects on an individual's life.

Chapter 15

The Moon at Work

THE MOON IS THE SECOND most important and influential planet in astrology (the Sun is the first). It is strongly associated with archetypal "feminine" qualities in a birth chart (whether the individual is male or female); maternal impulses, parental influences, compassion, nurturing instincts, imagination, and domesticity. The keywords associated with the Moon – responsiveness, instinct, intuition, fluctuation, and emotions – point to the Moon's strongest influences on an individual's psychological makeup and approach to the world.

In this chapter...
✓ The Moon through the signs
✓ The Moon through the houses
✓ The aspects of the Moon

THE MOON HAS A PROFOUND EFFECT ON NATURE AND HUMANITY

The Moon through the signs

WHEN YOU BEGIN interpreting the effects of the Moon in a sign, consider the sign's general characteristics, and then remember that the Moon's influence will encourage an individual to act out (and on) those characteristics intuitively and instinctively in almost all situations. The Moon also indicates how our intuition and instincts around certain issues and situations are shaped by our parents or other family members. The Moon's influence also underscores those inhibiting traits that may hold us back or disturb us, and suggests ways to overcome these inhibitions.

In the signs, the Moon works most beneficially when there are positive aspects — especially the conjunction — between it and the Sun or the chart's ruling planet (see "The aspects of the Moon" later in this chapter).

The Moon in Aries

You're very emotional, and your instinct is to react quickly (and sometimes thoughtlessly) to any issue that arouses passionate feelings. As a result, your reactions can sometimes be over the top. You also have a quick temper, especially if the Moon receives negative aspects from Mars or Uranus, but you're extremely decisive in your approach to problems and easily grasp all the facets of a situation. Sexually, you're easily bored and need adventure both in and outside the bedroom. You may be selfish: when challenged you certainly put yourself first — though you are quick to regret any misunderstandings. Sudden and careless actions may make you accident-prone.

The Moon in Taurus

From Taurus, the Moon makes you conservative and conventional. You're determined, but also self-absorbed, and occasionally very stubborn. Your emotional responses are heightened by the Moon, and you're warmly affectionate. Comfort is a necessity, rather than a vague ambition, you demand it in the bedroom first, and then everywhere else through the house! In fact you must be surrounded by comfortable, even luxurious, things — or else you can't relax and enjoy yourself. You're a sensualist, and love good food, good wine, and beautiful possessions.

The Moon in Gemini

Geminian versatility is magnified here. Faced with five or six things that you really must do, you throw yourself at all of them at once, rather than prioritizing tasks and dealing with them one at a time. Your love of reason may make you mistrust emotions (yours and others) and approach every aspect of life in a rational, analytic way. This approach may conflict with the Moon's more emotional and intuitive impulses, and you need to search for a healthy balance between these two very different attitudes toward life. Healthwise, watch for stress and tension; either can lead to digestive problems or exacerbate asthma. (Gemini is strongly associated with the lungs.)

The Moon in Cancer

Because the Moon rules Cancer, its influence from this sign is particularly strong. For one thing, it powerfully heightens your self-protective tendency in all situations. This can be unfortunate, because that hard shell you use to protect yourself often hides a wonderfully soft and gentle personality. You're especially emotional and intuitive, so don't hesitate to trust your emotions and rely on them. On the other hand, you can be overemotional, and this may encourage your powerful imagination to run riot: the result is constant worry, at best; serious depression, at worst.

The Moon in Leo

Leo's best qualities – positive energy and happy enthusiasm – are heightened here. You have considerable leadership powers and organizational abilities. Unfortunately, this placing of the Moon also encourages Leo's dogmatism, stubbornness, and need to be in charge of everything. People with the Moon in Leo often think they know best about everything, much to the irritation of those around them. Ironically, you may be very insecure at heart and appear more extroverted and outgoing than you really are. Nevertheless, your quick-acting sense of determination will work in your favor if used properly.

The Moon in Virgo

With the Moon in Virgo, you're able to react very quickly to situations, and you easily best the competition. Your fine resource of nervous energy will be helpful if it's positively expressed – but there may be a problem with lack of self-confidence and a tendency to worry, often unnecessarily. You're highly rational, but when you're nervous, you may dissolve into an agitated flood of words. You have a talent for debate and argument, and very sharp reflexes which help you to stand firmly on your own ground in controversy. Literary talent is often present, with this placing of the Moon.

The Moon in Libra

Here comes the peacemaker, with a real talent for identifying with and responding to the problems of other people – and you have the ability to express this talent tactfully and diplomatically. Your natural tendency is to remain very much above any disagreeable and contentious frays, to remain calm and unlikely to panic. But you also intervene in many situations, even when you're convinced one side is right, because you have a powerful need to bring out the best in others (and are very successful indeed at this), and you readily make others feel at ease.

The Moon in Scorpio

The moment you're challenged or provoked, the floodgates of emotion open. Whatever your reaction to a situation – positive or negative, analytical or intuitive – it will definitely be very emotionally expressed. You expect others around you to show the same enthusiasm for life that you have, and you don't hesitate to express your disapproval when they don't. Jealousy can be a major problem, on the homefront or at work. Remember that your powerful emotionality can be destructive when negatively channeled; but it's an enormously beneficial asset when used positively.

The Moon in Sagittarius

Optimism and enthusiasm are two keywords when this placing of the Moon occurs. Presented with an obstacle, you really blossom: you love a challenge, are eager to face it, and are quick to find a solution. (But do watch out for a tendency to overlook or even ignore small details which could be important!) You have a tendency to be restless and a rather strong urge to rush forward with things – physically or intellectually. Watch out for impatience and a tendency toward bluster; look for countering, calming influences elsewhere in the chart.

The Moon in Capricorn

From Capricorn the Moon encourages cool reactions and thoughtful, careful progress rather than any frivolous dashing about. You may tend to be undemonstrative with your feelings. Indeed, you may try to distance yourself from other (lesser?) mortals. You have a strong need to impress others, but you like to go it alone in everything and rarely accept any help, however well-intentioned. (This is often a mistake on your part!) On the other hand, you have a natural instinct for self-preservation, and this will prevent you from taking unwise and rash risks.

The Moon in Aquarius

People with the Moon in Aquarius often have a somewhat brittle response to others. Your innate charm and magnetic personality initially attract people's attention, but when someone tries to get close to you, you firmly push them away. It's almost as though you have something to hide, or simply like to appear mysterious and inscrutable. You often have unpredictable and surprising responses to situations, and you can be extremely stubborn about your position. Stubbornness and unpredictability make for an uneasy marriage and can be a real problem in your life. You have a definite romantic streak, but it's not at all obvious to others. Study the placements and influences of Mars and Venus in your chart for clues about how you express yourself in love.

The Moon in Pisces

Someone with this placing of the Moon always reacts first from his or her emotional core. For example, you are very easily moved – either to intense happiness or abject tears – by a piece of nostalgic music or a sentimental film. Your intensely romantic attitude toward everything can lead you into serious trouble. Indeed, you're so reluctant to hurt others that you often lie to them, because you believe the truth will be too painful. The fact is, such deception almost always makes matters worse and hurts both parties. Healthwise, you may have bad reactions to prescription drugs, so be on the alert whenever you're prescribed any. Under stress, you often turn to the use of tobacco, alcohol, or illicit drugs for release. Beware of your addictive tendencies!

The Moon through the houses

THE AREAS OF LIFE governed by the house in which the Moon is placed will be of singular importance to an individual and the key focus of the Moon's major influences: imagination and aspiration; maternal instincts and nurturing; the home and domestic security; stability and changeability. The more aspects the Moon receives (see "The aspects of the Moon" in this chapter), the greater its importance in the house. Lunar influences are further enhanced if Cancer is emphasized by the Sun sign or Ascendant, or if Taurus is the Sun sign or Ascendant.

The Moon in the first house

You have a deep concern for other people, and a need to care for and protect them. Your emotions and intuition are very strong forces indeed. You may have a rather sensitive digestive system, one which is easily upset by a careless diet. In women, the reproductive system can also be sensitive. If you're a man, your relationship with your mother may be quite complex and need a good deal of sorting out.

The Moon in the second house

You need security and won't function properly without it. A low bank balance, the possible loss of your home, a reduction in income (all of which, of course, are scary to most people) will throw you into utter panic and obsessive worrying. Your imagination will run wild, turning otherwise manageable bumps in the road of life into completely unnavigable terrain. Ironically – and despite your fierce need for security – money can run like sand through your fingers. You're a soft touch for all kind of appeals, especially those made by needy friends.

The Moon in the third house

You need to let everyone in the world know just how you feel about anything of importance, and you spend hours on the phone or the Internet. (Your phone bills are simply enormous!) You not only need and need to keep in constant touch with friends, you also are compelled to spread your ideas among the widest possible audience. Shrewd and lively in argument, you find it easy to communicate your feelings in any situation.

The Moon in the fourth house

A good, secure, satisfying family life is of paramount importance to you. If your domestic life is shaky or threatened in any way, your response is extremely bad and emotionally intense (and will affect every other area of your life). You may have great difficulty letting your children go when they grow up and decide to leave home. (This tendency is heightened if you also have the Moon or the Sun in Cancer.) In fact, a child of yours who moves away will be seen as not only ungrateful, but intent on undermining the whole of your family life. Even when you (reluctantly) accept this kind of situation, you worry incessantly about the well-being of your children. Those you love will find these tendencies of yours suffocating, and you must try to counter your overly "nurturing" instincts with work or hobbies that take the focus off the home.

The Moon in the fifth house

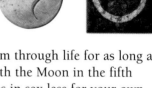

You are (or were) especially eager to start a family, and you're marvelously suited to bringing up children. You instinctively know the way to build a really sound relationship with them, and you easily and gently guide them through life for as long as they need you. This is also the house of sexual love, and with the Moon in the fifth house you're a wonderfully responsive partner, who indulges in sex less for your own pleasure than for the pleasure it brings your lover or spouse.

The Moon in the sixth house

The Moon in this house has a potent effect on health and well-being. develop healthy habits early in life and work hard at ridding yourself of tobacco, alcohol, or illicit drug addictions: you have a higher than usual chance of suffering the serious health consequences associated with these behaviors. Under stress, you may also use food in an addictive way, and anorexia or bulimia could be problems for you. Strive to maintain a healthy balance in your life, and not to let an occasional indulgence turn into a compulsion. If the Moon is in an Earth sign, you may find it easy to stick to a healthy routine once you're convinced it's necessary and valuable.

The Moon in the seventh house

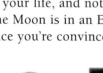

At best, this placement of the Moon encourages a splendidly warm, sensitive response to a lover or partner. At worst, it can encourage such a complete dependence on that partner, that he or she will feel like the two of you are joined at the hip! This can be claustrophobic for your partner, and it can weaken your own character.

The Moon in the eighth house

A good personal relationship is founded on your powerful feelings for sex, which you're able to express particularly well and enthusiastically. It's also very important that your partner has an equal (and uninhibited) enjoyment of sex. Complete trust in that partner is vital to your personal happiness. As is so often the case with people who have an intense sexuality, jealousy can be a serious problem.

The Moon in the ninth house

You probably have difficulty concentrating on any task at hand, and disciplined thought often eludes you. No matter how much you want to focus your whole mind on a specific subject or problem, you inevitably find that your powers of concentration waver. Successful resolutions to challenges and the right answers to problems are always just out of your reach. In truth, your judgment is frequently clouded by your emotions. Work extra hard at keeping your feet firmly on the ground, and look for steadying, intellectual influences elsewhere in the birth chart.

The Moon in the tenth house

This placing makes you sympathetic and understanding. People with the Moon in the tenth are almost always genuinely loved and admired – even idolized. You expend a good deal of emotion on behalf of others, attempting to understand their problems and doing your best to help. You frequently need change and variety in any chosen career, and you're likely to be the sort of person who can handle almost anything.

The Moon in the eleventh house

Here we find a mass of emotional contradictions. On the one hand, you may long to be a member of a warm and close-knit group; but on the other hand, you can't really open up and be at ease with many people. Or you are someone who may really long for love, and you don't keep that longing to yourself. In fact, you may openly plead, quite strongly, for affection – to the point that people are sometimes repelled by your approaches. Finally, if you're given the love you so strongly desire, you often find yourself unable to accept it unconditionally and happily. Obviously these are worrisome tendencies. Look to other areas of the chart for clues about how to solve these problems.

The Moon in the twelfth house

The Moon in the twelfth demands that you sometimes stop rushing about and take time to be alone, regardless of how extroverted and lively you are. If you don't recognize the necessity for constructive solitude, trouble will follow. You actually have an innate and instinctive need for withdrawal that comes from the deepest core of your personality. If you don't practice being happily alone from time to time, you'll inevitably feed your instinct for withdrawal with negative and escapist behavior, including experimenting with alcohol and drugs.

The aspects of the Moon

Study the aspects of the Moon quite carefully, because the Moon subtly but potently personalizes any planet it contacts, and this personalization will have a considerable effect on the planet's characteristics and their influence on your personality and life. For example, in contact with Mars, the Moon sharpens reactions; with Saturn, it adds caution; with Jupiter, it encourages enthusiasm. Also read over the discussions in the house and sign where the Moon is placed for additional clues to its influence in aspect. In general, the aspects of the Moon strongly affect one's instinctive and immediate reactions to everyday circumstances.

(For the Moon's aspects to the Sun, see the Sun's aspects to the Moon, p. 253.)

The Moon's aspects to Mercury

Conjunction

This brisk influence strengthens your natural instincts and gives you a strong but logical sense of intuition. Mercury will add to the qualities of the Moon-sign its own quick-thinking power, and imagination linked to practicality can be of great value in almost every area of your life.

Positive aspects

Your powers of concentration are good, and you have plenty of common sense, a practical outlook, the shrewdness of the Moon, and the cunning of Mercury. You make decisions on the basis of logic and intuition.

Negative aspects

Your critical acumen will be increased by negative aspects between the Moon and Mercury, and you'll sometimes make comments which are sharp and even unkind.

The Moon's aspects to Venus

Conjunction

You should be popular, affectionate, calm, serene, and instinctively aware of the needs of your partner. Any personal relationship will profit from these talents.

Positive aspects

You have all the positive traits of the conjunction, with optimism and perception added. You may be too charming – the sort of person who can "get away with anything."

Negative aspects

You have a powerful ability to love and a keen desire to be loved. As a result, you may tend to rush into relationships, ignoring signs of incompatibility until it is too late.

The Moon's aspects to Mars

Conjunction

The Moon boosts your physical and emotional energy levels, heightens your emotions, quickens your response to situations, and encourages a direct approach in all things.

Positive aspects

Here there is an encouraging link between your physical and emotional energies, and you should work to strengthen that connection. You should have good, robust health – and a willingness to use your well-balanced energies on behalf of others.

Negative aspects

Nervous and emotional tension can be heightened, and you may have a short temper and a volatile disposition. As a result, your sense of judgment can be faulty. Your tendency to take hasty or premature action should be resisted.

The Moon's aspects to Jupiter

Conjunction

You respond sensitively to other people and are happy to pass on your experience and knowledge (wonderful makings for a gifted teacher!). You're also kind and gentle, generous and charitable.

Positive aspects

Here we find positive influences similar to those in the conjunction (sensitivity, kindness, and generosity), but added to the mix are a heightened imagination and a marvelous capacity for philosophical exploration – sometimes down unconventional paths.

Negative aspects

Unfortunately, you're a rather poor judge of people, and you tend to overdramatize situations. To add injury to insult, you may frequently suffer from bouts of indigestion and biliousness, especially if you overindulge in rich food and alcoholic drink.

The Moon's aspects to Saturn

Conjunction

This rather heavy aspect can make you serious and gloomy in outlook, and rather sluggish emotionally. You're wonderfully hard working, however, and have a practical, matter-of-fact outlook on life.

Positive aspects

Common sense, determination and prudence are all aspected here, and they work to restrain any impulsiveness shown elsewhere in the horoscope. You approach work in a disciplined and practical way, and slowly build a solid reputation based on reliability and thoroughness.

Negative aspects

Inhibition and lack of self-confidence will sometimes make life difficult for you – and may even lead to depression when your outlook on life is especially negative. You do have a tendency to grumble, which irritates friends. These emotional aspects can gradually weaken your physical constitution, and you may be prone to chronic bouts of colds and flu.

The Moon's aspects to Uranus

Conjunction

This can be a splendid aspect, but its quality will be affected, as always, by other indications in the chart. The Moon's conjunction to Uranus is a very powerful aspect indeed, with potential for both positive and negative influences. It encourages a magnetic, dynamic, original, brilliant, and marvelously intuitive mind. But . . . Uranian perversity may color this extraordinary spectrum of qualities with murky undertones that may, for example, turn brilliant originality into troubling unconventionality.

Positive aspects

These aspects will positively fuel your emotions, allowing you to use your creative, energetic force in a positive and original way, either scientifically or artistically. You have a tendency, however (especially when young), to listen to someone's advice and then do exactly the opposite thing.

Negative aspects

Self-will can be a real problem here. But you can turn it into a positive force for you by single-mindedly channeling it into constructive ideas and actions. Physical exercise is an excellent countering remedy with this aspect.

The Moon's aspects to Neptune

Conjunction

Very fine aspects are working here, but do beware: you may be so idealistic, kind, and sympathetic that others take advantage of you. Your marvelous imagination, when creatively channeled, provides a wonderful foundation for personal and professional fulfillment.

Positive aspects

Both planets work well in these aspects, strengthening your imagination and emotions. Work consistently to channel your imagination positively; otherwise, vagueness and confusion may get in the way of your ability to freely express yourself. Many individuals with these positive aspects are psychically gifted.

Negative aspects

You have a sort of wistful weakness, together with an impractical attitude about life. You may find it hard to make any real progress in the world, and this may encourage you to look for the easy way out of difficult situations.

The Moon's aspects to Pluto

Conjunction

You express yourself with unusual freedom and force. In fact, your emotional level is so heightened that life with you may be a series of disturbingly strong outbursts of raw feelings. Disturbing for others, yes. But probably healthy for you: if you try to completely restrain your strong emotions, damage – in the form of self-combustion – may occur.

Positive aspects

Though your emotional level is generally high, you rarely make a scene – except to relieve tense situations. Do be careful that a chance remark of yours isn't woefully misunderstood or taken more seriously than intended.

Negative aspects

You may find it difficult to express your feelings, and the resulting emotional blockage can cause damage both to you and to significant others. This will almost certainly be the case if shyness or inhibition is emphasized elsewhere in the horoscope.

The Moon's aspects to the Ascendant

Conjunction

This aspect will accent the changeability and moodiness which are so much a part of the Moon's influence, and you'll feel this at the level of instinct, intuition, and response. More than most, you're keenly influenced by your surroundings and by the reactions of others.

Positive aspects

Here is a splendidly integrating influence on the personality; you should have no psychological difficulties in coming to terms with yourself. Common sense is strong and plentiful, and you have an innate ability to get on easily with others.

Negative aspects

However charming you may be, these aspects may make you rather prickly and impatient – qualities which can damage any relationship, even on first acquaintance. You may find you suffer from a niggling inner dissatisfaction which will fight to make itself felt and recognized.

The Moon's aspects to the Midheaven

Conjunction

Traditionally, it's often been said that this aspect appears in the chart of someone who is destined to be famous! You may certainly have a powerful ego and an especially magnetic appeal. You are often at your best when in charge of a considerable number of other people.

Positive aspects

The qualities of the zodiac sign at your Midheaven (refer to the topmost point of your birth chart) are greatly underscored and strengthened with these positive aspects. Additionally, your identification with, and need to express, these qualities is considerably heightened.

Negative aspects

With negative aspects between the Moon and the Midheaven, it isn't easy for you to realize your ambitions. And if you do, you may not be very satisfied with your success. The truth is, you often can't decide just what your ambitions are!

A simple summary

✔ The Moon is the second most influential planet in astrology, strongly associated with archetypal "feminine" qualities, including maternal impulses, compassion, emotions, nurturing, instinct, imagination, intuition, and changeability. Changeability is a driving force behind these lunar qualities when the Moon is prominent in a birth chart, and contradictory emotions and behavior are often seen in an individual; for example, deep compassion juxtaposed with extreme selfishness.

✔ The Moon's influence in the signs will encourage an individual to act out (and on) the sign's characteristics in an intuitive and instinctive manner. The Moon's influence also underscores inhibiting traits that may hold one back. In the signs, the Moon works most beneficially when there are positive aspects – especially the conjunction – between it and the Sun or the ruling planet of the chart.

✔ The areas of life governed by the house in which the Moon is placed will be of unique importance to an individual and will receive the full force of all the Moon's potent influences, especially if Cancer or Taurus is prominent in the birth chart.

✔ The Moon's aspects subtly but powerfully personalize any planet contacted. For example, in contact with normally sedate Jupiter, the Moon encourages enthusiasm. The aspects of the Moon strongly affect one's instinctive and immediate reactions to daily circumstances.

Chapter 16

Mercury at Work

WHETHER IN A SIGN, HOUSE, OR IN ASPECT, Mercury's singular influence is on the mind. Its specific placement and aspects in a birth chart indicate how an individual's mind works, whether it is instinctively and quickly, deliberately and slowly, intellectually and logically, or emotionally and intuitively. Mercury also influences the decision-making process and how we communicate with others.

In this chapter...

✓ Mercury through the signs

✓ Mercury through the houses

✓ The aspects of Mercury

IN MYTHOLOGY, MERCURY WAS THE MESSENGER GOD

Mercury through the signs

MERCURY IS ONE of the inferior planets (Venus is the other) whose orbit lies between the Earth and the Sun. From the Earth, Mercury always appears near the Sun. Similarly, in the birth chart Mercury can never be more than 28 degrees from the Sun.

Remember that each of the 12 zodiac bands (one for each sign) is only 30 degrees wide. Because Mercury is always within 28 degrees of the Sun, it can only be found in three signs: The same sign in which the Sun appears; the sign before the one in which the Sun appears; or the sign after the one in which the Sun appears.

> **DEFINITION**
>
> Mercury and Venus – the planets whose orbits lie between the Earth and the Sun (and thus the planets closer to the Sun than Earth) – are known as the **inferior** planets. Those planets farther from the Sun than Earth – Mars, Jupiter, Saturn, Uranus, Neptune, and Pluto – are known as the superior planets.

For example, if your Sun sign is Cancer, Mercury can only appear in Cancer, Gemini, or Leo. Put another way: if Mercury is in Cancer in your birth chart (and you drew up the chart correctly!), your Sun sign can only be Gemini, Cancer, or Leo. If you're an Aries, and your birth chart shows Mercury in Cancer, you'll need to go back to the drawing board!

Mercury in Aries

From Aries Mercury encourages decisiveness, quick thinking, and the ability to look at problems clearly and unflinchingly. If Mercury is in a negative aspect to Mars you may tend to be impulsive, but your natural decisiveness works well for you; you make the right choices and take positive, assertive action. You also come straight to the point – which doesn't mean that argument and debate won't be tolerated. Indeed, you enjoy both and take a special delight in offering provocative and stimulating suggestions. Your general outlook on life is positive and optimistic.

Sun sign Pisces

with Mercury in Aries

You're powerfully decisive, positive, and self-assured. You have a sparkling imagination and a great deal of creative potential. Pisces's high level of emotionality will be readily expressed. Indeed, it is easy for you to communicate your emotions, though if Mercury is negatively aspected by the Moon or Uranus you may experience some above-average tension, together with periods of positive excitement that alternate with periods of uncertainty. Piscean strength of will is increased here.

Sun sign Aries

with Mercury in Aries

This placement can mean that Arien action will be supported by the ability to think rapidly on your feet. On the other hand, you may have to watch out for a tendency toward rash hastiness rather than sure-footed speed, coupled with a decided lack of patience. Look to the Moon or the Ascendant for tempering influences.

Sun sign Taurus

with Mercury in Aries

Less cautious than a purely Taurean type, your actions are characterized by vivacity, speed, assertiveness, and immediacy. On the negative side, you tend to get impatient and irritated when your suggestions aren't met with immediate enthusiasm.

Mercury in Taurus

Stubbornness is almost inevitable, and flexibility must be nurtured so that your opinions don't become too firmly fixed. In the worst case scenario, you may become obsessional and overly attached to security. For the most part you are inclined to be generally cautious, practical, and conventional in your approach to life. Common sense and practicality, together with disciplined work habits, almost always prevail.

Sun sign Aries

with Mercury in Taurus

The more impetuous areas of the Arien personality will be stabilized by Mercury in Taurus. Your ability to think slowly and constructively is an asset and lessens your chances of making a reckless, rash, and wrong decision.

Sun sign Taurus

with Mercury in Taurus

Steady, reliable, and cautious, you are the epitome of the strong, silent type. You speak only when it's necessary, are slow to respond to new ideas, and are deliberate in your response to them. You may need an injection of vigor from somewhere else in the chart if you want to move forward in life.

Sun sign Gemini

with Mercury in Taurus

Like all Geminians, you're typically lively, quick, and versatile. But because Mercury rules that sign, the planet will have a strong effect here, adding considerable stability to your character. For one thing, you think more carefully and constructively than most pure Geminian types.

Mercury in Gemini

Gemini is Mercury's ruling sign and thus its influence here is greatly strengthened. There is an emphasis on communication: you need to exchange ideas, like to be heard, and will talk to anyone rather than keep your thoughts to yourself! You're quick on your feet where ideas are concerned and are usually involved in more than one task at a time. Your major difficulty is a serious addiction to the superficial, both in thought and action. In-depth examination of a subject is foreign to your nature. You'll probably be very impatient, and you won't have much sympathy with anyone whose mind works more slowly than yours. Cunning and craftiness are not unknown.

Sun sign Taurus

with Mercury in Gemini

You like routine but are less likely to be a slave to it than other Taureans. Versatility and adaptability will profit you without sapping the strength of your typical Taurean sense of purpose and determination.

Sun sign Gemini

with Mercury in Gemini

You need to be especially careful about the negative Geminian traits of superficiality and restlessness, but on the whole you are generally quick-witted, versatile, and able to talk yourself out of any situation.

Sun sign Cancer

with Mercury in Gemini

Mercury encourages you to change your mind, Cancer to change your mood. The combination of the two influences may be pretty volatile at times, but Mercury will at least curb your Cancerian tendency to be overly sentimental.

Mercury in Cancer

Nostalgia can be a problem for you. It's not that looking back isn't pleasurable from time to time, but a preoccupation with the past may damage your capacity to move forward and plan for the future. In fact, you downright dislike doing that, because you're innately apprehensive about the unknown. Remember that your imagination can work overtime – and negatively – so that every molehill which trips you up becomes an unclimbable mountain. Your imagination can work to your advantage, however, if creatively directed. Combined with your love of the past, your imaginative skills may be put to wonderful use – for example, in the study of history or the writing of historical romances. Watch out for a tendency to allow emotions to override logic – often to your disadvantage.

Sun sign Gemini

with Mercury in Cancer

Powerful intuition and instinctive responses are added to Geminian quickness of mind, and this placing of Mercury contributes a degree of sensitivity, especially when you're assessing the reactions of others. You're more likely to be sympathetic than critical.

Sun sign Cancer

with Mercury in Cancer

You have a very lively and potent imagination, but it must be properly and positively directed. An unbridled imagination can easily translate into excessive worry. And if there are indications elsewhere in the chart that you are prone to pessimism or depression, that worry can be magnified tenfold. Watch out, too, for a strong tendency toward moodiness, which may negatively impact those around you.

Sun sign Leo

with Mercury in Cancer

Leo optimism will help you overcome Cancerian worry. Mercury will add kindness, consideration, and sympathy. Mental flexibility and a degree of caution will act as stabilizing counters to Leo's more fiery influence, but your imaginative skills are nevertheless keen, and you put them to good use.

Mercury in Leo

With this placing of Mercury you have plenty of imagination, a good deal of emotional and nervous energy, and great organizational skills. Anything that needs to get done, will get done – sensibly and practically. You have terrific powers of concentration and are able to think creatively. But be careful about your tendency to be rather stubborn, inflexible, and dictatorial, especially when you are in the wrong. You're enthusiastic and optimistic, and you have keen communication skills (though you can sometimes be condescending). All of the upbeat qualities may be dampened somewhat by negative influences elsewhere in the birth chart, particularly any negative aspects between the Moon and Saturn.

Sun sign Cancer

with Mercury in Leo

Cancerian intuition is leavened by a degree of realism. You take a practical approach to new ideas and act on them deliberately and carefully. Good organizational skills are another asset, as is your positive outlook on life.

Sun sign Leo

with Mercury in Leo

You are probably drawn to dominate others, and this tendency can mar what would otherwise be a spectacularly enthusiastic, optimistic, and positively charged personality. Watch out, too, for a strong streak of stubbornness and try to develop more flexible attitudes toward your life.

Sun sign Virgo

with Mercury in Leo

Mercury rules Virgo, so its influence from that sign will be powerful, countering the Virgoan tendency to worry. Mercury will also help build self-confidence and optimism. The latter will temper your fixation on detail and help you see the larger picture.

Mercury in Virgo

Mercury rules Virgo as well as Gemini, and its influence is strengthened by that fact. The combination encourages an excellent ability to analyze problems and assess every aspect of them with thoughtful insight. Common sense and practicality rule here, and you're not happy if your feet aren't planted firmly on the ground. Watch out for a tendency only to feel safe when you know exactly what you have to do and how to do it – in every situation. This may lead to an over-preoccupation with detail and a tendency to be short-sighted about larger issues. (Jupiter's placement and aspects in your chart may, however, temper these latter tendencies.) You may have an excess of highly charged nervous energy. You need to find positive outlets for this to avoid possible stomach upsets and migraines.

Sun sign Leo

with Mercury in Virgo

Mercury is usually thought of as a quick-moving and even rash planet, but working from Virgo it can act as a brake on the overexuberant and overoptimistic side of Leo. Virgo's practical common sense will help prevent you from overreacting and temper your tendency to show off.

Sun sign Virgo

with Mercury in Virgo

Here we have a surplus of Virgoan traits, including the tendency to worry too much and to overcriticize both yourself and others. Personal shyness and a lack of self-confidence are also indicated.

Sun sign Libra

with Mercury in Virgo

Librans who might otherwise suffer from procrastination and indecision will find these tendencies easier to control when Mercury works for them from Virgo. You won't suffer from typical Libran laziness either.

Mercury in Libra

Mercury's powers of concentration are diluted by Libra, but you have a sympathetic heart and a keen desire both to make friends and to be good to them. It is sometimes a challenge for you to think clearly and quickly and as a result, you often adopt a lackadaisical attitude.

Sun sign Virgo

with Mercury in Libra

It's easy for you to relax with this combination of Sun sign and planet. Indeed, your attitude to life may be calm to the point of lethargy! (And this despite the fact that you sometimes suffer from nervous tension.) You never rush and you're reluctant to make decisions. You must recognize your tendency to indecisiveness and try to counter it.

Sun sign Libra

with Mercury in Libra

This placing of Mercury doesn't help a Sun sign Libran: it tends to make you even lazier than your Sun sign profile suggests! On the other hand, you may sometimes use the outward appearance of laziness to cover up a lack of self-confidence. Indecision is also more problematic than usual.

Sun sign Scorpio

with Mercury in Libra

A potentially excellent placement for Sun sign Scorpios, Mercury in Libra takes some of the edge off your prickliness and encourages you to listen sympathetically to others. Stubbornness will be less of a problem, and you'll be more relaxed and charming.

Mercury in Scorpio

This is a powerful placement: the logic and rationality of Mercury combines with the intuition and intensity of Scorpio. You go at a problem with great perseverance, determined to examine every aspect of it. You have the mind of a natural researcher and investigator, so much so that you may even have obsessional tendencies – especially if Mercury makes a negative aspect to Pluto. You may find it hard to be outgoing, preferring instead to look inward and self-analyze. Because it's difficult for you to open up, you may be unwilling or unable to discuss intimate matters with anyone. Since you keep your problems to yourself, they are that much more difficult to solve. Your partner or close friends may recognize this and try to help you unburden yourself, but often without much success.

Sun sign Libra

with Mercury in Scorpio

Libran indecisiveness will conflict with Mercury-in-Scorpio's determination and sense of purpose; with any luck the latter tendencies will win out. At worst, you may seem indecisive. Rely on your intuition to show you in which direction you should move – even if that move is slow in the making.

Sun sign Scorpio

with Mercury in Scorpio

The determination and sense of purpose which this combination offers may be so strong that you become obsessive about some aim or plan. Nevertheless, that aim or plan will have hatched from your powerful and trustworthy intuition, been carefully crafted in great detail, and will ultimately bear great fruit.

Sun sign Sagittarius

with Mercury in Scorpio

Sagittarians aren't fond of detail, but Mercury in Scorpio will remedy this and encourage cautious and unhurried enthusiasm. There's little chance of your being overly optimistic about anything.

Mercury in Sagittarius

Traditionally, most astrologers view Mercury in Sagittarius as a somewhat negative placement. But Mercury encourages intellectual stimulation, which is good for Sagittarians. In turn, you need to work at consistency in all your endeavors and try to avoid restlessness and superficiality. You have a quick and broad grasp of detail, which is useful in many situations, but avoid changing jobs or leisure activities too frequently. Try to develop a philosophical attitude about life and all should be well.

Sun sign Scorpio

with Mercury in Sagittarius

Mercury will liven up the somewhat heavy Scorpio influence, encouraging you not to take yourself too seriously or become too obsessive about personal problems. Born under this influence you'll be open-minded, frank, tolerant, and optimistic.

Sun sign Sagittarius

with Mercury in Sagittarius

This placement will make you almost too lively, and you will do well to look elsewhere in the chart for a steadying influence. If you can't find one, be careful about being too optimistic or becoming overwhelmed by your own enthusiasm.

Sun sign Capricorn

with Mercury in Sagittarius

The rather serious Capricorn nature can always do with an injection of positive optimism, and Mercury will offer just that when stationed in Sagittarius. Your dogged persistence and single-mindedness – great Capricorn advantages – may be somewhat less compulsive, and you'll have an easier and more relaxed attitude to life.

Mercury in Capricorn

There's no time for idle gossip when Mercury is in Capricorn. Instead, there's just plain straightforward speech, often tinged with pessimism (especially if the Moon and Saturn form negative aspects), but usually constructive and practical. Your mind works fairly slowly and cautiously, but every move you make is carefully calculated. Add to that the fact that you take a cool, rational view of a situation. You're very ambitious, and you achieve your goals with the determination and decisiveness that characterize most people with Mercury in Capricorn.

Sun sign Sagittarius

with Mercury in Capricorn

The overenthusiasm which can be a worry with Sagittarians will be steadied by Mercury working from Capricorn. This placement also encourages common sense, cautiousness, practicality, and the ability to cope with details.

Sun sign Capricorn

with Mercury in Capricorn

You often seem to be a plodder, and your mind certainly works in a very calculated way. Those qualities help you cope well with a variety of situations and plan your life with great foresight. You have a positive outlook, are lively and ambitious, and are eager and able to deal with any rival in any arena.

Sun sign Aquarius

with Mercury in Capricorn

Practicality will leaven the perversity which can dog Aquarians, and stubbornness can be less of a problem. Unconventionality, too, will be less marked – though you may swing between the two extremes of nonconformity and rigid conventionality.

Mercury in Aquarius

You tend to be intellectual, have a quick and original mind, and express unique opinions and ideas. You can, however, be extremely stubborn and perverse, especially when you're stressed. You may have a problem with nervous tension and find it very difficult to unwind (especially if Mercury is negatively aspected by Mars or Uranus). You're generally very friendly and helpful, and you're especially adept at analyzing and solving problems with precision and speed. Do try, however, to cultivate consistency in all your efforts.

Sun sign Capricorn

with Mercury in Aquarius

Your strong Capricorn tendency to "do the right thing" at all times may well conflict with your fierce Aquarian love of individuality and independent thought and behavior. All being well, life itself will teach you that if you want to be happy, there must be give and take between these two opposing forces.

Sun sign Aquarius

with Mercury in Aquarius

There isn't any shortage of individuality with this combination of planet and sign, but you're also stubborn and inflexible. Worst of all, you find it difficult to accept that you're being difficult!

Sun sign Pisces
with Mercury in Aquarius

This is an admirable combination in many ways: Pisces's emotionality is balanced by Aquarius's objectivity and humanity. You aren't as likely as some Pisceans to be overwhelmed by your feelings. Furthermore, your excellent intuitive powers are backed up by a strong streak of logic.

Mercury in Pisces

Inconsistency and vagueness are almost certain to plague you. For instance, while you may have plenty of sympathy for one friend in distress, you may treat other friends with infuriating carelessness and forgetfulness. In most difficult situations your attitude is either, "Everything will be all right," or, "That has nothing to do with me!" In other words, you take the line of least resistance, and friends must learn to forgive that in you. Interestingly, considering your effect on people, shyness and lack of self-confidence also may be problems for you. Your intuition is keen and generally accurate, but your vivid imagination can give you trouble. You always fear the worst in any situation: a partner is late from the office, and of course he or she has been abducted by aliens! Be sure to look for grounding, stabilizing influences elsewhere in your chart.

Sun sign Aquarius
with Mercury in Pisces

It may be difficult for those Aquarians with Mercury in Pisces to detach themselves from their emotions, which will be very strong. You'll be warmly sympathetic to others, and the strain of perversity and unpredictability found in most Aquarians will be softened by sensitivity to other people and their feelings.

Sun sign Pisces
with Mercury in Pisces

Confusion and muddle surround you, and you're so scatterbrained that your best intentions to get organized may never be realized. But you're a wonderfully sensitive, kindly person, and your vivid imagination helps you express yourself creatively.

Sun sign Aries
with Mercury in Pisces

Arien selfishness and aggression should be tempered by Mercury (unless Venus is exerting a strong influence elsewhere in your chart). You tend to be forgetful, particularly about minor things, which irritates you no end. You're likely to be less decisive than a pure Arien, but you're also far less inclined to Arien anger.

Mercury through the houses

THE AREAS OF LIFE *ruled by the house in which Mercury is found will be the focus of much thought and analysis on your part. Mercury will also influence how you think about those areas of life: Logically or intuitively; optimistically or pessimistically; sensibly or fantastically. Look for other influences in your chart that can help you determine if you think constructively (with a good dash of common sense), or if you're prone to flights of brilliant fancy (that have no backbone to them).*

Mercury in the first house

"Mercurial" is certainly the word which describes you best: you're talkative, quick-witted, changeable, and versatile. You have a tremendous need to communicate – and all the tools with which to communicate well – but you can muddy the message with your dual tendency to be superficial and restless. The positive aspects received by Mercury in your chart may act to counter your less-than-likable qualities. Mercury's aspects will also color your general outlook, particularly whether you approach life with optimism or pessimism.

Mercury in the second house

You love a bargain, and you strike a hard one. You especially enjoy bartering and probably play the market. Buying and selling shares is wonderfully engrossing and even profitable hobby for you – even on a small scale.
Your attitude toward money is very sound, and your flair for investment can be trusted. But beware: you may have terrible tendency to be taken in by get-rich-quick schemes.

Mercury in the third house

Communication is a major theme in your life, though you may be more interested in how you say something than in what you say! In fact, you're often not sure what's on your mind until it comes out of your mouth! You use that agile, quick mind and your keen powers of observation to learn a little bit about everything in general, but not a great deal about one thing in particular.

Mercury in the fourth house

Family is especially important to you. Nevertheless, you're often restless, may feel somewhat insecure in your home, and frequently think about "moving on." (This is particularly likely if the Sun and Moon are in negative aspect to each other – an aspect which often indicates inner discontent).

Mercury in the fifth house

Risk-taking – whether based on intuition, logic, or practicality – is probably one of your strongest traits. You're also a prize flirt, always able to say the most flattering and romantic things – and no doubt you reap an abundance of rewards! For you, planning a seduction is almost as enjoyable as following through on it! Unfortunately, your victims may make the mistake of assuming they are your one true love. Be prepared for trouble on that front!

Mercury in the sixth house

If there are indications elsewhere in your chart that you're likely to be a worrier, then worry will certainly be a big part of your life. Moreover, it can lead to physical problems – stomach upsets and headaches, for example. You tend to fixate on difficulties and problems, gnawing at them like a dog at a bone. A vigorous and well-planned exercise regimen will help counter this problem.

Mercury in the seventh house

You are an excellent partner, as long as you keep the lines of communication open. Try not to lean on your partner too much. If he or she is stronger-minded than you, you can fall into the trap of handing over all the decision-making to him or her.

Mercury in the eighth house

This placement makes for a rather serious person with a strong philosophical bent. The latter tendency can grow to overwhelming proportions – especially if Neptune and the Moon are badly aspected. You may find yourself so  concerned with the great unsolvable mysteries of life and death that you forsake real life almost entirely. On the other hand, this placing of Mercury often produces an above-average, inventive sexual drive, together with a significant (sexual) fantasy life.

Mercury in the ninth house

The ninth was once known as "the house of dreams," and individuals with Mercury here are sometimes daydreamers whose potential is never fully realized. You have a fascination for travel that's connected with your frequent compulsion to "get away from it all," as well as your belief that the grass is lusher in tropical climes. Of course, this is rarely the case.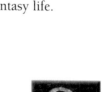

Mercury in the tenth house

You may find it quite difficult to settle down in one career. And even when you're settled, your aspirations and ambitions change from year to year, decade to decade. You need a job that provides as much day-to-day variation as possible. Otherwise, boredom may become a real problem for you.

Mercury in the eleventh house

A good and varied social life is very important to you. And while you may not have many close friends, you certainly have a wide range of acquaintances. You're also likely to be a valuable member of a group or committee which has great significance for you.

Mercury in the twelfth house

The twelfth house is all intuition and emotion, while Mercury is a logical planet – obviously there could be some conflict here, especially if Mercury is in a water sign. If your intuition can be rationalized and your emotions properly channeled, there'll be no problems, and a lot of benefit will be reaped.

The aspects of Mercury

MERCURY'S ASPECTS *emphasize the intellectual in any planet that it contacts. Mercury's influence can almost always be used positively, since the planet encourages a lively and expressive mind. Negative aspects, on the other hand, often produce accompanying stress and nervous tension (especially where Uranus is concerned).*

(For Mercury's aspects to the Sun, see the Sun's aspects to Mercury, p. 254. For Mercury's aspects to the Moon, see the Moon's aspects to Mercury, p. 269.)

Mercury's aspects to Venus

Note: Because Mercury and Venus are never more than 76 degrees apart, they can only form the conjunction, semi-sextile, sextile, and semi-square. Here we discuss all the aspects but the semi-square aspect, which is beyond the scope of this book.

Conjunction

Good powers of communication are emphasized here, and you find it easy to communicate with lovers, friends, and colleagues. Your lucky partner is treated to a generous dose of love, natural sympathy, and understanding.

The sextile

Open friendliness is the mark of this aspect, which traditionally encourages an interest and skill in craft work, particularly work with textured materials.

Mercury's aspects to Mars

Conjunction

This is a marvelously winning aspect that energizes and quickens the mind and supports a capacity for strenuous mental work. You're fast-thinking, decisive, assertive, and competitive.

Positive aspects

Here you find the same winning aspects highlighted by the conjunction, with the added benefit of a strong nervous system which easily shakes off strain and tension

Negative aspects

Your intellectual energy is sharpened, much as with the conjunction and the positive aspects, but nervous tension can be a problem. You have a tendency to act before you think.

Mercury's aspects to Jupiter

Conjunction

You have considerable brain power. If creativity is indicated elsewhere in the chart – in the arts or the sciences – you have a tremendous potential for substantial achievements.

Positive Aspects

Besides having a great mind, you're also good-natured and optimistic. You have a tendency, however, to be too easygoing.

Negative aspects

You may be a trifle absentminded and have a tendency to exaggerate and be careless. You're a healthy skeptic, but you ignore details. Remember to read the small print before you sign any contract or agreement.

Mercury's aspects to Saturn

Conjunction

This strong aspect encourages a serious outlook, common sense, caution, practicality, and a degree of pessimism. You may have excellent powers of concentration, and the ability both to develop and to carry out long-term plans.

Positive aspects

This aspect has a positive grounding effect on your personality, particularly if you're especially lively, optimistic, and enthusiastic. Here you use your mind carefully and methodically, and you always have the right thing to say. People depend on you a good deal, and you're known for your reliability.

Negative aspects

You have a passion for order and neatness that may border on the obsessional (and drive some people crazy!). You also may be rather narrow-minded, easily shocked, shy, and lacking in self-confidence.

Mercury's aspects to Uranus

Note: Aspects between these two planets are often found in the charts of professional astrologers!

Conjunction

You're fiercely independent, but you may also be stubborn and self-willed – especially if these tendencies appear elsewhere in the birth chart. You're original, quick-witted, and versatile, but you may be a private person who needs a good deal of your private space.

Positive aspects

The influences of the conjunction are seen here, including a need for independence. They are intensified if Leo or Jupiter is prominent in your birth chart, or if Mercury or Uranus is a personal planet.

Negative aspects

You have a bright and original mind, but nervous tension may cause you to be tactless and to speak first, think later.

Mercury's aspects to Neptune

Conjunction

Mercury's intellect combines with Neptune's imagination and inspiration. This can make for a charming and eccentric character – though you won't be celebrated for your common sense! Watch out for a tendency to engage in daydreaming

Positive aspects

The same influences seen in the conjunction – a fanciful combination of intellect, imagination, and inspiration – are graced with kindness, gentleness, and sensitivity.

Negative aspects

Native cunning – and a tendency to deceive – are emphasized here. If Mercury or Neptune is a personal planet, self-deceit and avoidance of reality may also be present. Look for helpful grounding influences – practicality, for example – elsewhere in the chart.

Mercury's aspects to Pluto

Conjunction

You possess great intuitive powers, enjoy self-analysis and problem-solving, and are gifted with the ability to think deeply and thoroughly about psychological issues. If there's a problem that can be solved through self-examination, you're the one who can do it. But watch out for a tendency to hold on too long to that problem, examining every facet of it to the point of mental exhaustion.

Positive aspects

You pay extraordinary attention to detail and enjoy studying a subject in great depth. You possess all the personal problem-solving skills highlighted in the conjunction. And if Mercury or Pluto are personal planets, you solve those problems even more quickly and easily.

Negative aspects

You tend to be secretive and to avoid discussing your personal problems. In fact, you can be stubbornly obsessive about protecting your private life, even when this causes problems for you and those around you.

Mercury's aspects to the Ascendant

Conjunction

You're quick thinking, versatile, and enjoy communicating your ideas – which you do very well indeed. Watch out for possible problems with your nervous system and for a tendency to be overly restless.

Positive aspects

Here we see the same aspects as in the conjunction – quick-wittedness, versatility, and the ability to communicate well – but they are less powerfully expressed here.

Negative aspects

Nervous tension can be a real problem here. And you express that nervousness in the way you communicate. For example, the more nervous you are, the more you talk – and the faster you talk! You also may worry too much about your health.

Mercury's aspects to the Midheaven

Conjunction

You probably won't be able to avoid flitting about. You may channel this restless tendency into a love of travel, but you're just as likely to fly from job to job. In fact, you feel compelled to do the latter. Just remember that you may have to pay a substantial physical and mental price for spending your whole life moving from here to there to here again.

Positive aspects

The same influences seen in the conjunction are also indicated here, but they have far less potency. Mercury exerts a more positive influence on these positive aspects, and restlessness will rarely be damaging.

Negative aspects

You may suffer from repeated bouts of nervous strain and tension, especially when you have to make decisions. This difficulty will be intensified if Mercury is a personal planet.

A simple summary

✔ Mercury's greatest influence – in a sign, house, or aspect – is on the mind and on how we think and problem-solve (fast or slow; logically or emotionally). The planet also strongly influences how we make decisions and how we communicate with others.

✔ Mercury is always within 28 degrees of the Sun. Therefore in a birth chart, Mercury can only be found in three signs: the sign in which the Sun appears, the sign before the one which contains the Sun, or the sign after.

✔ In the houses, Mercury influences how we think about the specific areas of life governed by the house in which Mercury is placed. For example, is our intellectual approach to a specific area or issue sensible or intuitive, optimistic or pessimistic?

✔ In aspect, Mercury emphasizes the intellectual component of any planet it contacts. In general, Mercury's aspects encourage quick-wittedness, imagination, and good communication skills. Occasionally these positive qualities are accompanied by nervous tension and stress.

Chapter 17

Venus at Work

VENUS INFLUENCES THE WAY we relate to and feel about others, from both a social and an economic perspective. The planet is strongly associated with the notion of partnership, both on a personal and professional level. Our attitudes and behavior toward love, sex, money, and possessions (and how we engage in and/or acquire them) are also influenced by Venus's placement in a sign, house, or an aspect. It is useful to remember, here, how often our feelings about love are similar to our feelings about money!

In this chapter...
✔ *Venus through the signs*
✔ *Venus through the houses*
✔ *The aspects of Venus*

VENUS WAS THE ROMAN GODDESS OF LOVE

Venus through the signs

VENUS IS ONE of the inferior planets (Mercury is the other; see Chapter 16) *whose orbit lies between the Earth and the Sun. From Earth, therefore, Venus appears near the Sun. Likewise, in the birth chart Venus can never be more than 48 degrees from the Sun.*

Remember that each of the 12 zodiac bands (one for each sign) is only 30 degrees wide. Because Venus is always within 48 degrees of the Sun, it can only be found in five signs on the birth chart: the same sign in which the Sun appears; or in either of the two signs before the one in which the Sun appears; or in either of the two signs after the one in which the Sun appears.

For example, if your Sun sign is Cancer, Venus can only appear in Cancer, Taurus, Gemini, Leo, or Virgo. Put another way: if Venus is in Cancer on your birth chart (and you drew up the chart correctly!), your Sun sign can only be Taurus, Gemini, Cancer, Leo, or Virgo. If you're a Pisces, and your birth chart shows Venus in Cancer, you'll need to recast your chart!

Venus in Aries

You're passionate, energetic, and enterprising. You may often take extreme risks in money-making ventures and must be careful about financial losses. More than many, you need sexual fulfillment to live a happy and stress-free life. And you won't tolerate a partner who isn't as enthusiastic in bed as you are.

Sun sign Aquarius
with Venus in Aries
The rather cool attributes of the Aquarian Sun are warmed by Venus from Aries. In an emotional relationship you're warm and intense, though you may hesitate if a partner wants to make a deeper commitment to the relationship.

Sun sign Pisces
with Venus in Aries
Here, the fiery passion of Aries wins out over the watery emotionality of Pisces. But Pisces adds tenderness to this passion, and you are therefore a splendid and caring lover.

Sun sign Aries

with Venus in Aries

Passion and enthusiasm, mixed with generosity and a certain amount of selfishness, make you an interesting lover. You crave independence and avoid instant commitments.

Sun sign Taurus

with Venus in Aries

You're highly emotional and very passionate. You're also an expressive, expert lover, but sudden emotional outbursts can capsize your love boat.

Sun sign Gemini

with Venus in Aries

You tend to overexamine and rationalize your relationships and must work hard at expressing your emotions. You may find that you have a greater talent for friendship than for passionate love.

Venus in Taurus

Venus rules Taurus, so its influence is intensified here. You're a hard worker and crave luxury and comfort, beautiful art, and good food. In the bedroom, you're a passive, sensual, romantic, and warm lover, and you easily express your affection. Possessiveness, however, may be a problem. Remember, your lover doesn't belong to you.

Sun sign Pisces

with Venus in Taurus

Pisceans with this placing of Venus will be steady, forthright, commonsensical, practical, and good with money. You're a reliable friend, though sometimes rather possessive. Your natural creativity is strengthened here.

Sun sign Aries

with Venus in Taurus

This combination of Aries with Venus in Taurus makes you seethingly passionate – so much so that you must work hard at tempering your fiery enthusiasm with a modicum of prudence. If you don't, you can seriously damage your personal and professional relationships. You may appear cautious and slow moving when it comes to love, but the object of your affection will have no doubts about your intentions . . . or the intensity of your passion.

Sun sign Taurus

with Venus in Taurus

You are quintessentially Taurean, a lover of sensuality, romance, money, and beautiful people and things. You prize emotional and financial security above all else, with good food and drink a close second. Since your metabolism is notoriously slow, not putting on excess weight is a real challenge.

Sun sign Gemini

with Venus in Taurus

If you want to be happy in love, express your emotions, which are warmer than with pure Geminians. You're quick-witted, love good conversation, and are rarely possessive (like most Taureans). But you have expensive tastes and love luxurious things.

Sun sign Cancer

with Venus in Taurus

You're a caring and sensitive lover, and life for you and those you love is generally happy. Take care, however, not to let Taurean possessiveness combine with your Cancerian need to protect: the combination will create a claustrophobic atmosphere which will drive away most people.

Venus in Gemini

You're a fun-loving friend and a lively, enthusiastic lover. Depending on your Sun sign (*see below*), you may not express your emotions well in love, but you're invariably a delightful friend. You're also a terrible flirt, and along with that comes a definite tendency to spread yourself around. Inevitably you try (or have tried) to juggle several relationships at once. You need a partner who can cope with this, and who's prepared to accept your considerable enthusiasm and passionate sexuality as compensation for any small deceits.

Sun sign Aries

with Venus in Gemini

Arien selfishness combined with Geminian flirtation can make you the kind of person who doesn't care who gets hurt as long as you get what you want.

Sun sign Taurus

with Venus in Gemini

All the Taurean charms are enhanced by this position of Venus –
warmth, sensuality, romance, and affection. Your Taurean
tendency
to sometimes be too possessive and serious-minded is
considerably tempered by the placement of Venus (which is
Taurus's ruling planet) in Gemini.

Sun sign Gemini

with Venus in Gemini

You have a strong tendency to engage in dangerously high levels of flirtation and
seduction. Your excuse for this behavior is typical: you believe that love doesn't enter
into flirtation and seduction, so they're not really important in the end. The latter is
an example of another of your bad tendencies – overrationalizing and de-emphasizing
important feelings (and often hurting others in the process). True romance and love will
elude you if you can't get these destructive influences under control.

Sun sign Cancer

with Venus in Gemini

The Cancerian tendency to be overemotional and worry
excessively is greatly tempered by Venus in Gemini, making for
a more balanced approach to love and life. In love, you need a
partner who has a mind as well as a body, and friendship is just
as important as passion. Cancer's faithfulness will generally win
out over Gemini's flirtatiousness! Outside the home, you're a
shrewd business person.

Sun sign Leo

with Venus in Gemini

Flirtatiousness is inevitable here, but an equal need for
genuine love and affection may help you to counter that
tendency when you believe you have found the right
lover. In a relationship, you need much more than love
and passion. Friendship, generosity, and the ability to enjoy
life, with all its ups and downs, are equally necessary.

Venus in Cancer

With Venus in Cancer you have a keen need for a very secure relationship. But be careful about mistaking claustrophobic overprotection for security! While you're loving, kind, and sympathetic, your driving desire to take care of your family may translate into being too emotional and too protective – both of which may do more harm than good.

Sun sign Taurus

with Venus in Cancer

Here love and affection are enhanced by sensual passion. Possessiveness, however, can be a problem, occasionally causing stormy times during a relationship. When a relationship ends, try to make a clean break. Clinging to a relationship long after it's over can be fatal. Trying to think logically and rationally may help. Applying your excellent business sense to the business of relationships may also be helpful.

Sun sign Gemini

with Venus in Cancer

The typical Geminian coolness is warmed by Venus in Cancer; emotions and romantic love are positively expressed – though you need an exciting and stimulating sex life, as most pure Geminians do. You're a marvelous friend and can communicate easily with those around you.

Sun sign Cancer

with Venus in Cancer

Worrying is a really big problem for you. Any relationship, however passionate and emotional, may be ruined by your constant concern about your lover or spouse. You're also driven to look after your friends and may be viewed as too possessive because of this. Try to keep a check on these tendencies, or you may push away the very people you care most for.

Sun sign Leo

with Venus in Cancer

Here, a high level of emotionality combines with Leo's naturally commanding manner, and your lover or spouse may feel emotionally dominated. Worse, you put your loved one on a pedestal, and you view any slips or actual falls as fatal to the relationship.

Sun sign Virgo

with Venus in Cancer

You're very emotional, but also shy and reserved, so you may have difficulty expressing your feelings. Worrying too much about a loved one will almost certainly be an element of any relationship. Watch out, too, for a tendency to overcriticize those you love.

Venus in Leo

As a lover or spouse, you are loyal and faithful. But you are also drawn to high drama – a tendency that can lead to trouble if not watched. You prefer a very comfortable, if not luxurious, lifestyle, and are driven to earn a good deal of money to support that style. You're a wonderfully exuberant, and entertaining, friend – though sometimes a bit bossy – and you are prized for your optimism and enthusiasm.

Sun sign Gemini

with Venus in Leo

You need sexual variety and you pursue it – even when that means being unfaithful to your current partner. Your partner, on the other hand, will never complain that life is dull with you. You bring to your relationships a wonderful sense of adventure and absolute enjoyment in all the simple pleasures that life has to offer.

Sun sign Cancer

with Venus in Leo

Here, Cancer's moodiness combines with Leo's commanding determination to call all the shots. This would be a dicey combination if not for the fact that you're such a caring, warm-hearted person. You're a faithful and extroverted partner, a constant and enthusiastic friend. Just keep an eye on the Leonine tendency to be bossy and the Cancerian tendency to be too emotional.

Sun sign Leo

with Venus in Leo

You're an enthusiastic, admiring, and buoyant partner, and you love nothing more than encouraging and supporting those dearest to you. But you do lean too strongly toward the extravagant and overly dramatic, and this can cause scenes and miscommunications (even though you are often "all talk, no action!"). Opt for diplomacy and tact over drama, occasional indulgences over out-and-out extravagance.

Sun sign Virgo

with Venus in Leo

Sexually, Virgo's modesty may clash with Leo's showiness, which can be confusing for both you and your lover. And please, watch out for your tendency to chatter . . . and chatter . . . when you're confused or nervous!

Sun sign Libra

with Venus in Leo

Venus rules Libra, so its influence, together with Leo's, will be quite strong here, making for a warm-hearted romantic who loves the good life. You're especially generous – even extravagant – with those you love and admire. But do watch for a tendency to try to buy others' affection.

Venus in Virgo

People with Venus in Virgo are naturally charming, unassuming, kindly, and genuinely modest. You're always willing to give practical help to someone in need. You may, however, be sexually nervous and inhibited. And you have a strong tendency to overcriticize and nag.

Sun sign Cancer

with Venus in Virgo

Cancerian moodiness plus the critical tendency which Venus encourages when in Virgo – you can see there might be a problem, especially as the Cancerian tendency to worry will be directed toward your partner

Sun sign Leo

with Venus in Virgo

Here we have Leo's imperious manner combined with Virgo's tendency to be overcritical. This is a recipe for certain trouble. Remember, too, that Leo's extravagance coupled with Virgo's caution can spell nothing but confusion. Recognize these less-than-lovely tendencies, try to control them, and look for positive countering influences elsewhere in your birth chart. On the plus side, you're a wonderfully lively and entertaining friend with terrific communication skills. Focus on both those traits!

Sun sign Virgo

with Venus in Virgo

Natural Virgoan modesty and gentility will charm almost everyone, but your lover or partner may find you rather frustrating in the bedroom. Try to remove these barriers between yourself and true fulfillment.

Sun sign Libra

with Venus in Virgo

Libran love and harmony and Virgoan shyness and inhibition make for a shaky mix. Try to find a balance between these two conflicting sides. When you do, people will find you a lively, talkative – though sometimes indecisive – individual who is a wonderfully loyal friend.

Sun sign Scorpio

with Venus in Virgo

At worst you may be obsessively concerned with sex – either vastly enthusiastic or extremely inhibited. At best, you're an energetic and thoughtful friend and partner. But do watch out for your tendency to be overly critical.

Venus in Libra

"Falling in love with love," could be your theme song, with this placement of Venus in Libra. You have an idealized, romantic view of love and prize simple affection as much as sex. You're a kind and sympathetic friend, have wonderful diplomatic skills, and a great love of luxury and comfort. On the negative side, you can be indecisive, resentful, sybaritic to a fault, and lazy – especially if the latter is indicated elsewhere in your birth chart.

Sun sign Leo

with Venus in Libra

Laid-back folk with this combination of signs and planets will love the good life, be generous to others as well as themselves, and make every outing or event you attend a special occasion.

Sun sign Virgo

with Venus in Libra

Venus working from Libra will help shy Virgoans relax and enjoy being in love.

Sun sign Libra

with Venus in Libra

All the Libran qualities – negative as well as positive – are emphasized here. And if the Sun and Venus are in conjunction, you'll be too Libran for words!

Sun sign Scorpio

with Venus in Libra

A dynamic Scorpio will have a rather surprisingly romantic side, with more sympathy and understanding for partners than seen in some purer Scorpios. But Libran resentfulness may join Scorpio jealousy to make life extremely difficult when problems arise.

Sun sign Sagittarius

with Venus in Libra

Unlike many Sagittarians, in love you enjoy the capture as much as the chase. You're less restless than is typical for your sign, and more romantic, exuberant, and philosophical.

Venus in Scorpio

People with Venus in Scorpio need all the elements of a happy love life if their relationship is going to be fulfilling and lasting: romance, a satisfying sex life, harmony, friendship, and affection. When all these positive elements are present, you should be able to cope with the almost inevitable (but usually occasional) displays of jealousy and resentfulness.

Sun sign Virgo

with Venus in Scorpio

Virgoan modesty will fight with Venus's sexy influence from Scorpio. You're probably extremely attractive, and if you can find just the right balance between Virgo and Venus . . . then Vavoom! will be the only word.

Sun sign Libra

with Venus in Scorpio

Behind the romance which is always a strong presence in Librans, there lies a sexual urge so dynamic that your initial air of romantic mystery lasts but a moment once you've made physical contact.

Sun sign Scorpio

with Venus in Scorpio

As we said in the introduction to this section – "Venus in Scorpio" (*see previous page*) – for a long-term and fulfilling love relationship, your partnership must include every element associated with a happy love life: romance, affection, friendship, harmony, and a satisfying sex life. It's a tall order, but one that individuals with this combination of planet and sign demand . . . and get! With this happy mix of love and harmony, you handle occasional jealousy and resentment with much more ease than typical Scorpios.

Sun sign Sagittarius

with Venus in Scorpio

Sagittarians are quite passionate to begin with, and Venus working from Scorpio may just overdo things a bit. For example, jealousy could be a very serious problem for you. And how your Sagittarian side will hate you for that!

Sun sign Capricorn

with Venus in Scorpio

You're sexually intense, but quite serious-minded as well. Not an easy combination, and you may never be able to enjoy the delicious high jinks you secretly desire.

Venus in Sagittarius

You often have more than one partner at the same time. This predilection for variety – together with a need for independence – may prevent you for quite some time from having a permanent relationship.

Sun sign Libra

with Venus in Sagittarius

Your insistence that you care for no one and don't need love is simply not true; you need romance as much as anyone else (though your lover will also have to be your friend). With this placement, you're a touch more rational than many pure Sagittarians.

Sun sign Scorpio

with Venus in Sagittarius

Scorpio jealousy combined with the Sagittarian need for freedom and a variety of lovers makes for a disturbing mix. Though Venus lightens Scorpio's intensity, it may not be enough to avoid trouble on the romantic front.

Sun sign Sagittarius

with Venus in Sagittarius

You love the chase above all else, and you so delight in romancing potential lovers that finally capturing them feels like an anticlimax! Your fickleness in love doesn't help matters at all.

Sun sign Capricorn

with Venus in Sagittarius

Serious Capricorns enjoy life more when Venus is in Sagittarius; you're less austere and more emotional. You enjoy a partner with ideas of his or her own, and in fact may draw inspiration from them.

Sun sign Aquarius

with Venus in Sagittarius

With a taste for sexual experimentation, you're also the last to rush into any long-term commitment.

Venus in Capricorn

Venus loves to love; Capricorn loves to get ahead in the world. The two ambitions don't sit well together. You may have difficulty expressing your feelings and your needs when in love.

Sun sign Scorpio

with Venus in Capricorn

Scorpio's deep intensity and Capricorn's cool calculation certainly doesn't suggest moonlight and roses in this combination! Watch out for a tendency toward ruthlessness in business, especially if you're keen to be number one on the corporate ladder.

Sun sign Sagittarius

with Venus in Capricorn

You take your love life quite seriously, though your Sagittarian passion is less strongly expressed here. You're loyal in love, but Capricornian discipline may conflict with Sagittarian freedom of action and expression.

Sun sign Capricorn

with Venus in Capricorn

Review the introduction to this section – "Venus in Capricorn." The problems are similar here, with a Sun-sign Capricorn, but greatly intensified. You have an additional tendency to let work get in the way of family life, but you're a faithful and loyal partner.

Sun sign Aquarius

with Venus in Capricorn

The Aquarian influence here may inhibit your having solid emotional relationships, and romantic impulses may actually be repressed. No matter how wildly attractive you are to others, you often present a cold and unapproachable face to the world.

Sun sign Pisces

with Venus in Capricorn

Earth and water mix well together, and so do Capricorn and Pisces. Venus will help temper the Piscean flow of emotions, and Capricorn's coolness brings much-needed caution and common sense.

Venus in Aquarius

You love the idea of a relationship, but you don't want the restrictions that come along with it. A pity, because you have a considerable capacity to enjoy straight-out romance.

Sun sign Sagittarius

with Venus in Aquarius

The passionate side of Sagittarius is cooled by Aquarius, and the love of independence is increased. You're a faithful partner, once committed, with a casual but glamorous image.

Sun sign Capricorn

with Venus in Aquarius

You often appear aloof, and sometimes give the impression that nobody is quite good enough for you. These attitudes are simply ruses, designed to help you put off expressing your emotions and making a commitment.

Sun sign Aquarius

with Venus in Aquarius

You have a fierce desire for love and admiration, but an even stronger need for independence. It's difficult – if not impossible – for you to make lasting commitments, because of the restrictions a relationship can put on your independent lifestyle.

Sun sign Pisces

with Venus in Aquarius

Here originality and sparkle combine with practical common sense. You easily distance yourself from your surface emotions and tend to rely on intuition instead. On the financial side, you should seek practical advice on all money matters.

Sun sign Aries

with Venus in Aquarius

Venus's cool detachment dilutes Arien passion, and the desire for a permanent relationship may be dampened by the need for independence. You have a flair for shrewd investment, but an unfortunate tendency to act too hastily in some money matters.

Venus in Pisces

You need to express all your emotions, and hopefully you will do so with someone who is worthy of you. Remember: You have a tendency to deceive yourself about the real intentions of possible partners. Others can easily take advantage of you as well. You're an easy touch and freely give money to what seem like good causes – whether they really are or not.

Sun sign Capricorn
with Venus in Pisces
The gullibility of Pisces is less operative when Capricorn is the Sun sign. At the same time, Venus in Pisces softens your cool Capricornian heart. Here you have the best of both worlds.

Sun sign Aquarius
with Venus in Pisces
The coolness of Aquarius is warmed by Venus from Pisces, and emotional involvements are less difficult for you. Piscean emotion will make Aquarian independence less impervious to attack from a possible lover!

Sun sign Pisces
with Venus in Pisces
Emotions can all too easily drown someone with this combination of planet and sign. Beware of becoming a doormat for anyone able to spin a good yarn.

Sun sign Aries
with Venus in Pisces
Warmth, kindness, and emotionality are combined here with assertiveness and inner strength – and a fine combination it is! You're charitable and kind, without being gullible or overcritical. What's more, you're very sexually exuberant with a receptive partner.

Sun sign Taurus
with Venus in Pisces
This combination brings deeply felt but very gentle emotions, unencumbered by typical Taurean possessiveness. You're a wonderfully sensual, passionate, and caring lover and partner.

Venus through the houses

IN THE HOUSES, Venus strongly influences how you handle all your deeply personal relationships, including love, marriage, and business partnerships, in the areas of life ruled by the house in which the planet appears. These influences are most strongly seen in the two traditionally Venusian houses: the second house (of money, possessions, business partnerships, and artistic endeavors) and the seventh house (of emotional relationships).

Venus in the first house

You need to be in a loving relationship; if you aren't in one, you may feel you're not living a full life. You're a graceful, charming person, innately kind and sympathetic, happy to have a relaxed and easy conversation any time. Indeed, you always seem to have time to spare. You may appear rather slow moving and laid-back in your approach to life, but no one should mistake your easygoing attitude for a lack of smarts – you've got plenty of brain power!

Venus in the second house

Don't let possessiveness run wild and unchecked! Family members may wind up on the mantelpiece, along with your other souvenirs and possessions! Collecting beautiful things will be an important part of your life, as will financial security. Your keen appreciation of beauty is heightened by Venus's presence in this house.

Venus in the third house

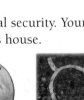

You have no difficulty communicating, even when what you have to communicate is difficult; and very often it will be because you love intellectual challenges and often study complex subjects slowly and meticulously. But you also like socializing, and will have no difficulty maintaining close relationships with friends and family.

Venus in the fourth house

Be it never so humble, there's certainly no place like home for those with Venus in the fourth house. You go to enormous lengths to ensure that your home is both beautiful and comfortable, and then you're very happy to

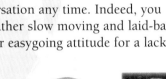

remain cozily inside it, surrounded by your family. But when the family grows up and begins to leave home, trouble starts. You'll hate it when your beautiful nest begins to empty. Be prepared!

Venus in the fifth house

A good, happy, fulfilling love life is important to everyone, but for those with Venus in the fifth house it's absolutely essential if they're to prosper and be happy. You probably have a pretty colorful love life already, sumptuously founded on romance and fantasy, and filled with luxurious comforts – no expenses spared. You may love the arts, too, and in fact have artistic ability yourself.

Venus in the sixth house

Weight-loss programs should really direct their advertising at those with Venus in the sixth. The planet in this placement does indeed seem to encourage people to eat, drink, and be merry to such an extent that extra

pounds – or kilos – are inevitable. This tendency toward overindulgence isn't helped at all by your keen dislike of exercise. As far as work goes, you will respond well to constructive criticism and thrive on a steady routine, but you do hate dirty or unpleasant working conditions.

Venus in the seventh house

You need a partner so much that you may rush into a commitment before really thinking it through. Once committed, it's all too easy for you to take on the

personality of your partner, through sheer love and admiration of him or her. Work hard at establishing a properly balanced friendship within the relationship, where good communication and mutual aims are as important as a happy and rewarding sex life.

Venus in the eighth house

You should have an extremely healthy and bouncy sex life. However, if Venus is inhibited by Saturn or Pluto, psychological problems may arise. Luckily, you have

generous reserves of insight and sympathy, both of which will help you resolve any inhibitions. This house is associated with inheritance – but don't hold your breath!

Venus in the ninth house

You love to travel and do it as much as you possibly can. You're a relaxed and philosophical person whose aim is to live happily in peace and quiet. Traditionally, astrologers have suggested that you tend both to marry people from overseas and to live abroad. In fact, this very often is the case.

Venus in the tenth house

You work better with others than on your own, and consequently you are not happy in a position of power which cuts you off from your colleagues. You don't cope well with responsibility anyway. Indeed, you're sometimes a bit lazy and lethargic.

Venus in the eleventh house

You move among a wide circle of acquaintances, and apart from enjoying a wonderful social life, you work well with others in charitable organizations or social justice groups. You thrive on admiration and the respect of your peers, and that can contribute to your motivation for working as hard as you often do for humanitarian and social causes.

Venus in the twelfth house

If ever there was a placing of Venus that encourages secret love affairs, this is it! Indeed, clandestine romances are frequently found in the lives of those with Venus in the twelfth. Frequently, however, it's an unrealized love affair that's kept secret, often because you are too shy to express your feelings, or for some reason can't.

The aspects of Venus

*IN TRADITIONAL ASTROLOGY, Venus is known as a beneficial planet – or more archaically, as a **benefic**. This means that its effects are almost always positive, and this is true with respect to the aspects it makes with the planets it contacts. Venus's influence in aspect is viewed as negative only when it tends to overexaggerate another planet's positive qualities; when excessive charm borders on superficiality or gentle sensitivity becomes thin-skinned vulnerability.*

(For Venus's aspects to the Sun, see the Sun's aspects to Venus, p. 254.
For Venus's aspects to the Moon, see the Moon's aspects to Venus, p. 270.
For Venus's aspects to Mercury, see Mercury's aspects to Venus, p. 292.)

Venus's aspects to Mars

Conjunction

Mars coarsens the effects of Venus, while Venus refines
the appetites of Mars: a very fine mix indeed. You have
a healthy appetite for all the good things of life, plenty of exuberance and enthusiasm,
as well as a fine ration of sensitivity and affection.

Positive aspects

Here we see the same influences as in the conjunction, but the *element* of
the planet in which the conjunction falls considerably modifies these
influences: air encourages detachment; earth indicates a need for security;
fire brings enthusiasm and passion; water underscores sensuality.

Negative aspects

Here we see the same influences as in the conjunction, but the *element* of
These aspects enliven your attitude to love and sex and increase your
appetite for a variety of things – especially sex. Chronic tension may be
a problem, and you may have to work at learning to relax before you
can enjoy your sex life.

Venus's aspects to Jupiter

Conjunction

Venus's conjunction with Jupiter
brings an excess of charm and
generosity, and so it's no surprise
that you're extremely popular.
You have a wonderfully
philosophical, unworried, and even idealistic outlook on life.

Positive aspects

Very popular and amusing, you find it easy to
deal with other people. These aspects also often
indicate a long life.

Negative aspects

Restlessness and occasional discontent are indicated here, both of which may encourage overeating and excessive drinking – and possible poor health.

Venus's aspects to Saturn

Conjunction

Shyness, inhibition, and a rather cool attitude about personal relationships may result from the conjunction of these two planets. It's difficult to know you or get close to you, and a happy love life may elude you.

Positive aspects

The tendency toward inhibition and shyness is less powerful here than in the conjunction. A love of luxury is emphasized, but with it possible financial difficulties.

Negative aspects

Inhibiting influences are very potent here, though you can conquer them if positive emotional energy is emphasized elsewhere in the birth chart. If not, consider getting professional help.

Venus's aspects to Uranus

Conjunction

You have great personal magnetism and enormous sex appeal, but you tend to keep potential partners at a distance. Watch out for an element of perversity in your life, and for excess nervous tension which needs positive expression.

Positive aspects

The effects felt here are similar to those of the conjunction, but they are far less intense. Moreover, creativity and originality are encouraged, and provide you with positive and constructive outlets for any nervous strain. The tendency to distance yourself from a partner, however, is even more strongly emphasized, and may perhaps cause an unhappy breakup.

Negative aspects

The negative aspects encourage strain and tension within personal relationships. You also have great difficulty relaxing, and the annoying tendency to say one thing but mean another.

Venus's aspects to Neptune

Conjunction

A romantic and idealistic attitude toward life is joined by great sensitivity (especially if the conjunction falls in Libra). This is a lovely, gentle combination of qualities, but one that can also leave you vulnerable to heartbreak.

Positive aspects

Sympathy and kindness add a delightful gentleness to your otherwise practical and down-to-earth personality. And this despite the fact that you often pretend your softer side doesn't exist!

Negative aspects

These aspects intensify any restlessness and discontent that appear elsewhere in your chart. Look at the position of the Sun and the Moon. If they're in negative aspect, you might be experiencing some serious stability problems. You could find yourself drifting from job to job, person to person, and never settling down.

Venus's aspects to Pluto

Conjunction

When you fall in love, you fall suddenly and deeply. When that love is reciprocated, you both share an enviable degree of high passion and deep sexual fulfillment. Interestingly, this powerful positive aspect also often indicates a gift for financial wheeling and dealing.

Positive aspects

You're highly sexual and emotional, qualities that must be satisfied with an equally passionate partner. It won't be difficult to attract that partner because you're distinctly attractive and possess a smoldering intensity.

Negative aspects

Your emotional energies may be blocked, and your intensity and passion unexpressed. If these are caused by specific problems, you'll find it difficult to talk about them to anyone close. Professional help may be the answer.

Venus's aspects to the Ascendant

Conjunction

A long-term and secure partnership is essential to you. You're warm and affectionate and should have little difficulty establishing a peaceful, harmonious life with the right person. You have a keen appreciation of beauty. Watch out for a sluggish metabolism that may be mistaken for laziness (or encourage weight gain).

Positive aspects

Here we find the need to give and receive love particularly emphasized. You're sympathetic and understanding, and have a full and happy social life.

Negative aspects

Extravagance, self-indulgence, resentfulness, and indecision are all possible influences of these aspects.

Venus's aspects to the Midheaven

Conjunction

You're a kind and considerate colleague at work, though you do perform better in a team than alone. If you find yourself in a position of authority, however, you're a sympathetic boss with good listening skills. Do watch out for your tendency not to be able to stick to a routine.

Positive aspects

The positive aspects are similar to those of the conjunction. You enjoy pleasant working conditions and work hard to have a good relationship with your colleagues – especially if your job is somewhat dull. Outside the office, your good social life is a source of great contentment.

Negative aspects

These aspects indicate that you may be working in a dull and unrewarding job, which encourages discontent and resentfulness on your part. Possibly because of an abiding unhappiness and resentment in your life, you're sometimes viewed as arrogant and conceited.

A simple summary

✓ Venus influences our attitudes and behavior toward love, sex, money, and possessions (and how we go about getting all four). The planet also affects how we relate to others, both privately and in business, in terms of partnerships and joint ventures.

✓ Venus is one of the inferior planets and is always located within 48 degrees of the Sun. Therefore it can only be found in five signs on the birth chart: the same sign in which the Sun appears, or in either of the two signs before or after the one in which the Sun appears.

✓ In the houses, Venus influences how we view and handle all our strong relationships, including love, marriage, and business partnerships, in the areas of life ruled by the house in which the planet appears. Venus's effects are most strongly seen in the two houses traditionally associated with the planet: the second house and the seventh house.

✓ Because Venus is a "beneficial" planet, its effects – especially in aspect – are almost always positive; it enhances or expands the better qualities associated with the planets it contacts. Negative influences of Venus in aspect usually occur as over-exaggerations of normally positive characteristics. For example, Venus may turn natural charm into irritating superficiality.

Chapter 18

Mars at Work

NAMED FOR ARES, the ancient Greek god of war, the fiery red planet Mars influences our sex drive, physical energy levels, competitiveness, initiative, and assertiveness. The presence of Mars in the birth chart also indicates how quick we are to anger or to respond to stressful stimuli, since it governs the flow of adrenaline in our systems. The planet is also strongly associated with how aggressively we interact with the everyday world – both physically and verbally – especially when confronted with problems or conflicts that require swift action and immediate resolution. On the negative side, Mars rules explosive and violent situations and objects, and encourages hasty decisions and rude behavior.

In this chapter...
✓ Mars through the signs
✓ Mars through the houses
✓ The aspects of Mars

MARS WAS STRONGLY ASSOCIATED WITH ACTION AND ASSERTION IN MYTHOLOGY

Mars through the signs

MARS'S ORBIT is farther from the Sun than the Earth's, and so unlike Mercury and Venus (which are always found in the zodiac signs near the Sun in a birth chart), Mars can fall in any sign of the zodiac. Whether you are male or female, Mars's placement in a sign strengthens the masculine nature of that sign's qualities and characteristics, particularly with regard to physical strength and aggressive tendencies, emotional stability when stressed, and the type of behavior exhibited when decisive action is called for.

Mars in Aries

You're a strong, assertive type who knows where you want to go and won't hesitate to set out on the journey – whatever that journey may be. Sadly, however, you may be the sort of person who doesn't think twice about stepping on other people's toes as you go for the gold. In fact, you forget that the people you step on as you climb up the ladder of success won't be inclined to give you much support when you take a fall. You may learn this lesson the hard way. Your sex drive will be forceful and uncomplicated – nothing subtle there – and since you don't get mired down in complex emotions, you'll rarely have to deal with psychological blocks or difficulties. In fact, you're an uncomplicated person in just about every way.

Mars in Taurus

Your ample sex drive will be expressed in a delightfully Taurean way, with great warmth and affection. But you do need affection in return – and emotional security. Taurean patience will steady the Martian influence when you lose your temper, but the explosion may still be considerable. When you're enraged, your anger doesn't allow you to consider the feelings of others, who may be hurt by your words and actions. The best effect on Mars from Taurus is to give you determination, firmness, and the ability to work very hard and tenaciously both at your career and your hobbies.

Mars in Gemini

You're very versatile and energetic, and you find it difficult to relax. It's a good idea to have a number of projects going at the same time, so you can switch from one to the other as needed. You'll find this a good way to relax, to expend some of your famous energy, and to enjoy a variety of challenges and pleasures. You also enjoy variety and experimentation in your sexual life. Sex – which you probably view as the most fun one can have in life – is likely to be enjoyed for as long as is physically possible (which may mean until the very last minute!). On the other hand, other forms of exercise are so boring to people with Mars in Gemini that you may never take any at all; and the results will be all too obvious.

Mars in Cancer

Those with this combination of planet and sign will be eager to start a family. In Cancer, Mars has a distinct and powerful influence on the sex life. You're a sensuous lover who knows just what pleases your partner most, and you're more than eager to see that he or she gets it! Watch out for the Cancerian caring spirit's tendency to turn possessive; so much physical and mental energy may be spent on the partner's behalf that the atmosphere can get claustrophobic. You have a pretty short fuse, too, and once it gets to the point of combustion, the explosion will be short, sharp, and destructive.

Mars in Leo

Mars fits well into the Leonine scheme of things, and those with this combination are good organizers and leaders – even when they tend to dominate those with less extroverted tendencies. You express your emotions positively and really love life, getting special pleasure from allowing and encouraging others to enjoy themselves – in sex as well as in other areas. You must watch your tendency to dramatize everything, however, and to make horrendous mountains out of innocent little molehills. You hate petty-mindedness, but you yourself indulge in exaggeration and bombast. Your temper is quick and blows up out of nowhere, though the storm is usually over as quickly as it began.

Mars in Virgo

Mars and Virgo aren't particularly happy bedfellows, and your sex drive may not be especially strong or well-balanced. You're somewhat short on passion, though you can feel deeply about the environment or nature. This combination of Mars in Virgo makes for general uneasiness all around. You can be edgy and tense, restless and nervous, and need continual activity to use up an excess supply of nervous tension, which easily erupts into anger. Learn to control emotional tension with the help of such techniques as yoga and deep relaxation. At work, there's a lot to be said for this combination; it fuels excellent working habits, especially an exceptional (and sometimes obsessive) attention to detail.

Mars in Libra

The romantic Libran approach to life, delightful as far as it goes, is spiced up in a welcome way by Mars. You still crave romance, love, and harmony in a relationship, but you're also more sexually active than the typical Libran. On the other hand, Mars will find it difficult work indeed to exert any authority from its placement in Libra. Even Mars's considerable energy can be drained by the Libran "I can't-be-bothered" attitude. One of the planet's effects will be to encourage you to fall in love at first sight, which often leads to heartbreak. You may be troubled by headaches (perhaps caused by slight kidney upsets), and you tend to quarrel over nothing. You aren't keen on exercise, either, though you enjoy the social side of a good health club, which may tempt you into action.

Mars in Scorpio

Stand back. Mars and Scorpio combined make a satisfactory sex life absolutely necessary – and satisfaction means excitement, variety, experiment, vigor, regularity . . . All right, that sounds like a good recipe for all of us! But Mars in Scorpio must be sexually fulfilled, or trouble and real unhappiness will follow. Beware of jealousy, while you're at it, though ironically, you're the one who's far more likely to give your partners cause to be jealous! In the most extreme circumstances, you may really go on the warpath and set out to revenge yourself, sometimes for quite imaginary betrayals. You're a real whole hogger, too, going for the gusto in food and drink as much as in sex. You put on weight, diet relentlessly, and then the moment you've got the weight off, you set about putting it right back on. For relaxation, martial arts and water sports may appeal to you.

Mars in Sagittarius

Sagittarian energy – physical and mental – receives a welcome boost from Mars, but do remember that this additional energy must be properly channeled. That shouldn't be much of a problem for you, because you enjoy working on a variety of projects, especially those which demand physical as well as mental exertion. Try to keep a balance between your physical and mental endeavors, and you'll usually enjoy successful results all around. You're probably quite versatile, too, but you should keep an eye on this, since you have a tendency to fly too easily from one job to another – or indeed one lover to another. Your craving for adventure, excitement, and even danger can extend to your love life as well. And a sneaking enjoyment of risk-taking may translate to a love of gambling – with the attendant danger of addiction.

Mars in Capricorn

Those with this placing of Mars have considerable powers of endurance, which are an obvious advantage in some jobs and leisure activities – and certainly not to be sneezed at in bed! You're ambitious, and Mars will spur you on toward your objectives. You cope well with any risks (particularly physical risks) and are unlikely to be foolish enough to take unnecessary ones. All this makes for excellent athletes and sportsmen and -women in general. With determination to come first in everything (except in bed), you do well in any endeavor. You take sex seriously and think before making a move.

Mars in Aquarius

Aquarius is not a sign known for generous emotions, and not even Mars can do much to change that. The planet's main influence will be to endow you with a kind of eccentric zaniness and a keen sense of fantasy. Unfortunately, you can also be stubborn, and your work life is decidedly uneven: you often go at a project with a giant burst of energy, which is soon followed by what appears to be lazy inactivity. Personally, you sometimes feel compelled to get on with life, but you simply can't summon up the energy to do so. Nervous strain and tension may result, and you usually refuse offers of help. You're simply too independent and individualistic to take kindly to advice. With this combination of sign and planet, you can work well on behalf of others, particularly in world organizations devoted to the relief of suffering.

Mars in Pisces

With this planetary placement, the Piscean sex drive must be imaginatively expressed. You have a combination of ready emotion and sexual energy which takes some satisfying. And it must be satisfied if it's not to stagnate and cause psychological difficulties. Conversely, other individuals with Mars in Pisces sublimate sexual satisfaction in favor of sacrifice on behalf of others. Such individuals may pursue a vocation geared to helping those in need. You're sometimes indecisive and have a tendency to avoid facing reality; you may also not have a great deal of self-confidence or assertiveness. When a problem arises, you may try to escape by pretending it doesn't exist, by refusing to discuss it, or by turning to drugs. Gullibility can be a disadvantage, too. Your imagination is colorful and should be used creatively.

Mars through the houses

MARS'S PRIMARY EFFECT *in the houses is to energize those qualities and areas of life that the house governs. Thus you will expend a great deal of energy in very specific ways – read Mars's house placement (see next page), your Sun sign description (in Part 2), and your rising sign description (in Chapter 4) for clues to where you may primarily direct those energies. It will be up to you to decide whether that energy is used in a healthy, positive fashion or in an aggressively destructive way.*

Mars in the first house

You have tremendous willpower and a fierce desire to win in whatever field you decide to work. You have no patience at all with those slower than yourself, and you don't suffer fools gladly. You're always in a rush and enjoy challenges. You're also decidedly inclined to be selfish in pursuing your own ends. You may tend to be careless, and that can lead to accidents.

Mars in the second house

The energy from Mars in this house will be directed toward acquiring a fortune. And you enjoy your money, are pleased to spend it, and even happy to have others spend it with you. Whether the money comes through cautious investments, physical work, or intricate financial dealings depends on the sign in which Mars is placed. You're sexually passionate, and you give your partners considerable pleasure. But they'd better respond as passionately as you, or they won't be around for long.

Mars in the third house

A good knock-down-drag-out argument is what you enjoy more than almost anything else. And if you're keen on a particular theory or cause, you pursue it with enormous conviction. You're quite inquisitive and need to find the answer to any question that occurs to you – and you get thoroughly impatient if that answer doesn't come quickly. You drive fast, with a lot of nervous tension; a course in advanced driving skills is highly advisable.

Mars in the fourth house

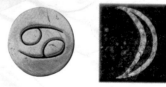

Family life, and often parenthood, will be welcomed when Mars is in the fourth house. The emphasis on the home may well give you an interest in do-it-yourself projects, and you probably spend a lot of time improving and redecorating your home. At the other end of the scale, you can become quickly bored by redecorating your surroundings and may move homes quite frequently.

Mars in the fifth house

An emphasis on sexual pleasure here should make for a very active and rewarding love life. You're an assertive lover, taking the lead in adventurous experimentation or simple, good fun. You obviously need a partner who's equally enthusiastic about joining in! You may be inclined to take risks, and the sign in which Mars is placed will give you clues about how to control and positively use this tendency. Beware the perils of gambling, however, which is an especially insidious form of risk taking.

Mars in the sixth house

Impatience with the petty things of life – the little everyday tasks that must be done – will bore the pants off you if you have Mars in the sixth house. At the same time you're a sturdy and enthusiastic worker, and you get through your daily routines with a sort of distasteful precision. Stress may affect you, especially physically, and can take the form of skin complaints. Positive aspects from the Sun, Moon, or ruling planet will bolster your physical strength and powers of recovery, and put some backbone into your nervous system.

Mars in the seventh house

You're really keen to make your partnerships work, and you put a lot of energy into them. Quarrels should be stopped before they start. Apart from that, Mars will be helpful in both your emotional and business life, encouraging joint interests. Your sex life will be positive and vigorous, and your sexual energy well channeled. There will still be plenty of energy left over, however, for you and your partner to share other interests, ensuring that the friendship within the partnership is lively and lasting.

Mars in the eighth house

You have a strong sex drive which must be expressed positively; otherwise you become generally dissatisfied and fed up with life. Watch out for a tendency to become obsessed with your own personality and emotions. You like to analyze every feeling and reaction. In the process, you waste an enormous amount of your time and energy – and usually get nowhere interesting. In the career arena, you may well be fascinated by the machinations of big business.

Mars in the ninth house

Mars exerts a brave influence from the ninth house: you're willing to tackle all sorts of challenges, and you approach those challenges with eagerness and joy. Your constant need to push forward in life may lead to frustration when advancement is slow or impossible, or when your plans are obstructed. If patience isn't indicated elsewhere in your chart, you respond to frustration with restlessness, which may be channeled into your love – indeed, your need – for travel.

Mars in the tenth house

There's an emphasis here on your career and/or professional life, where the probability of success is high. You can be argumentative and quarrelsome, as well as intolerant of people with slower minds. If Mars receives negative aspects from Uranus or the personal planets, nervous tension will build up and explosions may take place from time to time.

Mars in the eleventh house

You're a highly independent person who tends to be rather cool and detached. But you have a great enthusiasm for the social life, and you're probably a leader in your social circles. You're wonderfully adept at enthusing your friends to get involved in various projects, but do watch out for a tendency to bully them into action.

Mars in the twelfth house

This is an excellent placing of Mars for anyone who is in – or is thinking of going into – the caring professions. On a personal level, you may be rather secretive. It can be very difficult for you to share your own problems, however good you are at helping other people with theirs. You may well have a strong and colorful fantasy life.

The aspects of Mars

MARS INVIGORATES AND ENERGIZES *any planet it contacts, but the positive and negative influences of its aspects to these planets are perhaps more critically different and extreme than is generally seen with other aspected planets. On the positive side, Mars encourages singular action and achievement; on the negative side, it causes aggression and serious stress, both of which must be carefully managed.*

(For Mars's aspects to the Sun, see the Sun's aspects to Mars, p. 254.
For Mars's aspects to the Moon, see the Moon's aspects to Mars, p. 270.
For Mars's aspects to Mercury, see Mercury's aspects to Mars, p. 292.
For Mars's aspects to Venus, see Venus's aspects to Mars, p. 317.)

Mars's aspects to Jupiter

Conjunction

This aspect encourages action, enterprise, and the enthusiasm to tackle tasks from which others shrink. You can be overly argumentative, tempted to take risks, and you have a daring attitude toward money.

Positive aspects

Optimism, enthusiasm, and energetic action are emphasized here – but you find it easy to control yourself in an argument. You're physically active and lively and have a good mind in a healthy body.

Negative aspects

Restlessness is the main indication here. You also have a tendency to exaggerate and to overdo things in almost any area of life.

Mars's aspects to Saturn

Conjunction

There are times when you work until you drop; other times you lie about the house, lazily staring at your navel. Frustration for all accompanies this behavior!

Positive aspects

These aspects contribute endurance and determination; you delight in difficult conditions.

Negative aspects

Up, then down; hot, then cold; enthusiastic, then pessimistic; positive, then negative – all these roller-coaster emotions are emphasized here.

Mars's aspects to Uranus

Conjunction

Though you're stubborn and obstinate, you're also extremely determined and able, frank and outspoken – sometimes to the point of intolerance or fanaticism.

Positive aspects

Bright and active nervous energy will be a positive asset, as will originality and the ability to react quickly in almost any situation.

Negative aspects

Strain and tension will be increased if they're shown elsewhere in the birth chart, and argumentativeness and perversity will be encouraged.

Mars's aspects to Neptune

Conjunction

Your imagination will be keen, colorful, and active in a variety of areas, perhaps most especially in your sex life. You're warmly sensual, but if your sex life isn't satisfying, you get restless and have a difficult time resolving any intimate problems.

Positive aspects

Your sexual feelings are important to you, and you express them intensely but sensitively. Remember to keep a firm grip on reality, especially in love affairs.

Negative aspects

Negative escapism – smoking, drinking, taking drugs – is a distinct possibility here, particularly if you are under pressure.

Mars's aspects to Pluto

Conjunction

A fierce temper is almost inevitable if the conjunction is in Scorpio, or falls in Virgo and is joined by Uranus. Pent-up energy and emotion should be released in physical exercise.

Positive aspects

Both physical and emotional energy must be positively expressed, so physical exercise and a satisfactory partnership are desirable.

Negative aspects

You have lots of energy that can appear obsessional when it is driven by ambition. Beware of the tendency to see every molehill as a mountain.

Mars's aspects to the Ascendant

Conjunction

If Mars is in the first house, read the description of "Mars in the first house" (in this chapter) and multiply the planet's effects tenfold! And those effects will increase the closer Mars is to the Ascendant.

Positive aspects

You have great stores of physical energy that must be worked off at work or at play. You're independent and need plenty of action.

Negative aspects

You may have a tendency to overwork, especially if Mars is in the sixth house. If Mars is in the seventh house, a lively and sexually rewarding partnership is very necessary to you.

Mars's aspects to the Midheaven

Conjunction

A great will to succeed, together with ambition and independence, means that if you're really involved in your career, you'll be a winner.

Positive aspects

You have an infectious enthusiasm for your work and an ability to spur colleagues into action.

Negative aspects

You must develop patience if you don't want to offend colleagues with your constant complaining about how much slower than you they work. You, of course, work happily until you drop.

A simple summary

✔ Mars strongly influences sex drive, physical energy, competitiveness, initiative, and assertiveness. The planet also indicates how quickly we get angry or how positively (or negatively) we respond to stressful stimuli. Mars suggests how aggressively we react to everyday problems and how we communicate our aggressive tendencies to others.

✔ In the signs, Mars's placement strengthens the masculine side of a sign's qualities and characteristics, particularly with regard to physical strength, aggressive behavior, and how we solve problems. This holds true whether the birth chart is drawn up for a male or a female.

✔ In the houses, Mars energizes those qualities and areas of life governed by the house in which it is placed. Clues to how you express this excess energy – whether positively or negatively, constructively or destructively – can be found in the qualities and characteristics associated with both your Sun sign (in Part 2) and your rising sign (in Chapter 4).

✔ Mars singularly energizes the aspects to any planet it contacts, in either a positive or a negative fashion (with rarely a middle ground). On the positive side, the planet encourages decisive action and achievement; on the down side, it encourages aggression and severe stress.

Chapter 19

Jupiter at Work

JUPITER, THE LARGEST PLANET in the solar system, takes about 12 years to travel around the Sun and also through the 12 zodiac signs. The planet is associated with expansiveness, with physical and intellectual development, and with acquiring knowledge. On the positive side, Jupiter encourages a philosophical outlook, optimism, tolerance, and positively directed mental energies. On the negative side, it is associated with extravagance, gambling, wastefulness, blind optimism, and histrionic, disruptive behavior.

In this chapter...

✓ Jupiter through the signs

✓ Jupiter through the houses

✓ The aspects of Jupiter

ONCE RULER OF THE GODS, JUPITER'S INFLUENCE ON HUMANITY IS EXPANSIVE

Jupiter through the signs

TAKE TIME TO REVIEW THE QUALITIES of the Sun sign given in Part 2, bearing in mind the fact that Jupiter strongly influences one's intellectual or philosophical approach to the world. The planet is especially associated with learning and languages, with optimism, loyalty, and justice, and with self-indulgence and conceit.

Jupiter in Aries

Aries and Jupiter get on well together and make for people who are confident, broad-minded, and enthusiastic. You love freedom and have a real need to expand your life – perhaps through adventure or travel. You're keenly competitive; given the physical ability, you may become a highly successful athlete – though you must remember to regard sport as just a part of life and not the whole of it! If Jupiter is negatively aspected by the Sun, the Moon, or Mars, you may have a tendency to take undue risks, and it'll be worthwhile looking elsewhere in the chart for some calming influences. You're highly extroverted and don't hesitate to blow your own trumpet – even when the noise upsets others!

Jupiter in Taurus

Your basic desire to make money will often bring great success. With this placing of Jupiter you tend to have good instincts about investments, a flair for business, and a keen sense of timing. You're very sincere and have a warm sense of humor. You enjoy entertaining your friends and are particularly generous, taking the expansive view that money, like manure, needs to be spread around to do any good! You're also generous with yourself and love the sumptuous things in life, especially good food and wine.

Jupiter in Gemini

The ancient astrologers never much liked the idea of Jupiter in Gemini, and the planet certainly seems to be an unsettling influence. Jupiter encourages the Geminian's tendency to prefer a spattering of knowledge about almost everything in general, rather than a thorough knowledge of one thing in particular. This intellectual restlessness, together with your inclination to jump from one subject to another, means that you may not (or didn't) go far as a student. But it doesn't mean you can't achieve a great deal through your natural broad-mindedness and cleverness. Do try to remember, though, that there's no substitute for in-depth study. And if you try to get away too often with a crafty use of the bits of information you manage to acquire, you'll soon be found out.

Jupiter in Cancer

Jupiter has a wonderful influence in Cancer, boosting your innate intuitive and emotional gifts. You're naturally kind, sympathetic, understanding, caring, and protective, and you're concerned not only about the welfare of those close to you, but about the world at large. You work well in charitable organizations, whether in a professional or volunteer capacity. You pay a great deal of attention to your children – without spoiling them. And with a good imagination yourself, you'll be eager to strengthen and nurture your children's imagination. You're naturally shrewd in business and eager to broaden your knowledge of the field in which you choose to work. Your imaginative skills may be employed in creative work – writing, perhaps – but also in the fields of science and invention. You're inventive in the kitchen, too, and are quite possibly an excellent cook.

Jupiter in Leo

Jupiter is in a very extroverted mood in Leo, and the person with this placing in his or her chart will never be a shrinking violet. Indeed, you may tend to blow your own trumpet with a particularly raucous noise; showing off really can become a way of life. Not a lot of fun for those around you, especially since you can be pompous and bombastic at times. There are positive things about this placing, however, not the least of which are your optimism, generosity, enthusiasm – and your great ability to enthuse others. You're determined to live every moment of life to its fullest, and you simply hate wasting time. You really should learn to relax, occasionally. Unsurprisingly, perhaps, you may become a splendid actor; Jupiter in Leo will enable you to take center stage – and love it!

Jupiter in Virgo

You may well lack self-confidence and decisiveness, and be unable to act boldly when the situation demands it. However, you have a highly matter-of-fact attitude toward life. This can help you solve any problems that spring up because of your indecisiveness, and you should be able to choose an alternative – and better – course of action. Careerwise, you can go far. You're a natural, but healthy, skeptic – always an excellent quality – and your critical sensibilities are keen, provided you keep them under control and don't antagonize others too often.

Jupiter in Libra

This placement of Jupiter makes for a really attractive character – laid-back, sympathetic, charming, and friendly. But . . . you can be so laid-back that nothing ever gets done until tomorrow (which, of course, never comes!). You may also love the luxuries of life so much that whenever you have a little money everything stops – including work – so that you can take your time enjoying a plate of something good and a glass of something even better. Nor will you be especially keen on stretching your mind or accepting challenges. A partner may be able to help you be more grounded. Your need for a partner, by the way, will be great: you hate to be alone and you need to share. Be careful about relying too much on a partner , however, though he or she will certainly get ample love and affection in return.

Jupiter in Scorpio

Scorpio isn't a sign known for halfheartedness to begin with, but with Jupiter here you have a truly formidable power. You certainly want to live life to the fullest, even to the extent that burnout is possible if you're not careful. You need to be fully involved in almost every aspect of life – particularly in your career and love life – and you need to feel real satisfaction in all endeavors. Be careful about mental strain or breakdown, and if the latter occurs, look at those areas of your life where you may simply be trying too hard. Properly directed, all the energy of Jupiter in Scorpio can be of enormous advantage: you'll have tremendous staying power and the utmost determination to achieve your full potential. However, do watch out for your naturally suspicious nature; don't let it become obsessive. And keep an eye on your tendency to be vain and proud!

Jupiter in Sagittarius

Jupiter is Sagittarius's ruling planet, and thus works very strongly in this position. It's well worth your while reading over Sagittarius's Sun-sign characteristics (in Part 2). Don't be surprised if you possess a good number of that sign's qualities. You're optimistic and enthusiastic, which are terrific assets, unless you overdo them. A steadying influence from Saturn – if it appears in your chart – will help you temper any tendency toward being blindly optimistic or overenthusiastic. As you grow older you should become wiser, and in middle-age and even old age you will stretch yourself, always studying something new. Incidentally, you should be good at languages, and you love to travel.

Jupiter in Capricorn

You're sensible, accept challenges for what they are, and are never blindly optimistic about your chances of success. Common sense, caution, and hard-earned success characterize your approach to life. Sounds pretty dull, doesn't it? Add to that the fact that Capricorn's serious side makes you pessimistic and downbeat. But take heart: you can also be positive and extroverted. And you have a sense of humor that reduces others to helpless laughter while you remain poker-faced. Just watch out for a tendency to be your own worst enemy and to think you're always right. You won't make friends or influence people that way.

Jupiter in Aquarius

You're fairly tolerant and impartial when judging others, and you're sympathetic in an unsentimental way. Jupiter in Aquarius may make you especially sensitive to humanitarian issues, and you may explore those issues and search for solutions in a variety of positive ways: you're particularly effective at persuading others to work for good causes; you have a keen sense of justice; and you insist that fairness prevails in all situations. Jupiter generally tends to warm up Aquarius a bit, and friendship will be important to you. You're inventive and original, as well, and you could have scientific, musical, or literary talent – especially if this is indicated elsewhere in your chart.

Jupiter in Pisces

Jupiter's influence from Pisces will make you kindly, sympathetic, and caring. This placing of Jupiter is often found in the charts of people who work in the caring professions – as nurses and doctors, for instance – as well as in animal medicine. On the other hand, you may have difficulty acting on your innate caring nature. Some people with Jupiter in Pisces tend to be reclusive, and they express their sympathetic and nurturing instincts in prayer or contemplation. Your emotions run high, and you're powerfully imaginative and intuitive. In fact, these gifts are so potent that they may cause some trouble. For example, you may worry unnecessarily about your loved ones. Try to keep that tendency in check. You're naturally friendly, and with your sympathetic spirit you're able to build really good relationships with anyone you care about. Indeed, you may have a natural rapport with the whole human race!

Jupiter through the houses

JUPITER'S KEY PLANETARY INFLUENCE – *expansiveness* – *is generally considered a positive quality that can enlarge and enrich the favorable characteristics already present in a chart; so look mostly for positive effects on the areas of life governed by the house where Jupiter is present. On the negative side, a dangerous exaggeration of otherwise positive qualities may be indicated.*

Jupiter in the first house

You have a positive and enthusiastic outlook on life, which you believe in living to the fullest. Open and honest, you also believe others are that way, too. Sometimes you'll be disappointed to discover that not everyone is. Your love of life also includes a love of good food and wine, and you'll be no stranger to the Alka-seltzer bottle!

Jupiter in the second house

Here we find a big accent on money! You want to make it, and you take risks to make even more of it. You love spending it, especially on entertaining your friends and making your home as luxurious as possible. Jupiter will make you a generous partner, always ready with a handsome present – even when you can't really afford it.

Jupiter in the third house

This is the house of the mind, and Jupiter is concerned with intellect; so you need mental challenge and will take up any contests with enthusiasm and determination. You continue to educate yourself after school and university are done. You need to express your opinions, and as you're a good communicator, that is not difficult for you.

Jupiter in the fourth house

The chances are that you're very good indeed at homemaking, and you probably had a happy childhood. You have a positive attitude toward children, and you encourage them enthusiastically – if chaotically – by filling the house with books, CDs, computer software, and all modern aids to learning.

Jupiter in the fifth house

You are one of the world's great enthusiasts, but overenthusiasm can lead you into all sorts of difficulties – taking risks is definitely one of them. Your love life may be spectacularly varied, and you may have more partners in a decade than most people have in a lifetime. Exaggeration? Well, that's the keyword for Jupiter in the fifth house!

Jupiter in the sixth house

Generous and optimistic, you're also naturally helpful, rushing forward whenever anyone needs anything, giving your time and your money, but above all, giving your enthusiasm. If you don't watch your diet you may put on weight far too easily – and find it difficult to take off. Your slow metabolism makes exercise tedious and difficult.

Jupiter in the seventh house

In relationships, you tend to think that the grass is greener on the other side of the fence, and this attitude may lead you into trouble. Try to put your emotions aside and think rationally before you make any new moves on the love front. Self-analysis will be your best friend. In a partnership, you need someone who is your intellectual equal.

Jupiter in the eighth house

You're a great sexual enthusiast, and you need a partner who is equally enthusiastic and committed to sexual enjoyment and experimentation. If your partner can't match you on those terms, there will be trouble. Outside the bedroom, Jupiter in the eighth house makes for a good business person but even here, some self-control is vital.

Jupiter in the ninth house

You have a powerful intellect, a positive (and philosophical) outlook on life, great vision, and a creative imagination. You always want to acquire more knowledge, and you should give yourself plenty of opportunity to do this after your formal studies are over. You especially enjoy studying foreign languages.

Jupiter in the tenth house

You thrive in a position of power or control, and on the whole you exercise that power positively and competently. On the other hand, if you overhear someone referring to you as "pompous," take heed. Pomposity is a temptation you sometimes can't resist! In general, you attract attention, wherever you are and whatever you do.

Jupiter in the eleventh house

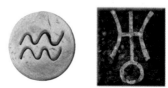

Almost everyone is your friend, because you're a social animal who has an enormous number of acquaintances. "We're just good friends" may be a phrase which seems more natural to you than anything more intimate, but this may hinder the development of something wonderful and more long-term.

Jupiter in the twelfth house

Peace and quiet is important to you, and your mind may well be more active than your body. Keep one foot on the ground, though, and do not live in the realms of philosophical speculation! Working alone is fine, but bring your work into the open to benefit other people.

The aspects of Jupiter

WHEN JUPITER IS WELL ASPECTED, *particularly with the Sun, Moon, Mars, or Saturn, it enhances an individual's positive traits. This is seen in the house and sign where Jupiter is placed, so read those house and sign descriptions (in this chapter) for Jupiter's influence when strongly aspected.*

(For Jupiter's aspects to the Sun, see the Sun's aspects to Jupiter, p. 255.
For Jupiter's aspects to the Moon, see the Moon's aspects to Jupiter, p. 271.
For Jupiter's aspects to Mercury, see Mercury's aspects to Jupiter, p. 293.
For Jupiter's aspects to Venus, see Venus's aspects to Jupiter, p. 317.
For Jupiter's aspects to Mars, see Mars's aspects to Jupiter, p. 332.)

Jupiter's aspects to Saturn

Conjunction

This conjunction encourages optimism, common sense, practicality, a sense of purpose, and the ability to be enthusiastic or restrained depending on circumstances. You have a positive outlook on life, except when Saturn brings a cloudy day and everything looks black.

Positive aspects

Common sense and enthusiastic optimism will be equally balanced, and sensible planning will result in good decisions and the talent to carry them through.

Negative aspects

Deal with restlessness and inner discontent if they are not to dominate your life. Try not to be affected by any disadvantages or criticism.

Jupiter's aspects to Uranus

Conjunction

A positive outlook, a bright and original mind, and a forward-looking and humanitarian approach to life are all aspected here. Watch out for occasional tension, which you can usually counter with positive action, interesting work, and engrossing hobbies.

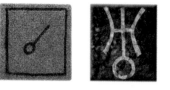

Positive aspects

You have a powerfully original turn of mind, a good sense of humor, and a compulsion to help others.

Negative aspects

You may be restless and eccentric, and you can feel discontented with, or unenthusiastic about, life in general. You can become obsessed with being independent, to the point that you reject help when it's offered.

Jupiter's aspects to Neptune

Conjunction

This conjunction is associated with all the finer, subtler humanitarian qualities – idealism, humility, spirituality, and optimism – and you have an obvious and enormous potential for doing good, as long as you avoid being simply a dreamer of dreams.

Positive aspects

This aspect shares with the conjunction the same humanitarian qualities, including idealism and humility, though there is a great need both for sensitivity to opposing forces and the ability to turn dreams into action.

Negative aspects

Forgetfulness added to dreaminess may mean that all your good intentions never see fruition.

Jupiter's aspects to Pluto

Conjunction

You need success and may seek it ruthlessly. Your enthusiasm to succeed in general can become downright obsessive. You're a magnetic leader with excellent powers of organization. Given your other qualities, you have great potential for doing good . . . or evil.

Positive aspects

You have great inner strength and can pursue any objective with a firm resolve (and ultimate success). You use your intelligence well and are especially adept at leading and organizing others.

Negative aspects

Beware of a tendency towards fanaticism and misusing your innate sense of power to mislead others – often by a show of sheer personal dynamism . . . and nothing else.

Jupiter's aspects to the Ascendant

Conjunction

The power of this conjunction depends to a great extent on whether Jupiter is in the first or the twelfth house. Jupiter's house placement is key to understanding how the conjunctive aspects will play out in your life, so do read over the descriptions of the first and twelfth houses (in this chapter). From the first house, this conjunction makes you enthusiastic, positive, and open-minded, though you have a tendency to exaggerate and to take both emotional and physical risks. From the twelfth house this conjunction makes you less extroverted and more thoughtful and reflective. You may also have a strong sense of vocation or calling to a very particular career or role.

Positive aspects

Here are the qualities of the conjunction – optimism, enthusiasm, open-mindedness, exaggeration, and risk taking – but at a less powerful level.

Negative aspects

You may have a tendency to show off or even be a bit of a bore! Look for other indications elsewhere in your birth chart that may weaken these tendencies – but watch out for them, nevertheless!

Jupiter's aspects to the Midheaven

Conjunction

Natural enthusiasm and optimism suggest a considerable potential for success – and a contented life as a result. Your optimism and enthusiasm are strong enough to carry you through most projects you undertake.

Positive aspects

You always meet a challenge head-on, and any successes you have will simply heighten your natural self-confidence and increase your sense of optimism and enthusiasm.

Negative Aspects

Showing off and exaggerating your accomplishments won't endear you to anyone; neither will your love of status and social position.

A simple summary

✓ Jupiter is the largest planet in the solar system and takes about 12 years to travel through the 12 zodiac signs. Expansiveness and all-round development are strong influences. At best, Jupiter can encourage optimism, tolerance, and energy. At worst, the planet is associated with gambling and blind optimism.

✓ Jupiter adds an intellectual or philosophical dimension to the characteristics of any Sun sign. The planet is associated with learning, languages, and justice.

At worst, Jupiter encourages indulgence and conceit.

✓ Jupiter's strongest influence has a positive effect on areas governed by the house in which it is placed, giving intellectual depth and an optimistic underpinning. It can encourage exaggeration or misuse other positive qualities.

✓ Jupiter's positive aspects, the Sun, Moon, Mars, or Saturn, enhance positive personality traits seen in the house or Sun sign where the planet is placed.

Chapter 20

Saturn at Work

SATURN REPRESENTS AUTHORITY – sometimes inner authority – and at times acts as a welcome warning flag in the face of emotional, psychological, or physical challenges and crises. Saturn says, "Don't!," when very often *not* pursuing a course of action is absolutely the right thing to do. On the other hand, Saturn can inhibit us just when we need to gather up our self-confidence and move forward with our lives. Thus a balanced reaction to – and considerable thought about – what Saturn "says" we should or shouldn't do is vital in managing the inhibiting influences of this powerful planet.

In this chapter...

✓ *Saturn through the signs*

✓ *Saturn through the houses*

✓ *The aspects of Saturn*

SATURN WAS THE FATHER OF ALL THE GODS IN ROMAN MYTHOLOGY

Saturn through the signs

REVIEW THE QUALITIES and characteristics of the Sun sign in Part 2. Then consider the effects Saturn's inhibiting influence may have on those qualities and characteristics. Remember, if you give in too readily to inhibition, you may doubt yourself and fail to act when you need to do so. Conversely, if you automatically reject Saturn's authoritative inner voice when it's pointing out real weaknesses in your character or your actions, you may run head first into disaster. Is this anybody's favorite planet? Well . . . it certainly has its depressing (and repressing) sides. But it also can restrain our wilder excesses. And that's a good thing.

Saturn in Aries

Aries suggests enthusiasm and action, Saturn caution and constraint; not a happy partnership. At times you'll appear strong and masterful, at others hesitant and weak. Obviously what you must do is use this planet's influence properly. Let Saturn temper your enthusiasm with common sense and caution – but without dampening your enthusiasm. Occasionally confusion may reign when Saturn shouts a cautionary opinion in one ear and Aries shouts an opposing one in the other. Learn to consider both opinions rather than clutching your head and not listening to either. You may feel the physical effects of Saturn's attempts to restrain your Arien energy as nervous tension. Seek out positive ways to let off your Arien steam, perhaps in sport or a form of physical exercise.

Saturn in Taurus

You tend to be rather a plodder, what with Saturn encouraging caution and Taurus giving you the patience to be cautious. But you love the idea of success, especially social success, and you climb deliberately toward your goal. You like comfort, and you won't want to make too many sacrifices for your success, even though Saturn will tend to whisper complaints in your inner ear about spending far too much money on luxuries. Watch yourself carefully if you're a parent: your children may not react well to the strict discipline and rigid routine which suits you, so try not to force it on them too heavily. And loosen up a little – emotionally. Don't be afraid to express your feelings and openly show kindness and consideration; you may have a tendency to repress these warm qualities because you think they weaken your authority.

Saturn in Gemini

This placing of Saturn is all about communication, and you should give some thought to the way you express yourself to others. You're economical with words, but what you say will be succinct, well-ordered, and extremely authoritative: people will not only listen to your opinions, but follow your advice. Typical Geminian running-off-at-the-mouth won't at all be your style. In fact, you may tend to be rather too taciturn – to the degree that people think you rude. Indeed, a certain harshness and sarcasm can make you a touch unlovable at times. Your natural sense of humor will help you lighten up when necessary, so that a seemingly offensive remark is witty enough to lose its cutting edge. And remember that people may take your flights of verbal fancy too seriously. ("Smile when you say that," is a good motto for you.)

Saturn in Cancer

This placing has two strong emphases: the family and worry. Well, maybe the two go together naturally. You certainly are very much concerned with family life and want to make a secure home for your partner and your children. Emotionally, you need to loosen up a little. You can be rather inhibited about expressing your feelings to your partner and even act timidly around him or her. This doesn't make for an especially good and trusting relationship. When challenged to act on something, you can creep into your shell and cower there until the need for a decision is over. You want to take action, but a quiet inner voice may insist that the consequences will be dire, or that you should rethink your options, or that doing nothing may be the best course of action . . . it hardly ever is. You may also be a prize worrier, especially if this tendency is indicated elsewhere in your birth chart. However, you're naturally shrewd, especially about money, and once you do make a decision, you have great tenacity and a strong sense of purpose.

Saturn in Leo

You can be autocratic and proud, and though you have great strength of will, this can easily translate into willfulness. Your serious attitude toward life may dampen the delightfully warm enthusiasm that this sign usually encourages. In fact, Saturn sends a cloud over Leo. Still, there is a positive side to Saturn's influence: the refusal to accept limitations; a real desire and determination to succeed; the willingness to put enormous effort into any project you support; the ability to cope with any situation that arises; and the capacity to organize others, especially in an emergency. But watch out for these Saturn-influenced dangers; your tendency to lose perspective, misplace your loyalties, and pursue a line of action simply because, "it's the right thing to do." Question this latter tendency in particular – what others expect you to do may not be what you should do.

Saturn in Virgo

You welcome routine and are at your best when you work methodically, plowing the same furrow with patience and enormous attention to detail. No shortcuts for you! All this makes you an excellent employee, but a hard taskmaster. For you, discipline is everything, and your tendency to insist that others match your high standards of perfection won't be appreciated. Try to temper your expectations of others with some tolerance – something you may find difficult to do. Ironically, you're modest about your own achievements, and you're not the most self-confident person in the world. In fact, you can be extremely shy. Try to recognize your own virtues without trumpeting them to the world. Your Saturnian inner voice tends to be sarcastic, cool, and distant, and it may criticize your every thought and potential action. That's fine, if it makes you look at life realistically and practically; it also can underscore your love of detail and careful planning. But don't let that critical inner voice prevent you from moving forward. Watch out for the tendency, when you're under stress, to take refuge in doing nothing and waiting for the storm to pass. The storm will pass, but it may take you along with it!

Saturn in Libra

The qualities of Saturn and Libra seem to mesh wonderfully: a strong sense of justice, sympathy for others, kindness, common sense, tact, diplomacy, fairness, impartiality, and flexibility . . . a marriage made in heaven! Yes . . . but. And the "but" relates mainly to the possibility that you may be intolerant of your colleagues or lover. You may also have a tendency to shrink from commitment, though one side of you will long for a permanent emotional relationship. Your tentativeness about commitment may be related to sexual inhibition or an inability to express your emotions freely. On the other hand, you're generous and kind, and you're always eager to help out and to please others. However, watch out for your strong tendency to expect too much appreciation and gratitude in return. You are among those who are famous for saying, "After all I did for you . . . "

Saturn in Scorpio

Saturn can have an especially inhibiting effect on your sex life, preventing you from expressing yourself as freely and generously as you might. Beware of being far too intent on your own pleasure and inconsiderate of your partner's. Actually, the effect of Saturn – when it's in Scorpio – isn't enormously positive in any sphere of life. You tend to have a rather dark and brooding side to your personality, coupled with a strong sense of purpose, dogged determination, and excess emotional energy when it comes to achieving any goal. At the worst end of the spectrum you may become strongly obsessive and maddeningly single-minded when you set your sights on a particular objective. A decidedly cruel and ruthless side to your nature may emerge and cause great problems. One positive aspect of Saturn's influence is that it strengthens your business sense. You also have a good – though very offbeat – sense of humor. Use it to lighten things up when you get too intense with your family, friends, or business associates.

Saturn in Sagittarius

In Sagittarius, Saturn insists that you develop your full intellectual potential – and encourages you to study until you've done so. This pattern of learning goes on throughout your life, not just at school. The planet also encourages you to speak your mind decisively and sometimes bravely, because your ideas and opinions won't necessarily be those of the majority. You want to act on your opinions, without delay; but you often find yourself hesitating (and then are puzzled about that hesitation). The fact is that a part of you is instinctively aware of the difficulties and drawbacks in many situations, and Sagittarian enthusiasm will be restrained by the cautious influence of Saturn. This isn't necessarily a bad thing. A measure of caution – a quality that one side of you despises – may well save your hide in situations where there's just too much going against you.

Saturn in Capricorn

You're determined but cautious, ambitious but practical, and you will make any number of sacrifices in order to realize your ambitions. But if Saturn is negatively aspected, your outlook will tend to be grim and downbeat, and your determination to take whatever life throws at you may be admirable but self-defeating. You may be too keen on achieving power, which will make those around you uncomfortable. They won't care much for your social climbing, either. You can also be rather stingy with your time and your money, especially if Saturn is badly aspected. Your family may feel neglected because you spend so much time at work. Of course, you'll reply that you're doing it all for them! However true that may be, your family needs personal attention as well as the money (and social position) you're working to give them. Saturn's no-nonsense "inner voice" will lay down the law so authoritatively that you'll have difficulty not obeying instantly. That's better than disregarding Saturn's cautious directives completely, but don't be cowed by them.

Saturn in Aquarius

In Aquarius, Saturn encourages determination, originality, humanitarianism, and the ability to know your own mind. But as always, there's a downside to Saturn's influence. That "originality," for example, may be refreshing, even astonishing, at age 18, but rather tired and stale at 80 – if it, and you, haven't matured with time. And while you do indeed know your own mind, you almost certainly also have an obstinate side to your nature which prompts you to express an opposite view just for the sake of being different. And if Saturn is negatively aspected, you can be very cunning in expressing that view. You may also find it a little difficult to form close friendships, preferring to distance yourself slightly from even your best friends. However, independence is important enough to you that you are able to put up with a degree of loneliness. Be aware that one side of your nature will want to be safe and secure, while the other will want to rebel and be unconventional. Watch out for the pull between those opposing camps.

Saturn in Pisces

Your instinct to shrink shyly away from public attention is attractive, in some ways. In other ways, your natural shyness can become real inhibition. Be careful about that. You're humane and sympathetic, and your natural sympathy for others is based on strong intuitive skills, on which you can always safely rely. You also can build on your intuitive gifts to counter any lack of self-confidence you have; the latter is one of the unfortunate effects of Saturn in Pisces. You must try to fight your tendency to think of yourself as unappealing and having little to contribute to life. On the contrary, you can contribute a great deal: your powerful imaginative and intuitive skills allow you to see – when others can't – both the problems and the rewards life has to offer. Watch out for a tendency toward swift mood changes and hypochondria, especially if Saturn receives negative aspects from the Moon.

Saturn through the houses

IT'S ALWAYS WELL WORTH looking carefully at the house in which Saturn is placed, because it will probably have a rather dampening effect on the areas of life covered by that house. The planet's effects won't be disastrous, by any means, but you will probably have to make a special effort to throw off Saturn's heavy influence in certain areas.

Saturn in the first house

You can be rather shy and lack self-confidence. You may be naturally cautious, conservative in your thinking and attitudes, and have a great deal of common sense.
Sometimes you may feel very pessimistic and incapable of dealing with life. On the other hand, you stick firmly to what you consider your duties in life.

Saturn in the second house

Even if you end up fabulously wealthy, money won't come easily to you: you'll have to work hard for every penny earned. The best way to build your finances is by wise investing – in the more secure stocks available – and not by risk taking. On the personal side, Saturn will tend to inhibit you emotionally, and you may have to work hard for emotional security as well.

Saturn in the third house

You're sensible and practical, with the ability to make long-term plans and stick to them. Those plans may tend to be on the conservative side, but they will pay off in the end. Quite a lot of your spare time will probably be spent studying – trying to fill in the gaps left by what you believe to be a faulty education.

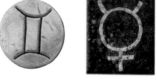

Saturn in the fourth house

Was your early life fairly Spartan and lacking in real affection? Were your parents perhaps overstrict and not altogether encouraging or warm? Was there a strong emphasis on discipline? If so, it will take you some time to come to terms with your past, and you may find it difficult to express your feelings and opinions because of an unconscious fear of criticism or a lack of appreciation.

Saturn in the fifth house

You may be creative, but slow to develop your creative talents. You take love very seriously, and you need a relationship. But it may take some time for you to make a real commitment, possibly because of your father's strong influence. This is especially true for men in their attitudes toward women, but also affects women's feelings about men.

Saturn in the sixth house

You work hard, with great attention to detail, but you may not care much for your job and believe that your work isn't worth the effort. When that happens, you grumble incessantly about it but you don't change job, because you don't like to take risks.

Saturn in the seventh house

You may be hesitant to form an emotional relationship, but you will be extremely faithful once you have entered into one – possibly with someone older than yourself.
Part of your hesitation is due to the fact that you consider a commitment a serious responsibility – so much so that you may stay single just to avoid that responsibility!

Saturn in the eighth house

Your sexual tastes are not conventional, and you may worry about "turning off" a partner. You'd be surprised how rarely that is the case. But do watch out for the demon jealousy. Your intuition will be strong and rarely let you down. Follow it!

Saturn in the ninth house

You probably don't like facing problems or challenges, and while you're capable of thinking deeply and seriously about problems, your mind isn't adventurous. Your solutions may be conventional and dull. Shyness and self-consciousness can be difficulties, especially if Saturn is negatively aspected by any personal planets.

Saturn in the tenth house

Saturn will sometimes seem to overload you with responsibility. You carry it well, however, because you are ambitious and have high aspirations. A warning: sometimes you're so preoccupied with fulfilling those aspirations that you neglect your family; this can cause a serious gap between you and those you love.

Saturn in the eleventh house

You may find it difficult to have close friendships, and when you do make friends, they may be quite a bit older. One reason you may be drawn to them is because you think they're more intelligent than you (not true!). Relax: You have a good social life; enjoy it!

Saturn in the twelfth house

You may want to retreat from the world and its worries, and you may only feel secure in your own little castle – with the drawbridge up. Don't turn into too much of a recluse. Remember that you need a certain amount of exercise. Join a gym or a yoga class to kill two birds with one stone: exercising your body and getting you out of the house.

The aspects of Saturn

Here we detail the main aspects made by Saturn to the three planets beyond it in the solar system: Uranus, Neptune, and Pluto. Since the following aspects hang around for a considerable length of time, they will appear in a great number of birth charts. While they tend to have an inhibiting effect on individuals, they are also stabilizing forces.

(For Saturn's aspects to the Sun, see the Sun's aspects to Saturn, p. 255.
For Saturn's aspects to the Moon, see the Moon's aspects to Saturn, p. 271.
For Saturn's aspects to Mercury, see Mercury's aspects to Saturn, p. 293.
For Saturn's aspects to Venus, see Venus's aspects to Saturn, p. 318.
For Saturn's aspects to Mars, see Mars's aspects to Saturn, p. 332.
For Saturn's aspects to Jupiter, see Jupiter's aspects to Saturn, p. 344.)

Saturn's aspects to Uranus

Conjunction

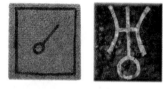

This conjunction occurs in the birth charts of individuals born between December 1986 and December 1989, and its energy flavors the characteristics of the whole generation born in those three years. If Saturn and Uranus are aligned with the Sun, Moon, Ascendant, or Midheaven in a birth chart, that person will probably be a leader of their generation with potent views and an ability to express them. This is a leader who craves individuality but needs guidance and discipline.

Positive aspects

You're outwardly conventional, but you have a sneaking sympathy for the unconventional. You have willpower, determination, and patience.

Negative aspects

You will sometimes be obsessively obstinate, and you may tend to be rather distant and cold. If you are in a position of authority, you won't find it easy to win your employees' loyalty.

Saturn's aspects to Neptune

Conjunction

This potent conjunction is like Saturn and Uranus's conjunction (see above), but Neptune weakens the determination as well as clouding judgment.

Positive aspects

Kind and sympathetic, you'll be idealistic but practical. These aspects will certainly encourage you to express any creative instincts you may have.

Negative aspects

This is a weak negative aspect and shouldn't be given too much importance. It indicates that you have talent but may hesitate to express it.

Saturn's aspects to Pluto

Conjunction

In Leo this aspect exerts a negative influence. It has an inhibiting effect on emotions, which makes for psychological problems. In Libra it is less punishing, and determination is the motto for this aspect.

Positive aspects

Determination and a good deal of energy are indicated, but these aspects will only operate strongly if the planets are personalized.

Negative aspects

With these aspects the phrase heard is, "I can't be bothered!" There may be obsessional behavior as well, which others find difficult to deal with.

Saturn's aspects to the Ascendant

Conjunction

Saturn in the first house lowers your self-confidence and makes you shy. But you're practical and your confidence will build over the years. Saturn in the twelfth house will show a tendency to lock yourself away.

Positive aspects

Practicality, common sense, and caution are aspected here. These are good influences, but watch out for a parallel tendency to be overemotional.

Negative aspects

Low vitality, a gloomy outlook – and are you a grumbler! If you recognize these tendencies, work on being cheerful. But we can't count on that.

Saturn's aspects to the Midheaven

Conjunction

If Saturn is in the tenth house its influence will be strong and load you with responsibilities – though never more than you can handle. Your ambition will be great – so strong, in fact, that you may miss out on the fun side of life. Read the discussion about Saturn in the tenth house in this chapter and take heed!

Positive aspects

You possess all the positive Saturnian qualities – practicality, common sense, discipline, and ambition – tempered by caution.

Negative aspects

You may have to put up with considerable frustration, but the obstacles in your way will build up your self-confidence and determination. You'll achieve your ambitions, but more slowly and steadily than you'd wish.

A simple summary

✓ Saturn represents the voice of inner authority and acts as a inhibitor on behavior. Saturn warns us about emotional, psychological, or physical challenges and says "Stop," when pursuing an action is wrong.

✓ Saturn has a repressing effect on the qualities of the sign in which it is placed. On the positive side, it can restrain our excesses in the more volatile Sun signs. On the negative side, Saturn's inhibiting influence may encourage the quieter, less confident Sun signs to hold back when they need to let go.

✓ Saturn has a dampening effect on the areas covered by the house in which it is placed. While its influence isn't overly restrictive in the houses, it can throw a cloud over personal issues.

✓ Saturn acts to inhibit certain behaviors and emotions, but is also a stabilizing force where too much emotionality is present.

Chapter 21

Uranus at Work

IN MYTHOLOGY, Uranus was the sky-god and father of the Titans, a race of giants who originally inhabited the Earth. As the story goes, Uranus was born of Gaia (Mother Earth), and later mated with her. From this forbidden union, the Titans were born to rule the Earth until they were overthrown by the Olympian gods and goddesses. Leading the Olympian charge was Saturn, who had Uranus castrated. But Uranus may have had the last – albeit ironic – word, because from his castrated genitals, the goddess of love, Aphrodite (later known as Venus), was born! Fittingly, perhaps, Uranus is associated with individualism, independence, radical thought, revolutionary change, and, ultimately, personal transformation. On the dark side of Uranus's influence, we find rebellion, wild eccentricity, and outright perversion.

In this chapter...

✔ Uranus through the signs

✔ Uranus through the houses

✔ The aspects of Uranus

URANUS HAS A PROFOUND EFFECT ON BOTH PERSONAL AND SOCIETAL CHANGE

Uranus through the signs

URANUS SPENDS ABOUT SEVEN YEARS in each sign of the zodiac, and so it will be in the birth chart of everyone born during a specific seven-year period. Generally, Uranus won't have a strong personal effect on everyday life; instead, it is one of the planets (Neptune and Pluto are two others) whose influences are "generational" and affect a whole group of people. If, however, Uranus is a personal planet in your chart, you should give its influences greater import, remembering that this is the planet of personal transformation.

Uranus in Aries

Unless it receives negative aspects, Uranus should give you originality and the motivation to express it to the world. You'll be happy looking for the new and different in whatever area you work. You may be rather erratic, and certainly not too patient, and your strong self-confidence won't make it easy to discipline you – or easy for you to discipline yourself!

Uranus in Taurus

Once you've made up your mind about something, that's it! And it will mostly be a waste of time trying to persuade you to change your opinions. You really must try to be more flexible, because stubbornness could be your downfall (especially if it's shown elsewhere in the chart). Watch your bank balance, as well: you can be too generous and extravagant, and your general attitude toward money is pretty eccentric.

Uranus in Gemini

You'll be original to the point of brilliance, but nervous tension could cause problems related to stress, especially if Uranus receives squares or oppositions from the Sun, Moon, or Mercury, or if it is in negative aspect to the Ascendant.

Uranus in Cancer

Cancer can make you moody, Uranus unpredictable – not an easy combination. If Cancer is a prominent sign in your chart, or Uranus is a personal planet, you may experience trouble if you don't take steps to get a handle on your emotions and think before you act.

Uranus in Leo

You can be stubborn, and you'll certainly be self-confident. Dynamic energy coupled with a desire for power can spell trouble, but you have a definite, and enormously positive, talent for leadership.

Uranus in Virgo

If other elements of your birth chart tend to make you nervous and apprehensive, this placing of Uranus won't help, but you'll have an original approach to problems, and you'll be especially good at analysis and research.

Uranus in Libra

You'll be strongly independent and a little cool in your approach to other people, but you are a caring and affectionate friend who'll be really sympathetic and kindly. This doesn't mean you'll want to jump into any relationship; you always think before you leap.

Uranus in Scorpio

Uranus is exalted in this sign, and works strongly from it, making you brave and daring – but likely to hide those emotions. You may appear calm on the surface while all sorts of things boil up inside you. This can lead to explosions.

Uranus in Sagittarius

Originality and an unusual slant to your mind will enable you to meet challenges in a really positive and unique fashion. You're mentally and physically adventurous, and ready to fight for good causes – from saving the dolphin to saving the planet.

Uranus in Capricorn

Everyone born during the same seven-year period will feel the effect of Uranus in Capricorn, which tends to make individuals rational, cool, and somewhat conservative. You may always feel that you have to "do the right thing," but you may sometimes shock yourself by your own unexpected reactions to certain people and events.

Uranus in Aquarius

Uranus rules Aquarius, and the planet's personal influence will lead you to be kindly and humanitarian. You can be unpredictable, however, and sometimes even intractable. More than many people, you're likely to keep your good looks well into old age.

Uranus in Pisces

Original, imaginative, inspirational, idealistic, kind, and sympathetic: that's St. Pisces when Uranus comes to visit! But if there's an emphasis on Pisces elsewhere in the chart, you may also be deceptive and gullible. Above all, avoid all drugs – even prescribed ones, if possible – like the plague.

Uranus through the houses

SUDDEN CHANGES *and unexpected developments may be linked to areas governed by the house in which Uranus is placed. Considerable stress may accompany these disruptions; a general remedy is to work at turning inner tension into positive action.*

Uranus in the first house

Fiercely original and independent, you may also be rather perverse and unpredictable. Look keenly at the characteristics of the Sun sign Uranus is in on your birth chart: they will be a vital part of your personality. If Uranus is negatively aspected, you may tend to suffer from emotional tension.

Uranus in the second house

You're clever with money, but may in fact be a little loony when it comes to looking after your cash. Furthermore, any financial problems that do crop up will probably be your own fault! Realize that you can make serious mistakes in this area, and don't let the occasional sudden gain convince you that you're a financial genius.

Uranus in the third house

With the help of positive aspects, you are cool, calm, and collected. You bring a measure of brilliance and originality to whatever you do, and you do it very well. You'll want to get to the heart of every question, and you will look for logical answers and solutions. You may occasionally be willful and stubborn.

Uranus in the fourth house

"Different" is the word people will apply to you, whether they mean it as a compliment or a criticism! You can be clever, and you can be perverse. You need a stable home environment, but not so stable that it restricts your personal freedom in any way.

Uranus in the fifth house

If you're artistic in any way, this placing of Uranus will encourage and help your creative endeavors, sharpening ideas and enabling you to express them well. You take emotional risks in your stride, and your love affairs will be positive, lively, and rewarding.

Uranus in the sixth house

Strain and tension can be a real problem for you; in fact, they may lead to a susceptibility to infections and then to illnesses. Watch your diet and try to learn to relax. Expending your energy carefully and in a balanced way – rather than in sporadic fits and starts – will help keep your nervous system on an even keel.

Uranus in the seventh house

You're attractive and shouldn't find it difficult to enter a relationship. However, you tend to be rather unsure in love about whether to rely on your heart or your head, and this may lead to difficulties. You also need your freedom – and a sympathetic partner who understands that need.

Uranus in the eighth house

You have an easy attitude towards money: if you have it – great; if you don't – well there are other things besides money . . . that attitude's fine, as long as it doesn't lead to bankruptcy. In love, you may vacillate between being wildly enthusiastic about your relationship or seeming not to care at all. This can be difficult for most partners.

Uranus in the ninth house

You're clever, original, and enthusiastic, with a need for excitement and new experiences. You crave both intellectual and physical journeys, and you may have a strong attachment to a foreign country or to one of its inhabitants.

Uranus in the tenth house

This placement will affect your choice of career, which very likely may be in the airlines industry, the space program, science, or astronomy. Interest in the caring professions is also indicated. Sudden changes of career aren't unknown here; people with Uranus in the tenth house have been known to throw away half a lifetime's experience in one field and start again in a new one.

Uranus in the eleventh house

You're friendly, but somewhat distant. You enjoy having a good social life – indeed, it's extremely important to you – but you may never get really close to other people or even to one special person. Unpredictability is also a feature of this placement.

Uranus in the twelfth house

An urge to help – to do charity work, perhaps – is associated with Uranus in the twelfth house. You are also excellent handling emergencies that require someone with a cool, analytical approach. The need or desire for a home life may take a decidedly second place to your career.

The aspects of Uranus

URANUS MOVES VERY SLOWLY, and because *Neptune and Pluto are even farther from the Sun than is Uranus, the aspects it makes to them remain operational for a very long time and for a great number of people. The influences of these aspects are therefore more generational than personal. Nevertheless, they should be looked at carefully for possible parallel influences in your personal life.*

(For Uranus's aspects to the Sun, see the Sun's aspects to Uranus, p. 256.
For Uranus's aspects to the Moon, see the Moon's aspects to Uranus, p. 272.
For Uranus's aspects to Mercury, see Mercury's aspects to Uranus, p. 294.
For Uranus's aspects to Venus, see Venus's aspects to Uranus, p. 318.
For Uranus's aspects to Mars, see Mars's aspects to Uranus, p. 332.
For Uranus's aspects to Jupiter, see Jupiter's aspects to Uranus, p. 345.
For Uranus's aspects to Saturn, see Saturn's aspects to Uranus, p. 357.)

Uranus's aspects to Neptune

Conjunction

This conjunction occurs roughly every 171 years. The innovative, independent humanity of Uranus marries the spiritual, arcane humanity of Neptune, making you particularly interested in environmental issues and ecology.

Positive aspects

You are original and imaginative, intuitive and logical. These are all first-rate qualities for anyone interested in the scientific fields, but are also marvelous traits for creative people in general.

Negative aspects

If there is tension elsewhere in the chart, these negative aspects will increase it. Relaxation techniques will be helpful if stress and tension become real problems.

Uranus's aspects to Pluto

Conjunction

Occurring once every 115 years or so, this conjunctive aspect is a real source of energy, often positively used to sweep away injustices. On the downside, the same energy may be used negatively and destructively – and is often linked to drug abuse.

Positive aspects

You may feel the need to make drastic changes from time to time, but you may also have some difficulty making those changes. Watch out for a preoccupation with achieving power.

Negative aspects

These negative aspects can be a source of tension, often manifested in your need to make changes – that you later come to regret – just for the sake of change.

Uranus's aspects to the Ascendant

Conjunction

You're original, fiercely independent, and have no difficulty attracting attention. But if Uranus is negatively aspected, watch out for a strain of stubborn perversity.

Positive aspects

These aspects increase originality, creativity, and inventiveness, and add a sparkling brilliance to the personality. If Uranus is in the fifth house, you're also likely to have a delightfully lively and spicy love life, though you will always maintain a strong streak of independence, even in a committed relationship.

Negative aspects

Negative aspects here produce tension, unpredictability, and even perversity (especially with a square aspect also present).

Uranus's aspects to the Midheaven

Conjunction

You feel the need to be in command and may be fiercely independent, even rebellious. You may drastically change the direction of your career several times during your life, and you may find yourself drawn to politics.

Positive aspects

The same dynamic independence, rebelliousness, and desire to lead are operative here, with an added emphasis on originality of approach to career and life changes. But be careful about changing directions too often!

Negative aspects

You may experience excessive tension in your work life, and bouts of stress at work are often precipitated by the remarks or actions of colleagues and superiors. Job insecurity, together with fear of the future, may result.

A simple summary

✓ Uranus encourages individuality, independence, and radical and revolutionary thought and behavior. It is often characterized as the planet of personal transformation. Its negative influences include rebellion, eccentricity, and perversion.

✓ Uranus spends about seven years in each zodiac sign, so it is in the birth chart of everyone born during a specific seven-year period. Uranus's influences are more generational – affecting whole groups of people – than individual, unless the planet is personalized in the birth chart.

✓ Uranus signals abrupt and unexpected changes and disruptions in the areas of life governed by the house in which it is placed. Considerable stress inevitably accompanies Uranian disruptions, but the changes the planet heralds may ultimately be for the better good.

✓ Slow-moving Uranus's aspects exert their influence for a long time and for a great number of people, and underscore cyclical changes and disruptions. Even though these effects are largely generational, they should still be studied carefully for clues to parallel personal changes.

Chapter 22

Neptune at Work

NEPTUNE, NAMED FOR THE GOD OF THE OCEANS, can have a potent transformative effect on entire generations. Slowly, over time, Neptune's influence can help change an entire generation's attitudes, lifestyles, social norms, and spiritual beliefs. On a personal level, Neptune is strongly associated with the highest of human ideals and pursuits, and with an individual's hopes, dreams, aspirations, and visions. On the negative end of the transformative spectrum, Neptune may encourage deceitfulness, indecision, addiction, and escapism.

In this chapter...

✔ Neptune through the signs

✔ Neptune through the houses

✔ The aspects of Neptune

IN ROMAN MYTHOLOGY, NEPTUNE RULED OVER THE EBB AND FLOW OF THE SEAS

Neptune through the signs

NEPTUNE TAKES 146 YEARS *to travel around the Sun and stays in one sign for about 14 years. The planet influences – as a group – all the people born within a specific time frame. There are few people alive today who have Neptune in Gemini, and no one is alive with Neptune in Aries, Pisces, or Taurus. These four are not covered here.*

Neptune in Cancer

If Neptune is a personal planet in your chart, it will heighten your sensitivity, emotion, and intuition; if it receives negative aspects, you may tend to take the easy way out when you find yourself in difficulties. Your imagination can also work overtime, so that you'll worry unnecessarily about nonexistent problems and situations. If you're creative, this placing of Cancer will give you a refined and sensitive attitude toward your work.

Neptune in Leo

Glamorous, and with a sense of drama, you'll express your emotions in a positive, lively, and enthusiastic way. This is a pretty strong influence at a personal level, and if Neptune is a personal planet and receives some positive aspects, both your imagination and creativity will be vividly highlighted. Quite often people with this placing have an interest in the arts, and particularly in photography.

Neptune in Virgo

If Neptune is a personal planet in your chart, or Virgo is a prominent sign, your imagination will be abundant and strongly expressed – maybe through writing. But remember that Virgo is an earth sign, so you may have a creative interest in farming or gardening. Neptune can tend to lower self-confidence when it's in Virgo, and you should remember your achievements rather than belittle them; you may then avoid the discontent and restlessness which the planet can also indicate when in this sign.

Neptune in Libra

Neptune won't have a particularly strong influence from Libra unless the sign is very much emphasized by other features of your birth chart. It does enhance your kindly sympathy with others, but if your chart indicates elsewhere that you might be rather

lazy, then Neptune will encourage an easygoing attitude toward life. If Libra is rising, note whether Neptune is in the first or twelfth house and read the corresponding description under "Neptune through the houses" in this chapter. If Neptune conjuncts the Ascendant, read the corresponding description under "The aspects of Neptune," also in this chapter. Both indications are important.

Neptune in Scorpio

If Neptune is a personal planet in your birth chart, it will build your emotional intensity; if it's well aspected, it will encourage natural talent and be a great help in achieving your ambitions. But it won't have a strong effect unless either Scorpio is stressed elsewhere in the chart, or your emotions and talents are also encouraged by other factors.

Neptune in Sagittarius

If Sagittarius is emphasized elsewhere in your birth chart, then this indication will do much to encourage your talent for leadership. Neptune's gentle encouragement may take several forms, but one will certainly be related to your feelings about the animal kingdom, and it could well manifest itself in your being a vegetarian and working for the greening of the planet.

Neptune in Capricorn

A naturally low emotional level may be further underscored by this placing of Neptune, which we would also expect to soften the colder, harsher qualities of Capricorn – especially if the sign is particularly prominent in your chart. You'll be a determined but fairly cautious individual. The tendency toward negative escapism which is sometimes seen in people under a strong Neptune influence will be less likely to be a problem with this placement.

Neptune in Aquarius

The humanitarian qualities of Aquarius should marry well with the gentle influence of Neptune, though the rather detached, cool, independent, and distant qualities of the sign don't match especially well with the sensitive emotional qualities of the planet. However, if the planet is well-placed in the birth chart, the two should work very well together.

Neptune through the houses

YOUR ATTITUDE *to the areas of life governed by the house Neptune occupies will tend to be fairly vague, uncertain, and indecisive. Certain events or problems will throw you into a state of confusion. Rather than realistically facing a challenge head-on, you may instead resort to taking the easiest way out. On the more positive end of its influence, Neptune may also encourage you to develop your spiritual, idealistic, and/or creative potential.*

Neptune in the first house

This placing of Neptune will probably weaken the effect of the Ascendant, and you'll find it a problem to get your life organized. You're more than likely to wriggle out of challenging situations, rather than facing up to them, and consequently you may not realize your full potential. You'll tend to be a dreamer and an idealist, but you won't give your dreams the chance to come true.

Neptune in the second house

An uneasy attitude toward money will tend to make you more generous than you need be, simply because you get confused when someone appeals to you for help. You can be financially gullible, too, so getting sound advice in money matters is really vital. Delightfully sentimental, your expression of love can be enchanting and imaginative, but you're very intense and need to keep your emotions under control.

Neptune in the third house

You should have an excellent, inventive, and vibrant imagination, but you may feel nervous about expressing it because you believe yourself to be less educated than others. This placing of Neptune sometimes seems to indicate that an individual's early education was unsettled or ineffectual. If you are the eldest child, your fierce jealousy of siblings may have clouded your early years.

Neptune in the fourth house

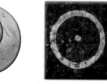

Your early life may not have been especially easy. You may have had a problematic relationship with your mother – whom you idolized. She may not have lived up to your expectations and may have failed to offer loving and encouraging guidance. The planet here suggests that your childhood should be carefully examined. Try to transform any shortcomings or lack of encouragement you experienced during childhood into positive learning lessons for your life as an adult.

Neptune in the fifth house

You may fall in love far too easily and fail to see any shortcomings at all in your lover. When, inevitably, these faults do show up, you'll be thoroughly disillusioned. Your love and sex life will be inventive, enthusiastic, and colorful, with the heart (or maybe another organ) always ruling the head. You may be too gullible where lovers are concerned, taking foolish risks – and not always emotional ones.

Neptune in the sixth house

An overactive imagination may result in bouts of hypochondria. But you may also be prone to bona fide allergies, particularly to foods and prescription medications. Holistic medicine appeals to you, and it often succeeds where conventional medicine fails. You will do your work in your own distinctive way, sometimes to the admiring dismay of colleagues.

Neptune in the seventh house

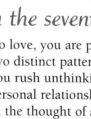

When it comes to love, you are prone to choose one of two distinct patterns: either you rush unthinkingly into a personal relationship, or you find the thought of a relationship so daunting that you don't start one to begin with! If you are in a relationship, you will expect much of a partner – perhaps too much. You're a romantic, too, which may not help. Try to drag yourself in the direction of practicality, and don't expect your partner to see to all the details of running house and home.

Neptune in the eighth house

If you have Neptune in Scorpio, everyone had better stand well back – or maybe, cuddle up real close. Neptune in the eighth house will have a strong effect on your sexuality, which will be richly inventive, creative, and rewarding – when positively expressed. Your sex life will be very important to you, and any inhibitions should be dealt with (if necessary with professional help). You'll be generous with money as well as love, though you should be cautious when investing.

Neptune in the ninth house

Idealistic and philosophical, you will tend to be studious and perhaps deeply religious. You may have to cultivate a degree of skepticism in order to use the whole of your mind and keep conviction in tandem with logic. Some people with Neptune in the ninth can cultivate dream recall to an unusual extent and are able to use the messages in their dreams toward productive ends in their waking life.

Neptune in the tenth house

High in the sky, Neptune in the tenth house usually indicates a colorful career with more changes of direction than is conventional. Your inner feelings may compel these changes, and "destiny," whatever that means to you, may also play a hand. You are a true romantic and use your imagination to good advantage. Provided you have a strong sense of direction, you are able to achieve your ambitions, however high you set your aims.

Neptune in the eleventh house

You enjoy an extensive social life, but your very enjoyment of people and your being frequently in their company means that they can take advantage of you – and sometimes they will. You enjoy working for charities, though as a rank-and-file member of a group, rather than as a leader. Responsibility worries you. If you must take it, be as practical and down-to-earth as possible, thus avoiding unnecessary tensions.

Neptune in the twelfth house

You tend to be a loner and are at your best working independently and out of the limelight. You need moments, and sometimes more than moments, of solitude, during which you can withdraw from the pressures of life and re-charge your batteries. You will do well in one of the caring professions; you understand and can identify with the suffering of others. This is an excellent placing for Neptune.

The aspects of Neptune

THE ASPECTS *between Neptune and the inner planets – the planets making the contact to Neptune – are most significant, though you should look carefully at the subtle effects of aspects to the Ascendant and Midheaven, which can be extremely influential.*

(For Neptune's aspects to the Sun, see the Sun's aspects to Neptune, p. 256.

For Neptune's aspects to the Moon, see the Moon's aspects to Neptune, p. 272.

For Neptune's aspects to Mercury, see Mercury's aspects to Neptune, p. 294.

For Neptune's aspects to Venus, see Venus's aspects to Neptune, p. 319.

For Neptune's aspects to Mars, see Mars's aspects to Neptune, p. 333.

For Neptune's aspects to Jupiter, see Jupiter's aspects to Neptune, p. 345.

For Neptune's aspects to Saturn, see Saturn's aspects to Neptune, p. 357.

For Neptune's aspects to Uranus, see Uranus's aspects to Neptune, p. 367.)

Neptune's aspects to Pluto

The only aspect Neptune and Pluto will make to each other in the lifetime of anyone living will be the sextile, which will appear in a very great number of birth charts. The sextile is the weakest of the positive aspects, so – especially in this context – it is not very important. If either planet is personalized, however, the sextile's positive influence will enhance your intuition and increase your emotional level.

Neptune's aspects to the Ascendant

Conjunction

In the first house the conjunction weakens the characteristics of the rising sign. Your determination will suffer and, while you will be a kind and sensitive person, your ability to motivate yourself will not be strong. In the twelfth house the conjunction works more positively. It will encourage you to do good work – out of the limelight. You also have a strong need for peace and quiet.

Positive aspects

While not very powerful, these positive aspects will soften the characteristics of the rising sign and color your imagination and intuition. And if Neptune is in Scorpio, your powers of seduction will be considerable!

Negative aspects

Neptune may encourage deceitfulness and a tendency toward losing touch with reality.

Neptune's aspects to the Midheaven

Conjunction

Changes of direction in your career will be likely and you will deal well with Neptunian concepts. See Neptune in the tenth house, earlier in this chapter.

Positive aspects

These fairly weak influences will help you if you follow a Neptunian career: photography, the caring professions, or dance, to name a few examples; or any career where inspiration and imagination are required.

Negative aspects

These negative influences encourage deviousness, underhandedness, and the desire (and often the ability) to pull the wool over other people's eyes.

A simple summary

✓ Neptune has a transformative effect on entire generations and encourages gradual change in a generation's prevailing attitudes, beliefs, and lifestyles. On a personal level, Neptune positively influences a person's hopes and highest aspirations. At its worst, the planet may encourage deceit and also self-destruction.

✓ Because Neptune takes 146 years to orbit the Sun, it stays in one zodiac sign for about 14 years. It therefore has a generational influence on large groups of people. In our time, the people born with Neptune in their Sun sign include Cancers, Leos, Virgos, Libras, Scorpios, Sagittarians, Capricorns, and Aquarians. There are very few people alive today who have Neptune in Gemini, and no one is alive with Neptune in Aries, Pisces, or Taurus.

✓ In the houses, Neptune tends to have a negative personal effect, encouraging uncertainty and indecision about the areas of life governed by the house in which it is placed. It can, however, encourage the development of spirituality and creativity.

✓ The aspects between Neptune and the planets it contacts exert the most potent influences in the birth chart; more subtle – but perhaps equally strong – influences may also be seen in Neptune's aspects the Ascendant and Midheaven.

Chapter 23

Pluto at Work

PLUTO, NAMED FOR THE ANCIENT GOD of the Underworld (the land of the dead), is sometimes associated both with the darker side of human existence (including catastrophic events and death), and with the sexual organs and human reproduction. In fact, Pluto's strongest influence may be on the unconscious and the unknown; buried emotions, psychological makeup, and secret motivations. Pluto is also strongly associated with personal obstacles and an individual's ability to overcome them. At the darkest end of the spectrum, Pluto may make some individuals devious and cruel.

In this chapter...
- ✔ *Pluto through the signs*
- ✔ *Pluto through the houses*
- ✔ *The aspects of Pluto*

IN MYTHOLOGY, PLUTO RULED OVER THE DEAD IN THE UNDERWORLD

Pluto through the signs

PLUTO IS THE SLOWEST MOVING of the planets, creeping along at the rate of one sign per 13 years at best, but, because of its eccentric orbit, often taking as many as 32 years to move through the sign. Pluto therefore has a generational influence. There is no one alive today with Pluto in Aquarius, Aries, Capricorn, Taurus, or Pisces – so you will not find them featured here – and the first people born with Pluto in Sagittarius arrived in 1995, when the planet started to totter slowly through that sign.

Pluto in Gemini

Those people still alive with Pluto in Gemini are characterized by their keen curiosity – and they have had much indeed to be curious about during the past century. They have skeptical minds and often test or challenge the status quo. They usually have an excellent rapport with younger people.

Pluto in Cancer

If Pluto is personalized or Cancer is strongly present, you can use your intuition and emotions powerfully and positively; if Pluto is negatively aspected by the Sun, Moon, ruling planet, or Ascendant, the flow of emotional energy is blocked, and there may be (or may have been) psychological troubles. But ample tenacity is also indicated here.

Pluto in Leo

Leonine leadership is emphasized here, but you need the support of a Leo or Pluto emphasis in the chart. The house position of Pluto will be important in deciding whether you are simply power-mad, or you are able to use your talents for the common good. You have a good business sense, coupled with a love of adventure, but you may be lacking a little in shrewdness.

Pluto in Virgo

Are you an obsessive? It's possible, especially if there are hints of this tendency elsewhere in your birth chart. Look at the influence of the Uranus/Pluto conjunction in Virgo, and its house placing. If the two planets are negatively aspected, you may find it difficult to express yourself openly.

Pluto in Libra

Pluto spices up Libra a little, but increases the Libran tendency to cause trouble just for the fun of it – often to test a partner's affection. With a Libran Sun or Moon, this placing of Pluto enlivens your sex life. But if Pluto is negatively aspected there may be sexual problems. Jealousy and possessiveness may be problems if Libra is prominent or Pluto is a personal planet.

Pluto in Scorpio

Since Pluto is Scorpio's ruling planet, its influence is increased here, and there is a distinct emphasis on darker undercurrents: sexuality with a dash of danger; nihilistic counterculture tendencies. It may be well to remember that the late 1970s heralded the onset of the AIDS epidemic and saw the emergence of the aggressive punk-rock movement. You may have found yourself (or indeed still are) struggling to cope with some very hard lessons. On the other end of the spectrum, the late 1980s through the mid-1990s marked the emergence of more positive and healing planetary influences. And making big money, especially in the world market, is strongly emphasized.

Pluto in Sagittarius

The planet and the sign are polar opposites in their influence. Pluto is restrictive, secretive, and possessive. Sagittarius is open, freedom-loving, and independent. It seems likely you'll have problems resolving these two influences. Hopefully the result of the conflict will be an airing out and resolution of problems through the wisdom of Sagittarius and its ruling planet, Jupiter.

Pluto through the houses

WHEN PLUTO FALLS in any house it emphasizes the difficulties or obstacles which may occur in those areas that the house governs. If Pluto is negatively aspected, you may even become obsessive about these problems.

Pluto in the first house

You'll be emotionally intense, wanting to explore every problem or situation to its depths – a very good placing for a researcher! But there will be obsessive tendencies and sometimes a need to dominate others. Your energy will often be expressed sexually, but in other areas your sense of purpose is strong and should lead you to success.

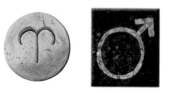

Pluto in the second house

A first-rate business person, you should be able either to make money or build your own small business empire – perhaps both. You could be obsessed with making money, and you may love collecting and owning things – sometimes collecting and owning people as well; trouble lies that way. Your emotional life will be intense and passionate, and Pluto's enhancement of your sensual expression makes you an excellent lover.

Pluto in the third house

Powerfully curious, you won't miss much – even if you seem not to be paying attention. Like a good poker player, you reveal little. This house emphasizes your need to communicate, but Pluto emphasizes a need to be silent! How you resolve that little problem will be shown elsewhere in your birth chart.

Pluto in the fourth house

Some frustration in childhood may have delayed your psychological development, but a keen intuition may have shown you the way around problems. You're probably capable of sufficient self-analysis to bring any conflict to a successful resolution.

Pluto in the fifth house

Your psychological development is important to you, and your success in this area will be reflected in your personal happiness, even if career gains and material success are less complete than you might wish. Your love life will be intense and happy as long as you don't expect too much of your lovers.

Pluto in the sixth house

Don't be too hard on yourself. Your powers of concentration are superb, and your energy will be positively directed and benefit you. Watch your weight, especially if you have any temporary emotional problems. Eating is no cure for them.

Pluto in the seventh house

Check your birth chart and note in which Sun sign Pluto resides; then read up on that sign in Part 2 – and pay attention! You probably need to be the dominant partner in an emotional relationship, and this may lead to stormy weather. Try not to dominate your lovers or consciously seek out a weaker personality than yourself as a partner.

Pluto in the eighth house

You have excellent intuition supported by a strong sense of logic: the best of combinations. You also possess a shrewd business sense and a strong emotional level. The latter, however, may not flow too freely in the sexual arena, and you may need some help there.

Pluto in the ninth house

A compulsive student with a delight in mental challenge, you could find that you allow tension and strain to build up just because you don't recognize how hard your mind is working. Unless you can attain perfection, you'll be dissatisfied, and this means that a lot of the time, you'll be dissatisfied!

Pluto in the tenth house

You need to be emotionally engaged in a career and must always have a recognizable goal. You have a strong will to succeed. Along with this you may sometimes suffer from a power complex, which can lead to ruthless behavior, especially if Pluto is joined by Uranus.

Pluto in the eleventh house

You may be a little too concerned about your friends' attitudes toward you. "What will other people think?" is a phrase which will occur to you far too often. Other people's opinions will worry you far too much – but even if you recognize this, you will find it hard to ignore them.

Pluto in the twelfth house

Secretive by nature, you may become reclusive, finding it very difficult to discuss your affairs with others or to go to them when you need help. A glamorous air of mystery may make you attractive to some people, but turning inward on yourself can make for great stress.

The aspects of Pluto

PLUTO IS THE MOST DISTANT PLANET in the Earth's solar system. Thus, here we deal only with Pluto's aspects to the Ascendant and Midheaven – where its influence on your emotional makeup and hidden motivations is very powerful indeed. Do double-check the time of your birth, however, since a deviation of just a few minutes can significantly strengthen or weaken Pluto's influence.

(For Pluto's aspects to the Sun, see the Sun's aspects to Pluto, p. 257.
For Pluto's aspects to the Moon, see the Moon's aspects to Pluto, p. 273.
For Pluto's aspects to Mercury, see Mercury's aspects to Pluto, p. 295.
For Pluto's aspects to Venus, see Venus's aspects to Pluto, p. 319.
For Pluto's aspects to Mars, see Mars's aspects to Pluto, p. 333.
For Pluto's aspects to Jupiter, see Jupiter's aspects to Pluto, p. 346.
For Pluto's aspects to Saturn, see Saturn's aspects to Pluto, p. 358.
For Pluto's aspects to Uranus, see Uranus's aspects to Pluto, p. 367.
For Pluto's aspects to Neptune, see Neptune's aspects to Pluto, p. 377.)

Pluto's aspects to the Ascendant

Conjunction

Review Pluto in the first and twelfth houses (in this chapter) for clues to your emotional makeup. You may have a great deal of emotional and physical energy, both of which need consistent and positive expression if you don't want to experience periodic burnout. You may have a dual tendency to be both guardedly secretive about your personal life and overenthusiastic about tackling work and life problems.

Positive aspects

You often have a deep-rooted need to make a clean sweep of the problems in your life and move on to bigger and better things. Indeed, you have a great capacity for successfully confronting and adapting to major changes.

Negative aspects

Watch out for the tendency to go overboard when making those changes, or to blow them out of proportion; the flip side of your abundant energy is a tendency to stagnate and do nothing at all when you experience frustration or opposition.

Pluto's aspects to the Midheaven

Conjunction

While you have potential for succeeding in your career, watch out for a tendency to fall in love with power for power's sake. You may also feel a need to change careers – or life goals – however successful you've been. Think hard about your motivations before doing so.

Positive aspects

Again, you have a marvelous facility for embracing change. You also cope well with sudden upheavals, provided you've been positively channeling your great reserves of emotional energy.

Negative aspects

When you are feeling less than energetic, your self-confidence and coping mechanisms may fail you, leaving you indecisive and shaky about making decisions.

A simple summary

✔ Pluto is strongly associated with the unconscious, the hidden, and the secretive. In the signs, houses, or aspects, Pluto points to unexpressed emotions, subtle psychological drives, and secret motivations.

✔ Pluto is the slowest moving of the planets and often takes as many as 32 years to travel through one zodiac sign. It therefore has a strong generational influence on large groups of people born in a specific time period.

✔ In the houses, Pluto underscores any problems or obstacles that could occur in the areas of life which the house governs. It may also be able to suggest ways of solving or overcoming these problems and obstacles.

✔ Pluto is the most distant planet in our solar system, and its most significant aspects are with the Ascendant and Midheaven, where the planet strongly influences one's emotional makeup and secret motivations.

PART FIVE

Chapter 24
Using Astrology in Everyday Life

USE IT . . . OR SIMPLY LOSE IT!

HALF THE FUN OF ASTROLOGY is using it in your *everyday life*. And here we talk about just how to do that, whether you're interested in astrology as a tool for better communication in your family, or as a guide to enhancing your love life, or as a sure-fire investment strategy, or as a divining tool for placing the best bet on next Saturday night's basketball game. Here you will also find a fabulous assortment of websites that feature every aspect of astrology and astrological applications, from the most esoteric realms of cosmobiology to buying and selling stocks or finding out whether your new fiancé is really the right choice for you.

We wrap up the book with those famous planetary tables we've been scaring you about, as well as an extensive glossary and a listing of astrological resources – including books, websites, schools, bookstores, magazines, and regulating institutions.

Chapter 24

Using Astrology In Everyday Life

THERE'S VERY LITTLE DOUBT that most people come to astrologers because they want to know about the future. And there's equally no doubt – as we've said before – that what astrology can tell us about the future is severely limited. Use it wisely as a guide, not as a prop in life.

In this chapter...

✓ Don't get confused

✓ Astrology as a prop

✓ The astrology of personality

✓ Seeking advice

✓ Love, sex, and relationships

✓ Business and career choices

✓ The family

✓ Your health

Don't get confused

ALTHOUGH SOME ASTROLOGERS *are psychics, and some psychics are astrologers, the two disciplines really shouldn't be confused. Generally, an astrologer will not tell you anything that he or she hasn't learned from a book, or from personal research. What he or she says may have first been published in Ptolemy's Tetrabiblios in the second century a.d., or in William Lilly's Christian Astrology in 1647, or in a modern textbook. But it certainly won't come from thin air!*

What astrology can do – in fact, what astrology does best – is help you live your life to the fullest by showing you what personality strengths you can energize and what weaknesses you can correct.

Astrology speaks to people about their personal problems, ambitions, dreams, family, relationships, work, and health. Astrology gives advice on a personal level, based on the indications in a birth chart. Indeed, that's astrology's main job – not prognostication – and one it does remarkably well.

Specialist astrologers

But astrology doesn't only confine itself to personal counseling. Some astrologers specialize in investment or business, offering advice on buying or selling stocks, hiring or firing employees, or starting new projects or business ventures. Some astrologers even specialize in the area of professional sports, forecasting the results of games and matches – with remarkable success. What astrology should never be is a crutch in your life – and we say "should" because there are always unscrupulous people out there, even among astrologers. Astrology isn't (and was never meant to be) a fallback system for answers and advice that you could (and should) easily come up with on your own.

■ **Looking at the** *birth charts of you and your partner will give you guidance on how to make a better relationship.*

INTERNET

www.astrosports-guide@loritek.com

If you're interested in using astrology to predict sports' results, this on-line site offers some terrific guidelines.

Astrology as a prop

ALL ASTROLOGERS HAVE HAD CLIENTS *who demand too much of them, who return again and again and again, asking more and more questions: "What should I do?", "Where should I go?", "How should I react?". If these people weren't leaning on an astrologer, they would be leaning on a priest or a psychiatrist, or an unfortunate partner, friend, or colleague.*

Astrology can't and shouldn't tell you how to act in any situation. What astrology offers instead are possible alternatives and approaches to a problem, a partner, a predicament.

Astrology can be a tool for helping make decisions, but the decisions are yours to make. There are, of course, other disciplines which offer this kind of advisory help – the Tarot, the Runes, the *I Ching* (the last as old and well-tried as astrology) – but astrology is the most subtle, complex, and dependable of these systems.

Seeking the truth

Of course you're going to be curious about what astrology has to say about you, your lovers, your friends, your career. Will you recognize yourself in the astrological mirror? Or will you discover someone strange and new? Your birth chart may certainly reveal some things about you that seem baffling or unbelievable. But astrology, like dreams, is a great truth-teller. The psychiatrist Sigmund Freud believed that the reason dreams speak in such a strange and confused language is that dreams tell us the truth about ourselves – and the truth is often too strange and frightening to be presented in simple, straightforward language and images.

The language of astrology is similar. Unlike dreams, however, astrology isn't likely to frighten you – though it often hints at characteristics and behaviors which you may not recognize. When an astrologer casts your birth chart, for example, you may learn that Mars was in Capricorn when you were born, and that that influence suggests you may be so wrapped up in your own ambitions that your personal relationships suffer.

At first that notion may seem absurd to you. But it will be strange indeed if there isn't a germ of truth in it; at the very least, it will be well worth thinking about.

INTERNET

www.astrologer.com/ psychast

If you're interested in exploring the fascinating world of psychological astrology, this web site is the place to visit.

393

The astrology of personality

GENTLY PRODDING PEOPLE *to look clearly at themselves, both at the inner self they hide from others and the outer self they present to the public, is what we mean by the "astrology of personality" – and it's what many astrologers believe astrology does best.*

In fact, it's fair to say that a properly cast birth chart creates a singular map of your personality – warts and all!

And while you may conclude that some of the characteristics shown in your birth chart are patently absurd, the truth is they're probably right on the money. Indeed, the more you study astrology, the more you will discover that what the chart has to say about your personality (and the personalities of others) is remarkably insightful. Those insights will enable you to know yourself better – and "know thyself" is a still a wonderful ideal!

Astrology the easy way

Unfortunately, and as with much else these days, many people want their insights – astrological or otherwise – delivered quickly, easily, and painlessly. And the computer now provides just that option. Many computer software programs offer the ability to cast a birth chart, complete with interpretations, in minutes. Similarly, many "astrological" web sites can throw up a birth chart in a moment – provided you type in an approximate time, date, and place of birth. Some sites charge a minimal fee for this service, others will provide a baseline birth chart for free, to entice you into joining their membership. You may be sorely tempted to use a computer as your personal astrologer, but we strongly caution against it.

The last statement is why most astrologers still like to draw a horoscope by hand, starting with the blank chart and gradually adding the various astrological elements to it (as this book teaches you to do). And for good reason.

Drawing up a birth chart by hand is akin to standing in a dark room, looking into a mirror, and seeing nothing at first. Stare long enough, however, and the outline of the face appears, followed by the eyes, nose, mouth, laugh lines, stress lines, and the color and texture of the skin. Eventually a complete portrait is staring you in the face. Likewise, as a birth chart slowly grows before an astrologer's eyes and the interpretations are laid upon it, the entire character of an individual takes unique form and substance.

Seeking advice

THE CHIEF WORK *of most professional astrologers is – and always has been – personal counseling. How counseling is handled has changed a bit over the past 100 years, of course, because of the growth and development of psychology. But basically, the kind of advice people were asking of Thrasylus, the astrologer of Imperial Rome, or of John Dee, the first Queen Elizabeth's astrologer, or of Simon Forman, a contemporary of Shakespeare, is the same kind of advice people seek today.*

Most people go to an astrologer with a problem. Many problems are emotional: "Should I stay with him?", or "Is she right for me", or "How can I cope now that she's left?" But people also bring practical problems to an astrologer: "Is this a good time to put my house on the market?", or "Should I buy a new car this month?", or "My cat's missing. Has she been stolen?"

■ **People often turn** *to the stars when going through an emotional crisis.*

Because astrology's been around for thousands of years, the questions people ask have usually been asked before, in one form or another, many times and of many astrologers. And contemporary astrologers have specific ways of answering them.

Generally, in answering a question or giving advice, astrologers rely on three things: their own life experiences; their uniquely personal interpretation of the birth chart; and techniques they have learned from astrological textbooks about answering specific questions.

In this respect, a good astrologer is similar to the astute doctor who recognizes in a patient the symptoms she read about in a textbook, but then uses her own medical experience and simple intuition to fine tune the diagnosis and offer the best treatment.

The astrological practice of answering specific questions is called horary astrology, an ancient and still very popular branch of astrology. In horary astrology, an individual asks a question, the astrologer draws up a chart for the time the question is asked, and then based on chart interpretation, intuition, life experience, and knowledge about the individual, the astrologer offers possible solutions.

Love, sex, and relationships

IF THERE'S ONE THING *that turns professional astrologers purple with fury, it's when newspapers or magazines publish a list of Sun signs showing what signs are compatible (or incompatible) with another. Almost every astrologer appearing on a call-in talk show will have had some sad character call and say, "I've met this marvelous person, but he's a Capricorn and I'm a Gemini, so it will never work, will it?"*

This is total and absolute nonsense.

Any Sun sign can have a wonderfully rewarding and loving relationship with any other Sun sign. Astrology is far too subtle to make such black-and-white assertions about relationships. In fact, no astrologer should warn away one person from another, even on the basis of comparing their two charts. The astrologer may certainly point out possible difficulties and rough patches, but the astrologer's credo always is (as we said at the beginning of this book), "The stars do not compel . . ."

INTERNET

www.users.evl.net/
~motive/HT-listy

This web site is designed for beginners who have an interest in horary astrology and in "predicting" specific events.

Tread especially carefully where the subject of sex is concerned. It preoccupies the minds of modern men and women far more than it did in previous eras – and it's an area astrologers are only beginning to examine in depth. Whether you're a beginning or advanced student of astrology, don't make rash assumptions about anyone's sexuality – whether those assumptions are about sexual passions, sexual taboos, or sexual preferences. Nobody, for instance, has yet discovered a reliable astrological indication of homosexuality, though many have tried.

Trivia...

The magnificent artist Michelangelo, who was also a homosexual, strongly asserted that the conjunction of Mercury and Venus in a birth chart indicated homosexuality, and that this had been the stated case of ancient astrologers since the time of Ptolemy. We believe the jury is still out on the point.

■ **Remember** – *don't make hasty assumptions about an acquaintance.*

Basic synastry techniques

The astrological technique of comparing two individuals' birth charts for compatibility is called synastry, and unfortunately it's too complex a technique to get into in this book. However, if you have your own and your partner's (or potential partner's) birth charts before you, there are some basic elements you can look for.

In general look at the positions and influences of the planets in both charts, and then look at the relationship between each planet in one chart to each planet in the other chart.

Just as with a single chart, look at the number of degrees which separate the planets – but across the charts. If, for example, your Venus makes an aspect to your partner's Mars, there is probably a very strong sexual attraction between the two of you. (See the accompanying chart for other interpretive tips about romance and compatibility.)

SIMPLE TIPS FOR TRUE ROMANCE

When looking at the two birth charts of potential (or actual) partners, keep these interpretive tips in mind:

✔ Venus in one chart conjunct Mars in the other suggests a positive, passionate, and compelling relationship.

✔ Venus in one chart square Mars in the other encourages a positive and harmonious relationship.

✔ Venus in one chart square Uranus in the other suggests a lively relationship with some tension.

✔ Venus in one chart conjunct Uranus in the other indicates emotional differences but a strong rapport.

✔ Venus in one chart trine or sextile Mars in the other points to possible frivolity and fickleness.

✔ Venus in one chart in opposition to Mars in the other suggests a lively and impulsive relationship.

✔ Venus in one chart trine Uranus in the other encourages a dynamic, but erratic, attraction.

✔ Venus in one chart in sextile or opposition to Uranus in the other indicates that impulsiveness may cause problems.

Business and career choice

THERE ARE MANY WAYS *in which astrology is useful for making business decisions and career choices. Some astrologers, for instance, specialize in the movements of stocks and shares, combining astrological knowledge of planetary movements and influences with known business cycles; these astrologers are often quite successful when offering investment advice. Some businesses employ astrologers (as they do people who analyze palms and handwriting) to help make employment assessments.*

One of the main uses of astrology in business is in comparing the charts of people working together at almost every level of employment. This is done in much the same way as for romantic partners (see previous page) – that is, planetary influences and aspects are compared across the charts of two or more individuals.

The perfect business partnership

Interestingly, the same astrological influences that indicate a romantic relationship may be unsuccessful are often the influences that make for an excellent business partnership. For example, considerable personality differences may signal problems ahead for a couple, but contrasting personalities are often great in business, where irritation and argument may spark new ideas and directions.

In interpreting the birth charts of potential business partners or coworkers, look for an opposition or trine between one person's Midheaven and the other's Ascendant: this indicates similar ambitions and aspirations. Strong aspects between each chart's Sun, Moon, rising sign, and/or Ascendant degree indicate compatibility. A strong relationship between the two charts' eighth houses encourages financial success.

If you are thinking of starting a business, or if you are trying to decide what business or career to go into, pay close attention to the placements and strength of the planets in your birth chart.

For example, Venus is associated with the beauty business and with luxury. A strong Moon suggests that the hotel or restaurant business would be fruitful. A dominant Saturn indicates that real estate may be an excellent choice.

INTERNET

www.citystats.co.uk

Fascinating business advice and tips on investing are offered at the Citystate Stockstars web site.

The family

WITHIN FAMILIES, there is almost always a strongly similar astrological pattern across the generations. Quite often we can see links between an adult family member's birth chart and that of a child in the family. This is particularly the case with grandparents and grandchildren (and perhaps one of the reasons for that unique bond).

You may find it especially useful to compare your children's birth charts to your chart and your spouse's. Of course, you will expect to find some close connections and similar characteristics – and you will. But you will also no doubt discover unexpected traits and qualities that may surprise you. It's a wise parent who knows his or her child as completely as possible, and astrology can be very helpful in closing generation gaps and indicating easier ways to communicate with your children.

Astrology and children

Of course, an astrologer cannot tell you precisely how your baby is going to grow up. Free will is always operative – especially with children! But an astrologer may be able to indicate whether a child will be closer to the mother or father and in what way; what childhood illnesses are most likely to occur and when; and what sort of school will best suit him or her.

Astrology is particularly helpful in indicating where a child's talents lie and in which direction he or she should be encouraged – for example, whether he will tend to be practical rather than artistic, or she will enjoy business management or public relations rather than fashion or music.

■ **Astrology can** *be used to highlight the strengths of our children.*

INTERNET

**www.egroups.com/list/
child-family**

If you're interested in studying astrology as it relates specifically to family and children, this web site offers some very interesting insights for you.

Health

THE ASTROLOGY OF HEALTH *is an enormously complex subject – one which demands a book of its own! Generally speaking, astrology has had a long-standing connection both with individual health (the direct influence of the Sun signs and ruling planets) and with the medical profession (which in the past often used astrology to make diagnoses and prescribe treatments).*

In particular, the Sun and the rising signs are great indicators of where you may be vulnerable to particular health problems.

■ **Consider alternative remedies**
that are tied to your Sun sign.

In fact, in Part 2 of this book, each Sun-sign description has a lengthy section on health alone. Just to recap, each sign is traditionally connected to a specific body part, organ, or organ system. And it is almost invariably true that those body parts, organs, or organ systems will figure prominently in an individual's life – either because there's an associated health problem or vulnerability; or, interestingly, because that area is remarkably strong and healthy!

Consider your birth chart

Apart from the general Sun- and rising-sign characteristics regarding health, look in your birth chart for the planetary influences and placements near the Ascendant, and in the first and sixth houses. Also consider the general influence and placement in the chart of the Sun and the Moon. Finally, consider the personality characteristics indicated by the chart. A strong emphasis on stress, tension, or undue worry, for example, may indicate related physical problems (such as high blood pressure) or psychological difficulties (such as anxiety or depression), or perhaps even a tendency toward hypochondria. Overly confident and optimistic people, on the other hand, may ignore the physical symptoms of poor health until a real problem develops.

INTERNET

www.medicine garden.com

The Athena web site, which can be found at the address given above, specializes in medical astrology.

A simple summary

✔ While many people consult astrologers because they want to know about the future, astrologers cannot (and should not) predict the future or pretend that they can.

✔ Astrology should never be used as a crutch. In the end, you must provide your own answers to your personal difficulties and make your own decisions. Astrology merely suggests, it never dictates a course of action.

✔ What astrology does best is draw up a complete picture of your personality, showing you how to maximize your strengths, minimize your weaknesses, take positive actions to combat your shortcomings, and make better decisions.

✔ Astrology shines brightest in the area of personal counseling, where it speaks truthfully about people's problems, ambitions, dreams, family, relationships, work, and health.

✔ Astrology, when used correctly, is also useful in business, finance, and sport.

✔ As far as romance is concerned, any Sun sign can have a wonderful relationship with any other Sun sign.

✔ Family members frequently share similar astrological indications. This is especially true between grandparents and grandchildren. Within the family, astrology can be a great tool for opening the doors of communication as parents can learn about the characteristics of their children and vice versa.

✔ Where health is concerned, the Sun and rising signs will point the way toward specific health problems, because each sign is associated with a particular body part, organ, or organ system. Personality characteristics that may make one vulnerable to certain illnesses can be seen in the birth chart.

Planetary tables

USE THE TABLES below to find the position of the Sun, Moon, and planets at the time of your birth. Find your birth year in the top column, and the month of birth in the left. Plot the position of each planet in the first, middle, or final section of the appropriate sign on your birth chart.

KEY TO GLYPHS FOR THE PLANETS

☉	Sun	♃	Jupiter
☽	Moon	♄	Saturn
☿	Mercury	♅	Uranus
♀	Venus	♆	Neptune
♂	Mars	♇	Pluto

KEY TO GLYPHS FOR THE SIGNS OF THE ZODIAC

♈	Aries	♎	Libra
♉	Taurus	♏	Scorpio
♊	Gemini	♐	Sagittarius
♋	Cancer	♑	Capricorn
♌	Leo	♒	Aquarius
♍	Virgo	♓	Pisces

	1910	1911	1912	1913	1914	1915	1916	1917	1918	1919	1920	1921	1922	1923	1924	1925	1926	1927	1928
1	20♒21.59	21♒3.51	21♒9.29	20♒15.19	20♒21.12	21♒3.00	21♒8.54	21♒14.37	20♒20.25	21♒2.21	21♒8.04	20♒13.55	20♒19.48	21♒1.35	21♒7.28	20♒13.20	20♒19.12	21♒1.12	21♒6.57
2	19♓12.28	19♓18.20	19♓23.56	19♓5.44	19♓11.38	19♓17.23	19♓23.18	19♓5.05	19♓10.53	19♓16.48	19♓22.29	19♓4.20	19♓10.16	19♓16.00	19♓21.51	19♓3.43	19♓9.35	19♓15.43	19♓21.19
3	21♈12.03	21♈17.54	20♈23.29	21♈5.18	21♈11.11	21♈16.51	20♈22.47	21♈4.37	21♈10.26	21♈16.19	20♈21.59	21♈3.51	21♈9.49	21♈15.29	20♈21.20	21♈3.12	21♈9.01	21♈14.59	20♈20.44
4	20♉23.46	21♉5.36	20♉11.12	20♉17.03	20♉22.53	21♉4.29	20♉10.25	20♉16.17	20♉22.05	21♉3.59	20♉9.39	20♉15.32	20♉21.29	21♉3.06	20♉8.59	20♉14.51	20♉20.36	21♉2.32	20♉8.17
5	21♊23.30	22♊5.19	21♊10.57	21♊16.50	21♊22.38	22♊4.10	21♊10.06	21♊15.59	21♊21.46	22♊3.39	21♊9.22	21♊15.17	21♊21.10	22♊2.45	21♊8.40	21♊14.33	21♊20.22	22♊2.08	21♊7.52
6	22♋7.49	22♋13.36	21♋19.17	22♋1.10	22♋6.55	22♋12.25	21♋18.22	22♋0.14	22♋6.00	22♋11.54	21♋17.40	21♋23.36	22♋5.27	22♋11.03	21♋16.59	21♋22.50	22♋4.30	22♋10.22	22♋16.06
7	23♌18.43	24♌0.29	23♌6.14	23♌12.04	23♌17.47	23♌23.26	23♌5.21	23♌11.08	23♌16.51	23♌22.45	23♌4.35	23♌10.30	23♌16.20	23♌22.01	23♌3.58	23♌9.45	23♌15.25	23♌21.17	23♌3.02
8	24♍1.27	24♍7.13	24♍13.01	24♍18.48	24♍0.38	24♍6.15	24♍12.09	23♍17.54	23♍23.37	24♍5.28	23♍11.21	23♍17.15	23♍23.04	24♍4.52	23♍10.48	23♍16.33	24♍22.14	24♍4.05	23♍9.53
9	23♎22.31	24♎4.18	23♎10.08	23♎15.53	23♎21.34	24♎3.24	23♎9.15	23♎15.00	23♎20.46	24♎2.35	23♎8.28	23♎14.20	23♎20.10	24♎2.04	23♎7.58	23♎13.43	23♎19.27	24♎1.17	23♎7.06
10	24♏7.11	24♏12.58	23♏18.50	24♏0.35	24♏6.17	24♏12.10	23♏17.57	23♏23.44	24♏5.33	24♏11.21	23♏17.13	23♏23.02	24♏4.53	24♏10.51	23♏16.44	23♏22.31	24♏4.18	24♏10.07	23♏15.55
11	23♐4.11	23♐9.56	22♐15.48	22♐21.35	23♐3.20	23♐9.14	22♐14.58	22♐20.45	23♐2.38	23♐8.25	22♐14.15	22♐20.05	23♐1.55	23♐7.54	22♐13.46	22♐19.35	23♐1.28	23♐7.14	22♐13.00
12	22♑17.12	22♑22.53	22♑4.45	22♑10.35	22♑16.22	22♑22.16	22♑3.59	22♑9.46	22♑15.42	22♑21.27	22♑3.17	22♑9.07	22♑14.57	22♑20.53	22♑2.45	22♑8.37	22♑14.33	22♑20.19	22♑2.04

	1929	1930	1931	1932	1933	1934	1935	1936	1937	1938	1939	1940	1941	1942	1943	1944	1945	1946	1947
1	20♒12.42	20♒18.33	21♒0.18	21♒6.07	20♒11.53	20♒17.37	20♒23.28	21♒5.12	20♒11.01	20♒16.59	20♒22.51	21♒4.44	20♒10.34	20♒16.24	20♒22.19	21♒4.07	20♒9.54	20♒15.45	20♒21.32
2	19♓3.07	19♓9.00	19♓14.40	19♓20.28	19♓2.16	19♓8.02	19♓13.52	19♓19.33	19♓1.21	19♓7.20	19♓13.09	19♓19.04	19♓0.56	19♓6.47	19♓12.40	19♓18.27	19♓0.15	19♓6.09	19♓11.52
3	21♈2.35	21♈8.30	21♈14.06	20♈19.54	21♈1.43	21♈7.28	21♈13.18	20♈18.58	21♈0.45	21♈6.43	21♈12.28	20♈18.24	21♈0.20	21♈6.11	21♈12.03	20♈17.49	20♈23.37	21♈5.33	21♈11.13
4	20♉14.10	20♉20.06	21♉1.40	20♉7.28	20♉13.18	20♉19.00	21♉0.50	20♉6.31	20♉12.19	20♉18.15	20♉23.55	20♉5.51	20♉11.50	20♉17.39	20♉23.32	20♉5.18	20♉11.07	20♉17.02	20♉22.39
5	21♊13.48	21♊19.42	21♊1.15	21♊7.07	21♊12.57	21♊18.35	21♊0.25	21♊6.07	21♊11.57	21♊17.50	21♊23.27	21♊5.23	21♊11.23	21♊17.09	21♊23.03	21♊4.51	21♊10.40	21♊16.34	21♊22.09
6	21♋22.01	22♋3.53	21♋9.28	21♋15.23	21♋21.12	22♋2.48	21♋8.38	21♋14.22	21♋20.12	22♋2.04	21♋7.39	21♋13.36	21♋19.33	22♋1.16	22♋7.12	21♋13.02	21♋18.52	22♋0.44	22♋6.19
7	23♌8.53	23♌14.42	23♌20.21	23♌2.18	23♌8.05	23♌13.42	23♌19.33	23♌1.18	23♌7.07	23♌12.57	23♌18.37	23♌0.34	23♌6.26	23♌12.07	23♌18.05	23♌23.56	23♌5.45	23♌11.37	23♌17.14
8	23♍15.41	23♍21.26	24♍3.10	23♍9.06	24♍14.52	23♍20.32	24♍2.24	23♍8.11	23♍13.58	23♍19.46	24♍1.31	24♍7.29	24♍13.17	23♍18.58	24♍0.55	23♍6.46	23♍12.35	23♍18.26	24♍0.09
9	23♎12.52	23♎18.36	24♎0.23	23♎6.16	23♎12.01	23♎17.45	23♎23.38	23♎5.26	23♎11.13	23♎17.00	23♎22.49	23♎4.46	23♎10.33	23♎16.16	23♎22.12	23♎4.02	23♎9.50	23♎15.41	23♎21.27
10	23♏21.41	23♏3.26	24♏9.16	23♏15.04	23♏20.48	24♏2.36	24♏8.29	23♏14.18	23♏20.07	24♏1.54	24♏7.46	23♏13.39	23♏19.27	24♏1.15	24♏7.08	23♏12.56	23♏18.44	24♏0.35	24♏6.26
11	22♐18.48	23♐0.34	23♐6.25	22♐12.10	22♐17.53	22♐23.44	23♐5.35	22♐11.25	22♐17.17	23♐23.06	23♐4.59	22♐10.49	22♐16.38	22♐22.30	23♐4.22	22♐10.08	22♐15.55	22♐21.46	23♐3.38
12	22♑7.53	22♑13.40	22♑19.30	22♑1.14	22♑6.58	22♑12.49	22♑18.37	22♑0.27	22♑6.22	22♑12.13	22♑18.06	21♑23.55	22♑5.44	22♑11.40	22♑17.29	21♑23.15	22♑5.04	22♑10.53	22♑16.43

	1948	1949	1950	1951	1952	1953	1954	1955	1956	1957	1958	1959	1960	1961	1962	1963	1964	1965	1966
1	21♒3.18	20♒9.09	21♒15.00	20♒20.52	21♒2.38	20♒8.21	20♒14.11	20♒20.02	21♒1.48	20♒7.39	20♒13.28	20♒19.19	21♒1.10	20♒7.01	20♒12.58	20♒18.54	21♒0.41	20♒6.29	20♒12.20
2	19♓17.37	18♓23.27	19♓5.18	19♓11.10	19♓16.57	18♓22.41	19♓4.32	19♓10.26	19♓16.05	18♓21.58	19♓3.48	19♓9.38	19♓15.26	18♓21.16	19♓3.15	19♓9.09	19♓14.57	18♓20.48	19♓2.38
3	20♈16.57	20♈22.48	21♈4.35	21♈10.26	20♈16.14	20♈22.01	21♈3.53	21♈9.35	20♈15.20	20♈21.16	21♈3.06	21♈8.55	20♈14.43	20♈20.32	21♈2.30	21♈8.20	20♈14.10	20♈20.05	21♈1.53
4	20♉4.25	20♉10.17	20♉15.59	20♉21.48	20♉3.17	20♉9.25	20♉15.20	20♉20.58	20♉2.43	20♉8.41	20♉14.27	20♉20.17	20♉2.06	20♉7.55	20♉13.51	20♉19.36	20♉1.27	20♉7.26	20♉13.13
5	21♊3.58	21♊9.51	21♊15.27	21♊21.15	21♊3.04	21♊8.53	21♊14.47	21♊20.24	21♊2.13	21♊8.10	21♊13.51	21♊19.42	21♊1.34	21♊7.22	21♊13.17	21♊18.58	21♊0.50	21♊6.50	21♊12.32
6	21♋12.11	21♋18.03	21♋23.36	21♋5.25	21♋11.13	21♋17.00	21♋22.54	22♋4.31	21♋10.24	21♋16.21	21♋21.57	22♋3.50	21♋9.42	21♋15.30	21♋21.24	22♋3.04	21♋8.57	21♋14.56	21♋20.33
7	23♌23.08	23♌4.57	23♌10.30	23♌16.21	22♌22.07	23♌3.52	23♌9.45	23♌15.25	23♌21.20	23♌3.15	23♌8.50	23♌14.45	22♌20.37	23♌2.24	23♌8.18	23♌13.59	22♌19.53	23♌1.48	23♌7.23
8	23♍6.03	23♍11.48	23♍17.23	23♍23.16	23♍5.03	23♍10.45	23♍16.36	23♍22.19	23♍4.15	23♍10.08	23♍15.46	23♍21.44	23♍3.34	23♍9.19	23♍15.12	23♍20.58	23♍2.51	23♍8.43	23♍14.18
9	23♎3.22	23♎9.06	23♎14.44	23♎20.37	23♎2.24	23♎8.06	23♎13.55	23♎19.41	23♎1.35	23♎7.26	23♎13.09	23♎19.08	23♎0.59	23♎6.42	23♎12.35	23♎18.24	23♎0.17	23♎6.06	23♎11.43
10	23♏12.18	23♏18.03	23♏23.45	24♏5.36	23♏11.22	23♏17.06	23♏22.56	24♏4.43	23♏10.34	23♏16.24	23♏22.11	24♏4.11	23♏10.02	23♏15.47	23♏21.40	24♏3.29	23♏9.21	23♏15.10	23♏20.51
11	22♐9.29	22♐15.16	22♐21.03	23♐2.51	22♐8.36	22♐14.22	22♐20.14	23♐2.01	22♐7.50	22♐13.39	22♐19.29	23♐1.27	22♐7.18	22♐13.08	22♐19.02	23♐0.49	22♐6.39	22♐12.29	23♐18.14
12	22♑22.33	22♑4.23	22♑10.13	22♑16.00	21♑21.43	22♑3.31	22♑9.24	22♑15.11	21♑20.59	22♑2.49	22♑8.40	22♑14.34	21♑20.26	22♑2.19	22♑8.15	22♑14.02	22♑19.50	21♑1.40	22♑7.28

	1967	1968	1969	1970	1971	1972	1973	1974	1975	1976	1977	1978	1979	1980	1981	1982	1983	1984	1985
1	20 ♒ 18.08	20 ♒ 23.54	20 ♒ 5.38	20 ♒ 11.24	20 ♒ 17.13	20 ♒ 20.59	20 ♒ 4.48	20 ♒ 10.46	20 ♒ 16.36	20 ♒ 22.25	20 ♒ 4.14	20 ♒ 10.04	20 ♒ 16.00	20 ♒ 21.49	20 ♒ 3.36	20 ♒ 9.31	20 ♒ 15.17	20 ♒ 21.05	20 ♒ 2.58
2	19 ♓ 8.24	19 ♓ 14.09	18 ♓ 19.55	19 ♓ 1.42	19 ♓ 7.27	19 ♓ 13.11	18 ♓ 19.01	19 ♓ 0.59	19 ♓ 6.50	19 ♓ 12.40	18 ♓ 18.30	19 ♓ 0.21	19 ♓ 6.13	19 ♓ 12.02	18 ♓ 17.52	18 ♓ 23.47	19 ♓ 5.31	19 ♓ 11.16	18 ♓ 17.07
3	21 ♈ 7.37	20 ♈ 13.22	20 ♈ 19.08	21 ♈ 0.56	21 ♈ 6.38	21 ♈ 12.21	20 ♈ 18.12	21 ♈ 0.07	21 ♈ 5.57	20 ♈ 11.50	20 ♈ 17.42	20 ♈ 23.34	21 ♈ 5.22	20 ♈ 11.10	20 ♈ 17.03	20 ♈ 22.56	21 ♈ 4.39	20 ♈ 10.24	20 ♈ 16.14
4	20 ♉ 18.55	20 ♉ 0.14	20 ♉ 6.27	20 ♉ 12.15	20 ♉ 17.54	19 ♉ 23.37	20 ♉ 5.30	20 ♉ 11.19	20 ♉ 17.07	19 ♉ 23.03	20 ♉ 4.57	20 ♉ 10.50	20 ♉ 16.35	19 ♉ 22.23	20 ♉ 4.19	20 ♉ 10.07	20 ♉ 15.50	19 ♉ 21.38	20 ♉ 3.26
5	21 ♊ 18.12	21 ♊ 0.06	21 ♊ 5.50	21 ♊ 11.37	21 ♊ 17.15	21 ♊ 23.00	21 ♊ 4.54	21 ♊ 10.36	21 ♊ 16.24	21 ♊ 22.21	21 ♊ 4.14	21 ♊ 10.08	21 ♊ 15.54	20 ♊ 21.42	21 ♊ 3.39	21 ♊ 9.23	21 ♊ 15.06	20 ♊ 20.58	21 ♊ 2.43
6	22 ♋ 2.23	21 ♋ 8.13	21 ♋ 13.55	21 ♋ 19.43	22 ♋ 1.20	21 ♋ 7.06	21 ♋ 13.01	21 ♋ 18.38	22 ♋ 0.26	21 ♋ 6.24	21 ♋ 12.14	21 ♋ 18.01	21 ♋ 23.56	21 ♋ 5.47	21 ♋ 11.45	21 ♋ 17.23	21 ♋ 23.09	21 ♋ 5.02	21 ♋ 10.44
7	23 ♌ 13.16	22 ♌ 19.07	23 ♌ 0.48	23 ♌ 6.37	23 ♌ 12.15	22 ♌ 18.03	22 ♌ 23.56	23 ♌ 5.30	23 ♌ 11.22	22 ♌ 17.18	22 ♌ 23.04	23 ♌ 5.00	22 ♌ 10.49	22 ♌ 16.42	22 ♌ 22.40	22 ♌ 4.15	22 ♌ 10.04	22 ♌ 15.58	22 ♌ 21.36
8	23 ♍ 20.12	23 ♍ 2.03	23 ♍ 7.43	23 ♍ 13.34	23 ♍ 19.15	23 ♍ 1.03	23 ♍ 6.53	23 ♍ 12.29	23 ♍ 18.24	23 ♍ 0.18	23 ♍ 6.00	23 ♍ 11.57	23 ♍ 17.47	23 ♍ 23.41	23 ♍ 5.38	23 ♍ 11.15	23 ♍ 17.07	23 ♍ 23.00	23 ♍ 4.36
9	23 ♎ 17.38	23 ♎ 23.26	23 ♎ 5.07	23 ♎ 10.59	23 ♎ 16.45	22 ♎ 22.33	23 ♎ 4.21	23 ♎ 9.58	23 ♎ 15.55	23 ♎ 21.48	23 ♎ 3.29	23 ♎ 9.25	23 ♎ 15.16	23 ♎ 21.09	23 ♎ 3.05	23 ♎ 8.46	23 ♎ 14.42	23 ♎ 20.33	23 ♎ 2.07
10	24 ♏ 2.44	23 ♏ 8.30	23 ♏ 14.11	23 ♏ 20.04	24 ♏ 1.53	23 ♏ 7.41	23 ♏ 13.30	23 ♏ 19.11	24 ♏ 1.06	23 ♏ 6.58	23 ♏ 12.41	23 ♏ 18.37	24 ♏ 0.28	23 ♏ 6.18	23 ♏ 12.13	23 ♏ 17.58	23 ♏ 23.54	23 ♏ 5.46	23 ♏ 11.22
11	23 ♐ 0.04	22 ♐ 5.49	22 ♐ 11.31	22 ♐ 17.25	22 ♐ 23.14	22 ♐ 5.03	22 ♐ 10.54	22 ♐ 16.38	22 ♐ 22.31	22 ♐ 4.22	22 ♐ 10.07	22 ♐ 16.05	22 ♐ 21.54	22 ♐ 3.41	22 ♐ 9.36	22 ♐ 15.23	22 ♐ 21.18	22 ♐ 3.11	22 ♐ 8.51
12	22 ♑ 13.16	21 ♑ 19.00	22 ♑ 0.44	22 ♑ 6.36	22 ♑ 12.24	21 ♑ 18.13	22 ♑ 0.08	22 ♑ 5.56	22 ♑ 11.46	21 ♑ 17.35	21 ♑ 23.23	22 ♑ 5.21	22 ♑ 11.10	21 ♑ 16.56	22 ♑ 22.51	22 ♑ 4.38	22 ♑ 10.30	21 ♑ 16.23	21 ♑ 22.08

	1986	1987	1988	1989	1990	1991	1992	1993	1994	1995	1996	1997	1998	1999	2000	2001	2002	2003	2004
1	20 ♒ 8.46	20 ♒ 14.40	20 ♒ 20.24	20 ♒ 2.07	20 ♒ 8.02	20 ♒ 13.47	20 ♒ 19.33	20 ♒ 1.23	20 ♒ 7.07	20 ♒ 13.00	20 ♒ 18.53	20 ♒ 0.43	20 ♒ 6.46	20 ♒ 12.37	20 ♒ 18.23	20 ♒ 0.17	20 ♒ 6.02	20 ♒ 11.54	20 ♒ 17.41
2	18 ♓ 22.58	19 ♓ 4.50	19 ♓ 10.35	18 ♓ 16.21	18 ♓ 22.14	19 ♓ 3.58	19 ♓ 9.44	18 ♓ 15.35	19 ♓ 21.22	19 ♓ 3.11	19 ♓ 9.01	19 ♓ 14.52	18 ♓ 20.55	19 ♓ 2.47	19 ♓ 8.33	18 ♓ 14.28	18 ♓ 20.16	19 ♓ 2.05	19 ♓ 7.51
3	20 ♈ 22.03	21 ♈ 3.52	20 ♈ 9.39	20 ♈ 15.28	20 ♈ 21.19	21 ♈ 3.02	20 ♈ 8.48	20 ♈ 14.41	20 ♈ 20.28	21 ♈ 2.14	20 ♈ 8.03	20 ♈ 13.55	20 ♈ 19.55	21 ♈ 1.46	20 ♈ 7.35	20 ♈ 13.31	20 ♈ 19.20	21 ♈ 1.06	20 ♈ 6.52
4	20 ♉ 9.12	20 ♉ 14.58	19 ♉ 20.45	20 ♉ 2.39	20 ♉ 8.27	20 ♉ 14.08	19 ♉ 19.57	20 ♉ 1.49	20 ♉ 7.36	20 ♉ 13.22	19 ♉ 19.10	20 ♉ 1.03	20 ♉ 6.57	20 ♉ 12.46	19 ♉ 18.40	20 ♉ 0.35	20 ♉ 6.24	20 ♉ 12.09	19 ♉ 17.56
5	21 ♊ 8.28	21 ♊ 14.10	20 ♊ 19.57	21 ♊ 1.54	21 ♊ 7.37	21 ♊ 13.20	21 ♊ 19.12	21 ♊ 1.02	21 ♊ 6.49	21 ♊ 12.34	20 ♊ 18.23	21 ♊ 0.18	21 ♊ 6.05	21 ♊ 11.52	20 ♊ 17.49	20 ♊ 23.41	21 ♊ 5.29	21 ♊ 11.16	20 ♊ 17.02
6	21 ♋ 16.30	21 ♋ 22.11	21 ♋ 3.57	21 ♋ 9.53	21 ♋ 15.33	21 ♋ 21.19	21 ♋ 3.14	21 ♋ 9.00	21 ♋ 14.48	21 ♋ 20.34	21 ♋ 2.24	21 ♋ 8.20	21 ♋ 14.03	21 ♋ 19.49	21 ♋ 1.48	21 ♋ 7.36	21 ♋ 13.24	21 ♋ 19.12	21 ♋ 0.58
7	23 ♌ 3.24	22 ♌ 9.06	22 ♌ 14.51	22 ♌ 20.45	23 ♌ 2.30	22 ♌ 8.15	22 ♌ 14.09	22 ♌ 19.51	23 ♌ 1.41	22 ♌ 7.30	22 ♌ 13.19	22 ♌ 19.15	22 ♌ 0.58	22 ♌ 6.47	22 ♌ 12.36	22 ♌ 18.24	23 ♌ 0.13	22 ♌ 6.05	22 ♌ 11.51
8	23 ♍ 10.26	23 ♍ 16.10	22 ♍ 21.54	23 ♍ 3.46	23 ♍ 9.21	23 ♍ 15.13	22 ♍ 21.10	23 ♍ 2.50	23 ♍ 8.44	23 ♍ 14.35	22 ♍ 20.23	23 ♍ 2.19	23 ♍ 8.11	23 ♍ 13.57	22 ♍ 19.49	23 ♍ 1.28	23 ♍ 7.19	23 ♍ 13.11	22 ♍ 18.55
9	23 ♎ 7.59	23 ♎ 13.45	22 ♎ 19.29	23 ♎ 1.20	23 ♎ 6.56	23 ♎ 12.48	22 ♎ 18.43	23 ♎ 0.23	23 ♎ 6.19	23 ♎ 12.13	22 ♎ 18.00	23 ♎ 23.56	23 ♎ 5.31	23 ♎ 11.32	22 ♎ 17.28	23 ♎ 23.05	23 ♎ 4.59	23 ♎ 10.51	22 ♎ 16.33
10	23 ♏ 17.14	23 ♏ 23.01	23 ♏ 4.44	23 ♏ 10.35	23 ♏ 16.14	23 ♏ 22.05	23 ♏ 3.57	23 ♏ 9.37	23 ♏ 15.36	23 ♏ 21.32	23 ♏ 3.19	23 ♏ 9.15	23 ♏ 14.59	23 ♏ 20.52	23 ♏ 2.48	23 ♏ 8.25	23 ♏ 14.21	23 ♏ 20.12	23 ♏ 1.52
11	22 ♐ 14.44	22 ♐ 20.29	22 ♐ 2.12	22 ♐ 8.05	22 ♐ 13.47	22 ♐ 19.36	22 ♐ 1.26	22 ♐ 7.07	22 ♐ 13.06	22 ♐ 19.01	22 ♐ 0.49	22 ♐ 6.48	22 ♐ 12.34	22 ♐ 18.25	22 ♐ 0.19	22 ♐ 5.59	22 ♐ 11.54	22 ♐ 17.44	22 ♐ 23.22
12	22 ♑ 4.02	22 ♑ 9.46	22 ♑ 15.28	21 ♑ 21.22	22 ♑ 3.07	22 ♑ 8.54	21 ♑ 14.43	22 ♑ 20.26	22 ♑ 2.23	22 ♑ 8.17	21 ♑ 14.06	22 ♑ 20.07	21 ♑ 1.57	22 ♑ 7.44	22 ♑ 13.37	21 ♑ 19.19	22 ♑ 1.13	22 ♑ 7.02	21 ♑ 12.40

	2005	2006	2007	2008
1	19 ♒ 23.19	20 ♒ 5.15	20 ♒ 11.03	20 ♒ 16.45
2	18 ♓ 13.31	18 ♓ 19.25	19 ♓ 1.11	19 ♓ 6.52
3	20 ♈ 12.35	20 ♈ 18.27	21 ♈ 0.10	20 ♈ 5.51
4	19 ♉ 23.42	20 ♉ 5.29	20 ♉ 11.10	19 ♉ 16.54
5	20 ♊ 22.51	21 ♊ 4.35	21 ♊ 10.15	20 ♊ 16.01
6	21 ♋ 6.49	21 ♋ 12.30	21 ♋ 18.11	21 ♋ 0.01
7	22 ♌ 17.42	22 ♌ 23.22	23 ♌ 5.05	22 ♌ 10.58
8	23 ♍ 0.47	23 ♍ 6.27	23 ♍ 12.14	22 ♍ 18.07
9	22 ♎ 22.26	23 ♎ 4.08	23 ♎ 9.56	22 ♎ 15.49
10	23 ♏ 7.46	23 ♏ 13.31	23 ♏ 19.19	23 ♏ 1.12
11	22 ♐ 5.17	22 ♐ 11.04	22 ♐ 16.52	22 ♐ 22.44
12	21 ♑ 18.35	22 ♑ 0.24	22 ♑ 6.08	21 ♑ 12.02

	1910	1911	1912	1913	1914	1915	1916	1917	1918	1919	1920

Month	1921	1922	1923	1924	1925	1926	1927	1928	1929	1930	1931
1	1♑ 7♑ 14♑ 20♒ 25♒ 31♒	1♑ 6♑ 12♒ 18♒ 24♒	1♑ 5♒ 13♒ 27♒	1♑ 14♑	1♐ 15♑ 24♑	1♐ 4♐ 12♑ 19♑ 26♑	1♐ 6♑ 12♑ 19♑ 25♒ 30♒	1♑ 5♑ 11♑ 17♒ 23♒ 28♒	1♑ 3♑ 9♒ 15♒ 22♒	1♑ 3♒ 24♑	1♑ 10♑ 26♑
2	1♒ 6♓ 12♓	1♒ 2♓ 10♒ 18♒	1♒ 7♑ 14♒ 27♒	1♑ 6♑ 15♒ 22♒ 29♒	1♑ 8♒ 14♒ 20♒ 26♓	1♒ 7♒ 13♒ 18♓ 24♓	1♒ 5♒ 11♓ 16♓ 23♓	1♒ 4♓ 13♓	1♒ 5♒ 15♒ 25♒	1♑ 16♒ 24♒	1♑ 4♑ 12♒ 19♒ 25♒
3	1♓ 5♓ 30♓	1♒ 9♒ 19♓ 26♓	1♒ 7♒ 14♓ 20♓ 26♓ 31♈	1♒ 6♓ 12♓ 17♓ 22♈ 27♈	1♓ 4♓ 9♓ 14♈ 19♈ 25♈	1♓ 7♈ 14♈ 30♈	1♓ 15♓	1♒ 19♓ 28♓	1♒ 8♒ 16♓ 23♓ 29♓	1♒ 4♒ 10♓ 16♓ 22♓ 27♈	1♒ 3♓ 9♓ 14♓ 19♈ 24♈ 29♈
4	1♓ 7♓ 15♈ 21♈ 27♈	1♓ 8♈ 13♈ 19♈ 23♉ 28♉	1♈ 5♈ 10♈ 15♉ 20♉ 25♉	1♈ 6♉ 12♉ 23♉	1♈ 2♉ 16♈	1♈ 28♈	1♓ 9♓ 18♈ 25♈	1♓ 5♓ 11♈ 17♈ 23♈ 28♉	1♓ 4♈ 10♈ 15♈ 19♉ 24♉ 29♉	1♈ 6♈ 11♉ 16♉ 22♉	1♈ 4♉ 12♉ 28♉
5	1♈ 2♉ 7♉ 11♉ 16♊ 21♊ 26♊	1♉ 3♉ 8♊ 13♊ 20♊	1♉ 2♊ 13♊ 22♊	1♉	1♈ 18♉ 26♉	1♈ 7♈ 14♉ 20♉ 25♉ 30♊	1♈ 7♉ 12♉ 17♉ 21♊ 26♊ 31♊	1♉ 3♉ 7♉ 12♊ 17♊ 22♊ 29♋	1♉ 4♊ 11♊ 21♊	1♉ 2♊ 18♉	1♉ 27♉
6	1♋ 8♋ 21♋	1♊ 2♋ 11♊	1♊ 25♊	1♉ 5♉ 14♊ 20♊ 25♊ 30♋	1♉ 7♊ 12♊ 17♊ 21♋ 26♋	1♊ 4♊ 8♊ 13♋ 18♋ 23♋ 30♌	1♊ 5♋ 11♋ 18♋ 29♌	1♋ 9♋ 24♋	1♊	1♉ 15♊ 24♊ 30♊	1♉ 5♉ 12♊ 17♊ 22♊ 27♋
7	1♋	1♊ 14♋ 21♋ 27♋	1♊ 3♊ 9♋ 14♋ 19♋ 24♌ 28♌	1♋ 5♋ 9♋ 14♌ 19♌ 25♌ 31♍	1♋ 6♌ 12♌ 19♌ 27♍	1♌ 7♌ 20♌	1♌ 15♋	1♋ 23♋ 31♋	1♊ 4♊ 12♋ 18♋ 23♋ 28♌	1♊ 5♋ 10♋ 15♋ 20♌ 24♌ 30♌	1♋ 6♋ 11♌ 17♌ 23♌ 29♍
8	1♋ 9♌ 14♌ 19♌ 24♍ 29♍	1♌ 6♌ 11♌ 16♍ 21♍ 27♍	1♌ 3♌ 8♍ 14♍ 21♍ 28♎	1♍ 7♍ 16♍	1♍ 28♌	1♌ 14♌ 22♌ 31♌	1♋ 13♌ 19♌ 24♌ 29♍	1♋ 5♌ 10♌ 15♌ 20♍ 25♍ 31♍	1♌ 7♌ 12♍ 18♍ 24♍ 31♎	1♌ 4♍ 11♍ 18♍ 27♎	1♍ 6♍
9	1♍ 4♍ 10♎ 16♎ 23♎ 30♏	1♍ 3♎ 10♎ 18♎	1♎ 8♎ 24♎	1♍ 10♍	1♌ 12♍ 19♍ 25♍ 30♎	1♌ 6♍ 12♍ 17♍ 22♎ 28♎	1♍ 3♍ 9♍ 14♎ 20♎ 27♎	1♍ 6♎ 12♎ 20♎ 28♏	1♎ 7♎ 18♎	1♎ 21♍	1♍ 6♍ 22♍ 29♍
10	1♏ 9♏ 30♏	1♎ 2♏ 6♎ 16♎	1♎ 5♍ 12♎ 21♎ 28♎	1♍ 8♎ 13♎ 19♎ 25♏ 31♏	1♎ 6♎ 12♎ 18♏ 24♏ 30♏	1♎ 4♎ 10♏ 17♏ 24♏	1♎ 4♏ 11♏ 20♏	1♏ 25♎	1♎ 12♎ 22♎	1♍ 11♎ 18♎ 24♎ 30♏	1♍ 5♎ 11♎ 16♎ 22♏ 29♏
11	1♏ 22♏ 29♏	1♎ 9♏ 16♏ 22♏ 28♐	1♎ 3♏ 9♏ 15♏ 21♐ 28♐	1♏ 7♏ 13♐ 20♐ 26♐	1♏ 6♐ 13♐ 21♐	1♐ 12♐ 20♐ 28♏	1♏ 7♏ 17♏ 22♏	1♎ 12♏ 19♏ 25♏	1♎ 6♏ 12♏ 19♏ 25♐	1♏ 5♏ 11♏ 18♐ 24♐ 30♐	1♏ 4♏ 10♐ 17♐ 24♐
12	1♏ 6♐ 12♐ 18♐ 25♑ 31♑	1♐ 5♐ 11♐ 18♑ 24♑ 30♑	1♐ 4♐ 11♑ 17♑ 24♑	1♐ 3♑ 12♑ 23♑	1♐ 11♐	1♏ 14♐ 23♐ 30♐	1♏ 3♏ 10♐ 16♐ 23♐ 30♑	1♏ 2♐ 8♐ 15♐ 21♑ 27♑	1♐ 8♐ 14♑ 20♑ 27♑	1♐ 7♑ 14♑ 23♑	1♐ 2♑ 21♐

Month	1932	1933	1934	1935	1936	1937	1938	1939	1940	1941	1942
1	1♐ 15♑ 23♑ 30♑	1♐ 9♑ 15♑ 22♑ 28♒	1♐ 2♑ 8♑ 15♑ 21♒ 27♒	1♑ 7♑ 13♒ 19♒ 26♒	1♑ 6♒ 13♒	1♑ 2♒ 10♑ 18♑	1♑ 7♐ 13♑ 25♑	1♐ 4♐ 13♑ 20♑ 27♑	1♐ 6♑ 13♑ 19♑ 25♒	1♑ 5♑ 11♑ 17♒ 23♒ 29♒	1♑ 4♑ 9♒ 16♒ 23♒
2	1♑ 5♒ 12♒ 18♒ 23♓ 29♓	1♒ 3♒ 9♒ 14♓ 20♓ 25♓	1♒ 7♓ 13♓ 23♓	1♒ 2♓ 16♒ 24♒	1♒ 27♒	1♑ 5♑ 14♒ 22♒	1♑ 8♒ 15♒ 22♒ 27♓	1♑ 2♒ 8♒ 14♒ 20♓ 25♓	1♒ 6♒ 11♓ 17♓ 23♓	1♒ 3♓ 11♓ 24♓	1♒ 10♒
3	1♓ 5♓ 10♈ 16♈ 23♈	1♓ 4♈ 26♓	1♓ 10♓ 29♓	1♒ 8♒ 19♓ 27♓	1♒ 7♒ 14♓ 20♓ 26♓	1♒ 7♓ 13♓ 18♓ 23♈ 28♈	1♓ 5♓ 10♓ 15♈ 20♈ 26♈	1♓ 8♈ 14♈	1♓ 4♈ 8♓ 21♓	1♓ 7♒ 16♓ 28♓	1♒ 9♒ 17♓ 24♓ 31♓
4	1♈ 10♈	1♓ 18♈ 27♈	1♓ 8♓ 15♈ 22♈ 28♈	1♓ 3♓ 9♈ 15♈ 20♈ 25♉ 30♉	1♈ 6♈ 11♈ 15♉ 20♉ 26♉	1♈ 2♈ 7♉ 13♉ 21♉	1♈ 2♉ 24♈	1♈ 6♈ 28♈	1♓ 7♓ 17♈ 25♈	1♓ 6♓ 12♈ 18♈ 24♈ 29♉	1♓ 5♈ 11♈ 16♈ 20♉ 25♉
5	1♈ 7♈ 16♉ 23♉ 29♉	1♈ 4♈ 11♉ 16♉ 21♉ 26♊ 31♊	1♈ 3♉ 8♉ 13♉ 17♊ 22♊ 27♊	1♉ 4♉ 9♊ 14♊ 21♊ 30♋	1♉ 2♊ 10♊ 30♊	1♉ 11♉	1♈ 17♉ 26♉	1♈ 8♈ 15♉ 21♉ 26♉ 31♊	1♈ 7♉ 12♉ 17♉ 21♊ 26♊ 31♊	1♉ 4♉ 8♉ 13♊ 18♊ 23♊ 30♋	1♉ 5♊ 11♊ 20♊
6	1♉ 3♊ 8♊ 13♊ 17♋ 22♋ 27♋	1♊ 4♊ 9♋ 14♋ 20♋ 28♌	1♊ 2♋ 8♋ 18♋	1♋ 21♊	1♊ 24♊	1♉ 5♉ 14♊ 21♊ 27♊	1♉ 8♊ 14♊ 18♊ 23♋ 27♋	1♊ 5♊ 9♊ 14♋ 19♋ 24♋ 31♌	1♊ 5♋ 11♋ 18♋ 26♌	1♋ 8♋	1♊ 15♊
7	1♋ 3♌ 9♌ 17♌ 28♍	1♌ 8♌ 25♌	1♋ 8♋	1♊ 14♋ 22♋ 28♋	1♊ 3♊ 9♋ 14♋ 19♋ 24♌ 29♌	1♊ 2♋ 5♋ 11♋ 16♌ 20♌ 26♌	1♋ 7♌ 12♌ 19♌ 27♍	1♌ 8♌ 17♌	1♌ 21♋	1♋ 24♋	1♊ 4♊ 13♋ 19♋ 25♋ 29♌
8	1♍ 11♌	1♌ 22♌ 28♌	1♋ 10♌ 15♌ 20♌ 25♍ 31♍	1♋ 3♌ 7♌ 12♌ 17♍ 23♍ 29♍	1♌ 3♌ 8♍ 14♍ 21♍ 28♎	1♍ 8♍ 16♍	1♍ 7♍ 21♍	1♌ 6♌	1♋ 12♌ 19♌ 24♌ 29♍	1♋ 6♌ 11♌ 16♌ 21♍ 27♍	1♌ 3♌ 8♌ 13♍ 19♍ 25♍ 31♎
9	1♌ 10♍ 16♍ 21♍ 26♎	1♌ 3♍ 8♍ 13♍ 19♎ 24♎	1♍ 5♍ 11♎ 17♎ 24♎	1♍ 4♎ 11♎ 18♎ 29♏	1♎ 6♎ 29♎	1♍ 15♍	1♍ 4♌ 11♍ 20♍ 26♍	1♌ 7♏ 13♏ 18♏ 23♎ 29♎	1♍ 4♍ 9♍ 14♎ 21♎ 27♎	1♍ 7♎ 13♎ 21♎ 28♏	1♎ 8♎ 17♎
10	1♎ 8♎ 14♏ 20♏ 27♏	1♎ 7♏ 14♏ 21♏ 31♐	1♏ 9♏	1♏ 13♎ 21♎	1♎ 21♎ 28♎	1♍ 9♎ 15♎ 20♎ 26♍	1♍ 2♎ 7♎ 13♎ 19♏ 25♏ 31♏	1♎ 5♎ 11♏ 18♏ 25♏	1♎ 3♏ 11♏ 19♏	1♏ 9♏ 21♏ 30♎	1♎ 8♎ 20♎
11	1♏ 3♐ 11♐	1♐ 17♏ 24♏	1♏ 3♏ 23♏	1♎ 10♏ 17♏ 23♏ 30♐	1♎ 3♏ 9♏ 15♏ 21♐ 28♐	1♍ 8♍ 14♐ 21♐ 27♐	1♏ 7♐ 14♐ 22♐	1♐ 11♐ 25♐	1♏ 11♏	1♎ 12♏ 20♏ 27♏	1♎ 7♏ 13♏ 20♏ 26♐
12	1♐ 6♐ 24♐	1♏ 13♐ 20♐ 27♐	1♏ 7♐ 13♐ 20♐ 26♑	1♐ 6♐ 12♐ 19♑ 25♑ 31♑	1♐ 4♐ 10♑ 17♑ 24♑	1♐ 4♑ 12♑ 28♑	1♐ 15♐	1♐ 3♏ 14♐ 23♐ 31♐	1♏ 9♐ 17♐ 23♐ 29♑	1♏ 3♐ 10♐ 16♐ 22♑ 29♑	1♐ 9♐ 15♑ 21♑ 28♑

Month	1943	1944	1945	1946	1947	1948	1949	1950	1951	1952	1953
1	1♑ 3♒ 13♒ 28♑	1♑ 7♑ 16♑ 25♑	1♐ 14♑ 23♑ 30♑	1♐ 10♑ 17♑ 23♑ 29♒	1♐ 3♑ 10♑ 16♑ 22♒ 28♒	1♑ 3♑ 9♑ 14♒ 20♒ 26♒	1♑ 6♒ 13♒ 23♒	1♒ 16♑ 24♑	1♑ 26♑	1♐ 5♐ 13♑ 21♑ 28♑	1♐ 7♑ 13♑ 20♑ 26♒
2	1♑ 16♒ 25♒	1♑ 5♑ 12♒ 20♒ 26♒	1♑ 5♒ 12♒ 18♒ 23♓	1♒ 5♒ 10♒ 15♓ 22♓ 27♓	1♒ 3♒ 8♓ 14♓ 22♓	1♒ 2♓ 21♒	1♒ 6♒ 26♒	1♑ 5♑ 15♒ 23♒	1♑ 3♑ 10♒ 17♒ 23♒	1♑ 3♒ 9♒ 16♒ 21♓ 26♓	1♒ 7♒ 12♓ 18♓ 23♓
3	1♒ 5♒ 11♓ 17♓ 23♓ 28♈	1♒ 3♓ 9♓ 14♓ 19♈ 24♈ 29♈	1♓ 6♓ 11♈ 17♈ 23♈	1♓ 4♈ 16♈	1♓ 6♓ 18♓ 28♓	1♒ 18♓ 27♓	1♒ 7♒ 14♓ 21♓ 27♓	1♒ 8♓ 14♓ 20♓ 25♈ 30♈	1♓ 6♓ 12♓ 16♈ 22♈ 27♈	1♓ 3♓ 8♈ 14♈ 25♈	1♓ 3♈ 16♓
4	1♈ 3♈ 7♈ 12♉ 17♉ 23♉	1♈ 4♉ 11♉	1♈ 18♈	1♈ 2♓ 17♈ 28♈	1♓ 9♓ 16♈ 23♈ 28♈	1♓ 3♓ 9♈ 15♈ 20♈ 25♉ 30♉	1♓ 2♈ 7♈ 12♈ 17♉ 22♉ 26♉	1♈ 4♈ 8♉ 14♉ 21♉	1♈ 2♉	1♈ 13♈ 25♈	1♓ 18♈ 26♈
5	1♊ 26♉	1♉ 6♉ 25♉	1♈ 7♈ 17♉ 24♉ 30♉	1♈ 5♈ 12♉ 17♉ 23♉ 27♊	1♈ 4♉ 9♉ 14♉ 18♊ 23♊ 28♊	1♉ 4♉ 9♊ 14♊ 21♊ 28♋	1♉ 2♊ 10♊	1♉ 21♉	1♉ 2♈ 15♉ 27♉	1♈ 7♈ 15♉ 21♉ 27♉ 31♊	1♈ 3♈ 8♉ 14♉ 19♉ 23♊ 28♊
6	1♉ 14♊ 24♊	1♉ 4♉ 11♊ 17♊ 23♊ 27♋	1♉ 4♊ 9♊ 14♊ 18♋ 23♋ 28♋	1♊ 6♊ 10♋ 15♋ 21♋ 28♌	1♊ 3♋ 9♋ 18♋	1♋ 29♊	1♊ 10♊ 22♊	1♉ 3♉ 15♊ 22♊ 28♊	1♉ 4♉ 9♊ 15♊ 20♊ 24♋ 29♋	1♊ 6♊ 10♊ 14♋ 20♋ 25♋ 30♌	1♊ 6♋ 12♋ 18♋ 27♌
7	1♊ 6♋ 11♋ 16♋ 21♌ 26♌ 31♌	1♋ 6♋ 11♌ 17♌ 22♌ 29♍	1♋ 3♌ 10♌ 17♌ 26♍	1♌ 7♌	1♋ 17♋	1♊ 12♋ 22♋ 28♋	1♊ 4♊ 10♋ 16♋ 21♋ 25♌ 30♌	1♊ 2♋ 7♋ 12♋ 17♌ 22♌ 27♌	1♋ 4♋ 8♌ 14♌ 21♌ 28♍	1♌ 8♌ 16♌	1♌ 28♌ 29♋
8	1♌ 5♍ 12♍ 19♍ 27♎	1♍ 6♍ 17♍	1♍ 17♌	1♌ 23♌ 29♌	1♋ 3♋ 11♌ 17♌ 22♌ 27♍	1♋ 2♌ 8♌ 12♌ 17♍ 23♍ 29♍	1♌ 4♌ 9♍ 15♍ 22♍ 29♎	1♌ 2♍ 9♍ 17♍ 28♎	1♍ 7♍	1♌ 12♌	1♋ 12♌ 20♌ 26♌ 31♍
9	1♎ 25♍	1♍ 12♍ 21♍ 29♍	1♌ 10♍ 17♍ 22♍ 27♎	1♌ 4♍ 9♍ 14♍ 19♎ 25♎	1♍ 6♍ 12♎ 18♎ 25♎	1♍ 4♎ 11♎ 18♎ 27♏	1♎ 7♎	1♎ 11♍ 21♍	1♍ 21♍ 27♍	1♌ 7♍ 13♍ 19♍ 24♎ 29♎	1♍ 5♍ 11♍ 16♎ 22♎ 28♎
10	1♍ 12♎ 19♎ 25♎ 31♏	1♍ 5♎ 11♎ 17♎ 22♏ 29♏	1♎ 3♎ 9♎ 15♏ 21♏ 28♏	1♎ 8♏ 15♏ 22♏ 30♐	1♎ 2♏ 10♏ 21♏	1♏ 18♎ 26♎	1♎ 4♎ 22♎ 29♎	1♍ 10♎ 16♎ 22♎ 27♏	1♍ 3♎ 8♎ 14♎ 20♏ 26♏	1♎ 6♎ 11♏ 18♏ 25♏	1♎ 5♏ 12♏ 20♏
11	1♏ 6♏ 12♏ 18♐ 25♐	1♏ 4♏ 10♐ 17♐ 24♐	1♏ 4♐ 12♐ 21♐	1♐ 21♏	1♏ 8♏ 23♏	1♎ 10♏ 17♏ 23♏ 29♐	1♎ 4♏ 10♏ 16♏ 22♐ 29♐	1♏ 3♏ 9♏ 15♐ 22♐ 28♐	1♏ 8♐ 15♐ 23♐	1♐ 10♐ 29♐	1♐ 7♏ 16♏
12	1♐ 8♑ 15♑ 23♑	1♐ 2♑ 24♐	1♐ 3♐ 12♐ 25♐	1♏ 13♐ 21♐ 28♐	1♏ 7♐ 14♐ 21♐ 27♑	1♐ 6♐ 13♐ 19♑ 25♑ 31♑	1♐ 6♐ 11♑ 18♑ 25♑	1♐ 5♑ 13♑	1♐ 2♑ 13♐ 20♐	1♐ 23♐ 31♐	1♏ 3♏ 10♐ 18♐ 24♐ 31♑

Month	1954	1955	1956	1957	1958	1959	1960	1961	1962	1963	1964
1	1♑ 6♑ 12♑ 18♒ 25♒ 30♒	1♑ 5♑ 11♒ 17♒ 24♒	1♑ 4♒ 13♒ 25♒	1♑ 10♑	1♐ 14♑ 24♑ 31♑	1♐ 3♐ 11♑ 18♑ 24♑ 31♒	1♐ 4♑ 11♑ 17♑ 23♎ 29♎	1♑ 3♑ 9♑ 15♒ 21♒ 27♒	1♑ 8♒ 14♒ 22♒	1♑ 2♒ 21♑	1♑ 7♑ 26♑
2	1♒ 5♓ 12♓	1♒ 15♒	1♒ 2♑ 15♒ 26♒	1♑ 5♑ 13♒ 20♒ 26♒	1♑ 7♒ 13♒ 19♒ 25♓	1♒ 6♒ 12♒ 17♓ 23♓ 28♓	1♒ 4♒ 9♓ 15♓ 22♓	1♒ 2♓ 25♒	1♒ 11♒ 26♒	1♑ 15♒ 24♒	1♑ 4♑ 11♒ 18♒ 24♒
3	1♓ 29♓	1♒ 9♒ 18♓ 25♓	1♒ 5♒ 11♓ 18♓ 24♓ 29♈	1♒ 4♓ 10♓ 16♓ 21♈ 26♈ 31♈	1♓ 3♓ 8♓ 13♈ 18♈ 24♈	1♓ 5♈ 14♈ 26♈	1♓ 11♓	1♒ 18♓ 28♓	1♒ 8♒ 15♓ 22♓ 28♓	1♒ 9♓ 15♓ 21♓ 26♈	1♓ 7♓ 12♓ 17♈ 22♈ 27♈
4	1♓ 7♓ 13♈ 20♈ 25♈ 30♉	1♓ 7♈ 12♈ 18♈ 22♉ 27♉	1♈ 3♈ 8♈ 13♉ 18♉ 23♉ 30♊	1♈ 5♉ 12♉	1♈ 3♉ 10♈	1♈ 28♈	1♓ 8♓ 16♈ 23♈ 29♈	1♓ 4♓ 10♈ 16♈ 22♈ 27♉	1♓ 3♈ 8♈ 14♈ 18♉ 23♉ 28♉	1♈ 5♈ 10♉ 15♉ 22♉	1♈ 2♉ 12♉
5	1♉ 5♉ 10♉ 15♊ 19♊ 25♊ 31♋	1♉ 7♊ 12♊ 20♊	1♊	1♉ 19♉	1♈ 17♉ 25♉	1♈ 6♈ 13♉ 19♉ 29♊	1♈ 5♉ 10♉ 15♉ 19♊ 24♊ 29♊	1♉ 6♉ 11♊ 16♊ 21♊ 24♋	1♉ 3♊ 10♊	1♉ 4♊ 11♉	1♉ 27♉
6	1♋ 8♋	1♊ 27♊	1♊ 24♊	1♉ 5♉ 13♊ 19♊ 24♊ 29♋	1♉ 6♊ 11♊ 16♊ 20♋ 25♋ 30♋	1♊ 3♊ 7♊ 11♋ 17♋ 22♋ 29♌	1♊ 3♋ 9♋ 17♋	1♋	1♊	1♉ 15♊ 23♊ 29♊	1♉ 3♉ 10♊ 15♊ 20♊ 25♋ 29♋
7	1♋ 13♋ 22♋	1♊ 14♋ 20♋ 26♋ 31♌	1♊ 7♋ 12♋ 17♋ 21♌ 26♌	1♋ 3♋ 8♋ 13♌ 18♌ 24♌ 30♍	1♋ 5♌ 11♌ 18♌ 26♍	1♌ 7♌	1♋ 2♌ 7♋	1♋ 23♋ 30♋	1♊ 4♊ 11♋ 17♋ 22♋ 27♌	1♊ 4♋ 9♋ 14♋ 18♌ 23♌ 29♌	1♋ 4♋ 9♌ 15♌ 20♌ 27♍
8	1♋ 2♋ 8♌ 13♌ 18♌ 23♍ 28♍	1♌ 5♌ 9♌ 14♍ 20♍ 26♍	1♌ 6♍ 12♍ 19♍ 26♎	1♍ 7♍ 16♍	1♍ 24♌	1♌ 9♌ 22♌ 30♌	1♋ 11♌ 17♌ 22♌ 27♍	1♋ 4♌ 9♌ 14♌ 19♍ 24♍ 30♍	1♌ 6♌ 11♍ 17♍ 23♍ 30♎	1♌ 3♍ 10♍ 17♍ 27♎	1♍ 6♍
9	1♍ 3♍ 8♎ 15♎ 22♎ 29♏	1♍ 2♎ 9♎ 18♎	1♎ 7♎ 20♎ 30♍	1♍ 6♍	1♌ 11♍ 18♍ 24♍ 29♎	1♌ 5♍ 11♍ 16♍ 21♎ 27♎	1♍ 7♍ 12♎ 18♎ 25♎	1♍ 5♎ 12♎ 19♎ 27♏	1♎ 7♎ 19♎	1♎ 17♍	1♍ 21♍ 27♍
10	1♏ 9♏ 26♏	1♎ 13♎	1♍ 11♎ 19♎ 26♎ 31♏	1♍ 6♎ 12♎ 18♎ 24♏ 30♏	1♎ 5♎ 11♎ 16♏ 23♏ 29♏	1♎ 3♎ 9♏ 16♏ 23♏ 31♐	1♎ 2♏ 9♏ 19♏	1♏ 23♎	1♎ 9♎ 23♎ 30♎	1♍ 11♎ 17♎ 23♎ 29♏	1♍ 3♎ 8♎ 14♎ 20♏ 27♏
11	1♏ 5♎ 12♏ 21♏ 28♏	1♎ 8♏ 15♏ 21♏ 27♐	1♏ 7♏ 13♏ 19♐ 25♐	1♏ 6♏ 12♐ 18♐ 26♐	1♏ 5♐ 13♐ 21♐	1♐ 26♏	1♏ 12♏ 22♏	1♎ 11♏ 18♏ 25♏	1♎ 5♏ 11♏ 18♏ 24♐	1♏ 4♏ 10♏ 16♐ 23♐ 29♐	1♏ 8♐ 15♐ 23♐
12	1♏ 4♐ 11♐ 17♐ 23♑ 30♑	1♐ 4♐ 10♐ 16♑ 23♑ 29♑	1♐ 2♐ 8♑ 15♑ 23♑	1♐ 2♑ 13♑ 29♐	1♐ 8♐ 17♐ 23♐	1♏ 14♐ 22♐ 29♐	1♏ 8♐ 15♐ 21♐ 27♑	1♐ 7♐ 14♐ 20♑ 26♑	1♐ 7♐ 13♑ 19♑ 26♑	1♐ 6♑ 14♑	1♑ 17♐

	1965	1966	1967	1968	1969	1970	1971	1972	1973	1974	1975

	1976	1977	1978	1979	1980	1981	1982	1983	1984	1985	1986

	1987	1988	1989	1990	1991	1992	1993	1994	1995	1996	1997

	1998	1999	2000	2001	2002	2003	2004	2005	2006	2007	2008

	1970	1971	1972	1973	1974	1975	1976	1977	1978	1979	1980	1981	1982	1983	1984

	1985	1986	1987	1988	1989	1990	1991	1992	1993	1994	1995	1996	1997	1998	1999

	2000	2001	2002	2003	2004	2005	2006	2007	2008

	1910	1911	1912	1913	1914	1915	1916	1917	1918	1919	1920	1921	1922	1923	1924	1925	1926	1927	1928

1929	1930	1931	1932	1933	1934	1935	1936	1937	1938	1939	1940	1941	1942	1943	1944	1945	1946	1947

1948	1949	1950	1951	1952	1953	1954	1955	1956	1957	1958	1959	1960	1961	1962	1963	1964	1965	1966

1967	1968	1969	1970	1971	1972	1973	1974	1975	1976	1977	1978	1979	1980	1981	1982	1983	1984	1985

1986	1987	1988	1989	1990	1991	1992	1993	1994	1995	1996	1997	1998	1999	2000	2001	2002	2003	2004

1910	1911	1912	1913	1914	1915	1916	1917	1918	1919	1920	1921	1922	1923	1924	1925	1926	1927	1928
JAN 1 ♈	JAN 1 ♈	JAN 1 ♉	JAN 1 ♉	JAN 1 ♊	JAN 1 ♊	JAN 1 ♋	JAN 1 ♋	JAN 1 ♋	JAN 1 ♌	JAN 1 ♌	JAN 1 ♍	JAN 1 ♎	JAN 1 ♎	JAN 1 ♏	JAN 1 ♏	JAN 1 ♐	JAN 1 ♐	JAN 1 ♐
FEB 24 ♈	JAN 20 ♉	APR 17 ♉	MAR 26 ♊	JUN 1 ♋	MAY 12 ♊	FEB 18 ♋	JUN 24 ♌	FEB 15 ♌	AUG 12 ♍	AUG 1 ♍	APR 1 ♎	OCT 1 ♍	SEP 22 ♎	APR 6 ♏	MAY 16 ♏	DEC 3 ♐	DEC 1 ♐	DEC 1 ♐
MAY 17 ♉	MAY 3 ♉	JUL 7 ♊	JUN 23 ♉	JUN 18 ♊	AUG 25 ♋	AUG 1 ♋	APR 3 ♋	JUN 5 ♌	OCT 19 ♍	DEC 31 ♍	OCT 8 ♎	DEC 31 ♍	SEP 14 ♍	DEC 31 ♏	DEC 6 ♏	DEC 31 ♐	DEC 31 ♐	DEC 31 ♐
DEC 15 ♉	AUG 18 ♉	DEC 1 ♉	DEC 7 ♊	JUL 13 ♋	DEC 31 ♋	AUG 27 ♌	DEC 31 ♌	DEC 31 ♍	OCT 8 ♎	DEC 31 ♍			DEC 31 ♏					
DEC 31 ♉	SEP 18 ♉	DEC 31 ♉			DEC 31 ♋	OCT 18 ♌		DEC 31 ♌	DEC 8 ♎									
	DEC 31 ♉					DEC 8 ♋			DEC 31 ♋									

1929	1930	1931	1932	1933	1934	1935	1936	1937	1938	1939	1940	1941	1942	1943	1944	1945	1946	1947
JAN 1 ♐	JAN 1 ♑	JAN 1 ♑	JAN 1 ♒	JAN 1 ♒	JAN 1 ♒	JAN 1 ♓	JAN 1 ♓	JAN 1 ♈	JAN 1 ♈	JAN 1 ♈	JAN 1 ♉	JAN 1 ♉	JAN 1 ♊	JAN 1 ♊	JAN 1 ♋	JAN 1 ♋	JAN 1 ♋	JAN 1 ♌
MAR 15 ♑	NOV 30 ♑	FEB 24 ♒	FEB 24 ♒	FEB 14 ♒	FEB 18 ♒	FEB 14 ♓	FEB 9 ♈	FEB 1 ♓	JAN 14 ♈	APR 3 ♉	MAR 20 ♉	FEB 28 ♊	MAY 9 ♊	APR 19 ♋	JUN 20 ♋	JUN 2 ♋	FEB 1 ♌	JUL 17 ♌
MAY 5 ♐	DEC 31 ♑	MAR 12 ♒	AUG 13 ♒	DEC 31 ♒	DEC 31 ♒	JUN 5 ♓	MAY 8 ♓	APR 3 ♈	JUL 1 ♉	JUL 6 ♉	DEC 31 ♉	JUL 10 ♊	DEC 31 ♊	DEC 31 ♋	AUG 2 ♋	AUG 2 ♌	DEC 31 ♋	OCT 10 ♌
NOV 30 ♑		NOV 27 ♒	NOV 20 ♒			JUL 8 ♓	SEP 1 ♓	OCT 18 ♈	DEC 31 ♉	SEP 22 ♈	NOV 21 ♉	DEC 31 ♊		DEC 31 ♋	NOV 22 ♋	AUG 2 ♌	DEC 31 ♋	
DEC 31 ♑		DEC 31 ♑	DEC 31 ♒			DEC 31 ♓	DEC 31 ♓	DEC 31 ♈		DEC 31 ♉	DEC 31 ♊				DEC 31 ♋	DEC 31 ♌		

1948	1949	1950	1951	1952	1953	1954	1955	1956	1957	1958	1959	1960	1961	1962	1963	1964	1965	1966
JAN 1 ♌	JAN 1 ♌	JAN 1 ♍	JAN 1 ♍	JAN 1 ♎	JAN 1 ♎	JAN 1 ♏	JAN 1 ♏	JAN 1 ♐	JAN 1 ♐	JAN 1 ♐	JAN 1 ♑	JAN 1 ♑	JAN 1 ♑	JAN 1 ♑	JAN 1 ♒	JAN 1 ♒	JAN 1 ♓	JAN 1 ♓
APR 4 ♌	APR 3 ♍	AUG 25 ♍	MAR 7 ♎	APR 23 ♎	OCT 23 ♎	OCT 19 ♏	JAN 23 ♏	JAN 13 ♐	JUN 16 ♐	DEC 31 ♑	JAN 5 ♑	DEC 31 ♑	JAN 4 ♒	APR 1 ♒	MAR 24 ♒	MAR 18 ♓	MAR 12 ♓	DEC 31 ♓
JUN 29 ♌	MAY 29 ♍	NOV 21 ♍	AUG 14 ♎	JUL 28 ♎	DEC 31 ♏	DEC 31 ♏	APR 3 ♏	MAY 14 ♐	OCT 5 ♐		DEC 31 ♑			DEC 31 ♒	AUG 10 ♒	SEP 17 ♓	DEC 31 ♓	
SEP 19 ♌	SEP 5 ♍	DEC 31 ♍	NOV 6 ♎	OCT 29 ♎		OCT 15 ♏	OCT 11 ♐	DEC 31 ♐							DEC 16 ♓			
DEC 31 ♍	DEC 31 ♍		DEC 31 ♎	DEC 31 ♎		DEC 31 ♏	DEC 31 ♐							DEC 31 ♒			

1967	1968	1969	1970	1971	1972	1973	1974	1975	1976	1977	1978	1979	1980	1981	1982	1983	1984	1985
JAN 1 ♓	JAN 1 ♈	JAN 1 ♈	JAN 1 ♈	JAN 1 ♉	JAN 1 ♉	JAN 1 ♊	JAN 1 ♊	JAN 1 ♋	JAN 1 ♋	JAN 1 ♌	JAN 1 ♌	JAN 1 ♍	JAN 1 ♎	JAN 1 ♎	JAN 1 ♏	JAN 1 ♏	JAN 1 ♐	JAN 1 ♐
MAR 4 ♈	FEB 20 ♈	APR 30 ♈	APR 16 ♉	MAR 30 ♉	JAN 10 ♊	MAY 14 ♊	JAN 8 ♋	JUN 26 ♋	JAN 14 ♌	AUG 10 ♌	JAN 5 ♍	MAR 9 ♎	SEP 21 ♍	SEP 13 ♎	MAR 26 ♏	MAY 7 ♏	NOV 14 ♐	NOV 17 ♐
MAY 30 ♈	MAY 13 ♈	DEC 31 ♈	JUL 10 ♉	JUN 19 ♊	FEB 21 ♉	AUG 2 ♊	APR 19 ♋	SEP 17 ♋	JUN 5 ♌	NOV 17 ♌	JUL 26 ♍	JUL 1 ♎	DEC 31 ♎	DEC 10 ♎	SEP 4 ♏	NOV 29 ♏	DEC 31 ♐
SEP 21 ♈	DEC 31 ♈		DEC 31 ♈	NOV 18 ♉	DEC 31 ♊	DEC 31 ♊	DEC 31 ♋	JUL 14 ♋	DEC 31 ♋	AUG 25 ♌	DEC 31 ♍	OCT 17 ♍	OCT 2 ♎		DEC 31 ♏	DEC 31 ♏	
DEC 31 ♈				DEC 31 ♉			DEC 31 ♋	DEC 31 ♋		DEC 31 ♌							

1986	1987	1988	1989	1990	1991	1992	1993	1994	1995	1996	1997	1998	1999	2000	2001	2002	2003	2004
JAN 1 ♐	JAN 1 ♐	JAN 1 ♐	JAN 1 ♐	JAN 1 ♑	JAN 1 ♑	JAN 1 ♒	JAN 1 ♒	JAN 1 ♒	JAN 1 ♓	JAN 1 ♓	JAN 1 ♈	JAN 1 ♈	JAN 1 ♈	JAN 1 ♉	JAN 1 ♉	JAN 1 ♊	JAN 1 ♊	JAN 1 ♋
NOV 16 ♐	FEB 22 ♐	FEB 14 ♑	FEB 9 ♑	FEB 7 ♑	FEB 5 ♒	FEB 2 ♒	JAN 29 ♒	JAN 22 ♓	APR 7 ♓	MAR 29 ♓	MAR 17 ♈	MAR 1 ♈	MAY 7 ♉	APR 21 ♉	MAR 27 ♊	JUN 4 ♊	MAY 12 ♋
DEC 31 ♐	MAY 9 ♐	JUL 7 ♑	JUL 10 ♑	DEC 31 ♑	DEC 31 ♒	MAY 21 ♒	APR 29 ♒	APR 17 ♓	DEC 31 ♓	APR 12 ♈	JUL 12 ♈	DEC 31 ♉	OCT 18 ♈	DEC 22 ♉	OCT 18 ♊	AUG 2 ♋	AUG 2 ♋
	NOV 14 ♐	NOV 12 ♑	NOV 9 ♑			JUN 30 ♒	AUG 20 ♒	OCT 3 ♓		AUG 23 ♓	OCT 26 ♈		DEC 31 ♉	DEC 22 ♉	DEC 31 ♊		
	DEC 31 ♐	DEC 31 ♑	DEC 31 ♑			DEC 31 ♒	DEC 31 ♒	DEC 31 ♓		DEC 31 ♓	DEC 31 ♈						

2005	2006	2007	2008
JAN 1 ♋	JAN 1 ♋	JAN 1 ♌	JAN 1 ♍
JUL 16 ♌	JUN 29 ♌	SEP 3 ♍	AUG 19 ♍
OCT 14 ♋	SEP 18 ♌	DEC 31 ♍	NOV 16 ♍
DEC 31 ♌	DEC 31 ♌		DEC 31 ♍

1910	1911	1912	1913	1914	1915	1916	1917	1918	1919	1920	1921	1922	1923	1924	1925	1926	1927	1928
JAN 1 ♑	JAN 1 ♑	JAN 1 ♑	JAN 1 ♒	JAN 1 ♒	JAN 1 ♒	JAN 1 ♒	JAN 1 ♓	JAN 1 ♓	JAN 1 ♓	JAN 1 ♈	JAN 1 ♈	JAN 1 ♈	JAN 1 ♉	JAN 1 ♈	JAN 1 ♈	JAN 1 ♓	JAN 1 ♓	JAN 1 ♈
DEC 31 ♑	DEC 31 ♑	FEB 1 ♒	DEC 31 ♒	MAR 1 ♒	DEC 31 ♒	FEB 1 ♓	DEC 31 ♓	APR 1 ♈	DEC 31 ♓	MAR 8 ♈	DEC 31 ♈	APR 25 ♉	FEB 15 ♈	DEC 31 ♈	NOV 4 ♈	DEC 31 ♈	APR 1 ♈	JAN 13 ♈
		SEP 5 ♑		JUL 25 ♒		AUG 17 ♓		DEC 31 ♈		OCT 22 ♈		SEP 1 ♈	DEC 31 ♈		DEC 31 ♈			DEC 31 ♈
		NOV 12 ♒		DEC 31 ♒		DEC 31 ♓				DEC 31 ♈		DEC 31 ♈						
		DEC 31 ♒																

1929	1930	1931	1932	1933	1934	1935	1936	1937	1938	1939	1940	1941	1942	1943	1944	1945	1946	1947
JAN 1 ♈	JAN 1 ♈	JAN 1 ♈	JAN 1 ♈	JAN 1 ♈	JAN 1 ♈	JAN 1 ♈	JAN 1 ♉	JAN 1 ♉	JAN 1 ♉	JAN 1 ♉	JAN 1 ♉	JAN 1 ♊	JAN 1 ♊	JAN 1 ♊	JAN 1 ♊	JAN 1 ♊	JAN 1 ♊	JAN 1 ♊
MAY 18 ♈	MAR 9 ♈	DEC 31 ♈	APR 22 ♈	DEC 31 ♈	JUL 7 ♈	MAR 28 ♉	DEC 31 ♉	MAY 8 ♉	DEC 31 ♉	JUN 17 ♉	APR 7 ♊	AUG 8 ♊	MAY 15 ♊	DEC 31 ♊	JUN 10 ♊	DEC 31 ♊	JUL 22 ♊	MAY 11 ♊
SEP 18 ♈	DEC 31 ♈		DEC 31 ♈		OCT 10 ♈	DEC 31 ♉		DEC 31 ♉		DEC 31 ♉	DEC 31 ♊	OCT 5 ♊	DEC 31 ♊		DEC 31 ♊		DEC 7 ♊	DEC 31 ♊
DEC 31 ♈					DEC 31 ♈							DEC 31 ♊					DEC 31 ♊	

Uranus

1948	1949	1950	1951	1952	1953	1954	1955	1956	1957	1958	1959	1960	1961	1962	1963	1964	1965	1966
JAN 1 ♊ AUG 31 ♋ NOV 12 ♊ DEC 31 ♊	JAN 1 ♊ JUN 10 ♋ DEC 31 ♋	JAN 1 ♋ DEC 31 ♋	JAN 1 ♋	JAN 1 ♋	JAN 1 ♋	JAN 1 ♋	JAN 1 ♋ AUG 25 ♌ DEC 31 ♌	JAN 1 ♌ JAN 28 ♋ JUN 10 ♌ DEC 31 ♌	JAN 1 ♌	JAN 1 ♌	JAN 1 ♌	JAN 1 ♌	JAN 1 ♌ NOV 1 ♍ DEC 31 ♍	JAN 1 ♍ JAN 10 ♌ AUG 9 ♍ DEC 31 ♍	JAN 1 ♍	JAN 1 ♍	JAN 1 ♍	JAN 1 ♍

1967	1968	1969	1970	1971	1972	1973	1974	1975	1976	1977	1978	1979	1980	1981	1982	1983	1984	1985
JAN 1 ♍	JAN 1 ♍ SEP 28 ♎ DEC 31 ♎	JAN 1 ♎ MAY 20 ♍ NOV 16 ♎ DEC 31 ♎	JAN 1 ♎	JAN 1 ♎	JAN 1 ♎	JAN 1 ♎	JAN 1 ♎ NOV 21 ♏ DEC 31 ♏	JAN 1 ♏ MAY 1 ♎ SEP 8 ♏ DEC 31 ♏	JAN 1 ♏	JAN 1 ♏	JAN 1 ♏	JAN 1 ♏	JAN 1 ♏	JAN 1 ♏ FEB 17 ♐ MAR 20 ♏ NOV 16 ♐ DEC 31 ♐	JAN 1 ♐	JAN 1 ♐	JAN 1 ♐	JAN 1 ♐

1986	1987	1988	1989	1990	1991	1992	1993	1994	1995	1996	1997	1998	1999	2000	2001	2002	2003	2004
JAN 1 ♐	JAN 1 ♐	JAN 1 ♐ FEB 15 ♑ MAY 27 ♐ DEC 2 ♑ DEC 31 ♑	JAN 1 ♑	JAN 1 ♑	JAN 1 ♑	JAN 1 ♑	JAN 1 ♑	JAN 1 ♑	JAN 1 ♑ APR 1 ♒ JUN 9 ♑ DEC 31 ♑	JAN 1 ♑ JAN 12 ♒ DEC 31 ♒	JAN 1 ♒	JAN 1 ♒	JAN 1 ♒	JAN 1 ♒	JAN 1 ♒	JAN 1 ♒	JAN 1 ♒ MAR 11 ♓ SEP 15 ♒ DEC 30 ♓ DEC 31 ♓	JAN 1 ♓

2005	2006	2007	2008
JAN 1 ♓ MAY 2 ♓ JUL 30 ♓ DEC 31 ♓	JAN 1 ♓ FEB 16 ♓ DEC 31 ♓	JAN 1 ♓ DEC 31 ♓	JAN 1 ♓ APR 2 ♓ DEC 31 ♓

Neptune

1910	1911	1912	1913	1914	1915	1916	1917	1918	1919	1920	1921	1922	1923	1924	1925	1926	1927	1928
JAN 1 ♋	JAN 1 ♋	JAN 1 ♋	JAN 1 ♋	JAN 1 ♋ SEP 23 ♌ DEC 14 ♋ DEC 31 ♋	JAN 1 ♋ JUL 19 ♌ DEC 31 ♌	JAN 1 ♌ MAR 19 ♋ MAY 2 ♌ DEC 31 ♌	JAN 1 ♌	JAN 1 ♌	JAN 1 ♌	JAN 1 ♌	JAN 1 ♌	JAN 1 ♌	JAN 1 ♌	JAN 1 ♌	JAN 1 ♌	JAN 1 ♌	JAN 1 ♌	JAN 1 ♌ SEP 22 ♍ DEC 31 ♍

1929	1930	1931	1932	1933	1934	1935	1936	1937	1938	1939	1940	1941	1942	1943	1944	1945	1946	1947
JAN 1 ♍ FEB 19 ♌ JUL 24 ♍ DEC 31 ♍	JAN 1 ♍	JAN 1 ♍	JAN 1 ♍	JAN 1 ♍	JAN 1 ♍	JAN 1 ♍	JAN 1 ♍	JAN 1 ♍	JAN 1 ♍	JAN 1 ♍	JAN 1 ♍	JAN 1 ♍	JAN 1 ♍ OCT 4 ♎ DEC 31 ♎	JAN 1 ♎ APR 17 ♍ AUG 3 ♎ DEC 31 ♎	JAN 1 ♎	JAN 1 ♎	JAN 1 ♎	JAN 1 ♎

1948	1949	1950	1951	1952	1953	1954	1955	1956	1957	1958	1959	1960	1961	1962	1963	1964	1965	1966
JAN 1 ♎	JAN 1 ♎	JAN 1 ♎	JAN 1 ♎	JAN 1 ♎	JAN 1 ♎	JAN 1 ♎	JAN 1 ♎ DEC 24 ♏ DEC 31 ♏	JAN 1 ♏ MAR 12 ♎ OCT 19 ♏ DEC 31 ♏	JAN 1 ♏ JUN 15 ♎ AUG 6 ♏ DEC 31 ♏	JAN 1 ♏	JAN 1 ♏	JAN 1 ♏	JAN 1 ♏	JAN 1 ♏	JAN 1 ♏	JAN 1 ♏	JAN 1 ♏	JAN 1 ♏

1967	1968	1969	1970	1971	1972	1973	1974	1975	1976	1977	1978	1979	1980	1981	1982	1983	1984	1985
JAN 1 ♏	JAN 1 ♏	JAN 1 ♏	JAN 1 ♏ JAN 5 ♐ MAY 3 ♏ NOV 7 ♐ DEC 31 ♐	JAN 1 ♐	JAN 1 ♐	JAN 1 ♐	JAN 1 ♐	JAN 1 ♐	JAN 1 ♐	JAN 1 ♐	JAN 1 ♐	JAN 1 ♐	JAN 1 ♐	JAN 1 ♐	JAN 1 ♐	JAN 1 ♐	JAN 1 ♐ JAN 19 ♑ JUN 23 ♐ NOV 21 ♑ DEC 31 ♑	JAN 1 ♑

Neptune

	1986	1987	1988	1989	1990	1991	1992	1993	1994	1995	1996	1997	1998	1999	2000	2001	2002	2003	2004
	JAN 1 ♑	JAN 1 ♑	JAN 1 ♑	JAN 1 ♑	JAN 1 ♑	JAN 1 ♑	JAN 1 ♑	JAN 1 ♑	JAN 1 ♑	JAN 1 ♑	JAN 1 ♑	JAN 1 ♑	JAN 1 ♑	JAN 1 ♒	JAN 1 ♒	JAN 1 ♒	JAN 1 ♒	JAN 1 ♒	JAN 1 ♒
	DEC 31 ♑	DEC 31 ♑	MAR 16 ♑	DEC 31 ♑	DEC 31 ♑	DEC 31 ♑	DEC 31 ♑	DEC 31 ♑	DEC 31 ♑	DEC 31 ♑	DEC 31 ♑	DEC 31 ♑	DEC 29 ♒	DEC 31 ♒	DEC 31 ♒	DEC 31 ♒	DEC 31 ♒	DEC 31 ♒	DEC 31 ♒
			MAY 9 ♑										AUG 23 ♑						
			DEC 31 ♑										NOV 28 ♒						
													DEC 31 ♒						

	2005	2006	2007	2008
	JAN 1 ♒	JAN 1 ♒	JAN 1 ♒	JAN 1 ♒
	DEC 31 ♒	DEC 31 ♒	FEB 22 ♒	DEC 31 ♒
			DEC 31 ♒	

Pluto

	1910	1911	1912	1913	1914	1915	1916	1917	1918	1919	1920	1921	1922	1923	1924	1925	1926	1927	1928
	JAN 1 ♊	JAN 1 ♊	JAN 1 ♊	JAN 1 ♊	JAN 1 ♊	JAN 1 ♋	JAN 1 ♋	JAN 1 ♋	JAN 1 ♋	JAN 1 ♋	JAN 1 ♋	JAN 1 ♋	JAN 1 ♋	JAN 1 ♋	JAN 1 ♋	JAN 1 ♋	JAN 1 ♋	JAN 1 ♋	JAN 1 ♋
	DEC 31 ♊	DEC 31 ♊	SEP 11 ♋	JUL 10 ♋	MAY 27 ♋	DEC 31 ♋	DEC 31 ♋	DEC 31 ♋	DEC 31 ♋	DEC 31 ♋	DEC 31 ♋	DEC 31 ♋	DEC 31 ♋	JUN 4 ♋	DEC 31 ♋	DEC 31 ♋	DEC 31 ♋	DEC 31 ♋	DEC 31 ♋
			OCT 20 ♊	DEC 28 ♊	DEC 31 ♋									DEC 31 ♋					
			DEC 31 ♊	DEC 31 ♊															

	1929	1930	1931	1932	1933	1934	1935	1936	1937	1938	1939	1940	1941	1942	1943	1944	1945	1946	1947
	JAN 1 ♋	JAN 1 ♋	JAN 1 ♋	JAN 1 ♋	JAN 1 ♋	JAN 1 ♋	JAN 1 ♋	JAN 1 ♋	JAN 1 ♋	JAN 1 ♋	JAN 1 ♌	JAN 1 ♌	JAN 1 ♌	JAN 1 ♌	JAN 1 ♌	JAN 1 ♌	JAN 1 ♌	JAN 1 ♌	JAN 1 ♌
	DEC 31 ♋	DEC 31 ♋	JUN 27 ♋	DEC 31 ♋	DEC 31 ♋	DEC 31 ♋	DEC 31 ♋	DEC 31 ♋	NOV 25 ♋	FEB 4 ♋	JUN 14 ♌	DEC 31 ♌	DEC 31 ♌	DEC 31 ♌	DEC 31 ♌	DEC 31 ♌	DEC 31 ♌	JUN 12 ♌	DEC 31 ♌
			DEC 31 ♋						DEC 31 ♋	DEC 31 ♋	DEC 31 ♌							DEC 31 ♌	

	1948	1949	1950	1951	1952	1953	1954	1955	1956	1957	1958	1959	1960	1961	1962	1963	1964	1965	1966
	JAN 1 ♌	JAN 1 ♌	JAN 1 ♌	JAN 1 ♌	JAN 1 ♌	JAN 1 ♌	JAN 1 ♌	JAN 1 ♌	JAN 1 ♌	JAN 1 ♍	JAN 1 ♍	JAN 1 ♍	JAN 1 ♍	JAN 1 ♍	JAN 1 ♍	JAN 1 ♍	JAN 1 ♍	JAN 1 ♍
	DEC 31 ♌	DEC 31 ♌	AUG 30 ♌	DEC 31 ♌	DEC 31 ♌	DEC 31 ♌	DEC 31 ♌	DEC 31 ♌	OCT 20 ♍	JAN 15 ♌	APR 11 ♌	DEC 31 ♍	DEC 31 ♍	DEC 31 ♍	SEP 7 ♍	DEC 31 ♍	DEC 31 ♍	DEC 31 ♍
			DEC 31 ♌						DEC 31 ♍	AUG 19 ♍	JUN 10 ♍				DEC 31 ♍				
										DEC 31 ♍	DEC 31 ♍								

	1967	1968	1969	1970	1971	1972	1973	1974	1975	1976	1977	1978	1979	1980	1981	1982	1983	1984	1985
	JAN 1 ♍	JAN 1 ♍	JAN 1 ♍	JAN 1 ♍	JAN 1 ♍	JAN 1 ♎	JAN 1 ♎	JAN 1 ♎	JAN 1 ♎	JAN 1 ♎	JAN 1 ♎	JAN 1 ♎	JAN 1 ♎	JAN 1 ♎	JAN 1 ♎	JAN 1 ♎	JAN 1 ♎	JAN 1 ♏	JAN 1 ♏
	SEP 1 ♍	DEC 31 ♍	DEC 31 ♍	DEC 31 ♍	OCT 5 ♎	APR 17 ♍	DEC 31 ♎	DEC 31 ♎	DEC 31 ♎	AUG 21 ♎	DEC 31 ♎	DEC 31 ♎	NOV 4 ♎	DEC 31 ♎	DEC 31 ♎	DEC 31 ♎	NOV 6 ♏	MAY 18 ♎	DEC 31 ♎
	DEC 31 ♍				DEC 31 ♎	JUL 30 ♎				DEC 31 ♎			DEC 31 ♎				DEC 31 ♏	AUG 28 ♏	
						DEC 31 ♎												DEC 31 ♏	

	1986	1987	1988	1989	1990	1991	1992	1993	1994	1995	1996	1997	1998	1999	2000	2001	2002	2003	2004
	JAN 1 ♏	JAN 1 ♏	JAN 1 ♏	JAN 1 ♏	JAN 1 ♏	JAN 1 ♏	JAN 1 ♏	JAN 1 ♏	JAN 1 ♏	JAN 1 ♏	JAN 1 ♐	JAN 1 ♐	JAN 1 ♐	JAN 1 ♐	JAN 1 ♐	JAN 1 ♐	JAN 1 ♐	JAN 1 ♐	JAN 1 ♐
	DEC 31 ♏	NOV 5 ♏	DEC 31 ♏	DEC 31 ♏	DEC 31 ♏	NOV 6 ♏	DEC 31 ♏	DEC 31 ♏	DEC 31 ♏	JAN 17 ♐	DEC 31 ♐	DEC 31 ♐	DEC 31 ♐	NOV 24 ♐	DEC 31 ♐	DEC 31 ♐	DEC 31 ♐	DEC 19 ♐	DEC 31 ♐
		DEC 31 ♏				DEC 31 ♏				APR 21 ♏				DEC 31 ♐				DEC 31 ♐	
										NOV 11 ♐									
										DEC 31 ♐									

	2005	2006	2007	2008
	JAN 1 ♐	JAN 1 ♐	JAN 1 ♐	JAN 1 ♐
	DEC 31 ♐	DEC 31 ♐	DEC 31 ♐	JAN 26 ♑
				JUN 14 ♐
				NOV 27 ♑
				DEC 31 ♑

Moon tables

THE MOON IS associated with the qualities that you have inherited from your parents, and influences your emotional level, and how you react and respond to situations. Consult the charts below to find your year of birth and the zodiacal glyph for your month of birth.

Refer to the Moon Table (*far right*) in which the days of the month are listed against a number. This number indicates how many zodiacal glyphs (*right*) you must count onward from the glyph of the month of your birth to reach your Moon sign. You may have to count to Pisces and return to Aries. For example, if you were born on May 14, 1978, the zodiacal glyph for your month of birth is Aquarius (♒). The Moon Table shows that for day 14, six signs have to be added. The Moon sign for this date of birth is therefore Leo (♌). The book in this pack, *Astrology and You*, contains interpretations for each Moon sign. If your Moon sign seems inaccurate, read the interpretations for the signs before and after the one indicated; one of the three will apply.

ZODIACAL GLYPHS

♈	Aries
♉	Taurus
♊	Gemini
♋	Cancer
♌	Leo
♍	Virgo
♎	Libra
♏	Scorpio
♐	Sagittarius
♑	Capricorn
♒	Aquarius
♓	Pisces

MOON TABLE

DAYS OF THE MONTH AND NUMBER OF
SIGNS THAT SHOULD BE ADDED

DAY	ADD	DAY	ADD	DAY	ADD	DAY	ADD
1	0	9	4	17	7	25	11
2	1	10	4	18	8	26	11
3	1	11	5	19	8	27	12
4	1	12	5	20	9	28	12
5	2	13	5	21	9	29	1
6	2	14	6	22	10	30	1
7	3	15	6	23	10	31	2
8	3	16	7	24	10		

The six moon tables below list the years 1910–2008, with a zodiacal glyph given for each month (JAN–DEC) of each year:

- Table 1: years 1910–1926
- Table 2: years 1927–1943
- Table 3: years 1944–1960
- Table 4: years 1961–1977
- Table 5: years 1978–1994
- Table 6: years 1995–2008

How to find your Ascendant

LOCATE THE LONGITUDE *of your birth place and your time of birth. Turn to the table here closest to the latitude of your birth. Find your date of birth and time of birth in the appropriate columns. Draw a line between these two points. The glyph to the right of this diagonal line reveals your ascendant. Note whether it crosses the top, middle, or bottom of the line.*

KEY TO GLYPHS FOR THE SIGNS OF THE ZODIAC

♈	Aries	♎	Libra
♉	Taurus	♏	Scorpio
♊	Gemini	♐	Sagittarius
♋	Cancer	♑	Capricorn
♌	Leo	♒	Aquarius
♍	Virgo	♓	Pisces

KEY TO GLYPHS FOR THE PLANETS

☉	Sun	♃	Jupiter
☽	Moon	♄	Saturn
☿	Mercury	♅	Uranus
♀	Venus	♆	Neptune
♂	Mars	♇	Pluto

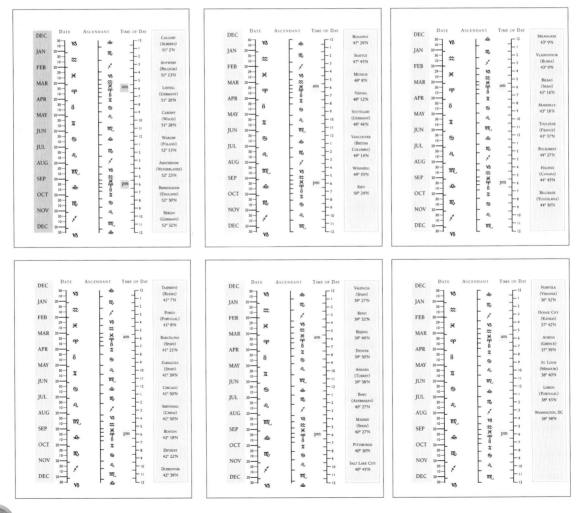

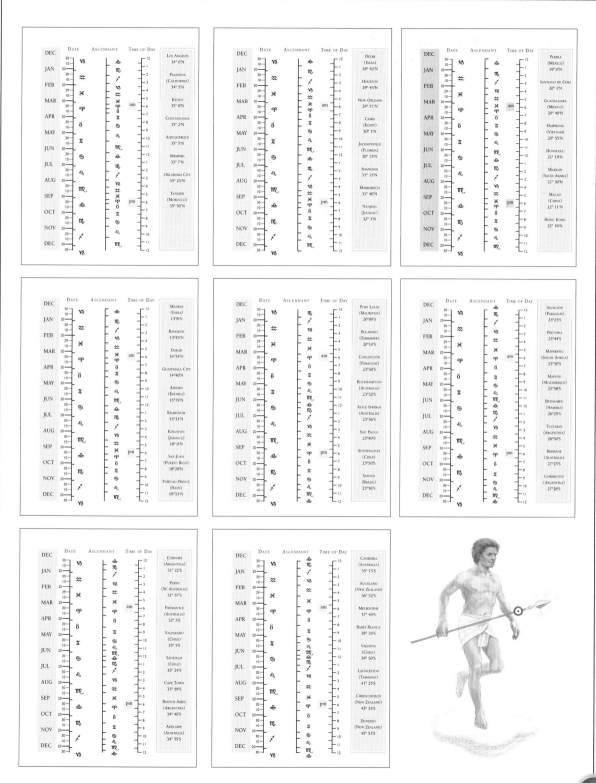

How to find your Midheaven

LOCATE THE LONGITUDE *of your birth place and your time of birth. Turn to the table here closest to the latitude of your birth. Find your date of birth and time of birth in the appropriate columns. Draw a line between these two points. The glyph to the right of this diagonal line reveals your Midheaven. Note whether it crosses the top, middle, or bottom of the line.*

KEY TO GLYPHS FOR THE SIGNS OF THE ZODIAC			
♈	Aries	♎	Libra
♉	Taurus	♏	Scorpio
♊	Gemini	♐	Sagittarius
♋	Cancer	♑	Capricorn
♌	Leo	♒	Aquarius
♍	Virgo	♓	Pisces

KEY TO GLYPHS FOR THE PLANETS			
☉	Sun	♃	Jupiter
☽	Moon	♄	Saturn
☿	Mercury	♅	Uranus
♀	Venus	♆	Neptune
♂	Mars	♇	Pluto

Table 1 — Cities
LE HAVRE 0° 7'E
ACCRA (GHANA) 0° 14'W
VALENCIA (SPAIN) 0° 22'W
ALICANTE (SPAIN) 0° 30'W
BORDEAUX (FRANCE) 0° 35'W
LOMÉ (TOGO) 1° 14'W
NANTES (FRANCE) 1° 33'W
CHERBOURG 1° 37'W

Table 2 — Cities
BOULOGNE 1° 37'E
ORLÉANS (FRANCE) 1° 55'E
BARCELONA (SPAIN) 2° 9'E
AMIENS (FRANCE) 2° 20'E
ARRAS (FRANCE) 2° 47'E
OSTEND (BELGIUM) 2° 55'E
BRUGES (BELGIUM) 3° 13'E
LAGOS (NIGERIA) 3° 30'E

Table 3 — Cities
KÖLN (GERMANY) 6° 58'E
BONN 7° 5'E
BASEL 7° 35'E
KANO (NIGERIA) 8° 32'E
ZÜRICH (SWITZERLAND) 8° 32'E
AJACCIO (FRANCE) 8° 43'E
STUTTGART (GERMANY) 9° 11'E
MILAN (ITALY) 9° 12'E

Table 4 — Cities
VIENNA 16° 23'E
BARI (ITALY) 16° 53'E
POZNAŃ (POLAND) 16° 55'E
BRINDISI (ITALY) 17° 56'E
STOCKHOLM (SWEDEN) 18° 3'E
SIMON'S TOWN (SOUTH AFRICA) 18° 26'E
SARAJEVO 18° 30'E
TROMSØ (NORWAY) 19° 0'E

Table 5 — Cities
SARAWAK (MALAYSIA) 113° 15'E
MACAU (CHINA) 113° 30'E
HANKOW (CHINA) 114° 17'E
BRUNEI (BORNEO) 115° 0'E
BALI (INDONESIA) 115° 19'E
FREMANTLE (AUSTRALIA) 115° 45'E
PERTH (AUSTRALIA) 115° 50'E
TIANJIN (CHINA) 117° 12'E

Table 6 — Cities
KYOTO 135° 45'E
ADELAIDE (AUSTRALIA) 138° 35'E
YOKOHAMA (KANAGAWA) 139° 38'E
AKITA (JAPAN) 140° 7'E
GEELONG (AUSTRALIA) 144° 21'E
MELBOURNE 145° 0'E
LAUNCESTON (TASMANIA) 147° 9'E

Each table column: Date (DEC–DEC by months with 10/20/30 intervals), Midheaven (zodiac glyphs), Time of Day (12–12, am/pm).

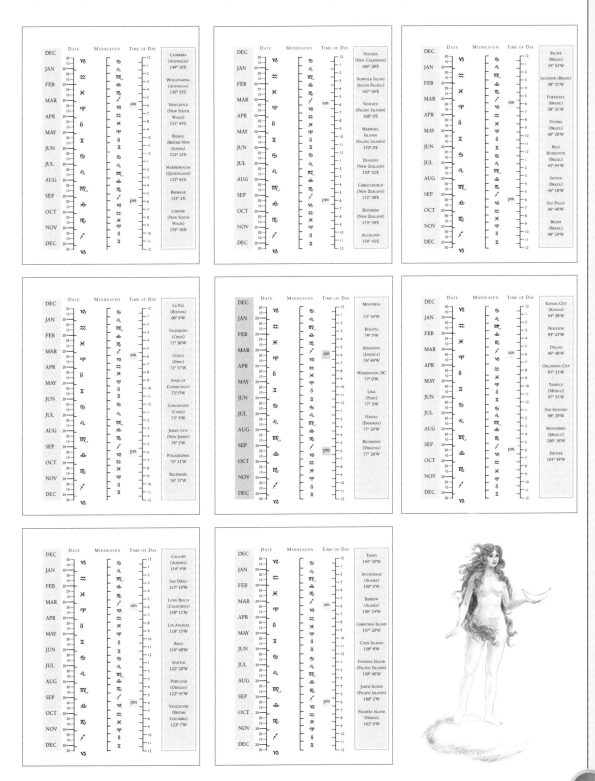

Midheaven Tables — location reference lists:

Location	Longitude
Canberra (Australia)	149° 10'E
Wollongong (Australia)	150° 53'E
Newcastle (New South Wales)	151° 45'E
Rabaul (British New Guinea)	152° 12'E
Maryborough (Queensland)	152° 42'E
Brisbane	153° 2'E
Lismore (New South Wales)	153° 16'E

Location	Longitude
Nouméa (New Caledonia)	166° 28'E
Norfolk Island (South Pacific)	167° 56'E
Vanuatu (Pacific Islands)	168° 0'E
Marshall Islands (Pacific Islands)	170° 0'E
Dunedin (New Zealand)	170° 32'E
Christchurch (New Zealand)	172° 38'E
Blenheim (New Zealand)	173° 59'E
Auckland	174° 45'E

Location	Longitude
Recife (Brazil)	34° 53'W
Salvador (Brazil)	38° 31'W
Fortaleza (Brazil)	38° 31'W
Vitória (Brazil)	40° 20'W
Belo Horizonte (Brazil)	43° 54'W
Santos (Brazil)	46° 18'W
São Paulo	46° 40'W
Belém (Brazil)	48° 29'W

Location	Longitude
La Paz (Bolivia)	68° 0'W
Valparaíso (Chile)	71° 38'W
Cuzco (Peru)	71° 57'W
State of Connecticut	73° 0'W
Concepción (Chile)	73° 3'W
Jersey City (New Jersey)	74° 2'W
Philadelphia	75° 11'W
Baltimore	76° 37'W

Location	Longitude
Montreal	73° 34'W
Bogotá	74° 5'W
Kingston (Jamaica)	76° 48'W
Washington, DC	77° 0'W
Lima (Peru)	77° 3'W
Nassau (Bahamas)	77° 20'W
Richmond (Virginia)	77° 26'W

Location	Longitude
Kansas City (Kansas)	94° 38'W
Houston	95° 23'W
Dallas	96° 48'W
Oklahoma City	97° 31'W
Tampico (Mexico)	97° 51'W
San Antonio	98° 29'W
Monterrey (Mexico)	100° 18'W
Denver	104° 59'W

Location	Longitude
Calgary (Alberta)	114° 4'W
San Diego	117° 10'W
Long Beach (California)	118° 11'W
Los Angeles	118° 15'W
Reno	119° 48'W
Seattle	122° 20'W
Portland (Oregon)	122° 41'W
Vancouver (British Columbia)	123° 7'W

Location	Longitude
Tahiti	149° 30'W
Anchorage (Alaska)	150° 0'W
Barrow (Alaska)	156° 24'W
Christmas Island	157° 20'W
Cook Islands	158° 8'W
Fanning Island (Pacific Islands)	159° 40'W
Jarvis Island (Pacific Islands)	160° 2'W
Palmyra Island (Hawaii)	162° 6'W

Resources

Books

Many astrological books are published each year, ranging from simple Sun-sign books to theoretical and philosophical treatises which tax the minds of very experienced astrologers, let alone complete beginners. Most of the books listed below are both helpful and accessible to a new astrology student. We don't provide publishing information because that will often be different in the United States than it is in the United Kingdom, Canada, or Australia. However, the stores we also feature below – which specialize in astrology books, tables, and tools – can supply most of the books we feature, as can any bookstore catalogue or web site.

The Rising Sign. Avery, Jean. An excellent look at the different influences of the rising sign in each of the zodiac signs.

Astrological Aspects. Carter, Charles E. O. One of astrology's great classics, this one provides everything you need to know about aspects.

Astrology for Beginners. Cornelius, Geoffrey, Maggie Hyde, and Chris Webster. A delightful A-to-Z astrology guide for beginners – done in cartoon format.

Astrology. Davison, Ronald C. One of the finest books available for an in-depth study of the planets' influences in each zodiac sign.

The Principles of Astrology. Harvey, Charles and Suzi. An excellent basic introduction to the study of astrology.

Astrology: Designs for Living. Kruger, Anna. A marvelous guide to using astrology in our everyday life, including astrological aids for stress reduction and decision making.

The Art of Chart Interpretation. Marks, Tracy. A fine guide to synthesizing, interpreting, and understanding all the components in a birth chart.

Parkers' Astrology. Parker, Derek and Julia. An illustrated guide to every aspect of astrology, which can train you from ground zero to advanced; so much so, in fact, that a thorough reading would probably allow you to pass the intermediate examinations of most astrological schools.

The Twelve Houses. Sasportas, Howard. A finely detailed exploration of the characteristics and influences of the 12 houses of the zodiac.

Aspects in Astrology. Tompkins, Sue. Every possible combination of aspects is expertly detailed and interpreted here.

Schools

If you are interested in becoming a serious astrology student, each of these fine schools offers an excellent curriculum. Write, phone, fax, or e-mail the schools first to get entrance requirements, etc. Some are geared to beginners; others are set-up for more advanced students. Also see "Astrological Schools – On-line" under *Internet Sites*.

United Kingdom
Faculty of Astrological Studies
54 High Street
Orpington, Kent BR6 0JQ
Phone: 07000-790143
Fax: 01689-603537
www.astrology.org.uk

The Astrological Lodge of London
50 Gloucester Place
London W1H 3HJ

The Mayo School
Alvara Gardens
Tregovethan
Truro, Cornwall TR4 9EN
www.astrology-world.com/mayoside.html

The Company of Astrologers
P. O. Box 3001
London N1 1LY
Phone: 01227 362427
E-mail: admin@coa.org.uk

The Centre for Psychological Astrology
BCM Box 1815
London WC1N 3XX
Phone: 0181-749 2330
E-mail: 106342.763@compuserve.com

Qualifying Horary Correspondence Course
Mongeham Lodge Cottage
Great Mongeham
Deal,
Kent CT14 0HD
Phone: 01304-375667

United States
The Kepler College of Astrological Arts and Sciences
4518 University Way NE, Suite 213
Seattle, WA 98105
Phone: 216-633-4907

Aquarius Workshops School of Astrology
P. O. Box 260556
Incino, CA 91426
Phone: 818-985-9221

Professional Astrologers, Inc.
1500 West El Camino Ave, Suite 130
Sacramento, CA 95833-1945

Australia
The International Astrological Guild of Educators
P. O. Box 141
Semaphore SA 5019
Australia
Phone: 61-88-8449-7660
Fax: 61-88-8242-2180
www.astrologicalguild.asn.au

Book Shops

Many of these book stores will hunt down rare or difficult-to-find astrology texts, and most provide you with a catalogue of their book listings.

United States
New York Astrology Center
545 8th Avenue, 10th floor
New York, NY 10018-4307
Phone: 212-947-3609
Fax: 212-947-3649

Minerva Books
1027 Alma Street
Palo Alto, CA 94301
Phone: 415-26-2006

The Kepler College of Astrological Arts and Sciences
4518 University Way NE, Suite 213
Seattle, WA 98105
Phone: 216-633-4907

Guiding Star
38 Miller Street, Suite 187
Mill Valley, CA 94941
Phone: 415-388-4827
www.crl.com/~guidstar

United Kingdom
Compendium
324 Camden High Street
London NW1 8QS
Phone: 020 7858944

Midheaven Bookshop
396 Caledonian Road
London N1 1DN
Phone: 020 76074133
Fax: 020 77006717
E-mail: 106063.420@compuserve.com

Ascella Publications
3, Avondale Bungalows
Sherwood Hall Road
Mansfield, Notts
Phone: 01623-634012
(mail-order only)

Australia
TS Bookshop
126 Russell Street
Melbourne, Victoria 3000
Phone: 03-9650-3955

Quantum Metaphysical Bookshop
113 Melbourne Street
North Adelaide, SA 5006
Phone: 61-8-267-1579
Fax: 61-8-267-1579

Adyar Bookshop
230 Clarence Street
Sydney, NSW 2000.
Phone: 61-2-267-8509

Canada
Full Circle Books
91 Bowmore Road
Toronto, ON M5W 1N5
Phone: 416-923-7827

Organizations

These organizations can provide you with names of reputable astrologers in your area, as well as educational resources.

United Kingdom
The Astrological Association
BM Box 3935
London WC1N 3XX
Phone: 020 77003746
Fax: 020 77006479
www.astrologer.com/aanet/index.html

United States
The American Federation of Astrologers
P.O. Box 22040
Tempe, Az 85285-2040
Phone: 602-838-1751
Fax: 602-838-8293

Australia
Federation of Australian Astrologers
20 Harley Road
Avalon NSW 2107
There are branches in each of the states.

Canada
Canadian Association for Astrological Education
4191 Stonemason
Crescent, Mississaiga
Ontario LSL 2Z6

Websites

There are many astrological sites on the Internet, some devoted to the wilder shores of the subject, some highly professional, and several certainly worth looking at. The following list is quite selective and offered with the caveat that many web sites come and go with depressing speed.

Astrology – General Information
www.bernadettebrady.com
Offers help to complete beginners who know nothing about astrology but who want to study it in a structured way.

www.astrologynow.com/about.Astrology
www.astrology.net
www.astropro.com/features/conxions
A good source for listings of newsgroups, newsletters, conferences, and mailing lists.

Astrological Books, Charts, and Maps
www.astrologyetal.com
A good astrology bookstore that stocks many second-hand books.

Astrological Magazines
There are several excellent on-line astrology magazines to which you can subscribe. Here are the best:

The Cosmic Times
www.onelist.com/subscribe/CosmicTimes

The Planetary Outlook
www.skyguides.com

Astrology World
www.astrology-world.com

Asmail
Aamail www.astrologer.com/aanet
This is the distinguished journal of the United Kingdom's Astrological Association.

The Mountain Astrologer
www.mountainastrologer.com
This is perhaps the best astrology magazine in the United States.

Astrological Schools – On-line
On-line College of Astrology
www.astrocollege.com

Classical Studies
www.leelehman.com

Astrological Theory and Techniques
www.members.tripod.com/~junojuno2
This is for the beginner who wants to study cosmobiology and other midpoint theories.

www.thenewage.com
Invited astrologers discuss the theory and technique of astrology here.

www.onelist.com/subscribe.cgi/JAAL
A site devoted to the astrological influences of asteroids, minor planets, and hypothetical planets.

www.egroups.com/group/all_ancient
The American astrologer Robert Hand has done wonderful work uncovering ancient astrological techniques and reconciling them with modern astrology. His work is discussed at this site.

Astrological Time Zone Information
www.astro.ch
This useful site gives time-zone changes around the world, together with adjustments for "summer time" or "daylight savings time" conditions.

Family and Relationship Astrology
www.egroups.com/list/child-family/
Family and children are the focus of this site.

www.efn.org/~patricia
An entertaining web site devoted to "astro-romance."

Financial Astrology
www.citystats.co.uk
This highlights astrology's use in the world stock markets.

Horary Astrology
The following websites have a special focus on horary astrology, a long popular method of astrological forecasting whereby an individual asks a specific question and a chart is drawn up for the moment the question is asked. Answers are then offered based on indications in the chart.
www.horary.com/w_lilly/wlmail
astroconsulting.com/FAQs/tableof.htm

Medical Astrology
www.medicinegarden.com
Medical astrology and holistic healing are featured here.

Psychological Astrology
www.egroups.com/list/chaos-stars/
Astrological interpretation is applied to psychology, the sciences, and the arts.

www.astrologer.com/psychast
This site explores the field of psychological astrology.

Sports Astrology
astrosports-guide@loritek.com
If you are interested in using astrology to predict sports results, this is the place.

Weather Astrology
indigo.weathersage

A simple glossary

Terms in italics are defined elsewhere in the glossary.

Affliction A *planet* is afflicted when it is unfavorably aspected by another planet.

Air sign See *element*.

Angle This word refers to the four angles of a birth chart – the top, the bottom, and each side – which form a cross within it. The top point is the *Medium Coeli* or *MC*, and is commonly referred to as the *Midheaven*; the bottom point is the *Imum Coeli* or *IC*; the left-hand point is the *Ascendant*; and the right-hand point is the *Descendant*.

Ascendant Traditionally, the Ascendant is the degree of the *zodiac* which is rising over the eastern horizon at the moment of your birth. Each degree takes about four minutes to rise. The *Ascendant* is also the *cusp* of the first *house*. Astrologers also call the *sign* that is rising on the eastern horizon the *Ascendant* or *rising sign*.

Aspects When two planets in a *birth chart* have a specific number of degrees between them (measured around the circumference of the birth-chart circle), one *planet* is said to be in aspect to the other. When they are 90° apart the planets are said to be in square aspect. Other aspects includes the trine (120° apart), the sextile (60° apart), the opposition (180° apart), the semi-square (45° apart), the sesquare (135° apart), the semi-sextile (30° apart), and the quincunx (150° apart). Planets are in *conjunction* when they occupy the same (or almost the same) degree. The influence of planetary aspects in a birth chart can be positive or negative in

character; and powerful, strong, moderate, or weak in strength.

Asteroids These are minor *planets* which some astrologers have brought into their systems. The most commonly used is Chiron.

Astrology The study of the influences on life on the Earth of the other celestial bodies in the *solar system*.

Astronomers The words astronomer and astrologer were interchangeable for centuries: astrologers were always astronomers, and vice versa. Today, however, astronomers confine themselves to studying the nature and movements of the celestial bodies in the known universe. Astrologers always have astronomical knowledge, but they study the ways in which celestial bodies affect life on Earth.

Birth chart A diagram – usually circular – showing the precise position of the Sun, the Moon, the planets, and the zodiac signs at the moment of an individual's birth. Traditionally, the word "horoscope" was always used instead of "birth chart," but today the terms are considered synonymous by astrologers. "Horoscope" is often (incorrectly) used to describe the brief, Sun-sign forecasts which are found in newspapers and magazines.

Birth time This is the precise time of birth, accurate to the minute, which astrologers use to cast a *birth chart*.

Cardinal sign See *quality*.

Chart ruler See *ruler of the horoscope*.

Conjunction Two planets are "conjunct" when they occupy the same (or almost the same) degree of the *birth chart*. Also see *aspects*.

Cusp This is the imaginary

line which separates a *sign* or *house* of the *zodiac* from the one before and after it.

Descendant In a birth chart, the point directly opposite the *Ascendant* (on the left-hand side of the circle) is the Descendant (on the right-hand side of the circle). The Descendant is also the *cusp* of the seventh house. See *angle*.

Detriment The influence of a *planet* is said to be somewhat weakened when it is in detriment. A planet is in detriment when it is in its *polar* sign, that is, when it is opposite the zodiac sign it *rules*. The Sun is in detriment when it is in Aquarius, the Moon in Capricorn, Mercury in Sagittarius, Venus in Aries, Mars in Libra, Jupiter in Gemini, Saturn in Cancer, Uranus in Leo, Neptune in Virgo, and Pluto in Taurus. Also see *exalt* and *fall*.

Duality See *gender*.

Earth sign See *element*.

Ecliptic The imaginary path which the Sun appears to follow around the Earth.

Element Astrologers divide the 12 *signs* of the *zodiac* among the four elements of fire, earth, air, and water. Aries, Leo, and Sagittarius are fire signs; Capricorn, Taurus, and Virgo are earth signs; Libra, Aquarius, and Gemini are air signs; and Cancer, Scorpio, and Pisces are water signs. The elements are also called the triplicities.

Elevation In astronomy, the elevation marks the distance – or altitude – of a *planet* above the horizon. In astrology, the planet which is nearest the *Midheaven* is said to be elevated.

Ephemeris A table listing the precise daily positions of the

Sun, Moon, and *planets* in a particular year. Annual ephemerides are published and are essential to an astrologer's work. They are also used for navigation and can be found on various web sites.

Equal house system A system of *house* division (the one used in this book) in which the 12 houses of the *birth chart* are of equal size. Many astrologers, however, use other house systems, notably the *Placidus System*.

Equator The imaginary circle drawn around the earth at its circumference.

Exalt The influence of a *planet* is stronger when it is exalted. In ancient times planets were said to be exalted in particular signs. Astrologers still respect this very well-established tradition and have added exaltations for the "modern" planets as well. The Sun is exalted in Aries, the Moon in Taurus, Mercury in Virgo, Venus in Pisces, Mars in Capricorn, Jupiter in Cancer, Saturn in Libra, Uranus in Scorpio, Neptune in Leo, and Pluto in Virgo. Also see *detriment* and *fall*.

Fall The influence of a *planet* is said to be weakened when it is in fall. A planet is in fall when it is opposite the sign in which it is *exalted*. The Sun is in fall when it is in Libra, the Moon in Scorpio, Mercury in Pisces, Venus in Virgo, Mars in Cancer, Jupiter in Capricorn, Saturn in Aries, Uranus in Taurus, Neptune in Aquarius, and Pluto in Pisces. Also see *detriment* and *exalt*.

Feminine sign See *gender*.

Fire sign See *element*.

Fixed sign See *quality*.

Gender Traditionally, the zodiac *signs* were said to

be either masculine/positive or feminine/negative, and astrologers still respect this tradition. The masculine/ positive signs are Aries, Gemini, Leo, Libra, Sagittarius, and Aquarius. The feminine/negative signs are Taurus, Cancer, Virgo, Scorpio, Capricorn, and Pisces. Here, the word "gender" does not refer to the male or female sex (a woman may have a masculine/positive sign; a man a feminine/negative side), but rather to the archetypal attributes associated with the masculine and the feminine. Symbolically, astrological gender is most like the Chinese concepts of *yin* (feminine) and *yang* (masculine).

Geocentric The (incorrect) idea that the Earth is the center of the solar system instead of the Sun. By necessity, astrologers cast birth charts from a geocentric perspective; they know full well, of course, that the Earth and planets revolve around the Sun.

Glyphs The symbols used by astrologers to represent the various *planets*, zodiac *signs*, and *aspects*; for example: ☉ for the Sun; ♉ for Taurus, and ♂ for the conjunction aspect between planets.

Horary astrology A method of astrological forecasting whereby an individual asks a specific question, the horary astrologer draws up a chart for the moment the question is asked, and then an answer is offered based on indications in the chart. Horary astrology was extremely popular prior to the 20th century, and William Lilly, the author of the first great astrology textbook written in English, was an expert. Some contemporary astrologers have taught themselves to use Lilly's methods, and they can still claim remarkable results.

Horoscope See *birth chart.*

House The circle of the *birth chart* is divided into 12 segments or houses, each of which symbolizes a particular aspect of life – for example, the home or work. The first house is placed immediately under the Ascendant line (or under the "9 o'clock" line). The balance of the houses (from two to 12) follow that segment consecutively in a counterclockwise direction. In the past, the houses were given descriptive names. Today they are simply numbered one through 12.

House division Throughout the history of astrology there have been a number of ways of dividing the *birth chart* into 12 *houses* which represent specific areas of life. This book uses the *Equal House system*, where each house is the same size (30 degrees wide). Other systems include Placidus, Regiomontanus, Campanus, Porphyry, and Morinus.

Imum Coeli/IC The Imum Coeli (IC), which means the "lowest part of the heavens," is the point located at the bottom of the *birth chart*, directly opposite the *Midheaven*. Also see *angle.*

Inferior planets Traditionally, the inferior planets are those whose orbits lie between the Earth and the Sun. Venus and Mercury are inferior planets. Also see the *superior planets.*

Interpretation This term is used to describe the conclusions reached by an astrologer after studying all the factors in a birth chart. An astrologer "interprets" a *birth chart* in much the same way that a weather forecaster interprets a weather map.

Masculine sign See *gender.*

Medium Coeli/MC The Medium Coeli, commonly called the *Midheaven*, is the topmost point of the birth chart, directly opposite the

Imum Coeli. Also see *angle.*

Medical astrology For many centuries there has been a strong association between medicine and astrology. Both birth-chart and horary astrology have been used to diagnose and treat illnesses, based on what is revealed of the physical characteristics of an individual and about possible treatments.

Meridian In a birth chart, the meridian is the line that connects the *Midheaven* (at the top of the circle) and the *Imum Coeli* (at the bottom), bisecting the circle and creating the left- and right-hand sides.

Midheaven See *Medium Coeli.*

Midpoint The halfway point (measured in degrees) between two significant components in a birth chart – for example, between two planets, two angles, or a planet and an angle (especially the Midheaven or Ascendant). Some astrologers believe these midpoints are key areas for interpretation in a birth chart. This is an additional (and quite complex) level of chart interpretation, variously called midpoint theory, cosmobiology, or the Ebertin method (after Reinhold Ebertin who invented the term).

Modern Planets Uranus, Neptune, and Pluto are known as the "modern" planets because of their relatively recent discovery. Some astrologers also include the *asteroids* as modern planets.

Mundane astrology A specific area of astrology related to the interpretation and forecasting of political, social, and world events and trends.

Mutable sign See *quality.*

Node The nodes of a *planet* are those points on the *ecliptic* where the planet crosses it going either north or south. Traditionally, the important nodes in a birth chart belong to the Moon;

its north node is called the Dragon's Head, the south node the Dragon's Tail.

Opposition See *aspects.*

Orbit The path of one celestial body around another celestial body: for example, the Moon's orbit around the Earth; the Earth's orbit around the Sun.

Placidus System A very popular system of *house division.*

Planet One of the celestial bodies that *orbits* the Sun. In our solar system there are nine major planets: Mercury, Venus, Earth, Mars, Jupiter, Saturn, Uranus, Neptune, and Pluto. In astrology, the Sun and the Moon are also traditionally considered to be "planets."

Polarity Each zodiac *sign* has an opposite sign (directly across from it) with which it shares a special relationship and is said to be in polarity. The zodiac polarities are: Aries/Libra, Taurus/Scorpio, Gemini/Sagittarius, Cancer/ Capricorn, Leo/Aquarius, and Virgo/Pisces.

Positivity See *gender.*

Precession of the equinoxes The term used to describe the gradual backward shift of zodiac *signs* over time, which is due to the Earth's rotation on its axis. As a consequence, the various constellations of stars (for which the zodiac signs were originally named) have slowly moved forward. The collective result is that the zodiac signs are no longer in the constellations that gave them their names.

Prediction Astrologers are often erroneously labeled as attempting to "predict" future events. In fact, it cannot be emphasized strongly enough that *astrology* cannot reliably predict certain events.

Progressed birth chart/Progressed horoscope In order to make observations about the future, astrologers by one means or another may "progress" a *birth chart* so that it represents a future period in time rather than the moment of birth. There are several ways of doing this, the most popular being the "day for a year" system. When a birth chart/ horoscope is progressed for a future date, the astrologer's interpretations are then called "progressions," not "predictions."

Quadrants The four quarters of the *birth chart*.

Quadruplicity See *quality*.

Quality The *signs* are assigned one of three qualities (also called quadruplicities): cardinal, fixed, or mutable. Aries, Cancer, Libra, and Capricorn are cardinal signs; Taurus, Leo, Scorpio, and Aquarius are fixed signs; and Gemini, Virgo, Sagittarius, and Pisces are mutable signs. Cardinal signs are said to encourage action; fixed signs to encourage resistance to change; and mutable signs to encourage adaptability and change.

Rectification Astrologers will often "rectify" an individual's *birth chart* – particularly if the exact birth time is not known – by studying the individual's personality characteristics and life events and then making suppositions from them about planetary influences and aspects. Often an arbitrary birth time, such as noon or sunrise, is also concurrently used to cast the chart. This is a difficult and often inaccurate technique and is generally considered a last resort measure.

Retrograde A planet is said to be retrograde when it appears (as seen from the Earth) to move backward through the *zodiac*. Ancient astrologers believed that a retrograde planet was a sinister omen. Modern astrologers believe that the retrograde motion merely slows down the actions and influences of the planet.

Rising sign The *sign* of the *zodiac* which was rising over the eastern horizon at the moment of your birth. Also called your *Ascendant*. In a *birth chart*, the rising sign or Ascendant always appears in the first 30-degree segment of the chart (under the Ascendant degree or "9 o'clock" line) of the chart. Each of the remaining 11 zodiac signs – in their proper order, but following the rising zodiac sign – are placed in segments two through 12, counterclockwise, around the birth chart. For example, if your rising sign

is Cancer, it is placed in segment one of the chart; then Leo is placed in segment two, Virgo in segment three, Libra in segment four, etc. The last or 12th segment of the chart would contain Taurus.

Ruler of the horoscope/Rulership The *ruling planet* of the *rising sign* (Ascendant) in the first 30-degree segment of a birth chart is called the *ruler of the horoscope*. The phenomenon itself is called *rulership*. For example, the planet Mercury rules Gemini. If Gemini is the rising sign in a chart, the chart ruler is Mercury.

Ruling planet Each zodiac sign is "ruled" by a specific planet and is uniquely influenced by the qualities and actions of that planet. In modern astrology Aries is ruled by Mars, Taurus by Venus, Gemini by Mercury, Cancer by the Moon, Leo by the Sun, Virgo by Mercury, Libra by Venus, Scorpio by Pluto, Sagittarius by Jupiter, Capricorn by Saturn, Aquarius by Uranus, and Pisces by Neptune.

Sidereal time Astrological time determined by the stars rather than by the Sun is called sidereal time. A sidereal zodiac is based upon the star constellations rather than the traditional zodiac *signs*.

Sign One of the 12 30-degree segments of the zodiac band: Aries, Taurus, Gemini, Cancer, Leo, Virgo, Libra, Scorpio, Sagittarius, Capricorn, Aquarius, or Pisces.

Solar system Earth's solar system primarily comprises the Sun, the Moon, the planets Mercury, Venus, Mars, Jupiter, Saturn, Uranus, Neptune, and Pluto, and other minor celestial bodies, including *asteroids* and *comets*.

Stellium A group of three or more planets in *conjunction* – that is, very close together in one area (a *sign* or a *house*) of a *birth chart* – which has a very powerful (and often disruptive) influence on an individual's character and life.

Sun sign The Sun sign is the *zodiac sign* that the Sun was traveling through (as seen from the Earth) at the moment of an individual's birth. For example, when you say, "I'm a Capricorn," you mean your Sun sign is Capricorn. Astrologers have come to view the Sun sign as representing the public image one presents to the world. (The *rising sign*, or *Ascendant*, represents an individual's hidden qualities or private image.)

Sun-sign astrology The most simplistic form of astrology dealing solely with the personality traits of someone born with the Sun in a specific zodiac sign (see *Sun sign*). Sun-sign astrology ignores the influences of other key astrological factors – for example, the *planets*, *houses*, and *aspects*. Popular newspaper and magazine "horoscope" columns are based solely on Sun sign characteristics and therefore are quite generalized.

Superior planets Those planets farther from the Sun than the Earth (that is, on the far side of the Earth) are called superior planets. They are Mars, Jupiter, Saturn, Uranus, Neptune, and Pluto.

Transit A planet's movement through a *sign* or *house*. Astrologers often use transits in an individual's birth chart to study possible future trends in that person's life.

Triplicity See *element*.

Unaspected planets *Planets* which do not make any of the *aspects* usually considered by astrologers are said to be unaspected. Opinions about such planets vary, but most astrologers believe that the qualities normally represented by the planets in question either go unrecognized or are under-utilized by the subject. Unaspected planets may sometimes also represent areas of considerable conflict in an individual's life.

Void of course A planet is considered "void of course" when it passes through a *sign* without making or receiving a single *aspect* from another *planet*.

Zenith A point in the sky immediately overhead. For example, the Sun is at its zenith at noon.

Zodiac The imaginary belt that follows the Sun's path around the Earth and which is divided into 12 30-degree sections called the *signs* of the zodiac.

Index

Acknowledgments

Cartoons courtesy of Barry Robson © Dorling Kindersley
Dorling Kindersley would like to thank the following for their kind permission to reproduce their photographs:
Bridgeman Art Library: 32, 34, 35, 37, 54, 55, 56, 57, 58, 59, 60, 61, 62, 63, 64, 65, 66, 68, 70, 71, 73, 74, 75, 76, 77, 78, 79, 80, 104, 116
Galaxy Picture Library: 24
Mary Evans Picture Library: 50
NASA: 390
Science Photo Library: 26, 94
Science and Society Picture Library: 40
Still Pictures: 16-17
Topham Picturepoint: 43, 47
Illustrations courtesy of Dorling Kindersley: 36, 49, 85,

216, 217, 218, 219, 220, 222, 223, 225, 226, 227, 229b, 231b, 232, 236, 237
All other illustrations courtesy of Foundry Arts/Douglas Hall and Foundry Arts/Jennifer Kenna.
All photo manipulation and imaging carried out by The Foundry.

All other images © Dorling Kindersley
For further information see: www.dkimages.com

Special thanks to Chester Kemp for his work on moon and planetary tables.

Dorling Kindersley would like to thank Neal Cobourne for the jacket design and Peter Jones for his editorial assistance.